The Organ Music
of J. S. Bach

II

Works based on Chorales

(BWV 599–771 etc)

by Peter Williams

CAMBRIDGE UNIVERSITY PRESS

CAMBRIDGE
LONDON NEW YORK NEW ROCHELLE
MELBOURNE SYDNEY

Published by the Press Syndicate of the University of Cambridge
The Pitt Building, Trumpington Street, Cambridge CB2 1RP
32 East 57th Street, New York, NY 10022, USA
296 Beaconsfield Parade, Middle Park, Melbourne 3206, Australia

© Cambridge University Press 1980

First published 1980

Printed in Great Britain at the
University Press, Cambridge

Library of Congress Cataloguing in Publication Data
Williams, Peter F.
The organ music of J. S. Bach.
(Cambridge studies in music)
Includes indexes.
Bibliography: p.
1. Bach, Johann Sebastian, 1685–1750. Works, organ.
1. Title. 11. Series.
MT145.B14W53 1978   786.6'22'4   77-71431

ISBN 0 521 21517 X

For Lucy and Daniel

Contents

Preface

Even were the *Neue Bach-Ausgabe* to be complete or near-complete, neither this nor any other book on Bach's organ music could claim to have the last word. Each generation must look anew at this incomparable body of music, re-examine it in the light of contemporary knowledge, view it in a way relevant to its own attitudes towards music and towards the role of the music scholar. Because it is now nearly thirty years since this music last received a complete commentary, the need for one has grown as the wider possibilities of contemporary musical research have made it opportune. Current attitudes are not always those of 1950, much less 1900.

One such 'current attitude' is to analyse the composer's creative method in general (e.g. what 'style' he is adopting) and in terms of his own contemporary music theory (e.g. whether his attention was focused on the *Figurenlehre*). Another is to place each piece against a background of its own source-material, not only to establish (or question) its authenticity but to supply the present-day performer with evidence for the piece as it stands. This book aims at satisfying these two current attitudes, both of which centre on the notes themselves – *as composed* on the one hand and *as preserved in the sources* on the other. It frequently refers to other attitudes or approaches, most notably those of the composer's admirers in the first decades after his death (Marpurg, Kirnberger etc), of the scientific scholars a century later (Spitta, Rust etc) and of the more recent commentators (Schweitzer, Keller etc). But each of these, including the earliest, wrote in musical and church contexts far removed from, and in some cases alien to, those of the composer in Weimar and Leipzig. All such approaches are therefore based both on fact and on conjecture; at best they serve to show what 'facts' and what 'conjectures' any one period will accept. Some of the big issues, particularly the dating of the organ works, allow room only for conjecture, however careful it might be; in a piece-by-piece commentary of this kind any such label as ' c1710–12 ' would require more expansive discussion than the context would allow and one best reserved for a more general survey of the music. Thus some questions have been left without summary conclusions, many pieces have been commented on from only one or two angles, and only a wide reading of the book will give the reader an idea of the several possible analytical approaches by this most carefully reasoning of all organ composers.

The present volume includes all the works based on chorales, including those of *Clavierübung III*; a similar volume includes all other works (BWV 525–598, 802–805, etc).

Preface

I wish to thank in particular the following for help and advice on questions that perhaps could not always have been answered by the composer himself: Dr Roger Bullivant (Sheffield), Dr Alison Cairns (Edinburgh), Mr Stephen Daw (Birmingham), Professor Dr Hans Klotz (Cologne), the Rev. Robin Leaver (Reading), the Rev. Theo Thermann (Freiberg) and the Johann-Sebastian-Bach-Institut, Göttingen (Dr Alfred Dürr, Dr Dietrich Kilian). Much encouragement was given by Dr Peter le Huray (Cambridge), and in its final form the book owes much to Mr Eric Van Tassel of the Cambridge University Press, whose advice on the content was as invaluable as it was on the presentation. As for the help of Mr Hans-Joachim Schulze (Bach-Archiv, Leipzig), I do not think the book could have been written without it, although he has no responsibility for any of the opinions or mis-statements.

July 1976   Peter Williams

Note on the Commentary

The commentary on each work is arranged in the following order:

Title. Throughout the present volume – works based on chorales – the title is that of the text as given in the chief source(s).

Sources. The first reference is to any known extant autograph MS or printed edition ('Published 1739' etc). Important 'copies' are then referred to, 'copy' being understood to mean 'written specimen' in general, not a reproduction of the autograph; the order implies only the approximate chronology and/or importance of the source. No attempt is made to provide a full *kritischer Bericht* or textual commentary to the pieces; the copies listed are those of particular importance, including any autograph, original engraving, reputed autograph, or early copy (perhaps of a version or draft earlier than the extant autograph), including lost or destroyed MSS. The names in round brackets after the MS number are those of the copyist or previous owner concerned. 'Late sources' does not necessarily indicate poor, unauthorized or unimportant sources, since some may derive more directly from an early good source than older copies. Where the basic source is good, other copies are often summarized as belonging to such groups of copyists as the 'Kirnberger circle' or 'Kittel pupils'. For further details of the MSS including fuller library references, see the List of Musical Sources; typical abbreviations in the commentary are:

Autograph MS P 271 = autograph copy extant, listed as P 271 (for which see the List of Musical Sources)

P 1109 (Penzel) = copy in the hand of or once in the possession of C. F. Penzel (for which see Index and List of Musical Sources)

Brief biographical details of the copyists etc are included in the Index.

Headings. Any subsidiary title (e.g. 'Fantasia super...') or direction (e.g. 'a 2 Clav. e Pedale') is taken from the chief sources. Often these are different from *BG* and subsequent editions. That most pieces were copied on two staves only underlines the doubts that must occasionally arise about what if anything is to be played by pedals, what the composer originally expected, whether he or another copyist gave the work a different aspect by later specifying pedals, etc. The history of three-stave organ notation, as distinct from an open score, is a subject of its own and deserves fuller treatment in a more general study.

Chorale. A brief account of the text and melody is given, without full hymnological details – still unclear in many cases – but including the chorale's chief associations, its use elsewhere in the music of J. S. Bach and its melodic form in one or another previous version. A few of the more significant hymnbooks have been referred to where useful as typical examples, particularly those widely used either in orthodox circles (e.g. Vopelius) or in pietist circles (e.g. Freylinghausen). Little reference to the standard classic 'Zahn' (see List of References) is made in this section, since (*a*) Zahn's lists of melodies were used by such later authors as Terry, who has been used instead, (*b*) Zahn's index system allows easy comparison of the various versions leading to J. S. Bach's melodies, and (*c*) there is still room for doubt on the exact history of certain melodies.

Only the first verse is quoted unless another verse can be or has been seen as relevant to the organ chorale concerned, though such quotation is no support for theories about text/music associations. The new translations into English are literal and, wherever possible, preserve the word order of the original. Information on the cantatas derives largely from Neumann 1967. As has been pointed out (Gojowy 1972), Bach cannot be shown to have depended completely on the known Lutheran year-plans of seasonal texts for his choice of which chorales to set in each cantata; and it is presumably true too that the organ chorales were not always associated exclusively with one day or season. Similarly, many hymns with specific associations in contemporary hymnbooks were not used in the organ works. Some texts seem to have had a special significance or some particular allusion for the composer himself, perhaps one not identified in the hymnbooks.

Commentary. The references to previous authors are selective and usually concern those of wide influence on players and writers during the last hundred years, whether old or new, worthy (Spitta) or idiosyncratic (Chailley). No attempt has been made to list the published views of all commentators on any one piece, but in some cases the main schools of thought are surveyed in outline. However, the commentary does include more general remarks on the collections themselves (*Orgelbüchlein*, 'The Eighteen', etc) and summarizes the changing conceptions of different generations of players and writers.

References are normally expressed in abbreviated form: thus 'Spitta I p595' = P. Spitta, *Johann Sebastian Bach*, vol. I (Leipzig, 1873), page 595. Abbreviations are explained with full details in the List of References.

Except where otherwise noted, bars are numbered including repeats, and the form 'b1/5' identifies a bar at its first appearance (as b1) and its identical repetition (as b5). An up-beat of half a bar's length or more is counted as the first bar (one of less than half a bar is 'bar zero').

Other questions – chronology, purpose, the instrument, registration, hymnology etc – as well as surveys of musical features common to many of the works (e.g. the use of paraphrase techniques or 'symbolism') are, in the present commentary, limited to questions arising from the stylistic nature of the single work then under discussion (e.g. the proportional tempos in BWV 672–674) or from the reliability or significance of the source-material for a given single work (e.g. the registrations in BWV 720). Any general discussion of these subjects deserves fuller treatment of the kind already referred to.

599–644   *Orgelbüchlein*

Autograph MS P 283. Title-page:

Orgel-Büchlein Worinne einem anfahenden Organisten Anleitung ge-
geben wird, auff allerhand Arth einen **Choral** durchzuführen, anbey auch
sich im **Pedal studio** zu **habilitiren**, indem in solchen darinne befindlichen
Choralen das **Pedal** gantz **obligat tractiret** wird. Dem Höchsten Gott
allein zu Ehren, Dem Nechsten, draus sich zu belehren. Autore Joanne
Sebast: Bach p.t. Capellae Magistri S. P. R. Anhaltini-Cotheniensis.

Little Organ Book, in which guidance is given to an inquiring organist
in how to accomplish a chorale in all kinds of ways, and at the same
time to become practised in the study of pedalling, since in the chorales
found therein the pedal is treated completely obbligato.

> For the highest God alone Honour,
> For my neighbour, that he may instruct himself from it.

Composed by Johann Sebastian Bach, p.t. [*pleno titulo*, 'with full
title'?] Kapellmeister to the Serene Reigning Prince of Anhalt-Cöthen.

The title-page of P 283 was written at Cöthen, later than almost all
of the contents. Although the make-up of the page does not suggest
that it replaced an earlier title (see *Dok* I p214), it cannot be assumed
that the album was originally planned, composed or copied out with
the expressed aims in mind; rather, such didacticism is more characteristic of other post-Weimar title-pages, particularly *Das Wohltemperirte Clavier*, I (1722) and the *Auffrichtige Anleitung* (Two- and
Three-part Inventions, 1723). The somewhat unclear term 'durchführen' was later used by C. P. E. Bach, almost certainly in connection
with P 283, when he referred in an undated letter to the chorale
melodies, each one of which 'in einer von den Stimmen gerade durch
geführt ist' ('is carried through directly [= without interludes?] in one
of the parts', *Dok* III p183). It suggests that instruction is given in
composing* chorales, not merely in performing them. Despite some
famous speculation, what the abbreviation 'p.t.' means is still uncertain, but it was not uncommon on documents both musical (*Das*

---

* And perhaps extemporizing. As long as keyboard improvisation was pursued as a
serious musical aim (i.e. until the twentieth century) it was generally assumed that
the highest form of extemporizing was that which was also most intricate on paper,
e.g. fugue. Tightly organized motivic harmonizations of the kind found in the
Orgelbüchlein must represent another extempore ideal. Either way, it has long been
pointed out that the album shows no 'calculated progressive difficulty' for the
organist, hence the bizarre suggestion that 'Bach did not intend the *Büchlein* for
publication in its present form' (Griepenkerl Peters v 1846).

Wohltemperirte Clavier, 1) and non-musical, and of itself tells one nothing specific about the album. The rhyming couplet of the title-page appears to be the composer's, written to the honour neither of the author (as e.g. Werckmeister's *Orgelprobe*, 1698) nor of a dedicatee (as Partita 1, 1726).

Questions concerning the sources, date, purpose (including hymnology) and musical style of the *Orgelbüchlein* can be summarized as follows:

(i) Sources. The contents of P 283, according to its present pagination, are:

	I	title-page
	II	—
	1	BWV 599
	2–3	BWV 600
	4	BWV 601
	5	BWV 602
	6+	BWV 603
	7	— (empty page, with the title of one chorale not set)
	8	BWV 604
	9	BWV 605
	10	BWV 606
	11	BWV 607
	12–13	BWV 608
	14	BWV 609
	15	BWV 610
	16	BWV 611
	17	BWV 612
	18	BWV 613
	19	BWV 614
	20–1	BWV 615
	22	BWV 616
	23	BWV 617
	24	BWV 618
½-slip {	23a	close of BWV 617
	24a	close of BWV 618
	25	BWV 619
	26	BWV 620
	27	BWV 621
	28–9	BWV 622
	30	BWV 623
½-slip	30a	close of BWV 624 (later copy?)
	31	BWV 624
	32	— (one title)
	33	'O Traurigkeit'
	34–8	— (four titles)
	39	BWV 625
	40	BWV 626
	41–3	BWV 627
	44	BWV 628

45	BWV 629
46–7	BWV 630
48–53	— (four titles)
54	BWV 631
55–8	— (four titles)
59	BWV 632
60	BWV 634
61	BWV 633
62–72	— (nine titles)
73	BWV 635
74–7	(three titles)
78	BWV 636
79–88	— (ten titles)
89	BWV 637
90	BWV 638
91–105	— (thirteen titles)
106+	BWV 639
107–12	— (six titles)
113	BWV 640
114	— (one title)
115	BWV 641
116–28	— (twelve titles)
129	BWV 642
130–48	— (seventeen titles)
149	BWV 643
150–76	— (twenty-seven titles)
177	BWV 644
178–82	— (five titles)

Two pieces (BWV 603 and 639) run over on to the following page for the last bar or two; others have their final bars written in tablature in the bottom margin (see the notes on each piece).

Some questions must await the publication of *NBA* IV/I *KB*: the date when the half-slips were written and/or included; when it was that the composer added the supplementary headings ('a 2 Clav. e Ped.' was written later than the titles,* presumably at the time the pieces were copied into P 283); why some pieces appear to be at early draft stage (e.g. BWV 599, 600) while others are written as fair copies (e.g. BWV 601, 636–644), yet others as fair copies amended later (BWV 631); whether the coloratura passages in (e.g.) BWV 641 were written in smaller notes merely for clarity or as a result of later re-working (almost certainly the former). If, as appears to be the case, all the titles were written into the album before the music was copied, it is striking that already two pages were allowed for some (e.g. BWV 608, 615). The half-slips and the completions in tablature show that, in the event, the page was too small for many of the pieces; but in no instance is a title crossed out because the previous piece needed a further page.

* It is possible, however, that the Latin–Italian phrase was merely written in a more cursive script than the clerical German of the chorale title, hence a discrepancy in the writing. A similar point could be made about P 271, the source of BWV 651–667.

Of the 46 settings themselves, three are or were meant to be duplications or alternatives: BWV 633/634, BWV 640 and 643 marked 'alio modo'. It is uncertain from P 283 itself whether 'alio modo' means 'another setting of the same melody to this text' or 'a setting of another melody sung to this text', though the former would be more usual. From these various questions and conjectures, it could be provisionally summarized that the original *Orgelbüchlein* was an album planned to hold a full – perhaps impractically full – repertory of organ chorales of which many had already been composed when the composer thought of compiling the album; some of them were (then or later) amended to a greater or lesser degree, and a few of them were added (and probably composed) later still.

Of the other numerous sources, none is complete or keeps the same order – a fact of very uncertain significance. J. T. Krebs copied twenty-nine chorales into P 801 (by c1714?) and six into P 802 (three of which are also in P 801), into which Walther also copied one. While the presence of ensuing empty pages in P 801 suggests Krebs was to have copied more of them, his order appears to be arbitrary, unlike J. G. Walther's in BB 22541/1–3, where some of the eight are grouped with organ chorales on the same melodies by other composers.* P 802 shows signs of being written not on the principle of (e.g.) technical difficulty or chronology but rather as studies in the different ways of setting a chorale (Zietz 1969 p178). It has been assumed that both copyists wrote out chorales from the various putative phases of the *Orgelbüchlein*, since Krebs includes both the revisions from P 283 and some 'earlier versions' (Dadelsen 1963), but P 283 cannot be proved to be the source for P 802 (Daw 1976). An early copy after P 283, once thought to be a second autograph and given by Guhr to Mendelssohn (letter to Fanny Mendelssohn, 18 June 1839), is now assumed to be the lost MS P 1216, a page of which is extant and was written in c1727/30 by C. G. Meissner, the so-called 'Hauptkopist B' (Arfken 1966 p51; Schulze 1968); it contained twenty-six chorales.†

Of the albums made by or influenced by the major copyists, Kittel (Lpz Poel 39) omits one chorale, Kirnberger (Brussels W . 12 . 102) omits two, Am.B. 46/47 and Dröbs (P 1108) three; Oley and a fellow copyist (P 1160), P 1110 (possibly begun or made for C. P. E. Bach?), Penzel (P 1109) and LM 4719 (late eighteenth century) all omit various chorales. However, in other copies (P 1113, P 1114) Oley includes some of those omitted in P 1160, and various explanations can be offered for any apparently incomplete source. As they stand, the smaller collections often appear to be arbitrary, e.g. BWV 600, 609, 635 and 617 in Lpz MB MS 7 (Mempell–Preller), because in this instance these separate copies have been bound into one album, only more recently. P 284 'obviously goes back to a Kirnberger source' (*NBA* IV/2 *KB* p44), but why it follows only approximately the order of P 283 cannot be

---

* It is striking that all but two of the melodies set by Buxtehude and contained in these three albums of Walther were also set by J. S. Bach.

† It may well have been the 'Mendelssohn Autograph' that supplied Schumann with copies of BWV 639, 614, 637 and 622, published by him in supplements to the *Neue Zeitschrift für Musik* (1839–41): L. P. Plantinga, *Schumann as Critic* (New Haven, 1967), pp89ff.

explained by other known autograph sources, by liturgy or hymnology, by performing difficulty, or by orthographic or page-turning convenience. Why P 284, Brussels W.12.102 and Am.B. 47 omit two particular chorales (BWV 631 and 634) is clearer: BWV 634 is a kind of duplicate, and BWV 631 can be omitted from each MS because its longer version (BWV 667) appears either in the same MS or in related MSS (Am.B. 46). During his last few years at Leipzig the composer is also likely to have kept a fair copy of the *Orgelbüchlein* with his other collections of organ music (*NBA* IV/3 *KB* p14), and further copies, though incomplete, were then made by such pupils as Kirnberger, including the added BWV 613 and the revised BWV 620.

It has been suggested (Zietz 1969 pp111ff) that the twenty-nine chorales in P 801, with the copies of the longer chorales ('The Eighteen') in P 802, were meant to serve 'obviously [as] a basis for the musical instruction given Krebs by J. S. Bach'. Certainly a group of *Orgelbüchlein* chorales forms a complement to a group of 'The Eighteen' for the instruction of a young composer or organist. In some cases, Krebs's copies may be from an older version than that known from P 283 (see BWV 638, 622, 621, 639, 640). However, despite a suggestion to the contrary (Zietz 1969 p133), Krebs's different order for the chorales can hardly be taken as evidence that he was copying from a source other than P 283. The non-homogeneous nature of the autograph handwriting and of the Krebs copy may suggest that both were prepared at least in part from an existing, perhaps incomplete source, directly or indirectly used as teaching material for the several Bach pupils (*ibid* pp134–5). The autograph and Krebs copies are similar in details of layout (despite the composer's attempting to squeeze the shorter pieces on to one page each) and thus are related.

(ii) Date. On the evidence of such handwriting details in P 283 as the note and clef forms (Dadelsen 1958 p80) as well as the stave-lines (Wolff 1963 p91), the following table expresses current views on the date and chronology of the *Orgelbüchlein* as it appears in P 283:

c1713/14
> BWV 599, 600, 601, 602, 603, 604, 605, 606, 607, 608, 609, 612 (or later?), 616, 617, 618, 619, 621 (or later), 622 (or later), 625, 626, 627, 628, 629, 630, 631a, 632, 635, 636, 637, 638, 639, 641, 642, 643

1714/16
> BWV 610, 611, 614, 615, 620 (620a), 623, 624, 633, 634, 640, 644 (or earlier)

Leipzig (c1740)
> BWV 613, and 'O Traurigkeit, o Herzeleid' (not at the same time; 'O Traurigkeit' perhaps later than 613)

However, this still cannot be regarded as a true chronology, since the copies in P 802, 801 may suggest in most cases yet earlier composition.

Indirect evidence from handwriting, hymnology and organ-building at Weimar both helps and confuses. Handwriting in contemporary cantata parts confirms that a group of *Orgelbüchlein* pieces was written out before the end of 1714 at the latest (Dürr *NBA* I/35 *KB* p42). While all but two of the texts of the hymns themselves occur in C. F. Witt,

Neues Cantional (1715), 'there is no evidence that any of the preludes could not have been composed until after the publication of Witt's book' (Emery Novello xv p.xi); also, while the order follows to some extent that of the same chorales in the Weimar *Gesangbücher* of 1708 and 1713, the three *Orgelbüchlein* melodies which appear only in the 1713 edition belong to three different phases in the hypothetical chronology (BWV 613, 615, 629). That the composer's friend and relative J. G. Walther (Weimar) also published two sets of chorale variations in 1713 is perhaps no coincidence. Details of the work on rebuilding the Weimar chapel organ are unfortunately not clear enough to throw any light on the date and purpose of the chorales; the period during which the organ appears to have been out of commission – soon after Whit 1713 to at least Easter 1714 (Schulze 1972 p9) – cuts across the chronology and would make it impossible for the well-represented Advent and Christmas chorales to have been set for performance on it during the new church year 1713–14. The watermark of P 283 (as of P 45, the score of BWV 152) is one known for paper dated to 1713–14 (Dürr 1977 p234).

Internal evidence and certain musical details may suggest an order in which chorales were composed – for example, in the way the pedal is used (Arfken 1966):

(1) basso-continuo quavers (e.g. BWV 605) following the chorale line and ending with it (e.g. BWV 642), even when they have a strong motif of their own (e.g. BWV 630)
(2) bass cadences timed only partly in relation to the cadences of the chorale lines (e.g. BWV 602)
(3) bass cadences independent of the ends of the chorale lines (e.g. BWV 611)

But such treatments reflect less a chronology than the composer's interest in variety. The 'Leipzig chorale' BWV 613, for instance, would qualify under the second category, yet its bass is derived from the melody to a degree unusual in the *Orgelbüchlein*, though certainly not unique to this piece. Nor is a derived pedal motif itself characteristic of a later date, since BWV 632 has a pedal even more closely developed from the chorale melody. Perhaps the derived *inner* parts of BWV 613 suggest that it was composed (as well as copied into the album) during the Leipzig period; but BWV 632 also has derived inner parts, rather more independently developed than those of BWV 613. On the other hand, the differences between BWV 620 and 620a do suggest a 'later revision', moreover of a kind far more radical and systematic than the 'Leipzig revision' of the so-called 'Weimar chorale' 'An Wasserflüssen Babylon' BWV 652a. This does not necessarily mean, however, that BWV 620a was revised at Leipzig.

(iii) Purpose. It has already been suggested above that the Cöthen title-page expressed a new aim for the *Orgelbüchlein*: the chorales are now 'instruction for beginners', useful perhaps to a busy teacher who is probably not going to play them himself again during services. But the original purpose is less certain. The dating already disposes of earlier theories that the collection was written to while away the time during the composer's detention at Weimar (6 November – 2 December 1717) and that it was left unfinished (*a*) because in the course of composition he moved to Cöthen, where there was no call for liturgical organ music, or (*b*) because he was promoted to *Konzertmeister* on 2 March 1714. However, it remains possible (*c*) that the collection was begun or continued with an eye to the new potential of the rebuilt organ, and (*d*) that it was left unfinished because of other work. But while many of the chorales set do suggest that the composer found particular inspiration in either their texts or their melodies, it is not known whether – and if so why – he had any order of priority. Schweitzer's claim that the chorales not set 'were those which do not lend themselves to musical description' is unfounded conjecture (Schweitzer 1905 p178). Nor is it certain which hymnbook was his chief source, although as was the case with the chorale texts in the Weimar cantatas (Neumann 1956) it was probably the Weimar *Geistreiches Gesangbuch* of 1713, before or after publication.

Terry's list of the 164 titles clarifies several important points and has been much used by commentators since (Terry 1921 pp31–61): although the contents follow such hymnbooks as Witt's *Neues Cantional* (1715), the exact plan of the album and the form of its melodies do not. Chorales are grouped in the first part according to season, ending with 'O Herre Gott, dein göttlich Wort' (Reformation Day text, listed immediately before BWV 635); in the second part, beginning with the Catechism Commandments BWV 635, the chorales are grouped to illustrate or trace aspects of the Christian life. However, no subtitles or other indications make it at all certain that there was a rigid plan of this kind. Of the non-seasonal chorales listed or set, the largest groups are those associated with penitence (11), Communion (9), time of trouble (17) and death (16); also included, though not as a group, are seven of Luther's Catechism hymns. The exact order follows no known hymnbook, particularly in the latter part. Similarly, all the melodies set can be found in no single known hymnbook, and the net would have had to be widened further had all the listed chorales been composed. Thirteen of the unset texts are Luther hymns, yet the composer's priority does seem to have been for 'orthodox' chorales against pietist – for example, the *Jesuslied* texts of the 1713 Weimar *Gesangbuch* are not listed. Otherwise, the preference was neither for nor against well-known texts, nor was it for or against melodies already set. That the seasonal part is well represented may be because the chorales were composed during the season concerned; the array of Advent and Christmas settings might also suggest that more than one 'cycle' was intended, and that the album was to have contained sufficient settings for two or more church years.

A larger question remains: What are the *Orgelbüchlein* chorales? Are they organ preludes to a congregational or choir hymn? Are they interludes between verses? Are they voluntaries to be played during the appropriate service without direct connection to a sung hymn? Many are little more than idealized harmonizations in four parts of a melody heard (as was by then normal in hymnbooks with melodies) in the top part. At least two quite different purposes or aims are possible. The album could have been planned as an organist's comprehensive hymnbook, even – since not all hymnbooks included melodies – for publication. Or perhaps the private conditions of the Duke's chapel services required unusual organ music of a kind not supplied by older types of organ chorale, i.e. those more 'in the Pachelbel manner' written for the town church of Weimar at the same period by J. G. Walther, who may then have been making his own collection (Krey 1956 p46).

Many of J. G. Walther's extant chorales have two particular details in common with those of the *Orgelbüchlein*, despite a very unequal level of achievement. These details are (1) canonic treatment of several cantus-firmus melodies (in particular those attached to Advent or Christmas), often combined with imitative or quasi-canonic accompaniments, and (2) use in the figurative harmonies of specific motifs such as the *suspirans* (see e.g. BWV 628). Although both of these details are in general fully traditional – e.g., the *suspirans* was found as a motif in every set of keyboard variations by the German organists – it is probable that Walther and J. S. Bach were working with them in the same town at much the same period. From there it would be no great step to think that the *Orgelbüchlein*, whatever else it was, was conceived as its composer's response to interests, even preoccupations, in compositional techniques shared by two organist friends in the same town. Whether it was a response by J. S. Bach to notions being realized by Walther, or whether Walther worked out his own versions of these techniques on the model of J. S. Bach's album – for example, publishing his variations on 'Allein Gott' as late as 1738 – cannot be shown, but various factors suggest Walther's work to have been the earlier and thus the *Orgelbüchlein* to be its composer's 'response'. These factors are (1) the wider canonic, motivic and harmonic invention of the *Orgelbüchlein*, (2) Walther's brief references to compositional devices as early as 1708 (*Praecepta*), and (3) the pedal parts of the *Orgelbüchlein*, which not only are more indispensable than is usually the case with Walther (hence the specific reference to pedals on the title-page?) but also lead to a more fully developed texture, whether or not it is canonic.

Early written references to *Orgelbüchlein* chorales do not explain their original function. In Marpurg's *Abhandlung von der Fuge* (Berlin, 1753), Figs. LI (2, 3, 4) and LII (1) quote the opening bars of BWV 633, 601, 626 and 623 on three or four staves as examples of contrapuntal treatments. In the Obituary, the volume is referred to as 'ein Buch voll kurtzer Vorspiele vor die meisten Kirchenlieder, für die Orgel' ('a book full of short preludes to [on? before?] most church hymns, for the organ': *Dok* III p86); but neither the precise meaning in 1754 of the term 'Vorspiel' nor its exact relevance to Weimar in 1715 can be known for certain. In c1765 C. P. E. Bach offered for sale a manuscript presumed to be the *Orgelbüchlein* autograph, and described the contents as follows:

Choräle...*manualiter* und *pedaliter* eigentlich für die Orgel gesetzt, ob man sie gleich recht gut auf dem Claviere spielen kann...Die mehresten sind nur kurz ausgeführt...bloss für die Orgel, ohne dass ein anderes Instrument oder Singestimme dabey ist (*Dok* III pp182–3).

Chorales...set especially for organ *manualiter* and *pedaliter*, although one can play them quite as well on the *Clavier*...Most of them are only short settings...for the organ alone, without any other instrument or voice taking part.

C. P. E. Bach introduced his offer by pointing out that none of the pieces had been printed in Birnstiel's edition of simple four-part chorales (1765), a fact which suggests that he saw them in this category.* Certainly the album as a whole can be neither purely didactic, since the order is inconvenient for pedagogic purposes, nor purely accompanimental, since many are too complex, too slow and (in the coloratura settings) too awkward for congregational use. The brevity of these chorales and their directness of melody may conform better than any other collection of J. S. Bach to Kauffmann's advice on playing preludes: 'die Melodie auf eine deutliche und vernehmliche Weise zugleich mithören lassen' ('at the same time let the chorale melody also be heard in a clear and distinct manner': *Harmonische Seelenlust*, 1733). But Kauffmann's Leipzig publication of 1733 gives no certain information on the practices in the Weimar court chapel in 1715, not least since hymns in a court chapel were probably dominated by the choir.

To what extent did Bach have a 'congregation' at Weimar? His strong emphasis on the chorale melodies themselves – prominent cantus firmus, without interludes – may suggest not that they were so composed in order to be intelligible to a common congregation but that he had the aim of invoking an orthodoxy, even dogma. The accompaniments and thus the mood of many *Orgelbüchlein* chorales cannot be proved to be due to any subjective interpretation (such as Schweitzer, Terry, Chailley etc have proposed) but are more likely meant to convey the biblical references or teachings behind the texts: to be bound to the cantus firmus is to be bound to the Word of God (Arfken 1965 pp101ff). Even the pitch of the chorales suggests that they prefaced or accompanied hymns for choir rather than congregation: the upper limit of the melodies varies from e″ (35 chorales) to f″ (7), to f♯″ (2) and to g″ (1), and although the organ pitch is conjectural (David 1951 p33) it was certainly higher than a′ = 440Hz. The very location of the organ – high in a top gallery above the altar, customary in the court chapels of Saxony and Thuringia – speaks against a direct relationship to the congregation. Such mundane considerations, while misleading if pressed beyond a certain point, do support the idea that the *Orgelbüchlein* chorales were more independent of any congregational hymn than an organist half a century later would have understood.

* In 1766, in a review of the Birnstiel edition of four-part chorales, J. F. Agricola advised organists to play them on two manuals and pedal (*Dok* III p188), i.e. as idiomatic organ music.

(iv) Musical style. The 'new' form found in the *Orgelbüchlein* chorales may be summarized as follows:

> contrapuntal harmonizations of a melody heard in the soprano
>   (exceptions: 611, 615?, 618)
> in four parts (excluding cadences)
>   (exceptions: 619, 634, 633, 639, all but the last canonic; at times in five parts: 599, 615)
> without interludes between the lines
>   (exceptions: 615, 617)
> beginning with the melody, alone or accompanied
>   (exceptions: 615?, 617, 619, 637)
> the ends of lines sometimes drawn out (e.g. 606)*

While other chorales in Bach's output are often described as 'of the *Orgelbüchlein* type' (BWV 683, 690, 709, 727, 730, 742, 743), various factors distinguish either their form or their harmonic style, either their texture or their organ idiom, from most of the album as outlined above (see the notes to these settings). The style of the *Orgelbüchlein* accompaniment – its motifs, any pedal quasi-ostinato etc – admits of great variety and dominates the chorale melody, whether one motif runs through all the parts (BWV 626) or through the middle parts (most chorales) or individually through each part (605). Most chorales also close with the motifs outrunning the melody, having produced their own impetus.

As to the form of the chorales, the spectrum is wide enough to allow two further important chorale types: the canon (9 examples) and the full coloratura setting (3). The canons may be at the fifth (4 examples) or octave (5), with the canon in the cantus firmus alone (5 examples) or in its accompaniment as well, whether strictly (2) or loosely (2). A type of canon that had been traditional – i.e. canon in the accompaniment above a plain cantus firmus (Scheidt, Weckmann etc) – is absent. On the other hand, the canon at the fifth is rare in organ music outside the *Orgelbüchlein*; Walther's octave canons result in far simpler harmony and a more clearly audible cantus firmus. In this respect, too, it is difficult not to think of the *Orgelbüchlein* as a response to methods of composition in which Walther took an interest.

Despite the amount that has been written on the *Orgelbüchlein* chorales, their general character is elusive. The relationship of melody to harmony is such as to present both in new lights, not only because of the harmonic inventiveness and its constantly new progressions, but because the relationship is as far removed from 'normal' hymn harmonizations as the form of the chorales is from the many 'normal' organ types. The motifs themselves are especially important in the general tone. Many of them can be seen in earlier chorale partitas or

---

* The meaning of the ⌢ signs at the ends of lines is difficult for the performer. While the signs cannot mean 'pause', since the motifs frequently continue uninterrupted, they could rather indicate the line-ends for purposes of rubato and articulation, as those at the ends of chorales suggest (or do not contradict) varying degrees of rallentando. Certainly it is illogical to claim that on the evidence of *Orgelbüchlein* notation, the ⌢ sign in the four-part chorale harmonizations is not to be marked by pulling up the tempo (Krey *BJ* 1956).

even song-variations. Such a motif as Ex. 1 gave unity to many a song-variation or chorale partita, not least to those of J. S. Bach himself.* But from the motif-cell new effects are produced, not simply

Ex. 1

because (as is often said) they are used in a more 'concentrated' manner; on the contrary, such a chorale as Steigleder's 'Vater unser im Himmelreich' (1627) already exploits a motif more single-mindedly than the caprice and inventiveness of the *Orgelbüchlein* would have allowed. The new effects are more those of a startlingly mature diatonicism, of an on-driving momentum towards cadence points, of a combining of different motifs – particularly the device of giving a conventional motif to the manuals above a new and striking motif in the pedals. Characteristic is the short suspension or tie in one part while the motif is heard in another. The total result of such details is unexpected, often capricious, never as calculating as the motivic play of (e.g.) J. G. Walther's 'Ach Gott und Herr' (see BWV 693 below). A doctrinaire exploiting of motifs is rare in the *Orgelbüchlein*, and it is significant that the chorale perhaps nearest to this danger is the one in the most antique form, i.e. the three-verse 'Christ ist erstanden' BWV 627. The composer's method of working is illuminated by the Leipzig fragment 'O Traurigkeit, o Herzeleid' – Ex. 2. This gives the

Ex. 2

appearance of having been composed *a 4* and not one part at a time, with the melody written down simultaneously as one of the four parts; both the phrase marks and the sign 'molt'adagio' were written in the same operation. Three motifs are introduced within only one and a half bars; the fragment includes a motif of repeated notes difficult to develop, along with two broken-chord motifs which are more pliable and would be more open to development, particularly in the bass and tenor lines. Motifs appear which are not used elsewhere in the album – similar in length and potential to other motifs (e.g. pedal of BWV 630) but nevertheless distinct. The adaptability of the alto and pedal motifs in b1 is striking: both could be easily fitted into b2, for example.

* It is an exaggeration to claim simply that 'in the *Orgelbüchlein* J. S. Bach transferred the song-variation to the sphere of the organ chorale' (Dietrich 1929 p28), without allowing for the fact that such motifs were common property by c1715.

While, as shown below, many motifs can be seen as conventional figures or *figurae* (Arfken 1965), outlined as such by theorists in classical teaching of harmony (Huggler 1935), their so-called symbolic significance has aroused much speculation during the last hundred years. Since few of them are simply graphic – even the falling motif of BWV 637 corresponds to a metaphor in the text, not a physical act – reasons have been found for seeing them as 'expressing' the objective dogma of the text concerned (Arfken 1965 pp101ff) and the chief meaning or atmosphere of the hymn (Vogelsänger 1972): that is, they suggest the whole text and not a single verse (Frotscher 1935 pp915ff), much less a single word. Some have seen a connection between the first verse of the text and each bar or idea in the organ chorale (Chailley 1974), a view flatly denied by others (Frotscher 1935 p917). In many cases it can be shown that the motifs are derived from the melody, but this is not incompatible with such expressiveness; the motifs 'contrapunctsweise zum gantzen Choral durch und durch geführt' ('contrapuntally developed through the whole chorale') by Praetorius in *Musae Sioniae* (1610) are chosen on textual rather than musical grounds (Vogelsänger 1972).* As so often in Bach, a traditionally based idiom or form is newly worked and becomes heavy with other possible meanings. Thus the canons for 'In dulci jubilo' BWV 608 and 'Gottes Sohn ist kommen' BWV 600 can be matched by J. G. Walther's (earlier?) canons on the same chorales, but the two composers' skills in four-part harmony are obviously not comparable; moreover, the line in the text 'trahe me post te' ('draw me after you') or even simply the word 'singen' suggests that the canon embodies some reference to the words. In most earlier canonic chorales, it is the accompaniment that was treated canonically, not the cantus firmus itself. The canonic treatment of the four Passion chorales BWV 618, 619, 620 and 624 may be less a specific reference than a symbol that 'Christ fulfils the will of his Father' (Dietrich 1929 p54), though the nature of symbolic interpretation seems to be such that few commentators have agreed on the image symbolized. Certainly it can be said that the closeness of canon both in interval and in metre give a distinctive character to the Passion chorales.

On the smaller formal level, the motifs may emphasize a word in the text: thus the accompanying motif derived from the first notes of the melody in BWV 632 and used throughout the movement (see Exx. 86–7 below) may well serve, at least in the composer's mind, as a reiteration of the opening words 'Herr Jesu Christ'. The way in which melody is treated in the three coloratura settings also suggests a close and natural link between technique and text: the hymns are concerned with prayer, complaint or trouble. Many of the motifs and the ways they are used suggest parallels between the *Orgelbüchlein* and Bach's partita movements or short settings by other composers (e.g. Buxtehude's 'Jesus Christus, unser Heiland' BUXWV 198); but only such movements as the last variation of 'O Gott, du frommer Gott' BWV

* The phrase 'durch und durch geführt' recalls the term 'durchführen' on the title-page of *Orgelbüchlein*.

767 actually resemble the *Orgelbüchlein* type either in technique or in musical quality. The technique and quality are better paralleled in some of the composer's contemporary work in church cantatas. Although for purposes of comparison the texture of cantata movements which incorporate a cantus firmus differs too greatly from that of an organ chorale – they are often more complex and detailed than the *Orgelbüchlein* settings – the Weimar cantatas do appear to work gradually towards using motifs not only in an inventive, concentrated form but also as if to imply an interpretation of the text: e.g. the sighing motif in 'Komm, du süsse Todesstunde' (BWV 161, 1715), the so-called tumult motif for 'Mit unsrer Macht' (BWV 80 no. 2, originally 1715), the French Overture details for 'Nun komm, der Heiden Heiland' (BWV 61, 1714). The last is the least graphic and most symbolic, since it does not picture or express but symbolizes the opening of a new church year, the 1st Sunday in Advent: overture = opening = Advent. In general, the motifs of the *Orgelbüchlein* provide examples of various allusions to the texts: allegory (falling Adam in BWV 637, flurrying angels in BWV 607), imitation (swaddling bands in BWV 603, knocking on 'the door of Heaven' in BWV 617), and general mood or *Affekt* ('uncertainty' in the diminished sevenths of BWV 637, sighs in BWV 618, festal mood in BWV 626). Both the terms and the resulting 'interpretation' of a certain chorale can be expressed in different ways, since music is not a language with a definable or replaceable vocabulary. But it remains fallacious, for instance, to expect to find in the organ setting of 'Nun komm, der Heiden Heiland' the French Overture rhythms used in BWV 61; the Advent chorale BWV 599 has no words, and it evokes rather than symbolizes.

---

599   Nun komm' der Heiden Heiland (*Orgelbüchlein*)

Autograph MS P 283; copy by J. T. Krebs (P 801), also in P 1160, P 1109 (Penzel), Brussels W.12.102 and Am.B. 47 (Kirnberger), Am.B. 46 and P 284 (Kirnberger circle), Lpz Poel 39 (Kittel), Danzig 4203/4 and late sources.

Two staves; second half of b7 corrected in tablature in P 283.

The TEXT is Luther's translation of Ambrose's Advent hymn *Veni redemptor gentium*, Erfurt 1524; in all hymnbooks from at least c1600, it was the chief hymn of the four Sundays in Advent (Gojowy 1972), given in Latin and German versions in several Leipzig books (Schein 1645, Vopelius 1682).

Nun komm, der Heiden Heiland,	Come now, Saviour of the heathen,
der Jungfrauen Kind erkannt,	acknowledged child of the Virgin,
des sich wundert alle Welt,	at whom all the world marvels
Gott solch Geburt ihm bestellt.	[that] God provided him with such
	a birth.

The following three verses concern the advent of Jesus, light in the darkness; the fifth verse is the doxology.

The MELODY was published with the text in 1524 and is a simplification of the Latin hymn (Ex. 3). Its form in BWV 659a, 660a and 661a

Ex. 3

BWV 36

corresponds to that in the Weissenfels hymnbook of 1714 (*NBA* IV/2 *KB* p76). Presumably because of its use over Advent, the melody was frequently set by Lutheran organ composers; in addition to BWV 599 (which opens the *Orgelbüchlein*, as the melody does many a hymnbook), 659, 659a, 660, 660a/b, 661, 661a and 699, it appears in three cantatas for the 1st Sunday in Advent, BWV 36 (1731), 61 (1714, 1723) and 62 (1724 etc). As in the versions used by Buxtehude and others, the harmonizations in the cantatas distribute the beat so that the accent lies on the first and fifth notes (as in Ex. 3); in the hymnbooks of Schein (1645) and Vopelius (1682) it appears on the second and fourth

(♩ ♩ ♩ ♩ | ♩ ♩ ♩ ♩ | ♩). In BWV 61 the melody appears in both sections of the first movement, a French Overture.

Since the time of Luedtke (1918 p54) there have been suggestions that the pedal rhythms of BWV 599 belong to the French Overture style, thus 'opening' the church year in an organ album; but neither the tempo nor the motifs themselves support this interpretation, particularly in comparison with BWV 61. Any *ouverture* allusions influencing the composer can have little bearing on the performer. More immediately striking is the series of falling phrases (Keller 1948 p151), particularly in the pedal and tenor lines; if this suggests the 'descente sur terre du Sauveur' (Chailley 1974 p196), the reference is symbolic rather than graphic, since the text does not itself refer to the Saviour as descending. In view of the 'talking figures' of musical rhetoric, it is as possible that the accompanying motif suggests a text of its own (Ex. 4). Indeed,

Nun komm, nun komm

Ex. 4

as has been pointed out already (Arfken 1965 pp46ff), the chorale does introduce many motifs heard later in the *Orgelbüchlein*. Not the least is that associated with texts referring to Life (♩♩♩), although not once does it appear as simple as it does in BWV 605, nor can any claim be made that BWV 599 as a whole is 'eine festliche Einzugsmusik für den Himmelskönig' ('a festive entrance-music for the King of Heaven': Arfken *op cit*). Conceptually, this is possible; perceptually, such an interpretation would be forcing a style of performance not otherwise obvious. Two details of composition are more striking: the motif *a* could have been continued or developed further than it is, and the chorale melody is much less prominent or even recognizable than in BWV 659–661. This appears to be due more to the density of motif (not least when it passes to the melody with its rhetorical rest in bb1, 8) than to the harmony itself, although it is true that the harmony is constantly inventing anew even when a previous passage could have been repeated (e.g. bb8–9 and bb1–2).

A stylistic allusion more in line with the chorale as a whole is that to the 'French prelude', associated in particular with lute and harpsichord preludes. One characteristic method of breaking a chord involved the very motif of BWV 599 (Ex. 5). Such 'chord-breaking' was

Ex. 5

L. Couperin, Prelude in G minor

known both to the 'old good French' masters admired by J. S. Bach (*Dok* III p288) and to German keyboard composers in the same tradition, e.g. Froberger and Fischer (likewise admired), who did not necessarily write out their opening chords in this way but left it to the performer. Similar 'French prelude' effects can be found elsewhere, e.g. the D major Toccata BWV 912 (bb112, 113) preserved in BB 40644 and P 804.

600

Gott, durch deine Güte (*Orgelbüchlein*)

Autograph MS P 283; copy by J. T. Krebs (P 801), also in P 1160, Brussels W . 12 . 102 and Am.B. 47 (Kirnberger) Am.B. 46 and P 284 (Kirnberger circle), Lpz MB MS 7 (Mempell–Preller), Lpz Poel 39 (Kittel), Danzig 4203/4 and late sources.

Headed in P 283 'Gott durch dein güte oder Gotts Sohn ist kommen', 'Man. Princip. 8 F.', 'Ped. Tromp. 8 F.'; two staves. In e.g. Brussels W . 12 . 102 headed 'Gottes Sohn ist kommen', 'im Manual, Principal 8 Fuss', 'Pedal, Trompete 8 Fuss'.

The TEXT of J. Spangenberg's *Gott, durch deine Güte* was published in 1544 to the same melody as *Gottes Sohn ist kommen*, being a hymn after the sermon 'von der Geburt Christi'.

Gott, durch deine Güte,	God, through your goodness,
wolst uns arme Leute	[we beg you] us poor people
Herze, Sinn und Gemüte	– heart, mind and soul –
für des Teufels Wüten	against the raging of the devil
am Leben und im Todt	in life and in death
gnädiglich behüten.	graciously to preserve.

The three verses are addressed to the Persons of the Trinity in turn.

The TEXT of J. Roh's Christmas hymn *Gottes Sohn ist kommen* was published in 1544 in a hymnbook of the Bohemian Brethren.

Gottes Sohn ist kommen	God's Son is come
uns allen zu Frommen	to all of us believers
hie auf diese Erden	here on this earth
in armen Gebärden,	in lowly guise,
dass er uns von Sünde	that he might free and release
freie und entbinde.	us from sin.

The eight verses that follow describe the purpose of Advent and Christmas, ending with a prayer for faith.

The MELODY was known in the fifteenth century and was published in 1544 to both texts in different hymnbooks; it belongs to the hymn *Ave ierarchia celestis et pia* (Terry 1921 p175). The melody (Ex. 6) is also used in BWV 703 and 724.

Ex. 6

BWV 318

The 'registration' indicates that the canonic voices are to sound at the pitch notated, and are to be distinguished by flue/reed stops. Although these specified stops were available on the Weimar court chapel organ, it is unlikely to be a registration in the normal sense. Written on two staves, the four parts present a canon between soprano and tenor, so composed and so copied out that the pedal can take either the tenor or bass; the 'short score' of P 283 makes either reading possible. At what point the composer added the registration is not yet known – it looks original – but since the Weimar pedal extended only to d' (as in the bass line) not e' and f' (as in the canonic tenor), it is possible that ambiguity led to the desire to clarify the canonic pitches (cf. also BWV 645 and 650). In conception and scoring, in the high pedal part and the metre of the canon, BWV 600 clearly forms a pair with BWV

608; in neither is the heading 'a 2 Clav.' authentic. The left hand is unlikely to be separately registered with 16' (*BG* 25.ii p.ix), since 'in the autograph the right hand parts are braced together, and the brace was extended to include the left hand as well' (Emery Novello xv p.xii) – i.e., the 8' registration served both hands.

The $^3/_2$ canonic treatment for a chorale melody found normally in duple time is also hinted at in J. G. Walther's F major setting of the same chorale (*Vers* 3, in BB 22541/1). Similarly, the almost doctrinaire

combination of three distinct rhythmic units –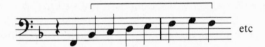

– is occasionally to be found less strictly observed elsewhere, e.g. Pachelbel's 'Nun lob mein' Seel' den Herren' (copied in P 803). The canon has been seen as expressing the sentiment of v2, that 'He comes again today to teach the people'(Chailley 1974 p124), a conjecture for or against which the evidence is poor.

The accompaniment itself has many details of interest characteristic of the composer's maturing style. Thus the pedal-like bass line incorporates the opening of the theme (Ex. 7) and returns to a common

Ex. 7  etc

shape in the 'interludes' between soprano phrases (bb4, 8, 12, 21 – Ex. 8). The alto, like that of BWV 608, remains within the ambit of

Ex. 8 b4

the right hand by contrary-motion figures; b1 of BWV 600 is conceived much as is b1 of BWV 608, all derived from the otherwise conventional *suspirans* figure (Ex. 9). Throughout, the harmony shows a masterful

Ex. 9 e.g. b2

diatonicism, in which organ-chorale canons can be seen developing into a new contrapuntally conceived harmonic language: see in particular bb8–13. This remains true even of those bars where a note-length has been altered to make the canon work (e.g. b10, pedal minims). Particularly mellifluous are those bars repeated in the second half (bb1–4 = bb18–21).

601 Herr Christ, der ein'ge Gottes-Sohn (*Orgelbüchlein*)

Autograph MS P 283; copy by J. T. Krebs (P 802 and P 801) and by J. G. Walther (Den Haag 4 G 14), also in P 1160 (Oley), P 1109 (Penzel), Brussels W.12.102 and Am.B. 47 (Kirnberger), Am.B. 46 and P 284 (Kirnberger circle), Lpz Poel 39 (Kittel; followed by figured-bass chorale BWV Anh.75), Danzig 4203/4 and late sources.

Headed in P 283 'Herr Christ, der ein'ge Gottes-Sohn oder Herr Gott, nun sei gepreiset' (first title only in other MSS; in P 283 the second may have been added by the composer afterwards); two staves.

The TEXT of E. Cruciger's Christmas hymn *Herr Christ, der ein'ge Gottes-Sohn* was published in Walther's hymnbook of 1524, becoming the chief hymn for the 4th Sunday in Advent. In Leipzig it was also sung on the 6th Sunday after Epiphany, and on the 13th and 18th Sundays after Trinity (Stiller 1970 pp220–1, 230–1), as elsewhere on Estomihi (Quinquagesima) or Michaelmas (Gojowy 1972).

Herr Christ, der einig Gottes-Sohn	Lord Christ, the only Son of God,
Vaters in Ewigkeit,	Eternal Father,
aus sein'm Herzen entsprossen,	sprouting from his heart,
gleichwie geschrieben steht,	as it is written,
er ist der Morgensterne,	he is the morning star,
sein Glänzen streckt er ferne	stretching his rays to the distance,
vor andern Sternen klar.	clear before other stars.

v5

Ertöt uns durch dein Güte,	Mortify us by your goodness,
erweck uns durch dein Gnad.	awaken us by your grace.
Den alten Menschen kränke,	Vex the old Adam
dass der neu' leben mag,	that he may live anew,
und hie auf dieser Erden	and here on this earth
den Sinn und alls Begehren	his mind and all [his] desires
und Gdanken hab zu dir.	and thoughts give to you.

The intervening verses are a meditation and prayer on Christmas.

The TEXT of *Herr Gott, nun sei gepreiset* was published in Babst's hymnbook of 1553, being a prayer *post prandium* (grace after meals); it was sung to the melody below from at least 1609 (Terry 1921 p184).

Herr Gott, nun sei gepreiset,	Lord God, now be praised,
wir sagen frohen Dank,	we give joyful thanks,
dass du uns Gnad' erwiesen,	that you have shown us grace
gegeben Speis' und Trank,	and have given us food and drink,
dein mildes Herz zu merken,	to remember your liberal heart,
den Glauben uns zu stärken,	to strengthen our faith,
dass du seist unser Gott.	that you are our God.

The MELODY was published with the first text and is adapted from the song *Ich hört ein Fräulein klagen* (Terry 1921 p184); its form in Ex. 10 was used in Cantata 22 (for Estomihi 1723). It appears also in

Ex. 10

BWV 22

BWV 698 and Cantatas 96 (18th Sunday after Trinity 1724 etc), 164 (13th Sunday after Trinity 1725?) and probably 132 (4th Sunday in Advent 1714).

An unusual binary form with two repeats, BWV 601 incorporates motifs heard elsewhere in the *Orgelbüchlein*, though never so simply. The bass motif is interpreted by Schweitzer as a 'motif de la quiétude joyeuse', already used by the composer in the final variation of BWV 767 (Schweitzer 1905 p349) and 'almost visually' a reference to the morning star (Chailley 1974 p129). But Dietrich finds that the bass motif is common in chorale variations of Buttstedt, Böhm and Vetter (1929 pp44–5), and other examples can be found in J. G. Walther. As in BWV 599, however, the *Orgelbüchlein* has a concentration of texture clearly beyond any conventional chorale variation and accordingly demands a performing tempo allowing for this. The accompanying motif is no static broken-chord harmonization but becomes extended towards the close of each line of the chorale, particularly in the left-hand phrase leading to the incomplete cadence in b10. Since the elements of praise and thanksgiving in the two hymn texts are not unrelated, neither need be sought in the music to the exclusion of the other. The opening itself – Ex. 11 – provides several elements characteristic of the

Ex. 11

piece and of the subtle techniques running through the album. Thus, motif *a* takes a different form in the pedal; motif *b* is an interpretation of the hymn melody, recurring (*rectus* or *inversus*) at key points in the chorale (bb1/5, 3/7, 8/14, 13/19);* both *a* and *b* are based on the AC♯ of the melody; the quasi-canonic nature of the alto and soprano

* On bar-numbering, see the Note on the Commentary, p.2 above.

in b1 is characteristic of an irregular but telling imitation between the voices, never pushed obtrusively nor dominated by any one motif (cf. the scale motifs of certain bars). If the alto in the example above is indeed derived from the soprano, it is in a hidden, intimate way that is new in organ chorales; at the same time, the resulting motif, though highly developed, is less consistently worked than that of (e.g.) BWV 643. Nor is it common for the (repeated) ends of each half to be so closely related (bb3–4 = bb13–14).

---

602   Lob sei dem allmächtigen Gott (*Orgelbüchlein*)

Autograph MS P 283; copy by J. T. Krebs (P 801), also in P 1160, Brussels W.12.102 and Am.B. 47 (Kirnberger), Am.B. 46 and P 284 (Kirnberger circle), Lpz Poel 39 (Kittel), Danzig 4203/4 and late sources.

Two staves.

The TEXT of M. Weisse's Advent hymn was published in 1531 for the Bohemian Brethren.

Lob sei dem allmächtigen Gott,	Praise be to Almighty God
der unser sich erbarmet hat,	who has been merciful to us,
gesandt sein'n allerliebsten Sohn,	sending his well-beloved Son
aus ihm geborn in Höchsten Thron.	born of him in the highest throne.

v2

Auf dass er unser Heiland würd,	So that he may become our Saviour,
uns freyte von der Sündenbürd,	freeing us from the burden of sin,
und durch seine Gnad' und Wahrheit	and through his grace and truth
führte zur ewigen Klarheit.	leading [us] to eternal light.

The following twelve verses relate the purpose of Christmas and the danger of 'not hearing the voice of the Son', and close with a doxology.

Ex. 12

1531

The MELODY (Ex. 12) was published with the text, and is derived from the melody of the hymn *Conditor alme siderum* or *Creator alme siderum* (*Liber usualis*, Vespers hymn for 1st Sunday of Advent). The versions used in BWV 602 and 704 have different openings.

As in BWV 599, the two motifs (pedal, manual) are complementary but distinct; that for the pedal is built on alternating notes typical of traditional alternate-foot pedalling. At times it brings the inner parts with it, unlike most *Orgelbüchlein* chorales (cf. BWV 625, where manuals and pedal share a motif). In particular, the tripling of the pedal motif in b5 leads to incidental parallel $\frac{6}{4}$ harmonies new at that period. The characteristic falling thirds in the melody in bb2, 3, 5 – more striking in the Gregorian version – perhaps suggested to the composer the various forms of the manual motif (Ex. 13). Similarly,

Ex. 13

b4

the Gregorian cadence suggested the close on A (cf. BWV 704). As b8 shows, the manual motif is no idle decoration of chords but itself motivates harmonic progression. Twice the bass motif begins in sequential suspensions and passes to emphatic repetition (bb1–3, 5–6), a third time eventually falling to the lowest note of the movement, in the final bar.

Despite attempts to show otherwise, it is difficult to feel sure that the two motifs, or their treatment, refer to any particular verse of the text. Vogelsänger (1972) suggests v2; Keller (1948 p152) sees in the falling bass a symbol for the 'coming down of divine Majesty', as in so many of the Advent/Christmas chorales in *Orgelbüchlein*; Chailley (1974 p186) thinks all the thirds and sixths refer to the union between the Father and 'his well-beloved Son'. Certainly a figure like Ex. 14

Ex. 14

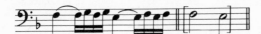

implies a desire to do more than merely vary plain minims by conventional 'divisions' of the kind recommended in composition manuals or theoretical studies of the period – e.g. Ex. 15.* Walther

Ex. 15

J. G. Walther, *Praecepta* 1708

suggests a *figura*; BWV 602 develops it beyond any conception Walther may have had of it. Nevertheless, it can only be conjectured whether the rhythmic idea ♪♪♪ is to be understood as a *motif de la joie* and whether, if so, it is a signal to the performer (tempo, registration etc) or rather offers insight into the working methods of the composer.

---

* Walther, *Praecepta*, 1955 edn p154.

603   Puer natus in Bethlehem (*Orgelbüchlein*)

Autograph MS P 283; copy by J. T. Krebs (P 801) and by J. G. Walther (BB 22541/1 and 22541/2), also in P 1160, Brussels W. 12.102 and Am.B. 47 (Kirnberger), Am.B. 46 and P 284 (Kirnberger circle), Lpz Poel 39 (Kittel), Danzig 4203/4 and late sources.

Two staves.

The Latin TEXT of the traditional Christmas hymn *Puer natus* was published by J. Klug in 1543 with a German translation; it became associated also with Epiphany, in particular v4 with its reference to the Magi (Stiller 1970 p224), though in Leipzig both Latin and German versions were sung over the whole period from Christmas Day to Epiphany, including New Year's Day (*ibid* pp50, 76).

Puer natus in Bethlehem,	A boy is born in Bethlehem,
Bethlehem,	Bethlehem,
unde gaudet Jerusalem.	wherefore Jerusalem rejoices.
Alleluia, alleluia.	Alleluia, alleluia.

The MELODY originated as the descant line (1553) to a tenor melody of 1543 of which a later version is used in BWV 607 (Terry 1921 p287). Apart from BWV 603, the descant melody is used in Cantata 65 (Epiphany 1724) (Ex. 16).

Ex. 16

BWV 65

The close of the chorale is uncertain. The last bar of P 283 has two beats, the second having a fermata and passing to a *custos* for B (flat or natural?); after this is a repeat mark between the staves, similar to those elsewhere in P 283 but here looking like an afterthought. 'It looks almost as if he meant the prelude to be repeated *ad lib.*, and to end eventually on the second beat of the bar' (Emery Novello xv p.xii), the repetition perhaps reflecting the twelve short, repetitive verses. Although such a close does not appear elsewhere in J. S. Bach, both the notation and the musical drive of the movement make such a 'second verse' plausible. Either way, the ending provided in the editions (*BG*, Peters, Novello, B & H) is less satisfactory than what appears to have been the composer's intention as understood by Walther and Krebs, i.e. closing on the second minim not the third and ending with open Gs.

The accompaniment to BWV 603 is in the classic *Orgelbüchlein* manner: a moving and intimate motif between the two hands is underpinned by a developed, almost ostinato descending motif in the pedal part, which is itself highly idiomatic. Both motifs syncopate the harmony and both have a persistent manner. Naturally the composer has been credited with picturing both swaddling bands (Ex. 17) and,

Ex. 17

in the pedal line, the steps of the revering Magi (Schweitzer 1905 p349) or the Saviour's descent to earth (Chailley 1974 p212). As the text refers to no swaddling bands, reverential steps or descending Saviour, such interpretations are conjectural. A key to the chorale text lies in its orthodox message of the purpose of the incarnation. The very importance of this text in Lutheran churches throughout the Christmas season suggests that it is no mere accumulation of Christmas images. Despite the fall within each pedal phrase, the overall impression is of a rising, intensive bass line; every line of the chorale sees a rising sequence in the bass below increasingly imitative and therefore increasingly tense inner parts.

604

Gelobet seist du, Jesu Christ (*Orgelbüchlein*)

Autograph MS P 283; copy by J. T. Krebs (P 801) and by J. G. Walther (BB 22541/1, with BWV 722), also in P 1160, P 1109 (Penzel), Brussels W.12.102 and Am.B. 47 (Kirnberger), Am.B. 46 and P 284 (Kirnberger circle), Lpz Poel 39 (Kittel), Danzig 4203/4 and late sources.

Headed in P 283 and Brussels W.12.102 (but not P 801) 'á 2 Clav. & Ped.'; two staves.

The TEXT of verses 2–7 of *Gelobet seist du, Jesu Christ* was derived by Luther from the Christmas sequence *Grates nunc omnes reddamus* and became in all hymnbooks a main hymn of the Christmas season (Gojowy 1972). The first verse is Low German of the fourteenth century (Stapel 1950).

Gelobet seist du, Jesu Christ,	Praised be you, Jesu Christ,
dass du Mensch geboren bist	that you are born a man
von einer Jungfrau, das ist wahr;	of a Virgin, that is true;
des freuet sich der Engel Schar.	the band of angels rejoices in it.
Kyrieleis.	Kyrie eleison.

The following six verses concern the incarnation, the light of the world, the Son 'leading us from the vale of misery'.

The MELODY was published with the text in 1524 and is ultimately derived from the plainsong of the Latin Sequence (Terry 1921 p169) – Ex. 18. In addition to the harmonization BWV 314, it appears in BWV

Ex. 18

BWV 314

697, 722, 722a and 723, in Cantatas 64 (3rd Day of Christmas 1723 etc) and 91 (Christmas Day 1724 etc), and in the Christmas Oratorio (1st and 3rd Days of Christmas).

The more conspicuous motif is heard in the pedal; the accompaniment is less motivic than in BWV 599 and, as in BWV 605, consists of broken two-part harmonies made rhythmically continuous (an early device known from e.g. Cantata 4). Again, the melody seems to have put the composer in the way of hidden lines. Thus the alto of b1 (Ex. 19)

Ex. 19

resembles the second line of the melody (b3), and the pedal motif itself (Ex. 20) may be derived (Vogelsänger 1972). Like others in the

Ex. 20

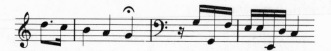

Orgelbüchlein, the pedal motif can be seen as typical of the tradition of alternate-foot pedalling; however, its falling line is not so much a derivation as an 'answer' to the rising inner voices, which in turn fall when it is inverted (penultimate bar). The placing of the pedal motif is carefully arranged, being neither repetitive nor predictable but leading to many clear cadences, including the final plagal close on G – which, in view of the similar key-scheme in BWV 697, is to be seen as quasi-modal.

   The first few bars show clearly some of the characteristics of the *Orgelbüchlein* melodic and harmonic style. The accompaniments not only lead to several *en passant* modulations but do so by the inner parts moving simply and by step (F, C and G major within three beats in bb1–2); accented passing-notes or short suspensions give momentarily involved harmonies, particularly of minor and dominant sevenths; at the same time, slight decorations of the melody itself, though in theory consisting of conventional *figurae*, present that melody in new guise and give it a lyricism that goes beyond pictorial or symbolic considerations. As is also common, the accompanying motif is not over-used, and could easily have been made to contribute more involved harmonies to the beginning of line 4 of the melody.

---

605 Der Tag, der ist so freudenreich (*Orgelbüchlein*)

Autograph MS P 283; copy by J. T. Krebs (P 801), also in P 1160, Brussels W.12.102 and Am.B. 47 (Kirnberger), Am.B. 46 and P 284 (Kirnberger circle), Lpz Poel 39 (Kittel), Danzig 4203/4 and late sources.

Headed in P 283 and Brussels W.12.102 'á 2 Clav. et Ped.' (*BG* 25.ii); two staves, last 4 bars in tablature (P 283).

The TEXT of the first two verses of the Christmas hymn *Der Tag, der ist so freudenreich* is an original fifteenth-century translation of the fourteenth-century hymn *Dies est laetitiae*; the three verses that follow were published in 1525. Text and melody appear in Klug's hymnbook (Wittenberg, 1529).

Der Tag, der ist so freudenreich	The day is so full of joy
aller Kreature;	for all creatures;
denn Gottes Sohn vom Himmelreich	because God's Son from Heaven
über die Natur	transcending nature
von einer Jungfrau ist geborn.	is born of a Virgin.
Maria, du bist auserkorn,	Mary, you are chosen
dass du Mutter wärest.	to be the mother.
Was geschah so wundergleich?	Was any event ever so miraculous?
Gottes Sohn vom Himmelreich	God's Son from Heaven
der ist Mensch geboren.	is born a man.

Amongst the Christmas images of the following four verses, the orthodox interpretation appears in v2.

Wär uns das Kindlein nicht geborn,	Had the child not been born to us,
so wärn wir allzumal verlorn;	we would be altogether lost;
das Heil ist unser aller.	the salvation is for us all.

The MELODY probably derives from the fifteenth century and was published in 1529. Apart from BWV 719, it is used only in the harmonization BWV 294 (Ex. 21).

Ex. 21

BWV 294

Only with difficulty does the text of vi fit the melody as used in BWV 605 (particularly lines 2 and 4), which suggests either that a later verse was in the composer's mind (v2? – Vogelsänger 1972) or that the setting was independent of any text. As in BWV 604, the inner motif is dispersed between two parts – a single line divided into two and producing inner harmonies. That it may be an early composition within the *Orgelbüchlein* period is suggested by the simple motif itself and its persistence throughout the chorale; also, as b11 shows, the notation for the figure is not quite consistent, nor is it clear if a real distinction is intended between the two notated versions ♪ 𝅘𝅥𝅮𝅘𝅥𝅮𝅘𝅥𝅮 𝅘𝅥𝅮𝅘𝅥𝅮𝅘𝅥𝅮 and ♪ 𝅘𝅥𝅮𝅘𝅥𝅮𝅘𝅥𝅮 ♪ 𝅘𝅥𝅮𝅘𝅥𝅮 (see b21 and b4/9). However, the dissonance in b3/8 (logical with the bass) suggests the mature harmony of the *Orgelbüchlein*. The falling bass figure is also characteristic, and 'early' signs in it are that each phrase begins and ends exactly with the chorale melody in the top part, that the end of each line of the melody leaves the middle parts with a void to fill (unlike e.g. BWV 604), and that the bass itself leads to many incidental cadences of falling fifths. The form of both melody and accompaniment emphasizes the mixolydian elements of the original hymn, and it is far from certain that the sudden f♮ in b3 evokes the 'coming of God's Son as a coming towards suffering' (Arfken 1965 pp46ff) or that the one in b18 evokes the line 'O, sweet Jesu Christ' (Vogelsänger 1972). It seems not to be agreed whether the left-hand motif incorporates the *motif de la joie* rhythm (Schweitzer 1905 p352, where this is called an Easter chorale), pictures the rocking cradle (Keller 1948 p153), or symbolizes the 'super/contra-natural' ('wider/übernatürlich') manner of the virgin birth (Arfken *op cit*). As in BWV 604 and elsewhere, the inner parts do sometimes resemble the melody (compare the alto of bb19–20 with line 5 of the melody), and the performer will find that if the notation is followed exactly, with rests taken as specified, many chords are without the third or its replacement (e.g. twice in the first two bars).

606   Vom Himmel hoch, da komm' ich her (*Orgelbüchlein*)

Autograph MS P 283; copy by J. T. Krebs (P 801) and by J. G. Walther (BB 22541/1 and 22541/2), also in P 1160, P 1109 (Penzel), P 1111 (Dröbs), Brussels W . 12 . 102 and Am.B. 46 (Kirnberger), Am.B. 47 and P 284 (Kirnberger circle), Lpz Poel 39 (Kittel), Danzig 4203/4 and late sources.

Two staves.

The TEXT of Luther's Christmas hymn was published in 1539, its first verse largely derived from the song *Ich komm aus fremden Landen her*; it was later associated with Vespers on the 1st Day of Christmas (Stiller 1970 p221) and with the whole Christmas season in all hymn-books (Gojowy 1972).

Vom Himmel hoch da komm ich her,	From Heaven on high I come,
ich bring euch gute neue Mär;	bringing you good tidings;
der guten Mär bring ich so viel,	of good tidings I bring so many
davon ich sing'n und sagen will.	of which I will sing and speak.

v2

Euch ist ein Kindlein heut geborn	To you is born today a little child
von einer Jungfrau auserkorn,	of a chosen Virgin,
ein Kindelein so zart und fein,	a child so tender and fine that
das soll eur Freud und Wonne sein.	he will be your joy and delight.

v15

Lob, Ehr sei Gott im höchsten	Praise, honour to God on the
Thron,	highest throne,
der uns schenkt seinen eigen Sohn.	who gives us his only son.
Des freuen sich der Engel Schar	Thus the band of angels rejoices
und singen uns solch neues Jahr.	and sings to us of such a new year.

The MELODY was published with the hymn in 1539 (Terry 1921 p304) as in Ex. 22. It is found in the organ works BWV 606, 700, 701, 738,

Ex. 22

1539

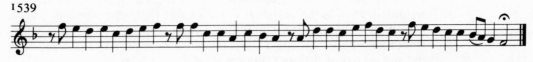

738a and 769 (five movements), three times in the *Christmas Oratorio* (1st and 2nd Days, twice to different texts) and as one of the movements of the E flat Magnificat BWV 243.

While the semiquaver motif produces runs characteristic of Christmas chorales concerned with the angels (cf. BWV 607, 701, 769), no line of BWV 606 is particularly scale-like. The inner parts, and the moments at which their motif reaches over to the hymn melody itself, follow rather the patterns traditionally made by the *figura suspirans* (Ex. 23).

Ex. 23

Such a figure may now and then lead to results superficially resembling those of other composers, such as the cadence of the first line in J. G. Walther's 'Vom Himmel hoch' *Vers* 1 – Ex. 24. But the texture of

Ex. 24

J. G. Walther, 'Vom Himmel hoch'

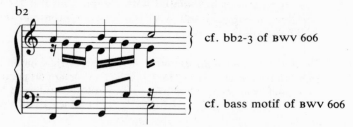

cf. bb2-3 of BWV 606

cf. bass motif of BWV 606

BWV 606 is characterized by a free use of the figure both *rectus* and *inversus*, as required either by the melody (also played in the right hand) or by the striding pedal (Schweitzer's 'thème de la démarche', a motif known in chorale partitas of Böhm, Buttstedt etc). Where the cantus-firmus crotchets are expanded to minims (bb3, 5–6, 8), it could be in order to allow the motif to develop and so to 'fill in' the pause implied in the fermata. But Bach's treatment of the melody is similar in BWV 700 and 769 and elsewhere. Striking is the syncopated version of the fourth pedal phrase, not only resulting in a rhythm comparable to that at the same point in 'Vom Himmel hoch' BWV 738 (b12), but also producing a texture similar to the opening and close of 'Da Jesus an dem Kreuze stund' BWV 621. As in the Easter chorale BWV 628, the inner motif finally spends its impetus by outrunning the melody not towards the full final chord as customary but towards bare Ds. Despite the similarity of motif between BWV 606 and 628, the details of its treatment are highly contrasted: in BWV 606, the motif passes between alto and tenor and is harmonized in thirds by them; in BWV 628, the motif produces a more spare texture and greater drive. As for the striding theme in the pedal, it is noticeable that while for line 1 such a contour is natural for a bass line keeping up quaver motion below such upper parts, by line 3 some ingenuity is required to give the bass the same kind of disjunct motion.

---

607   Vom Himmel kam der Engel Schaar (*Orgelbüchlein*)

Autograph MS P 283; copy by J. T. Krebs (P 801), Brussels W. 12. 102 and Am.B. 47 (Kirnberger), Am.B. 46 and P 284 (Kirnberger circle), Lpz Poel 39 (Kittel), Danzig 4203/4 and late sources.

Two staves; three in Brussels W. 12.102.

The TEXT of Luther's last Christmas hymn (Stapel 1950 p142) was published in 1543; its metre matches that of *Vom Himmel hoch da komm ich her*, to which tune it was frequently set (e.g. Freylinghausen 1741 etc).

Vom Himmel kam der Engel Schaar	From Heaven came the host of angels,
erschien den Hirten offenbar;	appearing openly to the shepherds;
sie sagten ihn'n 'Ein Kindlein zart	they said to them, 'A gentle child
das liegt dort in der Krippen hart.'	lies there in the hard crib.'

The following five verses centre on the orthodox message of Christmas as expressed by Luther:

v4

Was kann euch tun die Sünd und Tod?	What can sin and death do to you?
Ihr habt mit euch den wahren Gott.	You have with you the true God.

The MELODY was published in 1543 to the hymn *Puer natus in Bethlehem*; in 1553 it is found as the tenor to a soprano melody also associated with the latter text and used for BWV 603 (Terry 1921 pp286, 309). As comparison between BWV 603 and 607 shows, the melodies are closely related; the BWV 607 form is not used elsewhere by J. S. Bach.

The suggestion in *BG* 25.ii to use two manuals makes for ease of performance but separates the alto and tenor in a texture not naturally requiring it any more than in (e.g.) BWV 628; in other chorales, such as BWV 617, the two upper parts are more obviously paired. The tempo is also problematic but is in any case presumably slower than that of BWV 603. The cramped handwriting of P 283 makes it appear that the composer added the semiquaver runs to a harmonization already put on paper.

The descending scales for Christmas chorales (see also BWV 697, 701) are nowhere clearer than in the present movement where, at quarter-speed, the pedal follows the falling and rising figures, emphasizing the unsyncopated beats and marking each new line of the chorale by a rest. The resulting harmony is full of passing-note progressions in which most main beats are simple concords. The compass of the scale line gradually widens, not only running into the chorale melody itself (b5)* but eventually passing twice through three octaves and across the melody (bb15–18); at both points, the pedal passes in contrary motion. In this way the motif is exploited to a greater degree than in any known example by a comparable composer making use of such motifs (e.g. Buxtehude, 'Ich ruf zu dir' BUXWV 196). The bass line is most carefully composed, the first three phrases having four bars and the fourth phrase six bars, so that the bass gathers impetus towards the end even more strikingly than (e.g.) BWV 612 and 626. Similarly, while there is some

---

* The bar-numbering counts the first full-length bar as b1.

back-reference in the chorale (b3 = b7), other possible repetitions are in fact varied (b7 = b3, b15 = b6).

---

608   In dulci jubilo (*Orgelbüchlein*)

Autograph MS P 283; copies in P 1160, Brussels W.12.102 and Am.B. 47 (Kirnberger), Am.B. 46 and P 284 (Kirnberger circle), Danzig 4203/4 and late sources.

Two staves; in P 283 and e.g. Brussels W.12.102 no directions of any kind, except 'pedal' by the opening note of the tenor canon.

The TEXT of the fifteenth-century Latin–German Christmas hymn was printed in an early Lutheran hymnbook (Klug, *Geistliche Lieder*, 1535):

In dulci jubilo,	In sweet joy
nun singet und seid froh!	let us sing and rejoice!
Unsers Herzens Wonne	The rapture of our heart
liegt in praesepio,	lies in a manger,
und leuchtet als die Sonne	And shines like the sun
matris in gremio:	at his mother's bosom:
Alpha es et O, Alpha es et O.	You are alpha and omega.

v3

O patris charitas	O love of the father,
O nati lenitas!	O gentleness of the newborn!
Wir wären all verdorben	We should all have been lost
per nostra crimina,	through our sins,
so hat er uns erworben	so he earned for us
caelorum gaudia;	the joys of heaven;
eya wären wir da, eya wären wir da.	O that we were there.

Versions were known with three verses and with four.

The MELODY exists in variously embellished forms, e.g. BWV 368 (Ex. 25), and is used in BWV 608, 729, 729a and 751.

Ex. 25

BWV 368

The notation of BWV 608 has led to misunderstanding. Written out on two staves, the four parts enclose the lower canonic part as a tenor line at its required pitch, i.e. beginning at a and thus rising to f♯′. Because of the narrow pedal compass and the unsuitability of the bass line for pedals, the tenor line is played by pedal an octave lower than written, with 4′ stop. The 'short score' of P 283 thus notates the effect intended without further information on how to achieve it (cf. BWV 600).* Furthermore, like other old triple-metre Christmas hymns (e.g. BWV 603, 607) the movement is written in ³/₂, this time divided not into quavers and semiquavers but into triplet quavers. While the evidence is not conclusive, it is often assumed that the crotchets are to be played with the triplets, in the manner of bb25–30 notated with partial triplets ( ) in *BG* 25. ii – a passage presumably based on the later additions in P 283. And while it may remain true that the implied tonic pedal point or musette-drone running through the first twenty-four bars (compare BWV 751) is best realized by equal repeated crotchets in bb3, 4, 7, 8, the resulting inconsistency would be difficult to justify. Agricola's remark in 1769 (see notes to BWV 682) that J. S. Bach distinguished between dotted and triplet quavers unless 'extremely fast' is hardly relevant here, since there are no dotted notes in this piece, and in any case Agricola is not referring to this sort of organ music. However, there is one strong argument for not playing the crotchets as triplets: as in BWV 617, each voice subdivides the bar differently – into minims, crotchets and triplet quavers. Since after all the quavers 'should' strictly be triplet *crotchets*† (nine in a ³/₂ bar), it seems the composer intended to mark a distinction, both on paper and to the player.

The similarity of canonic treatment with J. G. Walther's 'In dulci jubilo' (BB 22541/2) is striking, but there is no evidence that Walther's setting is older. It is also striking that the harmonization BWV 368 decorates the melody with a motif not only found in the organ chorale (Ex. 26) but developed in most of the parts towards the end, including

Ex. 26

a diminished version in bb31–2. The canon is strict except for bb14–15. For the first twenty-four bars the accompanying line is also treated canonically; this feature – which arises from, and yet intensifies, the implied tonic drone – is a unique aspect of the chorale, despite a fitful tradition of canonic accompaniment from Scheidt to BWV 769. Thus BWV 608 crowns both canonic organ chorales and canonic treatments

* The canonic cantus firmus for pedal in the Premier Sanctus of F. Couperin's *Messe pour les paroisses* is also included within the two staves but marked to be played 'une octave plus bas'. Any 8′ pedal indication in other sources of BWV 608 confuses the issue and cannot now be authenticated.
† No doubt they are written as quavers 'to make the triplets more easily distinguishable' (Griepenkerl Peters v 1846).

of this particular melody. The accompanying motif is itself much developed, falling away in the first bar like that of BWV 600 and, also like it, running through to the final cadence. Again the accompanying motif produces accented passing-notes (of the characteristic *Orgelbüchlein* kind) and unusual syncopations in the repeated passage (bb10–16 = bb18–24). So naturally is the motif developed throughout that it appears to be neither contrived nor superimposed even when combined canonically against motif *a* above the unusually detailed final pedal point. Both the pedal point and the F♯ major chord of b25 may serve to depict the text, the former 'Alpha es et O', the latter 'leuchtet als die Sonne'.

---

609   Lobt Gott, ihr Christen allzugleich (*Orgelbüchlein*)

Autograph MS P 283; copy by J. T. Krebs (P801), also in P 1160, P 1109, Brussels W . 12 . 102 and Am.B. 47 (Kirnberger), Am.B. 46 and P 284 (Kirnberger circle), Lpz MB MS 7 (Mempell–Preller), Lpz Poel 39 (Kittel), Danzig 4203/4 and late sources.

Two staves.

The TEXT of N. Herman's eight-verse Christmas hymn was published in 1560, becoming a general Christmas hymn in many books and one for the 2nd and 3rd Days of Christmas in some (Stiller 1970 p222; Gojowy 1972).

Lobt Gott, ihr Christen alle gleich,	Praise God, you Christians all together,
in seinem höchsten Thron,	in his highest throne,
der heut schleusst auf sein Himmelreich	who today opens his Heaven
und schenkt uns seinen Sohn,	and gives us his son,
und schenkt uns seinen Sohn.	and gives us his son.

v8

Heut schleusst er wieder auf die Tür	Today he opens once again the door
zum schönen Paradies;	to beautiful Paradise;
der Cherub steht nicht mehr dafür.	the angel guards it no longer.
Gott sei Lob, Ehr und Preis,	To God be praise, honour and glory,
Gott sei Lob, Ehr und Preis!	to God be praise, honour and glory.

The MELODY was published with the hymn in 1580, having been earlier associated with another text (Terry 1921 p259). It appears in Cantata 151 (3rd Day of Christmas 1725 etc: Ex. 27) and to a different

Ex. 27

BWV 151

text in Cantata 195; it was harmonized in BWV 375 and 376 and set in the organ chorales BWV 609, 732 and 732a.

A comparison with BWV 606 shows BWV 609 to be less dominated by a single motif in the accompaniment, despite the similar motion, figuration and texture in the inner parts of the two chorales. In view of the unusually few tied notes and rests in BWV 609, its chief motif should be understood as in Ex. 28(i), not the form (ii) found in BWV

Ex. 28

606: the drawing of such clear distinctions between similar but different *figurae* in contemporary theory (e.g. J. G. Walther's *Praecepta* 1708) is borne out in many such *Orgelbüchlein* movements. The chorale BWV 609 is unusually homogeneous, and it is to be noted that the secondary motif Ex. 29 (also in BWV 603) is developed more fully and

Ex. 29

imitatively in another chorale, BWV 624. In the bass, the thrusting quavers of the pedal both rise and fall, by step and leap; the pedal line offers less a motif than a style. It is not clear why the motifs are mostly absent from b3, but the semiquaver motion is sustained simply, without the urgency of BWV 603 and 606, and without over-using the basic motif, as also in BWV 604.

---

610   Jesu, meine Freude (*Orgelbüchlein*)

Autograph MS P 283; copy by J. T. Krebs (P 801) and by J. G. Walther (BB 22541/1), also in P 1160, P 1109 (Penzel), Brussels W.12.102 and Am.B. 47 (Kirnberger), Am.B. 46 and P 284 (Kirnberger circle), Lpz Poel 39 (Kittel), Danzig 4203/4 and late sources.

Headed 'Largo' in P 283 (perhaps added later by the composer) and Brussels W.12.102 (but not in P 801); two staves.

The TEXT of J. Franck's six-verse hymn was published in 1653, soon becoming a popular *Jesuslied* in the hymnbooks (Stiller 1970 p234) in addition to its particular use on the 4th Sunday after Epiphany (*ibid* p225) and during Christmas in general, as in the Weimar hymnbook of 1708 (Gojowy 1972). The hymn was modelled on the song *Flora meine Freude, meine Seelenweide*, published in 1641 (Terry 1917 p261).

Jesu, meine Freude,	Jesu, my joy,
meines Herzens Weide,	pasture of my heart,

Jesu, meine Zier:
ach wie lang, ach lange
ist dem Herzen bange
und verlangt nach dir!
Gottes Lamm,
mein Braütigam,
ausser dir soll mir auf Erden
nichts sonst Liebers werden.

Jesu, my jewel:
oh how long, how long
has my heart been afraid,
and longed for you!
Lamb of God,
my bridegroom,
apart from you there shall be for me
nothing dearer on earth.

v2

Unter deinem Schirmen
bin ich vor den Stürmen
aller Feinde frei.
Lass den Satan wettern,
lass die Welt erzittern,
mir steht Jesus bei.
Ob es jetzt
gleich kracht und blitzt,
ob gleich Sünd und Hölle schrecken,
Jesus will mich decken.

Under your protection
I remain free of the tempests
of all [my] enemies.
Let Satan thunder,
let the earth tremble,
Jesus stands near me.
Although now
thunder roars and lightning flashes,
although both sin and Hell frighten,
Jesus will protect me.

The MELODY by J. Crüger was published with the text in 1653, taking slightly varied forms in different works of Bach (Ex. 30). As in

Ex. 30

BWV 64

Vopelius, the first and last lines are the same (Grimm 1969 p271). It appears in the organ chorales BWV 610, 713, 713a and 753, in Cantatas 64 (3rd Day of Christmas 1723 etc), 81 (4th Sunday after Epiphany 1724), 87 (different text, Rogation Sunday 1725) and 12 (no text, Jubilate Sunday (3rd after Easter) 1714 etc), in the motet BWV 227 (four chorales, one cantus firmus, one paraphrase) and in the harmonization BWV 358.

As a *Jesuslied* the chorale is relevant to Christmas and Epiphany as well as to contexts urging faith in adversity (Cantata 12), and it is not difficult to hear in its *Orgelbüchlein* setting a 'fervent longing' ('sehnsuchtsvolle Innigkeit', Spitta I p590) relevant to Advent rather than Christmas. The low pitch, the opening triad, the conspicuous use of the lowest note of the organ, and the 'Largo' direction join with the density of motif to produce this effect. The main cell of both manual and pedal motifs is Ex. 31, although (as in BWV 602, 606 and 609) the accompaniment achieves its greatest intensity when two of the parts

Ex. 31

are in simple thirds or sixths – an unusual by-product of the motivic technique in the *Orgelbüchlein*. Aided by the *largo* tempo, the shape of motif *a* can be made clear by phrasing, not least in the fermata b17.

As elsewhere in the *Orgelbüchlein*, the composer did not attempt to apply the motifs to every conceivable progression, despite their essential elasticity. More important is the nature of the pedal phrase, ostinato-like in its appearances, even running across the end of one chorale line (b4) and generally giving a longer-lined continuity than might be expected. Naturally it is the motifs that produce the striking harmonies, particularly the Ab–F♯–F♮ complexes in bb4, 18, 19. Bar 19 becomes a kind of rich-coloured version of b2. Indeed, it is striking that the composer does not employ repetition when the first line returns (compare b18 with b1) but only when the effect is somewhat hidden (compare b15 with b3).

---

611   Christum wir sollen loben schon (*Orgelbüchlein*)

Autograph MS P 283; copy by J. T. Krebs (P 801), also in P 1160, P 1109 (Penzel), Brussels W . 12 . 102 and Am.B. 47 (Kirnberger), Am.B. 46 and P 284 (Kirnberger circle), Lpz Poel 39 (Kittel), Danzig 4203/4 and late sources.

Headed in P 283 'Adagio', 'Corale in Alto' (both directions added after the music was copied?); in Brussels W . 12 . 102 'Adagio' and 'der C. F. im Alt'; in P 801 'Choral in Alto' (only); two staves.

The TEXT is Luther's adaptation of the Christmas hymn *A solis ortus cardine*, published 1524; in Leipzig and elsewhere it was often associated later with the 2nd Day of Christmas as a Vespers hymn (Stiller 1970 p222; Gojowy 1972).

Christum wir sollen loben schon,	We should indeed praise Christ,
der reinen Magd Marien Sohn,	son of the pure Virgin Mary,
soweit die liebe Sonne leucht'	as long as the dear sun shines
und an aller Welt Ende reicht.	and reaches to all the ends of the earth.

The alternative title for BWV 696, 'Was fürchtst du, Feind Herodes, sehr', is that of Luther's adaptation of the second part of the same Latin hymn, beginning *Hostis Herodes impie* (Terry 1921 p129):

Was fürchtst du, Feind Herodes, sehr,	Why are you so sore afraid, Herod,
dass uns geborn kommt Christ der Herr?	that Christ the Lord is born to us?
Er sucht kein sterblich Königreich,	He seeks no mortal kingdom,
der zu uns bringt sein Himmelreich.	he who brings his heavenly kingdom to us.

The MELODY is adapted from that of the Latin hymn, published 1524. Its form in Cantata 121 (2nd Day of Christmas 1724), which resembles that of BWV 611, is Ex. 32. In Witt, Scheidt, Scheidemann and J. G.

Ex. 32

BWV 121

Walther, the melody takes various forms, and the first full line appears in BWV 696.

Although P 283 could give the impression of presenting a short score leaving the organist to achieve the required effect in various ways (e.g. with cantus firmus on 4′ pedal and the bass in the left hand), in fact the spacing leaves no room for choice (cf. BWV 600, 608). Only in b14 is the layout ambiguous in that the usual reading may reflect a later emendation by composer or copyist: the bracketed 'upper pedal part' may be a left-hand part.

Except for the canonic BWV 618 and 633/634, no alto cantus firmus is found in *Orgelbüchlein*. It is striking that after the unusually dense 'Jesu, meine Freude', the spacing of BWV 611 is very wide: the opening notes span almost the whole extent of the keyboard, b6 achieving both C and c‴. Within the web of ascending and descending scale patterns the cantus firmus moves largely by step, obtrusive only in so far as its notes tend to be longer than those of the accompaniment. The *adagio* scales have led to the assumption that the composer is expressing not boisterous Christmas joy but rather a 'mystical contemplation', with an 'exaltation joyeuse dans ce soprano' (Schweitzer 1905 p353). Nevertheless, it is to be noticed also that the dorian character of the chorale melody is preserved and that its opening line (Ex. 33) has

Ex. 33

already been made scale-like, perhaps then suggesting both the scale patterns and (implied by the quasi-stretto between alto and tenor in b1) the rhythmic figure . A similar point can be made about BWV 612. The leaps belong chiefly to the accompaniment, and prepare motivic imitations in traditional manner; but the derivation of these motifs from the melody is unusual in the *Orgelbüchlein* and results in somewhat disguising the cantus firmus (Frotscher 1935 p923). The final setting of the chorale in Cantata 121 (2nd Day of Christmas

1724) is also lyrical and somewhat drawn-out, not least in a cadence that deserves comparison with BWV 611: Ex. 34. The 'modal' cadence

Ex. 34

BWV 121 (transposed up one tone)

of BWV 611 is also found in BWV 696. But the motivic concentration in BWV 611 is highly original and important in the composer's development. The inventive use of scale fragments of varying length is matched by a rhythmic fluidity equally untiring in its search for new forms. Thus, although there is a tied note across many of the beats, the exceptions, untied in all parts, are often at main beats (bb2, 4, 7, 12), and 'fluidity' is not therefore achieved by constant suspension or ties, despite the frequency of the suspended pedal rhythm.

---

612   Wir Christenleut' (*Orgelbüchlein*)

Autograph MS P 283; copy by J. T. Krebs (P 801), also in P 1160, P 1109 (Penzel), Brussels W.12.102 and Am.B. 47 (Kirnberger), Am.B. 46 and P 284 (Kirnberger circle), Lpz MB MS 1, Danzig 4203/4 and late sources.

Two staves; last 2½ bars in tablature in P 283.

The TEXT of C. Fuger's Christmas hymn *Wir Christenleut'* was published by 1593 (1586?); in Leipzig as elsewhere, it was sung on one or another of the Days of Christmas (Stiller 1970 p221).

Wir Christenleut'	We Christians
habn jetzund Freud,	now have joy
weil uns zu Trost Christus ist	because Christ for our comfort is
Mensch geboren,	born a man,
hat uns erlöst.	and has redeemed us.
Wer sich des tröst'	Who trusts in this
und glaubet fest, soll nicht werden	and believes firmly, shall not be
verloren.	lost.

The remaining four verses concern the message of Christmas:

   v3

Die Sünd macht Leid;	Sin causes sorrow;
Christus bringt Freud,	Christ brings joy,
weil er zu uns in diese Welt ist	for he is come to us in this world.
kommen.	

The MELODY – Ex. 35 – was published with the text in 1593 but is some years older. The versions of the melody differ in the repeat of line 1: see BWV 710.

Ex. 35

BWV 40

In P 283, dots between the lines of the stave at the beginning of b9 suggest that the section bb9–15 is repeated: this is plausible in view of similarities between the ends of b8 and b15. However, the music runs off the stave for the last two and a half bars in this MS and is completed in organ tablature – perhaps the reason why 'the autograph has no corresponding sign at the end of bar 15' (Emery Novello XV p.xii). The composer's intentions are unclear, not least since the text is not known to have been normally repeated; perhaps, on the contrary, bb9–15 were an optional omission, for several reasons – because the chorale melody is already unusually repetitive, b16 follows naturally on b8, and the two pedal-less lines (bb8–11) resemble an interlude in the four-part texture. However, BWV 632 provides a further example of a repeated second half to a chorale. A further detail of the notation in P 283 is that it looks as if the composer wrote out the cantus firmus first.

Whether or not the pedal line actually symbolizes 'une foi ferme en Christ le Sauveur' (Schweitzer 1905 p346; Chailley 1974 p251) cannot be demonstrated; but it is possible that the composer associated the 'glauben' of v1 with a striding pedal line, as shown in the later 'Wir glauben all'' BWV 680. The pedal phrase itself is of particular interest: it derives from the manual motif, simplifying it as well as accompanying it (Ex. 36) in much the same way as the pedal subject of BWV 664

Ex. 36

simplifies its manual subject (compare BWV 664 b10 with BWV 612 b1); the phrase-lengths are varied, the exact form of *b* being found untransposed in several bars (bb1, 3, 8, 11, 14); and the lowest phrase is the last, perhaps to be associated with the text line '[Wer] glaubet fest, soll nicht werden verloren' but developing the motif sequentially in a way familiar from the on-driving bass lines of later works (e.g. Fourth Brandenburg Concerto, last movement).

Ex. 37   (i)   (ii)

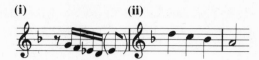

At the same time, the motif Ex. 37(i), used equally between the middle voices, and only occasionally varied, may well derive from a phrase which occurs no fewer than five times in the course of the chorale melody, Ex. 37(ii). Whether such derivation in BWV 611 and 612 is to be seen as the composer's way of 'confirming' the title and meaning of the chorale text (Vogelsänger 1972) can only be conjectured, but the inter-derivation – as if melody and motif were equally derived from each other – gives a kind of musical unity unexpected in a semi-ostinato movement. Equally original in organ music are the motifs themselves and the varied, changing texture they have led to. A comparison between the first two bars and the last three is instructive for the composer's use of motif in different parts, in different keys and with different harmonic implications, while the passage bb11–13 shows the half-speed development of the motif (two harmonies per bar) necessary when the melody includes repeated notes.

---

613   Helft mir Gottes Güte preisen (*Orgelbüchlein*)

Autograph MS P 283 (*c*1740; see below); copies in P 1109 (Penzel), Brussels W.12.102 and Am.B. 47 (Kirnberger), Am.B. 46 and P 284 (Kirnberger circle), Lpz Poel 39 (Kittel), Danzig 4203/4 and late sources.

Two staves.

The TEXT of P. Eber's six-verse hymn was published in 1569; it became associated in Leipzig and elsewhere with the Sunday after Christmas or (more often) New Year's Day (Gojowy 1972), having also been an Advent hymn in the 1693 Leipzig *Gesangbuch* (Stiller 1970 p223).

Helft mir Gottes Güte preisen,	Help me to praise God's goodness,
ihr Christen insgemein,	all you Christians,
mit Gsang und andern Weisen	with song and other melodies
ihm allzeit dankbar sein,	to be ever grateful to him,
vornehmlich zu der Zeit,	especially at the time
da sich das Jahr tut enden,	when the year draws to an end,
die Sonn sich zu uns wenden,	the sun turns towards us,
das neu Jahr ist nicht weit.	the new year is not far.

The MELODY, perhaps by Wolfgang Figulus, is one of two very similar melodies published with this text. The text was set to the other melody by Freylinghausen (1741 etc), a melody 'practically identical with the contemporary *Vom Gott will ich nicht lassen*' (Terry 1921 p180), and indeed the latter melody was recommended for the text in

Vopelius 1682. The version set in BWV 613 is also used in Cantatas 16 (New Year 1726?), 28 (Sunday after Christmas 1725) and 183 (Exaudi (Sunday after Ascension Day) 1726): Ex. 38.

Ex. 38

BWV 28

As in the fragment 'O Traurigkeit, o Herzeleid', the handwriting of BWV 613 shows characteristics suggesting that the piece was written into P 283 'during the Leipzig period, and probably only after 1740' (Dadelsen 1958 p80), or 'at least after 1730' (Dadelsen 1963). Whether it was composed then is not known; that the accompanying motif is clearly derived from the melody does not of itself demonstrate a late date (cf. BWV 635). In the varying texture, the use of both complete and incomplete cadences, the nature of the motifs themselves and their combinations and use, the movement is perfectly in accord with the type of chorale most represented in the *Orgelbüchlein*. Only the two pedal scales seem somewhat out of place; the bass line is otherwise pedal-like in a true organ texture, even when its phrases are apparently Corellian (bb7, 13–16). As in BWV 644, the scale motif throughout draws attention to the 'passing of time' but is not used in every bar, nor is the tempo languid.

While line 1 certainly provides the head of the motif, line 2 can be seen to influence its second phrase: Ex. 39. Such imitations built on

Ex. 39

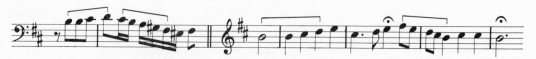

a repeated-note motif are often seen as 'speaking' (Schweitzer 1905 p384) or 'confirming' (Vogelsänger 1972) the opening line of the text, in this case one of praise. There is some repetition in the chorale (end b10 to middle b12 = end b12 to middle b14)* though not as much as in the melody itself (bb1–4 = bb5–8; bb15–16 = bb3–4). Surprising too is the number of dominant–tonic progressions (bb2–3, 6–7, 7–8, 9, 10–11, 12–13, 14–15, 15–16). In view of the following chorale, the chromatic line in the alto is noticeable (bb11, 13) for the text 'da sich das Jahr tut enden, die Sonn sich zu uns wenden'; but the chromatic line in the pedal six bars earlier has no such reference in any verse.

---

* Given repeat marks and not written out in P 283.

614   Das alte Jahr vergangen ist (*Orgelbüchlein*)

Autograph MS P 283; copy by J. G. Walther (BB 22541/1), also in
P 1109 (Penzel), Brussels W . 12 . 102 and Am.B. 47 (Kirnberger), Am.B.
46 and P 284 (Kirnberger circle), Lpz Poel 39 (Kittel), Danzig 4203/4
and several late sources.

Headed 'á 2 Clav. &. Ped.' in P 283 (*BG* 25.ii) and Brussels W . 12 . 102;
two staves.

The TEXT of the first two verses was published by C. Stephani in 1568;
vv3–6 followed in a publication of 1588 (J. Steurlein).

Das alte Jahr vergangen ist;	The old year has gone by;
wir danken dir, Herr Jesu Christ,	we thank you, Lord Jesu Christ,
dass du uns in so grosser Gefahr	that in such great danger you
so gnädiglich behüt' dies Jahr.	preserved us this year so graciously.

v3

Entzieh uns nicht dein heilsam Wort,	Do not deprive us of your wholesome word,
das ist der Seelen Trost und Hort;	which is the consolation and treasure of the soul;
vor falscher Lehr, Abgötterei	from false teaching and idolatry
behüt uns, Herr, und steh uns bei.	preserve us, Lord, and remain with us.

Three other verses contain prayers for the coming year, and the final
verse is a doxology.

The MELODY, attributed to Steurlein, is known from at least 1588
but is associated with this text only from 1608; its five melodic phrases
were distributed in different ways to make a stanza of eight lines
(*aabcdcde* in Steurlein), four (1687) or six (*aabcde* in BWV 288, 289,
614:* Ex. 40).

Ex. 40

BWV 288

The 'chromatic grief motif' has occasioned much speculation since
neither the text nor the aeolian melody, of themselves, seem to require
what has been described as 'the greatest intensity' (Spitta 1 p593) of
this organ chorale, a 'melancholy' (Schweitzer 1905 p355), 'a prayer,

* Repeating lines 1 and 4 of the text in each verse.

43

anxiety for the future' (Arfken 1965), marking the juncture between 'the past and the future' (Chailley 1974 p100). It has been shown that the final major chord of BWV 614, effectively an imperfect cadence, corresponds to the major ending found in some hymnbooks (Terry 1921 p140); it therefore does not necessarily refer in BWV 614 to the text, as was once supposed (Schweitzer 1905 p355). More recent approaches to Bach's chorale idiom could see the six falling and six rising chromatic notes as representing the twelve months of the year, in which case the six rising chromatic notes of BWV 613 can no doubt be explained in the same way. While the value of all such speculation is uncertain, the relationship of BWV 614 to the chorales on either side is clear. Whenever BWV 613 was composed, its three chromatic phrases either look towards or arise out of those of BWV 614; on the other hand, the sheer contrast with BWV 615 emphasizes the turning of the year. Thus the succession of these pieces forms a clear reference point in the church year which was not shown in the Weimar *Gesangbuch* of 1713.* The texts of both BWV 614 and 615 are addressed to Jesus; the first contains thanks and prayer, the second praise and joy, both presenting Jesus as the Saviour, though from somewhat different lines of approach. Both therefore exploit their key motif, giving it full expression and realization.

Within its basic character as one of the few coloratura chorales in the collection, BWV 614 also manages to include in its melody a clear reference to the accompanying motif (b5). The motif itself may therefore be seen as a kind of derivative; but more important is its own entity as a chromatic line answered in inversion (bb1, 3, 5, 6, 7, 11) or canonic stretto (e.g. alto, bass, soprano in bb3–5). This motif is exploited with great skill, with an 'objective' technique which does not of itself justify any 'melancholy' interpretation. Its exact form is also familiar from tradition – the so-called chromatic fourth found in such pieces as BWV 551 (Ex. 41) and labelled *passus duriusculus* by

Ex. 41   BWV 551

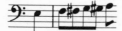

Schütz's pupil Bernhard (see BWV 625).† Unlike most *Orgelbüchlein* chorales, BWV 614 offers few other places where the motif could be introduced in the course of the twelve bars, especially as the composer has used it in so many ways, without regular stretto, regular answer or even regular phrase-length. For example, bb3–4 are neither a simple repeat nor an entirely new version of bb1–2. On the other hand, several of the cadences are noticeably straightforward in the pedal (bb2, 6, 8, 12), which gives a very firm anchor effect under the extraordinary rising 'sighing motif' of the final cadence. Nevertheless, the problem of BWV 614 remains: is the 'melancholy' heard in it during

---

* The hymns corresponding to BWV 614 and 615 are respectively nos. 39 and 29.

† Also found in D minor or *tonus primus*, from Sweelinck (*Fantasia Chromatica*) to Beethoven (Ninth Symphony, coda to first movement).

at least the last century justified by the 'objective' traditionalism of
its key motif?

---

615   In dir ist Freude (*Orgelbüchlein*)

Autograph MS P 283; copy by J. T. Krebs (P 801), P 1160, Brussels
W . 12 . 102 and Am.B. 47 (Kirnberger), Am.B. 46 and P 284 (Kirnberger
circle), Danzig 4203/4 and late sources.

Two staves; in P 283 and (e.g.) Brussels W . 12 . 102, no directions of
any kind.

The TEXT was published in 1598 by J. Lindemann as a two-verse hymn,
Liebe zu Jesu, . . . Weyhenachten Gesenglein ('Love of Jesu . . . a Christmas hymn': Terry 1921 p217).

In dir ist Freude	In you is joy
in allem Leide,	in all suffering,
O du süsser Jesu Christ!	O sweet Jesu Christ!
Durch dich wir haben	Through you we have
himmlische Gaben,	heavenly gifts,
du der wahre Heiland bist;	you who are the true Saviour;
hilfest von Schanden,	you help us from injury,
rettest von Banden.	you save us from fetters.
Wer dir vertrauet,	He who puts trust in you
hat wohl gebauet,	has built well
wird ewig bleiben, Halleluja.	and will live for ever, Hallelujah.
Zu deiner Güte	To your goodness
steht unser Gmüte,	our spirit holds fast,
an dir wir kleben	to you we cling
im Tod und Leben;	in death and life;
nichts kann uns scheiden, Halleluja.	nothing can separate us, Hallelujah.

The MELODY derives from G. G. Gastoldi's *balletto L'innamorato*,
published in 1591 and already a hymn tune in D. Spaiser's hymnbook
of 1609, becoming associated with *In dir ist Freude* by 1646. Included
in the Weimar *Gesangbuch* of 1713, the melody as it appears in BWV
615 is also very like the form in Witt's *Cantional* of 1715 (Terry 1921
p215): Ex. 42.

Ex. 42
Witt 1715

Alone of the *Orgelbüchlein* chorales, the melody of BWV 615 is split up and used as the basis of a web of thematic allusion, called the 'Böhmian manner' by some authors (Spitta I p593, Luedtke 1918 pp18–19); the melody as a whole only gradually becomes audible. Organ chorales by Böhm (e.g. 'Allein Gott in der Höh' sei Ehr'' in Walther's MS Kö 15839) and Buxtehude (e.g. 'Von Gott will ich nicht lassen' in the same source) can be found in which the melody passes from one voice to another, occasioning different treatments, often sectional and disparate. Similarly, quasi-ostinatos are not unknown in Walther's own works, e.g. for 'Dies sind die heilgen zehn Gebot' (Den Haag

Ex. 43

Walther
b2

4 G 14): Ex. 43. But the sum of BWV 615 seems greater than the parts; its varying but unified texture and its on-driving movement (despite internal repetition) are not to be found elsewhere.

There is the greatest possible change in musical mood between this and the preceding chorale (BWV 614). In BWV 615 the cantus firmus can be heard more or less continuously as follows:

text lines 1, 2	bb9–12, top part (12 bars)	A
3	bb13–16, alto, then top part	
4, 5	bb26–29, top part	
6	bb39–40, scattered through various parts	B
7–11	bb40–51, top part, middle lines decorated	C
12–16	bb52–end, ditto (12 bars)	

There are two major repeated sections:*

bb1–12   = bb18–29
bb39–50 = bb51–62

and it is not quite correct to describe the chorale as 'having interludes', despite most commentaries (e.g. Frotscher 1935 p925). In fact, within the main sections thus repeated, the technique – through-composition of a cantus firmus in the soprano, above a motivic accompaniment including a quasi-ostinato pedal part – is typical of the *Orgelbüchlein* as a whole. Less typical is the broken-up carillons of the opening, not only the ostinato but the manual figures in bb3, 5 etc; these are matched by the left-hand figure in the second half (bb40, 52).

In addition to its carillonesque ostinato, the pedal bears some of the cantus-firmus phrases (bb7, 24, 34, 48, 60), the last two of which are decorated (as in the right hand) and the middle of which quotes a line closer to Gastoldi's original (Ex. 44(i)). Nor is the pedal the only

Ex. 44

(i)   (ii)

* Given repeat marks and not written out in P 283.

quasi-ostinato: the melodic phrase Ex. 44(ii) also appears (in simple or decorated form) in each of the first eleven bars of the chorale, and again on their repeat beginning six bars later. Only a melody with such short, repeated phrases could be treated in such a manner, and the treatment is curiously evocative of the text itself, with its short phrases and repetitive rhythms. More traditional is the combination in bb48ff of one phrase of the cantus firmus with a decorated version of the preceding phrase (Ex. 45). The motif *a* is a decoration also familiar

Ex. 45 b48

from the Weimar chorale 'O Lamm Gottes unschuldig' BWV 656a, where however there is no thrusting bass to compel it onward in the same way; perhaps its turned trill also anticipates or copies the 'Hallelujah' figure at the end of 'Komm, heiliger Geist' BWV 651, where again it leads to harmonies far more conventional than the logical but at first puzzling bb48 and 60.* Despite a recent claim (J. Krause, *MuK* 1967 pp207ff), it is difficult to see that any ostinato motif of the movement is related in shape (and thus perhaps in 'meaning') to the rising *Kreuzstab* motif of Cantata 56.

616

Mit Fried' und Freud' ich fahr' dahin (*Orgelbüchlein*)

Autograph MS P 283; copy by J. T. Krebs (P 801) and J. G. Walther (BB 22541/1), also in P 1160, Brussels W . 12 . 102 and Am.B. 47 (Kirnberger), Am.B. 46 and P 284 (Kirnberger circle), Lpz Poel 39 (Kittel), Danzig 4203/4 and late sources.

Two staves; last 3 bars in tablature in P 283.

The TEXT of Luther's alliterative hymn is a version in four verses of the *Nunc dimittis* (Luke ii, 29–32), published Wittenberg 1524 and associated with the Burial Service (Luther 1542). In later hymnbooks it is associated with the end of the Epiphany period, with Mariae Reinigung (Purification of the Virgin) and, less often, with the 16th Sunday after Trinity (Gojowy 1972). As a prayer of thanksgiving, it shows Christian reconciliation with death, according to a 1527 sermon by Luther (Stapel 1950 pp222ff).

Mit Fried und Freud ich fahr dahin With peace and joy I now depart
in Gottes Willen; in God's will;

---

* The ninth followed by seventh is found in the same key in the cadence of the Loure from the French Suite in G BWV 816.

getrost ist mir mein Herz und Sinn,   my heart and mind are consoled,
sanft und stille;   soft and stilled;
wie Gott mir verheissen hat: as God has promised me,
der Tod ist mein Schlaf worden.   death has become my sleep.

The MELODY was published with the text, and the chorale was used in Cantatas 83 (Mariae Reinigung 1724), 95 (16th Sunday after Trinity 1723), 106 (funeral cantata, 1707?) and 125 (Mariae Reinigung 1725), and harmonized in BWV 382: Ex. 46.

Ex. 46

BWV 125

Of the three fully worked settings (BWV 95, 125, 616), the last is the least 'fluid'. Since Schweitzer's motif list of 1905, the rhythm

has been credited with symbolizing joy; but in BWV 616 the shape of the figure, and its moving by step without repetition or leap, suggests something more restrained. That the rhythm itself is not of prime significance – and therefore that its own 'meaning' is doubtful – is shown by the fact that the pedal bass motif contains the shape but not the rhythm; it has been simplified for pedal: Ex. 47. The rhythm,

Ex. 47   **(i)**   **(ii)**

however, is obtrusive and is only occasionally abandoned when the pedal has its own motif. Its phrase is often two beats long (cf. the short and long versions of a motif in BWV 625) and is developed both inverted (like the pedal version) and stretto. Several times it affects the cantus firmus itself, as is not uncommon when the motif is of archetypal simplicity (cf. BWV 606, 625, 642). However, the pattern is likely to be   rather than the form   which prevails in BWV 642. It is in the character of the *Orgelbüchlein*'s inventive use of motifs and motivic intensity to make such distinctions (see the note on BWV 609 in relation to BWV 606), and it would be unreasonable to claim both versions as *motifs de la joie*. Even within BWV 616, the in-turning shape that the rhythm sometimes takes (Ex. 48(i)) is essentially different from the scale-like shape (ii), as both are from the broken-chord version in the final half-bar. To separate the

Ex. 48　　(i)　　　　　(ii)

rhythm from such variety of melodic form can scarcely lead to a reliable interpretation of the composer's method; on the other hand, to see 'Fried' in the pedal form but 'Freud' in the manual form (Ex. 47(i) and (ii) respectively) as has been recently suggested (Chailley 1974 p192) requires a willingness to conjecture beyond the probable.

As in BWV 612, 607 and elsewhere, the pedal phrases are carefully graded towards the final cadence; each has a different length, and each begins with a rest at each new chorale line. The cadences formed at the ends of the pedal phrases are symmetrically arranged: plagal–perfect–plagal–perfect–plagal. But the line itself avoids the simpler symmetries (e.g. alternating the *rectus* and *inversus* forms of the motif), and throughout its fifteen bars it demonstrates the *Orgelbüchlein* characteristic of caprice enlivening tight organization. That such lines are not mere filigrees worked from simple motifs can be seen from the setting of the same chorale in Cantata 106, no. 3 (1707?), where the melody is accompanied by simple *suspirans* figures decorating the harmonies rather than directing them.

617　　　　Herr Gott, nun schleuss den Himmel auf (*Orgelbüchlein*)

Autograph MS P 283; copy by J. T. Krebs (P 801) and J. G. Walther (BB 22541/1–2), also in Brussels W . 12 . 102 and Am.B. 47 (Kirnberger), Am.B. 46 and P 284 (Kirnberger circle), P 603 (*c*1755–60), Lpz MB MS 7 (Mempell–Preller), Lpz Poel 39 (Kittel), Danzig 4203/4 and late sources.

Two staves; last half-bar in tablature in P 283.

The TEXT of T. Kiel's hymn was published in 1620, becoming associated with Mariae Reinigung (Purification of the Virgin) and, in pietist circles, with the ideas of death and resurrection (Freylinghausen 1741 etc).

Herr Gott, nun schleuss den Himmel auf!	Lord God, now unlock Heaven!
mein Zeit zu End sich neiget;	my time draws to a close;
ich hab vollendet meinen Lauf,	I have completed my course,
dess sich mein Seel sehr freuet;	which makes my soul rejoice;
hab g'nug gelitten,	I have suffered enough,
mich müd gestritten,	am tired with struggling,
schick mich fein zu,	send me off
zur ewig'n Ruh,	to eternal rest,
lass fahren was auf Erden	let go that which prefers to find
will lieber selig werden.	blessedness on earth.

The last of the three verses relates the text to the *Nunc dimittis*:

Lass mich nur, Herr, wie Simeon   Only let me, Lord, like Simeon
in Frieden zu dir fahren.   go to you in peace.

The MELODY was published with the text in a five-part setting (see Novello XV p52), from two voices of which a melody either gradually emerged or was deliberately formed in early-eighteenth-century hymnbooks. In Freylinghausen (1741) it takes the form shown in Ex. 49.

Ex. 49

Freylinghausen 1741

It is possible that the composer 'harmonized' the cantus firmus in BWV 617 (giving it a unique two-voice form) because of the ambiguous nature of the original melody, which emerged from two crossed parts. Such a 'double cantus firmus' can be seen as justifying the direction 'a 2 Clav. e Pedale' in *BG* 25.ii and elsewhere (Klotz 1975 p390).

Essentially a trio structure, BWV 617 shows a 'simplified' *Orgelbüchlein* arrangement of cantus firmus, running left hand and syncopated pedal. Neither of the latter lines is dominated by one particular motif; instead, both exploit several motifs which can combine variously with each other (Ex. 50). The broken-chord figure *c*, first used to lead back

Ex. 50

to the repeated section (bb7–11 = bb1–5),* comes into prominence when the harmony suddenly changes (bb18, 22, 23). Although BWV 617, unlike other *Orgelbüchlein* movements, has interludes between chorale lines and a short preface to the cantus firmus, in fact the chords concerned do not materially change, and harmonically speaking there is no reason for the 'interlude' rests in the right hand. Their purpose seems rather to draw attention to the running motifs *a* and *b* and to emphasize the non-stop character of the accompaniment. The text supplies several images which may be relevant to this texture: 'knocking on the gates of Heaven' (Schweitzer 1905 p348), 'the unease of worldly life' (Keller 1948 p157), 'the faltering steps of the aged Simeon' (Terry 1921 p190) and 'the course of life' running into lassitude (Chailley 1974 p136).

* Given repeat marks and not written out in P 283.

Whether they picture any such things or not, both manual and pedal figures are more useful for providing simple harmonic progressions to a complex tune than many other motifs of the *Orgelbüchlein* would have been. The time-signatures themselves suggest a careful working-out of the texture: three distributions of $^4/_4$ time ($\mathbf{C}$, $\mathbf{C}^{24}/_{16}$, $\mathbf{C}^{12}/_{8}$),* said to be 'completely independent rhythmically' (Finke-Hecklinger 1970).†

618

O Lamm Gottes, unschuldig (*Orgelbüchlein*)

Autograph MS P 283; copies in P 1109 (Penzel), P 1113 (Oley), P 603 (c1755–60), Brussels W.12.102 and Am.B. 47 (Kirnberger), Am.B. 46 and P 284 (Kirnberger circle), Danzig 4203/4 and late sources.

Headed in P 283 and Brussels W.12.102 'Adagio' and 'Canone alla quinta', the latter apparently added after the former in P 283; two staves; repeat marks as in *BG* 25.ii.

The TEXT is N. Decius's paraphrase of the *Agnus Dei*, published in 1542, and sung in particular on Good Friday between sermon and Communion, and in general in connection with the Passion (Freylinghausen 1741 etc).

vv 1–3

O Lamm Gottes, unschuldig	O Lamb of God, innocently
am Stamm des Kreuzes geschlachtet,	slain on the stem of the cross,
allzeit funden geduldig,	always found forbearing
wiewohl du warest verachtet:	although you were despised.
all Sünd hast du getragen,	All sin have you borne,
sonst müssten wir verzagen.	otherwise we should have despaired.

refrain vv 1, 2

Erbarm dich unser, o Jesu...   Have mercy on us, Jesu...

refrain v3

Gib uns dein' Frieden, o Jesu...   Give us your peace, Jesu...

The MELODY, at least the first line of which resembles that of a Gregorian *Agnus Dei* (*Liber usualis*, Mass IX), was published with the text but took two or more forms during the sixteenth century,

---

* The double time-signatures appear in P 283, but only $^{24}/_{16}$ and $^{12}/_{8}$ are used in P 801: i.e., any signification they may have had has not been upheld by Krebs.
† Even with regard to the notation on paper, this cannot be strictly true, since in P 283 the composer placed the paired quavers (e.g. in b19) so that the $^4/_4$ line is modified to agree with the $^{12}/_8$: i.e., the right-hand quavers become in performance.

Ex. 51

Anon 1598

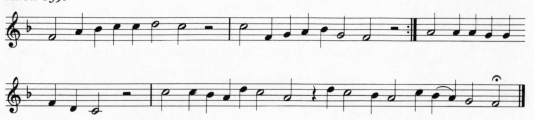

appearing in 1598 as Ex. 51 (Terry 1921 p281). A simpler version is harmonized as BWV 401 and used (with different line 6) as cantus firmus in the opening chorus of the *St Matthew Passion*, in BWV 618, 656 and 656a, and in the unnumbered organ chorale 'O Lamm Gottes, unschuldig'.

Like BWV 619, the movement does not begin with the cantus firmus; its canon is between the (first) tenor and alto, unlike the second tenor and soprano of BWV 619. To some extent, therefore, the two canonic movements are to be seen as related (in text, key and form) but contrasted (in metre, length and disposition and number of voices). Canonic treatment of at least certain phrases of the melody had also been attempted by earlier composers (e.g. Scheidt's 'O Lamm Gottes' in *Geistliches Konzert* no. 2, 1634). It is not out of the question that in order to make the canon clear P 283 presents a 'short score', enabling it to be played in various ways (cf. BWV 600), e.g. with double pedal, down an octave with 4' stop (cf. BWV 608).* To make the canon fit, the phrase-ends of the chorale melody are frequently altered, particularly to fit the last line, where the resulting bass/alto phrase resembles the fugally/canonically altered theme 'Ein' feste Burg' in the first movement of Cantata 80.

Whether or not the canon can be regarded as symbolizing the 'follower' of Jesus referred to in associated texts (Arfken 1965) or the 'following out' of God's will (Keller 1948 p158), it is clear that the accompanying motif (Ex. 52(i)), in both rising and falling forms,

Ex. 52   (i)   (ii)

has associations with Passion music (*St Matthew Passion* BWV 244, no. 35) and Christmas music (*Christmas Oratorio* BWV 248, no. 29). But it is scantily justified speculation to see this as a 'sobbing' figure, an 'idealized sigh', or an image for 'bearing sins' or 'dragging the cross',

---

* A forced parallel with the French technique of *quatuor à quatre claviers* as described by Dom Bedos (i.e. four parts on three manuals and pedal) has led commentators to suggest that BWV 618 'must be played' in Bedos's manner (Schrammek 1975 p103).

as often suggested. It is a motif useful in rising or falling form for situations requiring contrapuntal ingenuity and is by no means always used with verbal associations (e.g. *Goldberg Variations*, no. 15). Although its contrapuntal potential is clear in BWV 618, several of the lines it produces bear a decided resemblance to the obbligato line of a cantata aria (e.g. bb3, 7, 23), and its subsidiary motif (Ex. 52(ii)) is also violinistic. On the other hand, the final four bars use the motif as an adaptable means of harmonizing the canon and offer no distracting melody – a danger avoided in the other *Orgelbüchlein* canons by having one of the voices in the soprano.

619

Christe, du Lamm Gottes (*Orgelbüchlein*)

Autograph MS P 283; copies in P 1160, P 1109 (Penzel), Brussels W . 12 . 102 and Am.B. 47 (Kirnberger), Am.B. 46 and P 284 (Kirnberger circle), Lpz Poel 39 (Kittel), Danzig 4203/4 and late sources.

Headed in P 283 'in Canone alla duodecima a 2 Clav. et ped.' (*BG* 25.ii) as in Brussels W . 12 . 102; two staves.

The TEXT, another translation of the *Agnus Dei* (see BWV 618), was published in 1528, appearing with this melody in 1557.

vv1, 2

Christe, du Lamm Gottes,	Christ, Lamb of God,
der du trägst die Sünd der Welt,	who bears the sins of the world,
erbarm dich unser.	have mercy on us.

v3

Christe, du Lamm Gottes,	Christ, Lamb of God,
der du trägst die Sünd der Welt,	who bears the sins of the world,
gib uns deinen Frieden. Amen.	give us your peace. Amen.

The dorian MELODY – Ex. 53 – may derive from a simplified Gregorian tone (e.g. *Liber usualis*, Mass IV). It was used in Cantatas 23 (Estomihi (Quinquagesima) 1723 etc) and 127 (Estomihi 1725), in the mass movements BWV 233/233a, and in the chorale BWV 619.

Ex. 53

Anon 1557

In BWV 23 (last movement, middle verse) and BWV 619 the melody is treated in canon, whilst in BWV 233/233a and BWV 127 (first movement) it is incorporated with other chorale melodies; thus the composer habitually countered the melody's brevity with intricate contrapuntal

53

procedures. Both the five-part texture of BWV 619 and its three-bar introduction are unusual in the *Orgelbüchlein*, as is the modal change in the course of the work, from F to G (see also BWV 611, 620). The texture of five parts has been seen as 'after the model' of de Grigny (Klotz 1969a),* but the four upper voices are not paired in the same way (BWV 633 is more like de Grigny in this respect). The overlapping canonic lines of BWV 619, unlike those of BWV 618, contribute to the concentration of the work, as do the two major–minor progressions (bb8–9, 12–13) and chords created by the scale motif. Apart from the soprano f♮″ in b10, the canon is *per giusti intervalli* or in exact intervals.

Beginning canonically, the scale motif resembles that of the first variation of 'Vom Himmel hoch' BWV 769; it is present in every bar – sometimes *inversus*, often both *rectus* and *inversus* – and in the penultimate bar it hints at a derivation from the 'Amen' of the Gregorian chorale melody. As often in *Orgelbüchlein*, thirds between inner voices are important in the harmonic texture. In particular, the contrary motion of bb5–7 and 10–11 produces original harmony not actually required to solve the canon but arising from its inventive use of motifs; much the same can be said of BWV 600. The three lines developing the scale motif can be played on the manuals, but a rescoring of the movement to enable the pedal to take both canonic voices is not possible as long as the 'short score' in P 283 is assumed to present the required octave pitch. Although the heading 'alla duodecima' may just possibly be an autograph *addition*, and the canon might therefore be playable at the fifth an octave below on the pedals, the upper canonic voice does have the hallmarks of a top part, which the 'alto' does not.

---

620   Christus, der uns selig macht (*Orgelbüchlein*)

Autograph MS P 283 (superimposed improvements to BWV 620a); also in P 1160, P 1109 (Penzel), Brussels W.12.102 and Am.B. 47 (Kirnberger), Am.B. 46 and P 284 (Kirnberger circle), Lpz Poel 39 (Kittel), Danzig 4203/4 and late sources.

Headed in P 283 'in Canone all'Ottava'; two staves, last 6 bars in tablature in P 283; three staves in Brussels W.12.102.

The TEXT of M. Weisse's hymn is a version of the fourteenth-century Passiontide hymn *Patris sapientia, veritas divina*, published 1531 in the first German hymnbook of the Bohemian Brethren.

Christus, der uns selig macht,	Christ, who makes us blessed,
kein Bös's hat begangen,	committed no evil,
ward für uns zur Mitternacht	was for us at midnight
als ein Dieb gefangen,	taken like a thief,

* I.e. two parts on each manual, above pedal – hence the suggestion to register the Fantasia BWV 562 in this manner (Schrammek 1975 p102).

geführt vor gottlose Leut	led before godless people
und fälschlich verklaget,	and falsely accused,
verlacht, verhöhnt und verspeit,	ridiculed, jeered and spat on,
wie denn die Schrift saget.	as the Scripture says.

The remaining seven verses follow the events of the Passion, ending with a prayer:

deinen Tod und sein Ursach	your death and its cause
fruchtbarlich bedenken.	to consider fruitfully.

The MELODY was adapted from *Patris sapientia*, which was already metrical and not Gregorian. It is used in BWV 283, 620 and 747 – Ex. 54 – and a later version of the melody in the *St John Passion* BWV 245, nos. 21 and 65.

Ex. 54

BWV 283

The original version of the chorale copied into P 283 is BWV 620a; 'later he worked over bars 1–19, drastically revising them...his attempt to revise bar 20 ended in complete illegibility, and he left bars 21–25 [in tablature] untouched...the Yale MS [LM 4719] gives this prelude with its last bars revised in the style of bars 1–19' (Emery Novello XV p.xxi). Thus *BG* 25.ii presents a mixture of revised and unrevised versions, as given in the Kirnberger copy, Brussels W.12.102. Judging by the ink and the style of handwriting, the revisions were made at the same period in which BWV 613 was added to the album; the greater rhythmic activity given by the new syncopations and semiquaver figures make the composition less doctrinaire, less simply based on one chief (quaver) figure. Perhaps this argues that the composer was less loyal to *Figurenlehre* techniques in Leipzig than in Weimar; but it should be noticed that the resulting syncopated figure bears some resemblance to sections of the chorale melody (e.g. alto bb3–4, a truncated and chromaticized version of the opening cantus-firmus line).

As in BWV 629, the canon at the fifteenth (not the octave) is in the outer parts; and as in BWV 618 and 619, its accompanying parts also begin canonically and continue to be highly imitative. The melody itself requires alteration to fit canonically – by entering early (b6 etc) or by holding back (b15 etc), both devices familiar in Palestrina imitation. The nature of the melody in the bass assures a series of clear diatonic progressions, but the harmony is extremely well sustained without halting cadences. From b3 the chromatic motif becomes increasingly prominent, perhaps in association with the text 'kein Bös's' (end of b3), 'als ein Dieb gefangen' (b9), 'verklaget' (bars 15–16), 'verlacht, verhöhnt' (b18), as already foretold 'in the scripture' (bb20–end). However, the nature of the hymn as a whole (its *scopus*) makes such treatment relevant throughout, despite the fact that in the cantatas such chromatic motifs may often be a concrete allusion to the words being sung (e.g. Ex. 55). The fierce *scopus* of the hymn also justifies the

Ex. 55

BWV 2 (1724), no. 5

b34

durch's Kreuz ———————— das Wort

syncopation, which need not be understood as picturing (e.g.) the bonds binding the falsely accused prisoner (Chailley 1974 p97). As in BWV 614, the chromatic motif is partly the traditional 'chromatic fourth' (tonic falling to dominant by step), partly not; the originality of harmony in b9 and b16, for example, arises from other chromatic phrases, such as the mediant to the submediant. The strikingly mature four-part harmony of the movement seems to arise equally from such chromatics and from the need to 'explain' harmonic cruxes thrown up by the outer canon.

The combination of wailing chromatics and vigorous rhythms has naturally led to poetic interpretation of this movement. The 'original version' BWV 620a lacks much of the rhythmic energy and so emphasizes the chromaticism. Moreover, a particularly characteristic passage (bb8–10) is largely repeated later (bb19–21) including the unique low C♯. Many harmonic details are original (e.g. b15), but while the revised version allowed the false relation in b22 (c–c♯'), it is striking that the composer apparently altered the bass of the canon in b11 to avoid a similar but more obtrusive progression (f'–F♯). Indeed, the difference between b11 and b22 in this respect – as conveyed in the P 283/*BG* 25.ii version – may be significant to an understanding of J. S. Bach's contrapuntal harmony. In b11, a pedal F♯ would produce with the soprano an antique false relation unlikely with such a tenor line, which itself belongs to a later, diatonic conception of the accented passing-note; in b22, the fourth quaver is yet more dissonant (F♯ c♯ c' g'), but the dissonance is an incidental result of the passing-notes and is not part of the canonic framework.* Equally, though differently,

---

* In (e.g.) LM 4719 (Novello xv p65), the c' is delayed by a semiquaver rest, the F♯ by a dotted quaver: i.e., both are reduced to short semiquaver passing-notes by one means or another. It is not known whether this is because the last bars were 'revised in the style of bars 1–19' (*ibid*) and, if so, whether the composer authorized the revision. But judging by the fact that b20 in LM 4719 has also been altered more than such 'revision' would itself justify (compare it with b9), it does not seem that all variant readings in the last six bars had such justification and hence authority.

original is the progression over bb15–17. The lightening of the harmonic texture as a B minor chord rises to a clear G major, the passing to another temporary B minor chord, a C seventh, a highly chromatic turn to A major/minor, then a B seventh: the whole passage deserves the closest possible attention and examination. The harmonies are not at all obvious from the canonic cantus firmus, which in itself suggests the mild triadism of a Walther canon. As with b22, it is the two accompanying motifs that produce the inventive harmonies or at least – since harmony and motif are equal – that justify and express them.

620a

Christus, der uns selig macht (*Orgelbüchlein*)

Autograph MS P 283; Schelble–Gleichauf.

The handwriting of P 283 shows clearly that the original version of this chorale (BWV 620a) was revised; as with some of the headings in this MS, it is as yet unclear when the revision was made, but it appears (since Schelble–Gleichauf is a later source) that some copyists knew the unrevised version. While the harmonies and the chromatic motif remain largely unchanged in BWV 620, the first accompanying motif has become syncopated and its lines now incorporate semiquaver figures, as can be seen from the original alto line of bb1–3 – Ex. 56.

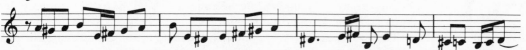

It is clear that the new syncopations and figures of BWV 620 will produce more pungent harmonies; but it is not known whether in another copy the composer revised the final six bars (written in tablature in P 283) to conform to the new style.

621

Da Jesus an dem Kreuze stund (*Orgelbüchlein*)

Autograph MS P 283; copy by J. T. Krebs (P 801, also P 802 fragment only), also in Brussels W.12.102 and Am.B. 47 (Kirnberger), Am.B. 46 and P 284 (Kirnberger circle), P 1109 (Penzel), P 1111 (Dröbs), P 1114 (Oley), Danzig 4203/4 and late sources.

Two staves.

The TEXT of J. Böschenstein's Passiontide hymn is based on the Seven Last Words (cf. the hymn *Stabat ad lignum crucis*) and was sung on Good Friday.

Da Jesus an dem Kreuze stund	As Jesus hung upon the cross,
und ihm sein Leichnam war verwundt	and his body was wounded
so gar mit bittern Schmerzen;	with so much bitter pain;
die sieben Wort, die Jesus sprach,	the Seven Words which Jesus spoke
betracht in deinem Herzen.	consider in your heart.

Verses 2–8 relate the Seven Words.

v9

Wer Gottes Mart'r in Ehren hat,   Who holds God's martyr in honour,
und oft gedenkt der sieben Wort,   and thinks often of the Seven Words,
des will Gott eben pflegen,   him will God cherish,
wohl hier auf Erd'n mit seinem Gnad,   here on earth with his favour,
und dort im ewigen Leben.   and there in eternal life.

The MELODY is of uncertain origin from the first half of the sixteenth century, associated with several texts and resembling other melodies. By at least the end of the seventeenth century, the melody (Ex. 57)

Ex. 57
Görlitzer Tabulaturbuch, 1650

was closely associated with the text above and was used as the basis for fugues by more southerly composers (J. E. Kindermann, J. Krieger, Pachelbel (?), J. K. F. Fischer), perhaps for liturgical use during Lent. It occurs rarely in more northerly parts of Germany and appears in no known Bach cantatas.

The sources of BWV 621 show a rare instance of varied cantus firmus. In P 801 the end of the third line reads e' a' g♯', and the lower parts harmonize it accordingly; the form in P 283 is as in Ex. 57, 'the usual form' as left by Scheidt (Zietz 1969 p121).

Since Spitta (I p593), the syncopated bass motif has been seen as 'symbolizing the condition of the man hanging', or picturing it by means of a motif in which one can 'see a sinking body' (Schweitzer 1905 p348). The similarity between the first one and a half bars (from which the rest springs) and the close of the Christmas chorale BWV 606 (bb8–9) then requires some special explanation; no doubt it would be that Christmas and Good Friday are closely connected. As in other chorales (e.g. BWV 606) the bass has a different motif from the middle voices, which again produce some important passages in thirds (also as BWV 606). The density of the chorale is shown in its constant reference to motif, in the compact harmony, and in the total absence of rests (cf. BWV 602, 609). At the end of each chorale line the bass presses forward, never pausing until the final cadence. Compared to the traditional 'objective' ricercare treatment of this melody, BWV 621 does invite speculation on the cross figure Ex. 58 and on the drooping bass and imploring tenor (Keller 1948 p159); but the text itself is in the main concerned not with the incidents of the crucifixion, but only with it as the setting for the Seven Words. The musical texture itself

Ex. 58

is particularly intricate: not only does each part have its own motif or prevailing rhythm, but the tenor and bass motifs (each heard five or more times) consistently avoid easy formula or contrapuntal convenience. Moreover, the voices are 'paired'; soprano and bass work in particular with or against each other, alto and tenor work often in thirds. Further concentration is given by the characteristic 'inner modified repetition' (bb1 and 7; bb4 and 8).

622

O Mensch, bewein' dein' Sünde gross (*Orgelbüchlein*)

Autograph MS P 283; copy by J. T. Krebs (P 802), also in P 1109 (Penzel), P 1160, Brussels W.12.102 and Am.B. 47 (Kirnberger), Am.B. 46 and P 284 (Kirnberger circle), Lpz Poel 39 (Kittel), Danzig 4203/4 and late sources. On first being written into P 283 'the melody was kept very simple', and the arabesques 'show by being in smaller notes and paler ink that they were added later' (*BG* 25.ii p.xii); hence copied into P 802 with fewer ornaments (Zietz 1969 pp114–15).

Headed in P 283 'adagio assai: á 2 Clav. & Ped', written later than the title; same headings in (e.g.) P 802; two staves, three in P 802; at end, 'adagissimo' in P 283 etc, 'più adagio' in Brussels W.12.102.

The TEXT of S. Heyden's Passion hymn was published in 1525.

O Mensch, bewein dein Sünde gross,	O man, weep for your great sin,
darum Christus seins Vaters Schoss	for which Christ left the bosom of his father
äussert und kam auf Erden;	and came to earth;
von einer Jungfrau rein und zart	of a Virgin pure and gentle
für uns er hie geboren ward;	he was born here for us,
er wollt der Mittler werden.	to be a mediator.
Den Toten er das Leben gab	He gave life to the dead
und legt' dabei all Krankheit ab,	and put away all sickness,
bis sich die Zeit herdrange,	until the time came on
dass er für uns geopfert würd,	that he should be sacrificed,
trüg unsrer Sünden schwere Bürd	bearing the heavy burden of our sins
wohl an dem Kreuze lange.	long on the cross.

The following twenty-two verses alternate between the crucifixion story and the 'great sin' that led to it.

The MELODY by M. Greitter was also published in 1525 and was associated with this text from the later sixteenth century; it is harmonized in BWV 402 and used in the final chorus of Part I of the *St Matthew Passion* (BWV 244, no. 35, originally from the 1725 version

Ex. 59

BWV 402

of the *St John Passion*): Ex. 59. The melody is also sung to the Whitsuntide hymn *Jauchz, Erd und Himmel, juble hell* (1537).

There have been few attempts to interpret this most celebrated of organ chorales in a symbolic or pictorial manner, though naturally the final line has led to parallels being drawn with the text itself ('Kreuze', 'lange'). In theory the coloratura manner is that of Buxtehude, but the figuration is much more original than is often assumed, and at the same time is less instrumental than (e.g.) BWV 659. Many of the patterns are unique and have a mysterious melodiousness (e.g. end of b2, beginning of b20, etc), perhaps reflecting the fact that one or two appear to be 'later additions'.* Many figures are more familiar and were found in repertories of *figurae*: Ex. 60(i). At least one of these was the result of second thoughts: the demisemiquaver figures in the right hand at bb14 and 22 were originally simple pairs of semiquavers. Some figures have different associations at different tempos: e.g., the first in Ex. 60(i), at a faster tempo, is characteristic

Ex. 60

(i)

(ii)

---

* Since the piece is on two staves in P 283, it must remain possible that some arabesques were written in smaller notes and in paler ink (see above) for reasons of clarity, the three staves in P 802 making this unnecessary.

of French Overtures. But the whole movement gives the impression of inspired caprice rather than a mere catalogue of *figurae* or *effetti* (cf. BWV 680), not least since the melody does return twice to plain cantus-firmus crotchets and is by no means coloratura throughout. Below the coloratura line, the accompaniment keeps its strict, often imitative, two parts and becomes increasingly motivic; and the prevailing movement in the inner parts progresses gradually from crotchets to semiquavers, reaching a particular intensity with the soprano *a* figure (b21: 'bearing the heavy burden') and the chromatic climax in the bass (bb19–23). At the same time, the coloratura becomes more and more wide-ranging – a very unusual feature in such a style. Several of these characteristics can be seen in the composer's revision of b21. Originally it seems to have been as in Ex. 60(ii), which he crossed out and replaced by the present b21, with its smoother figure over the first two beats and wider coloratura over the third. In general, the middle parts are less derived but more active than those of BWV 659, although the continuo-like pedal parts of the two settings have much in common and frequently (though not always) move in similar ways. In view of the length of BWV 622, the changes in texture are highly desirable; other details also affect the colour of the scoring, such as the many D♭s. Clearly the general conception of the movement may hand on various individual conventions but rises to an overall effect beyond the details; the effect was one imitated by younger composers (e.g. J. C. Vogler's 'Jesu Leiden', copied by J. T. Krebs in P 802 and by J. G. Preller in Lpz MB MS S x 14).

The coloratura effectively disguises not only the chorale melody but also the form of the hymn. Yet its four sets of three lines each are followed by the composer; in particular, the rhyme-scheme *aab* is mirrored in the two sets of dominant–dominant–tonic cadences at the end of the first six lines. The repetitions within the chorale melody are only partly followed in the chorale setting. Bar 8 can be seen as a kind of variation of b2 – see Ex. 61 – whereas b7 is quite different

Ex. 61

from b1, despite the melody. Such examples offer insight into the optional ways of harmonizing and decorating that the composer already had in his repertory by 1715; the invention seems limitless.

In view of the great length of the original hymn (and considering the Whit associations of the melody), it is reasonable to see the chorale in particular relation to VI of the text. Although such key words as 'bewein', 'Sünde', 'Toten', 'Krankheit', 'geopfert', 'schwere Bürd', 'Kreuze' and even 'lange' are bound to be suggestive, it is misleading to seek specific references to such words just at the equivalent moments in the melody. Nothing in the music specifically suggests 'Toten' or 'schwere Bürd', though a fully systematic 'musical sign-language' could have supplied them. 'Geopfert' (bb19–20) is preceded, not accompanied, by the chromatic bass; even 'Kreuze' precedes and does not coincide with the well-known Cb chord. Nevertheless, the reference to 'lange' does seem clear: Ex. 62. The Cb chord can be

Ex. 62

Kreu-ze ___ lan - - ge.

understood as a preparatory chromaticism: Eb minor for the Eb major cadence (Bullivant, *MR* 1959). Lesser preparatory chromaticism also colours the setting in BWV 244, where however 'Kreuze' is not treated conspicuously; but in the BWV 245 version (Eb major) the chord is indeed Cb. In BWV 622, the Cb and the following chord resemble both Neapolitan- and augmented-sixth progressions but are not exactly either; a similar triad at the end of Pachelbel's E flat Fantasia (copy by J. G. Walther) is inessential and demonstrates the twist to the minor not uncommon in the works of Froberger, Buxtehude and others (Ex. 63). Not the least original aspect of the Cb progression in BWV 622 is

Ex. 63

b33

the chords before and after it, simple but again outside convention (cf. the Pachelbel example).

623

Wir danken dir, Herr Jesu Christ (*Orgelbüchlein*)

Autograph MS P 283; also in P 1109 (Penzel), P 1160, Brussels W. 12.102 and Am.B. 47 (Kirnberger), Am.B. 46 and P 284 (Kirnberger circle), Danzig 4203/4 and late sources.

Headed 'Wir danken dir, Herr Jesu Christ, Dass du für uns gestorben bist' (second line added later); last 1½ bars in tablature in P 283; two staves, three in Brussels W. 12.102.

The TEXT of C. Fischer's Passiontide hymn (different, after the first line, from other texts beginning thus) was published in 1568.

Wir danken dir, Herr Jesu Christ, We thank you, Lord Jesu Christ,
dass du für uns gestorben bist, that you died for us,
und hast uns durch dein teures Blut and with your precious blood have
gemacht vor Gott gerecht und gut. made us righteous and good before God.

The remaining three verses are a prayer:

und schöpfen draus die Zuversicht, and give us the confidence
dass du uns werdst verlassen nicht. that you will not forsake us.

The MELODY was associated by the end of the sixteenth century with several texts; one form in 1597 is as in Ex. 64 (Terry 1921 p334).

Ex. 64

Anon 1597

In the theory of motif associations, the pedal and accompanimental rhythms can be seen as referring either to 'joyful thanksgiving' or (in the bass) to an 'expression of confidence'; in its actual working-out, however, the motif takes various forms differing in length and therefore in phrase-conception: Ex. 65. Such use or treatment of motif suggests

Ex. 65

an essentially different approach from that of (e.g.) BWV 643, with its (mostly) constant length of motif. Moreover, the ending of chorale lines on dominant sevenths (bb4, 16) seems to undermine any 'confidence' felt to be evoked by the motif itself, as it does in other chorales using dominant sevenths in such a way (e.g. 'Mein teurer Heiland', *St John Passion* BWV 245, no. 60). While the middle parts follow the *Orgelbüchlein* style of accompaniment, the pedal motif is rather cello-like, more so than the variant of the figure found in the G major Prelude BWV 541. Particularly good use is made of rhetorical rests and of 'displacement' of the motif across bar-lines, and all three lower parts show an inventiveness in the use of a simple motif-cell unknown in contemporary organ music by other composers but familiar also in (e.g.) BWV 640. Although basically only a three-note figure, the motif produces different patterns in each bar yet leaves the chorale melody clear and as if merely 'harmonized', unlike the settings of melodies in the chorales either side of it (BWV 622, BWV 624). This impression of chorale harmonization is due largely to the way the notes of the chorale melody are harmonized in an overall progression, but 'decorated' by the dactyl figure between beats. As Marpurg pointed out in *Abhandlung von der Fuge* (1753), 'die beyden Mittelstimmen machen eine blosse Gegenharmonie' ('the two middle voices produce a mere counter-harmony', *Dok* III p45), but this hardly suggests a full awareness of the harmonic nuances of the piece, or gives any hint that a second motif (*a* in Ex. 65) shows a tendency to emerge (bb7, 8, 11, 14, 15, 16).

624   Hilf Gott, dass mir's gelinge (*Orgelbüchlein*)

Autograph MS P 283; also in P 1109 (Penzel), P 1160, Brussels W.12.102 and Am.B. 47 (Kirnberger), Am.B. 46 and P 284 (Kirnberger circle), Lpz Poel 39 (Kittel), Danzig 4203/4 and late sources.

Headed in P 283 'á 2 Clav e ped'; two staves, pedal throughout in tablature in P 283; three staves in Brussels W.12.102.

The TEXT of H. Müller's 'Ballad of the Passion' was published in 1527 and appeared in early Lutheran hymnbooks.

Hilf, Gott, dass mirs gelinge,	Help me, God, that I succeed,
du edler Schöpfer mein,	my precious creator,
die Silben reimweis zwinge	in composing verses
Lob und Ehren dein,	to your praise and honour,
dass ich mag fröhlich heben an,	that I may joyfully begin
von deinem Wort zu singen,	to sing of your Word,
Herr, du wollst mir beistan.	Lord, support me.

The following twelve verses recount the story of the Passion and Ascension, with reference to the scriptures.

The MELODY used in BWV 624 combines features from several versions of the melody associated with the text by 1545 (Terry 1921 p203); it is not known if the composer had a further source, but the

Ex. 66

Freylinghausen 1741

harmonization BWV 343 resembles other versions, e.g. Freylinghausen 1741 (Ex. 66). Probably the difficulty of producing a canon from the third (fifth) phrase as it appears here occasioned the change in BWV 624 to an earlier version at that point. However, J. G. Walther uses a similar composite form in a setting of the same chorale with varied but at times similar canonic treatment.

Like BWV 618, the movement incorporates a canon at the fifth in adjacent voices; for the fifth and sixth lines (bb9–13) it is a canon at the fourth. The intervals of the canonic answer are not strict and the rhythms require alteration in b13.* Non-stop passage-work runs across or through the left hand and in the process presents a texture not unlike BWV 617: the alto is 'as a shadow cast by a body behind itself' (Spitta I p592). But it is difficult to agree that the movement is 'animated' because of the triplets (Terry 1921 p204), that the syncopated bass expresses 'lassitude' (Schweitzer 1905 p348) or that the canon 'translates the invitation to the Master' to help the Christian sing praises (Chailley 1974 p145). Further factors in common with BWV 617 are the repeat of the opening section (bb1–4 = bb5–8) and the curious fact that without the left hand the harmonies are already complete, particularly in BWV 624. The final cadence, for example, already carries the dissonant bass leading-note under a soprano pedal point heard in the more richly harmonized chorales BWV 721, 727 and 659. As in BWV 607 and 617, the left hand includes several distinct motifs, some scale-like, some doubling back. The three chorales present such obbligato lines in different rhythmic guises: ♪♪♪♪♪♪ (BWV 607),

♪♪♪♪♪♪♪♪♪♪♪ (BWV 617) and ♪♪♪♪♪♪♪♪♪♪♪ (BWV 624). All three have a compass of about three octaves from G (BWV 624 has the largest, G–ab″), and in all three the left hand only gradually emerges through and above the cantus firmus. The bass lines, though equally motivic, react in three different ways to such left-hand figures; that of BWV 624 seems particularly independent, not only because of the sophisticated treatment of accented and unaccented passing-notes (in all voices) throughout the movement, but because in the cantus firmus itself each line ends on a weak beat.

625

Christ lag in Todesbanden (*Orgelbüchlein*)

Autograph MS P 283; copies in P 1113 (Oley), P 1111 (Dröbs), Brussels W . 12 . 102 and Am.B. 47 (Kirnberger), Am. B. 46 and P 284 (Kirnberger circle), Danzig 4203/4 and late sources.

Two staves.

* The shortening of the c♯′ suggests that changes in a canon may also be made in order to accommodate an accompaniment.

The TEXT is one of Luther's two Easter hymns (see BWV 626), a seven-verse hymn built on the sequence *Victimae paschali laudes* for its vv4 and 5. It was published in 1524 and later became the chief Easter hymn in Leipzig and elsewhere (Stiller 1970 p226; Gojowy 1972).

Christ lag in Todesbanden,	Christ lay in the bonds of death
für unsre Sünd gegeben,	given for our sins,
der ist wieder erstanden	he is risen again
und hat uns bracht das Leben.	and has brought us life.
Des wir sollen fröhlich sein,	for this we should be joyful,
Gott loben und dankbar sein,	praising and thanking God,
und singen Halleluja,	and singing Hallelujah,
Halleluja.	Hallelujah.

v4

Es war ein wunderlich Krieg,	It was a wonderful battle,
da Tod und Leben rungen;	as Death and Life wrestled;
das Leben behielt den Sieg,	the victory went to Life,
es hat den Tod verschlungen.	it has swallowed up Death.
Die Schrift hat verkündet das,	Scripture has announced
wie ein Tod den andern frass,	how one death ate up the other death;
ein Spott aus dem Tod ist worden.	thus death has been mocked.
Halleluja.	Hallelujah.

The MELODY (Ex. 67) is drawn from the older hymn *Christ ist erstanden* (Terry 1921 p117). Bach commentators have pointed out that

Ex. 67

BWV 277

the sharpened second note of the melody is not often found in older versions, and its extensive use in Cantata 4 is therefore the more striking; both in late hymnbooks (e.g. Freylinghausen 1741) and in late organ chorales (e.g. Telemann 1736) it is still usually unsharpened. But while Cantata 158 (different text) has no sharp, it does appear in the organ chorales BWV 625, 695 and 718, in the harmonizations BWV 277–9 and in such earlier cantatas as Bruhns's 'Hemmt eure Tränenflut'. Scheidt and Böhm used both forms in their organ chorales, Scheidt within one set of variations ('Christ lag in Todesbanden', *Tabulatura nova* 1624).

Like that of BWV 616, the chief accompanying motif can take either a single or a double form (Ex. 68(i)), and both are developed throughout, joining finally in the last bar. As the juxtaposition of b14 and b15 shows,

Ex. 68

(i)   **(ii)**

single   double

the motif is related to the chorale melody (Ex. 68(ii)). In the same bars, the pedal also gives it in augmentation. The supposed significance of the motif is conjectural, suggesting to some 'the bonds of death' (Schweitzer 1905 p349), to others 'the rolling away of the stone' (Keller 1948 p161); at twice the speed, it resembles the cello motif at 'Gewalt' ('power') in *Versus* III of the early Cantata 4: Ex. 69. As in BWV

Ex. 69

BWV 4, *Versus* III

b24

etc

718, it is the tied suspensions here and there that have been seen as 'the bonds of death' (Chailley 1974 p85), though why just at these points is unclear.

The essential vigour of the motif in BWV 625 is assured when it rises into the chorale melody at its highest point (Ex. 70), despite the rising

Ex. 70

b10

Gott   lo - ben   und   ihm___   dank-bar sein

chromatic phrase or *passus duriusculus* in the pedal at the same moment. Although the movement begins as densely as 'Jesu, meine Freude' BWV 610, its tension is less sustained (e.g. end of b8) and its motifs are sometimes neglected (e.g. first half of b14).

---

626   Jesus Christus, unser Heiland (*Orgelbüchlein*)

Autograph MS P 283; copy by J. T. Krebs (P 801), also in P 1109 (Penzel), P 1113 (Oley), Brussels W . 12 . 102 and Am.B. 47 (Kirnberger), Am.B. 46 and P 284 (Kirnberger circle), Lpz Poel 39 (Kittel), Danzig 4203/4 and late sources.

Two staves.

The TEXT of Luther's three-verse Easter hymn was published in 1524 (Erfurt, Wittenberg); it is one of Luther's two Easter hymns (see also BWV 625).

Jesus Christus, unser Heiland,
der den Tod überwand,
ist auferstanden,
die Sünd hat er gefangen.
Kyrie eleison.

Jesus Christ, our Saviour,
who overcame death,
is risen,
and has taken sin prisoner.
Kyrie eleison.

The MELODY appeared with the text in 1529; the version used in BWV
626 and 364 closes with a different 'Kyrie eleison' phrase, first found
in 1585 (Terry 1921 p229): Ex. 71. The five melodic phrases have an
approximate form *abcab*.

Ex. 71

BWV 364

The same motif (Ex. 72(i)) runs through all three accompanying parts,
not in order but in constant succession so that it appears in every half-bar.
The syncopated figure can be seen as picturing the rise from death,
either symbolizing the triumph in that rise or translating the image of
'taking death prisoner'. However, by nature it resembles motifs often

Ex. 72   (i)   (ii)

found in compound-time variations of secular or chorale partitas, e.g.
the Gigue of Buxtehude's set 'Auf meinen lieben Gott' BUXWV 179 (in
J. G. Walther's MS Den Haag 4 G 14): Ex. 72(ii). Again thirds between
the inner voices are important though not, as in other one-motif
chorales (BWV 601, 623),* between bass and tenor. As in BWV 620, there
is a repeated bar, a kind of embedded back-reference: b7 is much like
b2. However, although as a consequence of the *abcab* pattern of the
chorale melody itself the last line is the same as the second, it is here
reharmonized with new modulations and progressions; yet each phrase
actually begins and ends with much the same chords as before (bb3–4
E minor – A minor, bb8–9 E minor – A minor). As with the bass line
of BWV 616, examination of the similar but different use of motifs over
these bars gives particular insight into the composer's method. Although
there is only marginally a greater use of sevenths in b8 than in b3,
the surprise B♭ of b8 can be seen to be crucial in giving a colour
unknown in b3; a reversing of the bars shows how naturally the simple
B♭ (with its hints of the Neapolitan sixth?) leads to the final cadence.
It also gives a new slant on the motif itself, whose second note
otherwise is always diatonic.

---

* The 'monothematic' accompaniment of these three chorales is the reason for their
early use as contrapuntal examples in Marpurg's *Abhandlung von der Fuge* (1753),
Figs. LI (3, 4) and LII (1).

627   Christ ist erstanden (*Orgelbüchlein*)

Autograph MS P 283; copy by J. T. Krebs (P 801), also in P 1160,
Brussels W . 12 . 102 and Am.B. 47 (Kirnberger), Am.B. 46 and P 284
(Kirnberger circle), Lpz Poel 39 (Kittel), Danzig 4203/4 and late
sources.

Headed in P 283 and P 801, 'Vers 1', 'Vers 2', 'Vers 3'; two staves.

The TEXT of the Easter carol was published in 1529; it is said to be
three, perhaps four, centuries older. In Leipzig and elsewhere it came
to be sung on all the days of Easter, and on all the Sundays of
Eastertide before the sermon (Stiller 1970 p226).

Christ ist erstanden	Christ is risen
von der Marter alle;	from all torment;
des solln wir alle froh sein,	therefore we should be joyful,
Christ will unser Trost sein.	Christ will be our consolation.
Kyrieleis.	Kyrie eleison.
Wär er nicht erstanden,	If he had not risen
so wär die Welt vergangen;	the world would be lost;
seit dass er erstanden ist,	since he has risen,
so lobn wir den Vater Jesu Christ.	we praise the father of Jesu Christ.
Kyrieleis.	Kyrie eleison.
Halleluja,	Hallelujah,
Halleluja, Halleluja!	Hallelujah, Hallelujah!
des solln wir alle froh sein,	therefore we should be joyful,
Christ will unser Trost sein.	Christ will be our consolation.
Kyrieleis.	Kyrie eleison.

The MELODY was published with the text in 1529 and may be of
similar age; it was printed in 1513. The three verses of the text are
given a melodic form *A A B*; neither BWV 276 (three verses) – Ex. 73
– nor the Easter Cantata 66 (v3 only) gives the melody in the same
form as BWV 627.

Ex. 73

BWV 276

The form of BWV 627 is unique in the *Orgelbüchlein*, and it was no doubt its three verses that led C. P. E. Bach to count the contents as '48 Chorälen', not 46, in the subtitle added to the title-page of P 283 (*Dok* I p214). The comparable three-verse text 'Christe, du Lamm Gottes' keeps the same melody throughout; but see also 'O Lamm Gottes' BWV 656. Why BWV 627 has three such verses is not known; the particular importance of this hymn over the Easter period may have made three separate or at least unlinked settings desirable, in addition to providing the organist with harmonizations for a continuous three-verse hymn, should they be required.

Although each *Vers* develops its own motif and makes a group of movements apparently similar to those of other chorales by such composers as J. G. Walther, BWV 627 is not a set of variations but is through-composed. Moreover, its cantus firmus is presented in the form of a *cantus planus*, with minims uncharacteristic of the *Orgelbüchlein* (but cf. BWV 635). The motifs themselves, however, are typical of conventional chorale settings. Each *Vers* has two such motifs (Ex. 74).

Ex. 74

Thematic relationships can also be found. Thus the opening melody (especially with its sharpened leading-note) traces the same notes as the opening line of 'Christ lag in Todesbanden' (cf. Ex. 67); motifs *b* and *f* can be seen to relate to the melody, e.g. Ex. 75. Motifs *a* and

Ex. 75

c are similar, as are *b*, *d* and *f*; motif *e* can be found augmented to quavers throughout *Vers* 2, as it can in the pedal of *Vers* 3 at bb49–51. Such relationships can easily arise within the motivic language of the *Orgelbüchlein* and have the effect of integrating the three movements.

Other factors of the motivic character are that the pedal takes fewer rests at the beginning of the cantus-firmus phrases as the movements proceed, and that the three movements become increasingly more flowing, from the syncopations of b1 to the fluid cadence at the end.

At the same time, the rigid cantus firmus accompanied by busy figuration emphasizing the $^4/_4$ nature of the piece leads to a texture unusual in the *Orgelbüchlein*, one which (despite its four parts) is close to the aims of a Pachelbel or a Walther. The *suspirans* figure of *Vers* 3, for example (motif *e*) is clearly more regular and conventional in its treatment than the same figure in BWV 628 or 630, even when it affects the cantus firmus in b49. Throughout, the harmonic progressions, particularly the cadences, are straightforward and orthodox, perhaps as an expression of respect for a classic hymn said to have been especially admired by Luther. Yet Spitta heard in it 'a powerful Life streaming with ever-increasing energy through the three verses' (Spitta I p590) and others have seen motif *a* as a symbol of life (Arfken 1965) or motif *b* as a syncopated picture of Christ cutting through the bonds of death (Keller 1948 p161). The three verses do seem to increase in tension or at least in flow, and cannot be regarded merely as an exercise in Waltherian *figurae*; that element, however, should not be underestimated. The striking fair copy of the piece in P 283 might itself suggest that this movement was somewhat older than other parts of that compilation.

---

628   Erstanden ist der heil'ge Christ (*Orgelbüchlein*)

Autograph MS P 283; copies in P 1160, P 1109 (Penzel), Brussels W . 12 . 102 and Am.B. 47 (Kirnberger), Am.B. 46 and P 284 (Kirnberger circle), Lpz Poel 39 (Kittel), Danzig 4203/4 and late sources.

Two staves.

The TEXT is a translation of the fourteenth-century carol *Surrexit Christus hodie*, published at Nuremberg in 1544 and taking various forms in the sources.

Erstanden ist der heilige Christ,	The holy Christ is risen,
Halleluja, Halleluja,	Hallelujah, Hallelujah,
der aller Welt ein Tröster ist,	who is a comforter of all the world,
Halleluja, Halleluja.	Hallelujah, Hallelujah.

The nineteen verses (with their refrain of 'Hallelujah' in every other line) relate the meeting of the three Marys with the angel at the opened tomb.

The original MELODY of the Latin carol (Ex. 76) was published by 1531; the version in BWV 628 follows later hymnbooks. BWV 306 is a harmonization of a melody which follows the same harmonic

Ex. 76
Anon. 1531

framework and which was published as a descant to the first one in 1555 (Terry 1921 p164).

As has been pointed out (Schmitz 1952 p95), contemporary German theorists such as Printz (1696) and Walther (1732) compare and contrast the particular *figurae* in their books on composition, e.g. the *suspirans* and *corta* (Ex. 77). It is thus the more striking that not only

Ex. 77

does BWV 627 itself incorporate both figures in different forms, but it is followed by three Easter chorales that alternate them:

> *suspirans* in BWV 628
> *corta* in BWV 629
> *suspirans* in BWV 630

The juxtaposition of motifs in BWV 628/629/630, united by a common sense of triumph, is patent; that the following chorale, BWV 631, also uses the *figura corta* (also in triple time) is less material, since four unset chorales were listed between BWV 630 and 631 in P 283.

Although in their different ways the rising alto, tenor and bass of the first bar of BWV 628 do justify the hearing in it of some reference to the Resurrection, there seems no reason for seeing the pedal alone as carrying the 'motif de la résurrection' (Schweitzer 1905 p357): both alto and tenor are even more potentially graphic. Moreover, in the latter half of the movement both pedal and manual motifs fall as much as they rise (showing the 'fall of the world without the Resurrection', according to Chailley 1974 p118), and the final octave D recalls a similar effect at the close of one of the Christmas chorales (BWV 606). Characteristic of the *Orgelbüchlein* is the partly imitative motif between the manual parts, supported by a constant (but different) pedal motif which in this case is unusually regular in its entries and in its lengthening at every fourth bar. The added passing-notes in the melody hint at the *suspirans* figure and may be related, since crotchets are not unimportant in the movement (Ex. 78). Either way, the upsurge of bb1–2 is undeniable.

Ex. 78

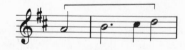

629   Erschienen ist der herrliche Tag (*Orgelbüchlein*)

Autograph MS P 283; copies in Brussels W.12.102 and Am.B. 47 (Kirnberger), Am.B. 46 and P 284 (Kirnberger circle), Lpz Poel 39 (Kittel), Danzig 4203/4 and late sources.

Headed in P 283 'a 2 Clav. & Ped. in Canone', as in Brussels W.12.102; two staves.

The TEXT of N. Herman's Easter hymn was published in 1560; in Leipzig it became particularly associated with the 2nd and 3rd Days of Easter (Stiller 1980 p226) and occasionally with Quasimodogeniti, the 1st Sunday after Easter (Gojowy 1972).

Erschienen ist der herrliche Tag,	The day of splendour has come,
dran sich niemand gnug freuen mag:	for which none can rejoice enough:
Christ, unser Herr, heut triumphiert,	Christ, our Lord, triumphs today,
all sein Feind er gefangen führt.	he has led into captivity all his enemies.
Halleluja.	Hallelujah.

Less ballad-like than *Erstanden ist der heil'ge Christ*, the hymn's fourteen verses return to the theme:

Sein' Raub der Tod musst geben her,	His robbery Death must give up,
Das Leben siegt' und ward ihm Herr.	for Life triumphed and became his master.

The MELODY by Herman was published with the text. It is used in Cantatas 67 (Quasimodogeniti 1724) and 145 (3rd Day of Easter 1729?: Ex. 79).

Ex. 79

BWV 145

Although the rhythm of the motif – ♫ ♪ ♫ ♪ etc – is also found accompanying the words 'et expecto resurrectionem' in the B minor Mass, there appears to be a further musical rationale for its development in BWV 629; see the note in BWV 628. The motif frequently marks out or encompasses the 'resurrection fifth' (Ex. 80) found in the melody of BWV 629 and in the bass of BWV 628. Both the canon

Ex. 80

and the motif are developed more consistently here than in J. G. Walther's $^3/_2$ D minor setting of the chorale in BB 22541/3. As in the other *Orgelbüchlein* canons, the motif runs through to the end, ending (like BWV 600) more succinctly than BWV 608.

The octave canons (BWV 600, 608, 629) have a rejoicing $^3/_2$ metre clearly different in mood from the canon of BWV 619. Two are particularly triadic, a factor which with their octave or *diapason* canon perhaps symbolizes perfection (Krey 1956 pp54ff). As in BWV 620, the lower canonic voice is also the bass of the harmony throughout; twice in particular it requires alteration to fit canonically (bb8, 11–12), whereas both voices usually have to change in BWV 620. As in BWV 619 and 620, the inner parts are imitative and at times quasi-canonic; their thirds and sixths present those intervals in a quite different light from the Passion chorale BWV 624 (where they appear in the canonic voices), particularly in the final upsurge. The thirds and sixths not only arise often through reciprocal imitation but themselves present a contrapuntal device of the period, the *canon sine pausa* (cf. BWV 670 etc), i.e. a kind of 'simultaneous imitation' resulting in parallel motion, shown at its clearest in bb1–2.

---

630   Heut' triumphiret Gottes Sohn (*Orgelbüchlein*)

Autograph MS P 283; copy by J. T. Krebs (P 801) and J. G. Walther (BB 22541/3), also in P 1114 (Oley), P 1109 (Penzel), Brussels W . 12 . 102 and Am.B. 47 (Kirnberger), Am.B. 46 and P 284 (Kirnberger circle), Lpz Poel 39 (Kittel), Danzig 4203/4 and late sources; published 1795 (Breitkopf).

Two staves.

The TEXT of the Easter hymn was first published by C. Stolzhagen in 1591 and was included amongst the Easter hymns in most later books (Gojowy 1972). In Leipzig it was sung at the beginning of the two major services during all three days of Easter and on Ascension Day (Stiller 1970 p76).

Heut triumphiret Gottes Sohn,	Today God's Son triumphs,
der von dem Tod erstanden schon,	having risen from the dead,
Halleluja, Halleluja,	Hallelujah, Hallelujah,
mit grosser Pracht und Herrlichkeit,	with great splendour and magnificence,
des dankn wir ihm in Ewigkeit.	therefore we thank him for ever.
Halleluja, Halleluja.	Hallelujah, Hallelujah.

The following five verses continue the praise and Hallelujahs.

Ex. 81

Gesius 1601

The MELODY – Ex. 81 – was published with the text in 1601 (B. Gesius?), and BWV 630 conforms more closely to this form than does the harmonization BWV 342 (Terry 1921 p198), which may have been a movement in the lost cantata for the 2nd Day of Easter 1729 (Neumann 1967 p245). The repeated Ds at the end of BWV 630, fitting the syllables 'Halleluja', seem to have been added by the composer, or they may reflect a local custom of singing a refrain here; those at the end of each *Vers* of BWV 627 clearly have a different effect.

The *suspirans* motif in the accompaniment suggests comparison with other chorales (see notes on BWV 628). While the pedal motif theoretically resembles those of other chorales, such as the falling fifth of BWV 628 or the pedal of the *molt'adagio* fragment 'O Traurigkeit, o Herzeleid' (cf. Ex. 2), it properly contains two ideas, one falling and one rising: Ex. 82. They are always paired and always appear at the

Ex. 82

cf. BWV 601

same point in the chorale lines, i.e. halfway through the new bar. Naturally, it is the final extension of *a* that has drawn the attention of players and commentators alike, just as both pedal motifs draw attention away from the melody itself. Terry (1921 p200) sees a resemblance to an aria in the Ascension Day Cantata 43 (no. 7), which seems to agree with Arfken's placing of the chorale amongst those for Ascension Day (Arfken 1966).

In the pedal line as a whole it is 'possible to see a hero pressing down his enemies' (Schweitzer 1905 p349), an interpretation conforming to the general sense or *scopus* of the text: 'Er liegt im Staub, der arge Feind' ('He lies in the dust, the wicked enemy'). It should not be forgotten, however, that the final pedal and manual phrase decorating the plagal cadence derives from traditional ways of 'breaking' a chord, as shown in a simple example by Buxtehude – Ex. 83. (See also the comparison with French preludes made in BWV 599.) Such

Ex. 83   Buxtehude, Prelude in G minor, BUXWV 163

b3

a motif particularly fits the repeated Ds at the end of BWV 630, as it does the held Ds in the Buxtehude example. The motif follows the *Orgelbüchlein* style of imitative development, occasionally creating a harmonic progression (e.g. end of b15), but more usually 'added' to (in the sense of decorating) one that is already clear. There is also an unusual number of sixths. The nature of the melody normally requires constantly new adaptation of motifs (compare b11 with b3), but back-reference is possible (b19 = b7 (and 23); compare b9 with b1).

---

631   Komm, Gott Schöpfer, heiliger Geist (*Orgelbüchlein*)

Autograph MS P 283; see also BWV 631a, 667 ('pro organo pleno'), 667a, 667b.

Two staves.

The TEXT is Luther's paraphrase of the ninth-century Vespers hymn for Whitsunday, *Veni creator spiritus* (Erfurt 1525); it is a stricter translation than the contemporary version by Thomas Münzer (Stapel 1950 pp154ff). As the Whit cantatas suggest, it is another hymn – *Komm, heiliger Geist, Herre Gott* – that seems to have been the one most closely tied to the Lutheran liturgy for Whit; the present hymn has a more general connection with 'gifts of the Holy Ghost' (Freylinghausen 1741). Luther seems to have changed the order of verses of the *Veni creator spiritus*.

Komm, Gott Schöpfer, heiliger Geist,	Come, God the creator, Holy Ghost,
besuch das Herz der Menschen dein,	visit the hearts of your mankind,
mit Gnaden sie füll, denn du weisst,	fill them with grace, for you know
dass sie dein Geschöpfe sein.	that they are your creatures.

The next five verses, following the Latin text, list the attributes of the Holy Ghost: the comforter, the living fire strengthening the weak, the finger of God, the Spirit directing faith.

v7

Gott Vater sei Lob und dem Sohn,	Praise be to God the Father, and to the Son,
der von den Toten auferstund,	who rose from the dead;
dem Tröster sei dasselb getan	praise be to the comforter,
in Ewigkeit alle Stund.	for ever in eternity.

Ex. 84

Anon 1535

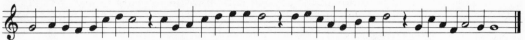

The MELODY – Ex. 84 – is a simplified adaptation of the Gregorian melody and was published with the text. Further versions followed, e.g. Klug (1529) and Crüger (1640). The melody was used in BWV 631, 631a, 667 etc, and was harmonized in BWV 370 and BWV 218 (by Telemann).

It is not known whether the shorter version of this movement (BWV 631) preceded the longer (BWV 667), but since BWV 631 conforms to the somewhat exceptional nature of the *Orgelbüchlein*, it might be conjectured that it is the earlier. It is not clear why Spitta thought that the pedal has 'scarcely anything to do' and therefore makes the piece unsuited to the musical aims of the *Orgelbüchlein* (Spitta 1 p601). In figuration, though not in ornamentation, BWV 631 corresponds to BWV 667, as BWV 631a does to BWV 667a/b. However, it is still unknown (*a*) whether the sources of BWV 631a show the shorter version of the movement in P 283 before the composer added ornaments and extra figuration, (*b*) whether its form in P 283 was always that of the present BWV 631, (*c*) whether BWV 631a is a 'simplification' made by the composer or somebody else, or (*d*) whether there is any further explanation for the differences between BWV 631 and 631a.

Although the concept of BWV 631 follows the *Orgelbüchlein* type – chorale-like melody in soprano with a common motif (often in thirds) in inner voices above a distinct pedal motif – it has a startling gigue-like character unique in the collection. As first copied into P 283, BWV 631a is the older version; it was then revised, much as BWV 620a was, by the introduction of a few more varied rhythmic groups of semiquavers. The result – BWV 631 – is a movement less uniform in figuration but richer in (specified) ornaments.

It is a sign of the exceptional nature of BWV 631 that commentators have had to search far for images, claiming (e.g.) that the middle parts symbolize the scattered tongues of fire (Steglich 1935 p122), or that the $^3/_8$ metre expresses a Trinity of which the rhythm $\lceil^{7}\ ^{7}\ \wp$ represents the Holy Ghost as the third Person of three (Arfken 1965). As Terry noticed, the bass line is similar to that of the harmonization BWV 370, and it is also to be observed that the off-beat figure is used both to change the chord on the third quaver (b7 etc) and to reinforce that already heard on the first two (b5 etc). Either way, the pedal produces straightforward harmony, whilst its off-the-beat rhythm creates syncopations that were not foreseen by the theorists of the day as they catalogued *figurae* and described the effect of an occasional rhetorically placed rest. Such a pedal seems to have been totally unknown. (See also BWV 667.)

The direction 'organo pleno' in BWV 667 is there perhaps for cyclic reasons (see introduction to BWV 651–668) and for the sake of the pedal cantus firmus in the second half; it is not relevant to BWV 631.

631a   Komm, Gott Schöpfer, heiliger Geist

Autograph MS P 283 (see BWV 631); copies in P 1160, P 1109 (Penzel), Lpz Poel 39 (Kittel), P 1216 ('Mendelssohn Autograph'), Danzig 4203/4 and late sources.

The two main differences between BWV 631a and 631 are that BWV 631a has no ornaments and has somewhat simpler figuration. The smoothness of the revised version BWV 631 may reflect the composer's (?) desire to soften too overt a gigue style. Examples may be seen in the penultimate bar, Ex. 85. In such figuration, BWV 631a corresponds to the first eight bars of BWV 667a/b.

Ex. 85
BWV 631a   BWV 631

632   Herr Jesu Christ, dich zu uns wend' (*Orgelbüchlein*)

Autograph MS P 283; copy by J. T. Krebs (P 801), also in P 1160, P 1109 (Penzel), Brussels W. 12. 102 and Am.B. 47 (Kirnberger), Am.B. 46 and P 284 (Kirnberger circle), Lpz Poel 39 (Kittel), Danzig 4203/4 and late sources; also a reputed autograph in private possession (London).

Two staves.

The TEXT, said to be by Duke Wilhelm II of Sachsen–Weimar, was published in 1648 and was sung every Sunday in Leipzig and elsewhere as a prayer-chorale immediately before the sermon, when the priest had entered the pulpit (Stiller 1970 p103).

Herr Jesu Christ, dich zu uns wend,	Lord Jesu Christ turn to us,
dein' Heilgen Geist du zu uns send,	send us your Holy Spirit,
mit Hilf und Gnad er uns regier	let him rule us, with his help and grace,
und uns den Weg zur Wahrheit führ.	and show us the way to truth.

v3

bis wir singen mit Gottes Heer:	until we sing with God's host
'Heilig, heilig ist Gott der Herr!'	'Holy, holy is the Lord God!'
und schauen dich von Angesicht	gazing on you face to face
in ewger Freud und selgem Licht.	in eternal joy and blissful light.

The fourth verse is a doxology.

Ex. 86

1648

The MELODY – Ex. 86 – was known from 1628; the number of organ settings (cf. BWV 632, 655, 655a/c, 709, 726, 749) probably reflects its position in the service and the need for an organ interlude at that point. There are no cantata settings, but a harmonization BWV 332.

Both the manual motif in its *rectus* form and the pedal line are clearly derived from the chorale melody: Ex. 87. The melody itself is made

Ex. 87

to flow with passing-notes, perhaps to the point of being sometimes disguised. The bass line is more than a little similar to that of BWV 655, as too the manual writing of both chorales has much in common during the penultimate line (BWV 632 b12 – BWV 655 b63) and elsewhere. The bass is unusually conceived, not as a quasi-ostinato but as a quasi-canon at the fifteenth:

bb1–3	line 1
b4 (last 3 notes) – b6	line 2 (anticipated ½ bar earlier)
b8	line 3 (anticipated in b7)
b9	line 4 (fourth below)
b13	line 3 (repeated)
b15	line 4 (fourth below, repeated)*

Not only does the bass take the opportunity to diminish parts of lines and introduce them at different points, but at least twice it avoids a more usual or straightforward canon: the canon does not of itself demand either the diminution in b1 or the alteration of the diminished line in b11. The conception is unusual, not least in that it is combined throughout with the motif *a* derived from the chorale melody itself. In turn, motif *a* can be seen to govern the inner parts in that all the semiquaver figures are broken chords almost without the usual runs or *suspirans* figures, not least when the figure rises about the melody and becomes itself sweetly melodious.

* In P 283 the last two lines are not written out but given repeat marks.

It is not known why the composer repeats the second half of the melody; but combined with the constant quoting of the notes associated with the opening syllables 'Herr Jesu' the device does have the effect of underlining the text. A *motif parlant* of this kind 'confirming' the vocative text is not out of place for the prayer-chorale before the sermon. Although Spitta perhaps overstates it when he claims that the chorale bears 'traces of the Böhm type' (I p592), both Böhm's and J. G. Walther's sets of variations on 'Herr Jesu Christ, dich zu uns wend' (both in the MS Den Haag 4 G 14) do make use of a full range of motifs for accompaniment and devices for treating the chorale melody, for example Variation 6 of Walther's set: Ex. 88. But the distance in Weimar from the Town Church to the court chapel is only too clear.

Ex. 88

633

Liebster Jesu, wir sind hier (*Orgelbüchlein*)

Autograph MS P 283 (where it follows BWV 634); copy by J. T. Krebs (P 801), also in P 1113 (Oley), P 1109 (Penzel), Brussels W . 12 . 102 and Am.B. 47 (Kirnberger), Am.B. 46 and P 284 (Kirnberger circle), Lpz Poel 39 (Kittel), Danzig 4203/4 and several late sources.

Headed in P 283 'distinctius' (added), 'Forte' above top stave, 'Pia' between staves, 'Ped' above third stave (the only three-stave movement in P 283); headed in P 801 'alio modo distinctig'.

The TEXT of L. Clausnitzer's hymn was published in 1663 for 'use before the sermon'.

Liebster Jesu, wir sind hier,	Dearest Jesu, we are here
dich und dein Wort anzuhören;	to listen to you and your word;
lenke Sinnen und Begier	direct our minds and desires
auf die süssen Himmelslehren,	to the sweet teachings of heaven,
dass die Herzen von der Erden	that our hearts be drawn from earth
ganz zu dir gezogen werden.	wholly towards you.

The following two verses continue the prayer.

The MELODY was published in 1664 and reshaped for this text in 1687 (Terry 1921 p251): Ex. 89. Apart from the harmonization in BWV 373, the melody was used in the chorales BWV 633, 634, 706 (twice),

Ex. 89

1687

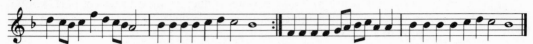

730, 731 and 754. For the role of the prayer-chorale before the sermon, see BWV 632; for the relationship of BWV 633 to other settings, see BWV 706. Krebs's order in P 801 is BWV 706.i, 706.ii, 634, 633 – thus presenting a pair of settings for each version of the chorale melody.

Unlike BWV 633, BWV 634 has the repeat written out; the heading (later?) 'for two manuals' is in 634 only, but the rubrics 'forte' and 'piano' are in 633 only.* There is less activity in the inner parts in BWV 634 at the beginning and end of each line. In P 283, the five voices on three staves are more spaciously written out in BWV 633. The unusual term 'distinctius' ('more distinctly') may refer to the way the music is written out, and to nothing more significant; or perhaps it warns the player that the parts are *forte* and *piano*. Either way, it is unlikely to refer (as Keller claims) to the fact that the melody of b1 is 'plainer' in BWV 633 than in BWV 634 (Keller 1948 p163). It is possible that on recopying the chorale the composer used the opportunity to take out the uncanonic decoration in b1 of BWV 634 and to put in four more references to the key motif of the movement, in b1 and b11.

The key motif is a group of four quavers taking various shapes, e.g. Ex. 90(i) in the manuals and 90(ii) in both pedal and manual parts;

Ex. 90
    (i)   (ii)

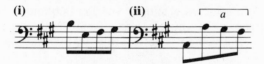

a perhaps springs from the first notes of the melody. In the first bar there are to be found not only the beginning of the canon at the fifth (i.e. fourth below) but also four versions of the motif in the manuals and one in the pedal; the opening harmonies are therefore made more complex by accented passing-notes, and this occurs wherever the pedal motif enters. Most bars have some unusual harmonic progression occasioned by the motivic accented passing-notes. The canon is strict, *per giusti intervalli* (cf. BWV 619), and keeps to the melody in the version found at the period (Terry 1921 p253); it may well symbolize the 'hearts drawn from earth wholly towards you'. Although the motion of the chorale is quiet, there is a richness of canonic and motivic harmony – each crucial to the nature of the movement – that justifies the amount of repetition in the setting. The overall form of the chorale is *ababcb*, as can be seen in the pedal line, which follows this pattern: virtually the same five-bar phrase is played three times, ending each

* This detail of BWV 633 is preserved in Marpurg's quotation from it in *Abhandlung von der Fuge* (1753), Fig. LI (2).

time with the same semibreve A. The pedal line thus helps to produce the most integrated chorale of the *Orgelbüchlein* from a formal point of view. The five parts themselves reflect the distribution of parts known in de Grigny (two upper pairs above pedal), unlike the canon of BWV 619 (one canonic line in each hand).

---

634   Liebster Jesu, wir sind hier (*Orgelbüchlein*)

Autograph MS P 283 (where it precedes BWV 633); copy by J. T. Krebs in P 801 (precedes BWV 633, follows BWV 706.ii), Lpz Poel 39 (Kittel), Danzig 4203/4 and late sources.

Headed in P 283 'in Canone alla Quinta à 2 Clav & Ped', with brackets pairing off four upper voices (as in *BG* 25.ii); in P 801 'alio modo'; two staves.

For TEXT and MELODY see BWV 633.

For the relationship of this chorale to other settings, see BWV 633 and 706; as in P 801, some later sources group BWV 706, 634 and 633 together. Although it is certainly possible that the three chorales before the sermon (BWV 632–634) were intended as Trinity hymns, like the three unset texts that were to follow in the *Orgelbüchlein* plan in P 283, it is difficult to find a justification for this idea in the fact that BWV 634 was written out a second time 'more distinctly' (Terry 1921 p40). Similarly, although BWV 633 is neither a 'variant' (Schmieder *BWV* p445) nor an 'alternative' version (Lohmann B&H 6597 p.v) in the usual senses of those terms, it can hardly be thought of as an independent movement contributing to form a clear group of three pieces.

For the differences between BWV 633 and 634, see BWV 633. The significance of the two directions 'a 2 Clav. e Pedale' and 'forte'/'piano' in the two movements is unclear on several counts. (*a*) Were they later additions? (*b*) If so, were they written in at the same time, or (*c*) was 'forte'/'piano' later or (*d*) earlier? (*e*) Is there any distinction intended between the two phrases? Two-manual organ music, at least by 1750, could have either instruction, and it is unlikely that the composer meant to imply something different between 'a 2 Clav.' and 'forte'/'piano'. Answers to the other questions are very uncertain. It could be that BWV 634 was originally intended as a single-manual movement, since it does not need two manuals as pressingly as (e.g.) BWV 624 or 604 (for reasons of part-writing or solo colour respectively); both moments of awkward part-crossings in this piece (bb2/7 and 13) arise because the left hand is of thematic importance (see Ex. 90, in BWV 633). Although its canonic distribution is different, similar things could be said of BWV 619, also in five parts. But however one conjectures about the 'original intention' of the movement – presumably the first of the

pair to be written – it is clear that its thinner motivic texture in bb1,*
6 and 11 results in simpler harmony.

---

635   Dies sind die heil'gen zehn Gebot' (*Orgelbüchlein*)

Autograph MS P 283; copy by J. T. Krebs (P 801), also in P 1114 (Oley),
P 1111 (Dröbs), Brussels W . 12 . 102 and Am.B. 47 (Kirnberger), Am.B.
46 and P 284 (Kirnberger circle), Lpz Poel 39 (Kittel), Lpz MB MS
7 (Mempell–Preller), Danzig 4203/4 and late sources.

Two staves.

The TEXT is Luther's versification (with preparatory and closing
stanzas) of the Ten Commandments, published Erfurt 1524; a shorter
version (Wittenberg 1524), beginning *Mensch, willst du leben seliglich*,
is one of the unset chorales in P 283. The hymn was particularly
associated in Dresden and Leipzig with the 13th Sunday after Trinity.

Dies sind die heilgen zehn Gebot,	These are the holy Ten Commandments,
die uns gab unser Herre Gott	which our Lord God gave to us
durch Mosen, seiner Diener treu,	through Moses, his true servant,
hoch auf dem Berge Sinai.	high on Mount Sinai.
Kyrie eleison!	Kyrie eleison!

The following nine verses list the commandments; the eleventh describes the commandments as given for man 'to learn how he should
live before God'; the twelfth is a prayer for help from 'Lord Jesus
Christ who is become our mediator'.

Ex. 91

BWV 298

The MELODY was published in 1524 with the text, and is probably
an adaptation of the pilgrim song *In Gottes Namen fahren wir* (Terry
1921 p148), though the order of priority might be the reverse. It is
harmonized in BWV 298 (Ex. 91), set for organ in BWV 635, 678 and
679, and used without text in Cantata 77. The last four incorporate
references to the number ten: BWV 77 has ten trumpet entries (i.e.

* In P 283, the soprano at the end of b1 originally had the rhythm ♪♪♪ still seen in
  the canonic alto in b2; the present soprano figure is a later revision by the composer.

separate phrases); BWV 635 contains ten entries of the subject proper (i.e. those in which the last two notes are a semitone apart); BWV 678 is the tenth chorale in *Clavierübung III*; BWV 679 has ten simple entries. The ten entries of BWV 635 are not immediately recognizable, nor are the ten semitones encompassed by the g–f′ *ambitus* of the fugue subject in BWV 679.

Although the manual and pedal motifs derived from the cantus firmus resemble those of BWV 632 in technique, the concept is different, since the cantus firmus remains throughout in minims, and the same motif is found in all parts and persists throughout, but without canonic implications. Although the subsidiary semiquaver line (made up of different *figurae*) can be found to circumscribe the first cantus-firmus line (Ex. 92), its purpose is not so much to form a paraphrase as to

Ex. 92

d = a inversus
c = b mirror

adapt constantly to the harmonies produced by the three other parts, and to sustain a motion otherwise endangered by so many repeated motifs. When these semiquavers pass to the bass line, they open out into the shape typical of alternate-foot pedalling; and alternate semiquavers in these phrases produce further reference to the first cantus-firmus phrase and to the motifs – e.g. b11 (with *d*), b18 (with *b*). The overall harmonic plan, with a G-mixolydian framework moving towards G minor as both tonic and dominant, is followed in the late setting of the same chorale, BWV 678.

The result of these various factors is a striking chorale to open the Catechism section of the *Orgelbüchlein*, to begin 'Part II' after the seasonal or *de tempore* section. Although the twofold use of repetition – appearing in the repeated notes in the derived motif, and in the unusual number of times that the motif is introduced – can be seen as constantly referring to or 'confirming' the text (Vogelsänger 1972), commentators have often resisted the idea of numerological allusion (or 'number symbolism') in the chorale, assuming instead that the composer 'was expressing the idea of insistence, order, dogma – anything but statistics' (Grace c1922 p123). Since, moreover, the motif appears no fewer than twenty-five times in the accompaniment – a possible exception to the *Orgelbüchlein* rule that motifs are not exhaustively treated – Schweitzer had to exercise ingenuity in order to count only ten, for which he has been much criticized (Schweitzer 1905 p345). But significant or not, it is true that there are ten diatonic entries, i.e. those preserving the exact intervals (GGGGGABC) in the *rectus* form. Also, if the final bar is read as a minim (cf. BWV 621), there are exactly twenty bars in a movement whose cantus firmus is notated in time-values twice as long as usual.

The use of a repeated motif that is a whole bar in length leads to each of those bars having a harmonic entity unique in the *Orgelbüchlein*, with a similar scope or shape for each bar. The main beats 1 and 3 usually produce the framework of a harmonic progression; beat 2 is frequently an accented passing-note chord, beat 4 almost always so. The plainest and most mellifluous bar is the penultimate, preparing the plagal cadence (cf. the penultimate bar of BWV 678). To counteract potential repetitiveness, four motifs enter halfway through their bar and run across the usual bar-by-bar entries. Throughout, the harmony, both as a whole and in detail, is a convincing and imaginative development of diatonicism.

---

636 Vater unser im Himmelreich (*Orgelbüchlein*)

Autograph MS P 283; also in P 1109 (Penzel), P 1113 (Oley), Brussels W.12.102 and Am.B.47 (Kirnberger), Am.B.46 and P 284 (Kirnberger circle), Lpz Poel 39 (Kittel), Danzig 4203/4 and late sources.

Two staves.

The TEXT is Luther's versification of the Lord's Prayer, published Leipzig 1539, and is a rather freer version than previous German translations of the *Pater noster*.

Vater unser im Himmelreich,	Our Father in Heaven,
der du uns alle heissest gleich	who bids us all to be equal
Brüder sein und dich rufen an	brothers and to call to you,
und willst das Beten von uns ha'n,	and desires prayer from us:
gib, dass nicht bet allein der Mund,	grant that we pray not only with our mouths,
hilf, dass es geh' aus Herzensgrund.	help us to speak from our hearts.

v9

Amen, das ist, es werde wahr,	Amen, that is, so be it.
stärk unsern Glauben immerdar,	Strengthen our faith always,
auf dass wir ja nicht zweifeln dran,	so that we have no doubts [concerning]
was wir hiermit gebeten han	what we here have prayed
auf dein Wort, in dem Namen dein.	on your word, in your name.
So sprechen wir das Amen fein.	So we say Amen.

Verses 2–8 take the first line of each section of the Lord's Prayer.

Ex. 93

1539

The MELODY was published with the text in 1539 and has remained unusually close to the original: Ex. 93. It may be based on an earlier song (Terry 1921 p302). The melody is used in four authentic organ chorales (BWV 636, 682, 683, 737) and four others of less certain authorship (BWV 760–3), in the *St John Passion* (BWV 245, no. 9, verse 4) and (to other texts) in three cantatas (BWV 90, 101, 102), and is harmonized in BWV 461.

As in BWV 625 and elsewhere, the accompanying motif appears as both a single and double cell (Ex. 94). It may be the demands of the latter

Ex. 94

that occasion an alteration in the chorale melody in b3 (b′ instead of g′) since it also produces an unexpected bass line in b1 (cf. harmony of third beat). Indeed, the motif is unusually varied, particularly in comparison with that of BWV 635. The mingling of *rectus* and *inversus* forms is quite unrigid and even apparently arbitrary, but a relationship is probably to be found between the motif and the first phrase of the melody (Ex. 95 – notice that all the notes of this phrase are incorporated

Ex. 95

in the second motif of Ex. 94). Schweitzer's description of such bass figures as 'motifs de la quiétude' (1905 p349) is justified in so far as in this case its ramifications imply, even compel, a quiet tempo – the first beat of b1, for example, contains two clear chords as well as an accented passing-note and therefore requires an unhurried tempo. Keller's ingenious demonstration that the contrapuntal lines can in some cases be shown to be 'derived from' one of the simple four-part chorale settings (1948 p150) begs too many questions about priority but does nevertheless add weight to the view that certain *Orgelbüchlein* movements are in the nature of decorated harmonizations.

Yet this impression must be due at least in part to the motifs themselves, since BWV 683 follows a similar harmonic framework without ever being regarded as a 'decorated harmonization'. Since the motifs of BWV 636 are broken chords, they are the more intrinsic to the harmony. Moreover, although there are no repeated bars in BWV 636, the movement is given increased integration by certain recurring features; the pedal approaches several cadences with the figure Ex. 96 or a variant, and there is in most bars an inner voice made more sustained by suspensions. Naturally, part of the special singing quality

Ex. 96

of BWV 636 is owing to the melody itself, which, though in some ways similar to that of BWV 637, has a greater degree of diatonicism.

---

637   Durch Adams Fall ist ganz verderbt (*Orgelbüchlein*)

Autograph MS P 283; copy by J. T. Krebs (P 802, P 801), also in P 1109 (Penzel), Brussels W . 12 . 102 and Am. B. 47 (Kirnberger), Am. B. 46 and P 284 (Kirnberger circle), Lpz Poel 39 (Kittel), Danzig 4203/4 and late sources.

Two staves.

The TEXT of L. Spengler's hymn was published in 1524; it was sometimes associated later with Sexagesima or the 21st Sunday after Trinity (Gojowy 1972), and in general with penitential texts 'vom menschlichen Elend und Verderben' ('of human misery and ruin', Freylinghausen 1741 etc).

Durch Adams Fall ist ganz verderbt	Through Adam's fall is totally spoiled
menschlich Natur und Wesen,	all human nature and being,
dasselb Gift ist auf uns geerbt,	the same poison is bequeathed to us
dass wir nicht konnten gnesen,	from which we cannot be delivered
ohn Gottes Trost, der uns erlöst	without the solace of God, who has
hat von dem grossen Schaden,	redeemed us from the great hurt
darein die Schlang Eva bezwang,	by which the serpent forced Eve
Gottes Zorn auf sich zu laden.	to draw God's anger down upon herself.

The remaining eight verses concern the need for and power of the Saviour; the central lines are:

v7

Wer hofft in Gott und dem vertraut,	Who hopes in God and trusts in him
der wird nimmer zu Schanden.	will never come to harm.

The MELODY was published with the text in 1535 but is said to be still older (Terry 1921 p152): Ex. 97. It is used in the chorales BWV 637 and 705, and in Cantatas 18 (Sexagesima 1713/14, 1724) and 109 (21st Sunday after Trinity 1723).

Ex. 97
1535

One of the most original of all *Orgelbüchlein* chorales, BWV 637 has perhaps the biggest repertory of motifs: Ex. 98. All are adaptable in

Ex. 98

and the rhythms

a texture of constant semiquavers. There are several common factors: each chorale line begins with a form of motif *b*, with its internal chromatic tension; the pedal enters after the first strong beat of each chorale line – except the last, where the entry is delayed and is therefore the more striking; and in addition to the repeated first section (not written out in P 283) an important repetition is incorporated (line 6 = line 3 = line 1) which is not the case in the setting in Cantata 18. The chromatic elements are far removed from the simpler *passus duriusculus* of BWV 614: here they are largely decorative in the manuals and involve diminished sevenths in the pedals (but there are fewer diminished sevenths in the fifth line). At least twice the cantus firmus seems to be fleetingly but dissonantly 'presenting' full diminished-seventh chords (b9 first beat, b15 last beat), which though logically treated helps to create unease. The greatest unease, however, is caused by the quick changes of harmonic direction occasioned chiefly by the fact that the lower note of the pedal motif *a* is often a (temporary) leading-note, albeit one that may not be resolved: within six beats in bb13–14, for example, the keys temporarily established by this means are D minor, G minor, Bb major (?), G minor, E minor, G major. In the last two bars, the progression towards the A major cadence is simple enough but is coloured by diminished-seventh lines off the beat (pedal) and diminished-seventh harmonies (four in the last five beats). It easily escapes notice that the final cadence is very similar to that of BWV 638.

The broken bass is not only a musical allegory of 'falling' but also a good example of the rhetorical figure *tmesis*, serving in its gaps or rests to express the effect (*Affekt*) 'suspirantis animae', 'of a sighing of the spirit', in Athanasius Kircher's words (Schmitz 1970 p72). The falling seventh (*saltus*) produces 'a series of almost irremediable stumbles or falls' (Terry 1921 p152) – complete falls expressing the Lutheran dogma of original sin through which the constant cantus firmus expresses the constant trust in Jesus expounded in the other verses of the text (Arfken 1965). It is possible that the major/minor change inherent in motif *b* relates or refers to the 'verderbt' of vi (Keller 1948 p164) and the chromatic phrases to the evil serpent of line 7 (Chailley 1974 p111); but such efforts at interpretation would go against Spitta's view that the whole text is involved, not merely an occasional image from it (I p593). Comparison with Buxtehude's setting of the melody (BUXWV 183) confirms Spitta's point, for there the connection between word and musical device is more precisely placed and limited – i.e., the falling bass accompanies line 1 only

('Durch Adams Fall...'), the chromatic phrase or *passus duriusculus* accompanies line 3 only ('dasselb Gift...'). But in BWV 637, falling basses and chromatic phrases run through the whole setting. To Krebs, the movement served as an example of chromatic chorale settings: in P 802 it follows Walther's chromatic formulae in his 'Was Gott thut das ist wohlgetan'. For a recent examination, see Budday 1977.

---

638 Es ist das Heil uns kommen her (*Orgelbüchlein*)

Autograph MS P 283; copies by J. G. Walther (P 802) and J. T. Krebs (P 801, 'earlier version' than P 283 (Dadelsen 1963)), also in P 1113 (Oley), P 1109 (Penzel), Brussels W.12.102 and Am.B. 47 (Kirnberger), Am.B. 46 and P 284 (Kirnberger circle), Danzig 4203/4 and late sources.

Two staves.

The TEXT of P. Speratus's hymn was published in 1523; in Leipzig it became associated with Septuagesima, in several other centres with the 6th Sunday after Trinity (Stiller 1970 pp224–5, 229), and occasionally elsewhere with other Sundays such as the 1st after Epiphany (Gojowy 1972). The text proclaims a doctrine central to early Lutheranism.

Es ist das Heil uns kommen her	Salvation comes to us
von Gnad und lauter Güte;	through grace and pure generosity;
die Werk die helfen nimmermehr,	good works never help
sie mögen nicht behüten.	and may not preserve us.
Der Glaub sieht Jesus Christus an,	Faith looks to Jesus Christ
der hat gnug für uns all getan,	who has done enough for us all;
er ist der Mittler worden.	he has become the mediator.

The following thirteen verses explain the doctrine further.

The MELODY was published with the text and was used in Cantatas 9 (6th Sunday after Trinity c1732/5), 86 (Rogation Sunday 1724), 117 (?), 155 (2nd Sunday after Epiphany 1716 etc) and 186 (7th Sunday after Trinity 1723): Ex. 99.

Ex. 99
BWV 155

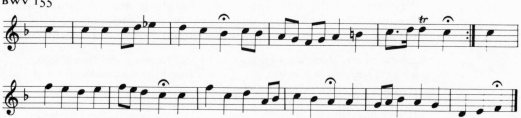

As in BWV 606 and 609, the rhythmic pattern – crotchets for the melody, quavers for the bass, and semiquavers (sometimes in sixths) for the inner parts – is particularly clear in BWV 638. The bass quavers, for instance, rest at the end of each phrase and thereby serve to emphasize the structure. Again, the *suspirans* figure Ex. 100 (the second note

Ex. 100

usually an accented passing-note) may derive from the melody but is perhaps too common a figure for such an origin, even when doubled or extended. The *suspirans* at the end of the second line (b4 third beat) is found in P 283 but not in P 802 or P 801, which supports the idea that the autograph version is later (Zietz 1969 p118). Whereas the pedal marks the ends of the lines with firm perfect cadences (affirming the power of faith?), the semiquavers run non-stop, clearly to produce a different effect from the constant semiquavers of either BWV 637 or 639. Whether or not they do represent the 'powerless good works' inferior to grace (Arfken 1965), it is striking that the highest phrase of the setting occurs at the word 'Glaub' in VI (b9). This is also the point at which the bass, after beginning line 5 in the same way as lines 1 and 3, modulates immediately. Arfken concludes that in Lutheran terms, text and music are particularly close in BWV 638, in which case the contrast with BWV 637 (which immediately precedes it and is also a doctrinal hymn) is unequivocal, since they are concerned with patently different aspects of salvation.

---

639   Ich ruf' zu dir, Herr Jesu Christ (*Orgelbüchlein*)

Autograph MS P 283; copy by J. T. Krebs (P 802), Lpz MB MS 3 (W. N. Mey), P 1109 (Penzel), Brussels W.12.102 and Am.B. 47 (Kirnberger), Am.B. 46 and P 284 (Kirnberger circle), Lpz Poel 39 (Kittel), Danzig 4203/4 and late sources. For a later arrangement, see BWV Anh. 73, p. 331 below.

Headed in P 283 'á 2 Clav. & Ped'; two staves in P 283, three in P 802.

The TEXT of J. Agricola's hymn was published in 1529; it became associated with various Sundays after Trinity, in Leipzig (but not Weimar) with the 3rd Sunday after Epiphany and 4th Sunday after Trinity (Stiller 1970 pp225–9; Gojowy 1972). Vopelius gives it for the 3rd and 5th Sundays after Epiphany, Septuagesima, Sexagesima, etc.

Ich ruf zu dir, Herr Jesu Christ,	I call to you, Lord Jesu Christ,
ich bitt, erhör mein Klagen;	I beg, hear my complaint;
verleih mir Gnad zu dieser Frist,	grant me grace at this time,
lass mich doch nicht verzagen.	let me not despair.
Den rechten Glauben, Herr, ich mein,	The true faith, Lord, I aspire to,
den wollest du mir geben,	which you will give me,
dir zu leben,	[is] to live in you,
mein'm Nächsten nütz zu sein,	to be of use to my neighbour,
dein Wort zu halten eben.	to keep your word.

All five verses are a prayer for faith, grace and strength.

The MELODY was published with the text and was used in two Cantatas for the 4th Sunday after Trinity, 177 (1732 etc) and 185 (1715 etc): Ex. 101. See also BWV Anh. 73, below.

Ex. 101

BWV 185

Although the clear distinction between the parts – the crotchets of the melody, the quavers of the bass, and the semiquavers of the alto – recalls the textural technique of BWV 638, the trio lines of BWV 639 (the only trio in the *Orgelbüchlein*) clearly create something quite new. Each trio line can be seen, clearly and unequivocally, to have an *Affekt* or means of expression – quiet, melodious soprano, gently throbbing bass, smoothly flowing accompaniment. The cello-like middle obbligato line* has suggested to some that BWV 639 is a cantata transcription like BWV 649 (Rust *BG* 25.ii p.vii). Others have observed that the phrasing of the middle line (not given in P 802)† suggests string bowing marks of a kind described by Scheidt for groups of four semiquavers which, by their nature, form what Scheidt calls an *imitatio violistica* (Kloppers 1966 p200). Although it contains no bowing marks, the lute obbligato in the *St John Passion* BWV 245, no. 31 offers something of a parallel, since the bass consists throughout of repeated quavers. Certainly BWV 639 has the most basso-continuo-like pedal part of the whole collection, with harmonic suspensions (b3) but not accented passing-notes. As the examples show, the middle line contains chiefly broken-chord *figurae* and thus in effect supplies two or more harmonic voices to the texture (Ex. 102).

Ex. 102

‡ or its inversion

---

* In P 802 this line is written an octave lower from b3 onwards. No doubt Zietz is right to say (1969 p117) that this octave-change is only notational and of no musical significance – see e.g. the awkward line produced across bb2–3.
† In P 283 the phrasing of the inner line in the middle section is unclear; but probably the intention was to slur each group of four semiquavers.

The melody itself is somewhat decorated in the first half, including in b2 a figure often regarded as a 'Hallelujah motif' – an example, therefore, that serves as a warning against easy labelling. Whether the decorations are the result of (incomplete) additions by the composer is not yet clear (cf. BWV 622), but he is unlikely to have meant anything significant by leaving the second half undecorated; it is certainly not out of place for the performer to add ornaments. Those found in J. T. Krebs's copy in P 802 (mordents in bb4, 14, 16, 18, trill in b13) are either merely suggestive or, if meant literally, unimaginative.

While the three-part conception of the movement could be adopted in theory for many a chorale melody, the character of the movement seems committed to supplication, natural for plaintive prayer. Scarcely a better example could be found for at least some of the qualities which Mattheson associates with F minor: 'gelinde...gelassene...tieffe... etwas Verzweifelung...Melancholie' ('gentle, calm, deep, somewhat despairing, melancholy', J. Mattheson, *Das neu-eröffnete Orchestre* (Hamburg 1713), pp248–9). Moreover, although searching for images in the 'heart-beating' pedal line, the 'restive' middle voice etc is based too much on mere conjecture, it can be pointed out that other settings of the melody are noticeably 'objective'. Pachelbel's fugue and Buxtehude's fantasia on this melody create no precedent for BWV 639; on the contrary, of all the *Orgelbüchlein* preludes BWV 639 seems the most untraditional in texture and in its conception of the chorale melody.

640

In dich hab' ich gehoffet, Herr (*Orgelbüchlein*)

Autograph MS P 283; copy by J. T. Krebs (P 801), also in P 1160, Brussels W.12.102 and Am.B. 47 (Kirnberger), Am.B. 46 and P 284 (Kirnberger circle), Lpz Poel 39 (Kittel), Danzig 4203/4 and late sources.

Headed in P 283 'alio modo', two staves; in P 283, P 801 and P 1216 ('Mendelssohn autograph') preceded by unused staves (for unwritten first setting of chorale?).

The TEXT of A. Reusner's hymn, based on Ps. 31, was published in 1533; in several hymnbooks (but not those of Leipzig) it was later associated with the 23rd Sunday after Trinity (Gojowy 1972) and in a general way with 'spiritual struggle and victory' (Freylinghausen 1741 etc).

In dich hab' ich gehoffet, Herr;	In you have I put my hope, Lord;
hilf, dass ich nicht zuschanden werd	help me to avoid disgrace
noch ewiglich zu Spotte.	and eternal derision.
Das bitt ich dich:	This I beg of you:
erhalte mich	sustain me
in deiner Treu, mein Gotte.	in your faithfulness, my God.

The opening may allude to the final lines of the *Te Deum*. Six further verses continue the prayer:

v3

Mein Gott und Schirmer, steh mir bei   My God and protector, stand by me

and close with a doxology.

The MELODY – Ex. 103 – was printed in 1536 to the text *Christ ist erstanden* but is known from the fifteenth century (Terry 1921 p213).

Ex. 103

Anon 1560

It was associated with the text *In dich hab' ich gehoffet, Herr* from 1560; for the melody more commonly used by J. S. Bach, see BWV 712. The title occurs for two consecutive numbers in the *Orgelbüchlein*, of which the composer set only the second, headed 'alio modo'; perhaps the other melody was to have been used for the first.

As in BWV 636, the accompanimental motif can probably be derived from the melody (Ex. 104). But it is a measure of the motivic identity

Ex. 104

of *Orgelbüchlein* chorales that despite similarities the figuration of BWV 636 and that of BWV 640 remain distinct and different, even when the motif is extended (e.g. tenor in bb1 and 6, bass in b9). The motif, imitative by nature, also gives many opportunities for thirds (more so than in BWV 636); but as in BWV 636, 637 and 614, the pedal is broken up in familiar fashion. Indeed so much do the harmonic progressions suggest a simple four-part chorale harmonization underlying the movement that in comparison the pedal appears particularly disjunctive, in b1 (for example) drawing out the dominant harmony and altering the chorale melody in the process. The incidental use of seventh and augmented chords in what is basically a series of simple harmonies (e.g. the last two bars) is a telling demonstration of the kind of harmony the composer had created by 1715. But in general, homogeneity in the movement is aided by the amount of tonic and dominant harmony, including the repeated section bb7–8 (bb1–2) where the composer not only adds a further pedal motif but also de-syncopates the chorale melody as it appeared in the first phrase and so gives it back its hymnbook form. Although the motif yields a rhythm ( ) which is abstracted by Schweitzer as a *motif de la joie* (1905 p352), its angularity combined with the low, rich tessitura suggest no light jubilation. Moreover, as b1 immediately shows, one or another voice is always at pains to produce a continuity of semiquavers, and there is no isolated dactyl rhythm of the kind frequently found in chorale-partita movements.

---

641   Wenn wir in höchsten Nöthen sein (*Orgelbüchlein*)

Autograph MS P 283; copy in P 1160, Brussels W.12.102 and Am.B. 47 (Kirnberger), Am.B. 46 and P 284 (Kirnberger circle), Danzig 4203/4 and late sources.

Headed in P 283 'á 2 Clav & Ped'; two staves.

The TEXT of P. Eber's seven-verse hymn was first printed in 1560, founded on J. Camerarius's hymn *In tenebris nostrae* (1546).

Wenn wir in höchsten Nöten sein	When we are in the greatest distress
und wissen nicht, wo aus noch ein,	and do not know where to turn,
und finden weder Hilf noch Rat,	and find neither help nor advice,
ob wir gleich sorgen früh und spät,	although we are anxious equally by
	day and night,
so ist dies unser Trost allein,	then is this our only comfort,
dass wir zusammen insgemein	that all of us together
dich anrufen, o treuer Gott,	call on you, O true God,
um Rettung aus der Angst und Not...	for rescue from care and distress...

The MELODY, by Louis Bourgeois, was published in 1543 (Geneva) and 1567 (Wittenberg), and was associated with this text from 1588. According to Terry (1921 p316) the 1588 form is Ex. 105. It is harmonized in BWV 431 and 432 and used in the organ chorale BWV 668.

Ex. 105
1588

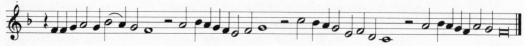

For the relationship of BWV 641 to its contemporary (?) and later re-working, see also BWV 668 and 668a. Spitta observed that the 'deathbed chorale' was founded on an earlier work (II pp759–60); he noted also that the accompanimental motif is clearly derived from the melody (1 pp590–1): Ex. 106. The derivation is somewhat clearer in the BWV 668 version since its melody is less decorated than in BWV 641; but other imitations intersperse the lines in BWV 668 and thus

Ex. 106

disguise the fact that motif *a*, both *rectus* and *inversus*, runs through the accompaniment to all lines of the chorale melody. Most appearances of the motif are *inversus* in BWV 641, unlike BWV 640 – a further element of contrast between pairs of chorales? Either way, the relationship between melody and motif is no more obvious to the ear than in most *Orgelbüchlein* movements.

That the melody of BWV 641 is so highly decorated suggests a quite different performing tempo from BWV 668, as do conversely the fore-imitation and interludes of the latter: BWV 641 must be about half the speed of BWV 668. But the absence of chromaticism (cf. the coloratura movement BWV 614) and a shorter, more restrained melodic line around g'–b' (cf. the coloratura movement BWV 622) help to produce an organ chorale of direct beauty rather than rhetorical effects. In theory the derived motif 'confirms' the opening line of the text, and it can be found in every half-bar: yet it must be an exaggeration to see the accompanying lines as 'constantly repeating' the words 'When we are in greatest distress' (Schweitzer 1905 p357), not least because four notes cannot in any case allude to a whole line of text. Such tenor motifs as the AAG of bb2 and 6 are not insistent: on the contrary, they produce slow-moving, enriched harmonies with appoggiaturas, and the role of such a figure as the *inversus* of motif *a* is comparatively far less prominent. In general the motif is worked into a three-part harmony above which the melody is constantly introducing appoggiaturas within or in addition to mordents of various kinds, while the prominence of thirds and sixths, though not extreme, gives the whole a sweet gentleness.

Unlike most of the coloratura figures in BWV 614 and 622, those in BWV 641 centre on turning phrases, each time so written as to lead to the next note of the melody on the next crotchet beat; the coloratura thus colours the interval of time or musical space between the notes of the melody, which are placed just as they would be if there were no decoration. This is a quite different technique from (e.g.) BWV 639 and does suggest that it was feasible to 'simplify' the melody in order to produce the form of it found in BWV 668. Alternatively – depending on which came first – the latter supplies a melody which could be readily coloured for its version in BWV 641. In P 283, some of the coloratura is written in smaller notes, as if to confirm such hypotheses; but this was almost certainly done for clarity only, in a fair copy from which it is impossible to guess the genesis of the movement. Naturally, some of the figures in BWV 641 can be found elsewhere; the second half of b1 in (e.g.) b1 of the chorale BWV 622, or the second beat of b2 in (e.g.) b2 of BWV 639. But in conception BWV 641 is unique; like BWV 639 and 643, it presents a model for its particular kind of expressiveness.

---

642   Wer nur den lieben Gott lässt walten (*Orgelbüchlein*)

Autograph MS P 283; copy by J. T. Krebs (P 802, P 801), also in Brussels W.12.102 and Am.B. 47 (Kirnberger), Am.B. 46 and P 284 (Kirnberger circle), Lpz Poel 39 (Kittel), Danzig 4203/4 and late sources.

Two staves.

The TEXT by G. Neumark was published with its melody in 1641. In Leipzig, Dresden and Weissenfels, it was associated with the 5th Sunday after Trinity (Stiller 1970 p229).

Wer nur den lieben Gott lässt walten	He who allows dear God to rule him
und hoffet auf ihn allezeit,	and hopes in him always,
den wird er wunderbar erhalten	will be wonderfully sustained by him
in aller Not und Traurigkeit.	in all distress and sadness.
Wer Gott, dem Allerhöchsten, traut,	He who trusts in God the most high
der hat auf keinen Sand gebaut.	has not built on sand.

v7

Sing, bet und geh auf Gottes Wegen,	Sing, pray and go in the path of God,
verricht das Deine nur getreu	only perform your duties faithfully,
und trau des Himmels reichem Segen,	and trust the rich blessing of heaven,
so wird er bei dir werden neu.	so that it becomes new again for you.
Denn welcher seine Zuversicht	For he who puts his confidence
auf Gott setzt, den verlässt er nicht.	in God will not be forsaken.

The MELODY appears in two strongly characterized forms, in duple and triple time: Ex. 107. Further uses: organ chorales BWV 642, 647, 690, 691, 691a; Cantatas 21 (3rd Sunday after Trinity 1714 – perhaps earlier – and 1723; also *per ogni tempo*), 93 and 88 (5th Sunday after Trinity 1724, 1726), 179 (11th Sunday after Trinity 1723), 27 (16th Sunday after Trinity 1726 etc), 84 (Septuagesima 1727), 166 (Cantate

Ex. 107

G. Neumark 1657

BWV 179

Sunday (4th after Easter) 1724), 197 (wedding cantata, first four lines altered); harmonized in BWV 434. For Cantatas 27, 84 and 166, the melody was used with the text of the funeral hymn *Wer weiss, wie nahe mir mein Ende*.

Although by nature BWV 642 seems to some 'serene' rather than 'animated', Schweitzer claims that the *motif de la joie* (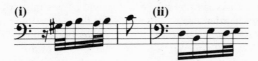) 'gives the confidence' described in the text (Schweitzer 1905 p352) and thus 'expresses' one kind of joy. However, the motif takes that form in BWV 616, but here it is rather ♪ , as in Ex. 108(i), which changes not only its aspect but any code meaning given it. Moreover, a distinction then becomes clear between manual and pedal motifs (Ex. 108(ii)). This rhythmic distinction presents the dactyl/anapaest

Ex. 108   (i)   (ii)

rhythm in yet another guise, and with other examples in the *Orgelbüchlein* (BWV 602, 605, 615, 616, 618, 620, 621, 623, 627 (vv1 and 2), 629, 637 and 640) this chorale helps to complete a repertory of this most adaptable of motifs. That the manual motif of BWV 642 generally occurs in thirds and the pedal motif in isolation furthers the distinction between the two.

Unusually for the *Orgelbüchlein*, new chorale lines beginning on an up-beat are held back for interlude-like development of the motifs (bb5/10, 12–13). This corresponds with treatment at the same points in another setting of the melody, BWV 690, where the harmony too is very similar and its motif (a simple *suspirans*) equally fertile. Since BWV 642 and 643 belong to the earliest chorales of the *Orgelbüchlein* to be composed (Dadelsen 1963), it is not surprising that they have in common such features as harmonization by sequence (e.g. bb13–14 of BWV 642, b15 of BWV 643), in both cases realized with characteristic thirds or sixths. The two chorales are also nearer to the form and style of a decorated harmonization than (e.g.) BWV 644: i.e., the harmony changes on each beat in a way familiar from simple four-part chorales, the motif-figures reinforce the sense of $^4/_4$ more than do the gliding scales of BWV 644, and so on. But certain non-motivic moments in the bass line of BWV 642 (e.g. in bb3–4) give the movement greater independence than any simple harmonization.

643 Alle Menschen müssen sterben (*Orgelbüchlein*)

Autograph MS P 283; copy by J. T. Krebs (P 801, now a fragment only), also in P 1160, P 1109 (Penzel), Brussels W.12.102 and Am.B. 47 (Kirnberger), Am.B. 46 and P 284 (Kirnberger circle), Lpz Poel 39 (Kittel), Danzig 4203/4 and late sources.

Headed in P 283 'alio modo'; two staves.

The TEXT of J. G. Albinus's hymn was written for a funeral in 1652, and was published in that year; it was later associated in general with texts 'of Heaven and the heavenly Jerusalem' (Freylinghausen 1741 etc).

Alle Menschen müssen sterben,	All mankind must die,
alles Fleisch ist gleich wie Heu;	all flesh is as grass;
was da lebet, muss verderben,	what lives must perish,
soll es anders werden neu.	if it is to become something new.
Dieser Leib der muss verwesen,	This body must wither away,
wenn er anders soll genesen	if it is to attain
zu der grossen Herrlichkeit,	to the great splendour
die den Frommen ist bereit'.	which is prepared for the righteous.

The remaining seven verses look increasingly towards:

v6

O Jerusalem, du schöne,	Jerusalem the fair,
ach wie helle glänzest du!	O how brightly you shine!

The MELODY probably dates from *c*1660 and was published in Weimar by 1681. It is probable that for BWV 643 the composer took the simplest form of each line from the various available versions of the melody. For comparison, see a 1687 form (Terry 1921 p93): Ex. 109. A similar

Ex. 109

Anon 1687

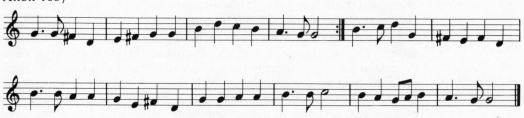

point could be made about versions in later pietist hymnbooks (e.g. second tune as given in Freylinghausen). The text is also listed in P 283 for another setting immediately before BWV 643.

Whether or not the motif derives from the opening notes of the melody, or from the final cadence (Ex. 110), or from anywhere else, BWV 643 certainly provides a good example of a single motif running through

Ex. 110

an entire chorale: more than that, it is an example unique in the *Orgelbüchlein*. It is to be expected that *a* itself can be found as a decorative figure in the partitas of Böhm and Vetter (Dietrich 1929 p45); but as with the dactyl rhythm common elsewhere, a motif in the *Orgelbüchlein* presents in itself different faces in different settings. It is a question of rhythmic and harmonic content. Thus motif *a* occurs frequently in the bass of BWV 602; however, the middle note of the three creates a discord on most half-beats in BWV 643 but not in BWV 602, and in the latter it is approached by a tied note (not a tmetic rest) and is in any case only one of two motifs. The simplicity of repetition and the question-and-answer technique between manual and pedal in BWV 643 would give a new face to any motif. The web of motivic allusion in the chorale is unbroken, yet the overlapping between pedal and manual (which in b1 begins halfway through the motif) gives both continuity and variety. Thus the five bars which begin with two Bs in the melody (bb3, 4, 11, 14, 15) are harmonized differently but have specific details in common (e.g. second half of bb3 and 14, first half of bb11 and 15); there are no duplicated bars or parts of bars, despite the actual and implied sequences from first bar to last; and harmonic tension, combined with a modifying of the motif, occurs exactly where it is most required, i.e. at the three-quarter point (b12). Despite its sophistication, however, deploying the motif so often in thirds and sixths (as in the similarly 'early' BWV 642) makes a contrast with the more disparate texture of the 'late' fragment 'O Traurigkeit, o Herzeleid'; it would be an exaggeration, however, to see this as an aid to dating.

But the secret of this celebrated movement cannot lie in its motivic competence. Rather it comes from the underlying simplicity of its judicious four-part harmony below a melody almost as undecorated as the soprano cantus firmus of BWV 627 and 635. But this too is no full explanation. Spitta must be right to find that not even such moments of 'indescribable expressiveness' as the first beat of the last bar (melody with motif *a*; false relation) are open to specific pictorial interpretation (I p590); yet since Schweitzer (1905 p350) the movement has been confidently accredited with expressing in some way the 'celestial happiness' invoked in the text. This accords with the associations of the text by 1715, when its last verse was used to close Cantata 162. Certainly the pedal motif alone saves the movement from lugubriousness, and adaptable Christian sentiment may allow the player to see this death as 'only a rebirth to a new life' (Chailley 1974 p49). But the 'blissful contemplation' heard in such chorales as BWV 643 or 601 cannot be assumed to have been an activity of early-eighteenth-century German Lutheran organists, even if simplicity of harmony and unity of motif would now be an agreed means of showing it.

644   Ach wie nichtig, ach wie flüchtig (*Orgelbüchlein*)

Autograph MS P 283; also in P 1160, P 1109 (Penzel), Brussels
W . 12 . 102 and Am.B. 47 (Kirnberger), Am.B. 46 and P 284 (Kirnberger
circle), Lpz Poel 39 (Kittel), Danzig 4203/4 and late sources.

Two staves.

The TEXT of M. Franck's eight-verse hymn was published in 1652.
It was not in the regular *Liedplan* or seasonal hymn-list at Leipzig
(Stiller 1970 p223), but it became occasionally associated with the 20th
Sunday after Trinity (Gojowy 1972) and with 'death and resurrection'
(Freylinghausen 1741 etc). It is not clear why BWV 644 gives the first
line as it appears in the even-numbered verses; Cantata 26 follows VI,
'Ach wie flüchtig, ach wie nichtig' (but see Böhm's setting, cited below).

Ach wie flüchtig, ach wie nichtig　　　Ah how fleeting, ah how vain
ist der Menschen Leben!　　　is the life of man!
Wie ein Nebel bald entstehet　　　As a mist soon rises
und auch wieder bald vergehet,　　　and as soon disperses again,
so ist unser Leben, sehet!　　　behold! so is our life.

v8

Ach wie nichtig, ach wie flüchtig　　　Ah how vain, ah how fleeting
sind der Menschen Sachen!　　　are the things of man!
Alles, alles was wir sehen,　　　All, all that we see
das muss fallen und vergehen.　　　must fall and decay.
Wer Gott fürcht', wird ewig stehen.　　　He who fears God will survive for
　　　ever.

The MELODY was published with the text in 1652 and is found in
various forms; that used in Cantata 26 (24th Sunday after Trinity 1724)
and BWV 644 has simpler outlines (perhaps conflated from several
versions with that intention, as in BWV 643): Ex. 111. A reiterated

Ex. 111

rhythm in Franck's original version (♩. ♪ ♪ ♪) matches the 'first-
line refrain' technique of the text.

A classic example of *Orgelbüchlein* motivic technique, BWV 644 is based
on two different motifs (manual, pedal) which are unbroken in their

flow from beginning to end, producing a texture and harmonic pattern some way removed from any patent 'decorated harmonization' of the melody. Scale motifs *rectus* and *inversus* being particularly adaptable, some care is clearly taken in BWV 644 to present the combination in varied and inventive ways. Thus although the motif is basically two beats long, half of it often appears alone; and while contrary motion is useful, it alternates with similar motion in thirds (examples of both in b9). The bass motif begins like many 'middle-period' Bach works (e.g. Cantata 161, Organ Sonata no. 2 BWV 526.i) but its full ostinato pattern (Ex. 112) is unusual in its constancy to the end (cf. BWV 628) and is interrupted only to avoid repetition (bb2, 4).

Ex. 112

That scale patterns also accompany the cantus firmus in the opening chorus of Cantata 26 (1724) is clearly a sign of associations in the composer's mind. But it is an over-simplification to see the cantata movement as 'only a kind of enlargement' of the organ chorale (Schweitzer 1905 p344) since the motif is about twice as fast: the counterpoint of contrary motion, frequent accented passing-notes (Walther's 'transitus irregularis', *Praecepta* p151) and pacing bass of BWV 644 compel a slower tempo. Whether the vanity of life can be heard in the pizzicato bass (Keller 1948 p166) or its mist-like qualities in the 'gliding semiquavers' (Terry 1921 p92) is open to conjecture. The only clear graphic reference is in the 'flüchtig' semiquavers; and even these were known in the repertory of figuration found in chorale variations. For instance, Partita 4 of Böhm's 'Ach wie nichtig, ach wie flüchtig' in Kö 15839* begins as in Ex. 113. As bb3–4 show, Böhm

Ex. 113

Böhm, 'Ach wie nichtig', Partita 4

makes no sustained attempt to develop the motif fully; moreover, the 'harmonic rhythm' (which affects the tempo) is also simpler and more like that in Cantata 26. Similarly, although in this and every variation of his partita Böhm also keeps to the sequence underlying bb5–8 of

* It is not known whether Böhm's setting was composed before BWV 644 or not.

BWV 644, he does so with different motifs and without the continuity between chorale lines seen in BWV 644. This alone gives the Böhm setting 'objectivity' in its use of motif. Often in the *Orgelbüchlein* it is the degree as much as the manner of motivic development that seems to have encouraged graphic/symbolic interpretation from commentators in this century.

645–650 *Schübler Chorales*

Published 1748/9? Title-page:

Sechs Chorale von verschiedener Art auf einer Orgel mit 2 Clavieren und Pedal vorzuspielen verfertiget von Johann Sebastian Bach Königl: Pohln: und Chur-Saechs: Hoff-Compositeur Capellm: u: Direct: Chor: Mus: Lips: In Verlegung Joh: Georg Schüblers zu Zella am Thüringer Walde. Sind zu haben in Leipzig bey Herr Capellm: Bachen, bey dessen Herrn Söhnen in Berlin und Halle, u: bey dem Verleger zu Zella.

Six Chorales of various kinds to be played as preludes on an organ with two manuals and pedal, prepared by Johann Sebastian Bach, Royal Polish and Electoral Saxon Court Composer, Kapellmeister and Director of the *chorus musicus*, Leipzig. Published by Johann Georg Schübler at Zella in the Thuringian Forest. To be had in Leipzig from Kapellmeister Bach, from his sons in Berlin and Halle, and from the publisher in Zella.

The origin, date, order, purpose and musical style of the *Schübler Chorales* are related.

(i) Origins. Five of the six pieces are transcriptions of arias from known Leipzig cantatas, three of which are so-called chorale-cantatas. The original keys of the transcriptions are unaltered; the bass figures of the originals are left unrealized. It is not known who prepared the printer's copy (see Wolff 1977a). Four of the five bear the titles of the first verses of their respective hymns (for the exception, see BWV 650). Only BWV 646 is not known to be based on a cantata aria, and details of its keyboard idiom suggest that it may be an original organ piece. However, the usual assumption that the other five *Schübler Chorales* are organ transcriptions of vocal–instrumental originals, not vice versa,* is supported not only by several musical details (e.g. pedal line of BWV 645, alto line of BWV 647) but also by the dates of the respective sources and by the absence of known copies of BWV 645–650 that antedate the engraving. As with *Clavierübung III*, manuscript copies of the collection, though numerous, appear to derive directly or indirectly from the engraved edition.

(ii) Date. The *terminus post quem* date of 1746 is provided by the appointment of W. F. Bach to the Liebfrauenkirche, Halle on 16 April

---

* The dates of the cantatas and of the printed organ volume would not of themselves make it impossible for the organ version to have been written before the cantatas, regardless of the date of publication. Transcribing a cantata movement as a wordless organ chorale is the nearest the composer seems to have come to rewriting a sacred work as an instrumental piece.

1746 and his removal from Dresden. At what point during the following four years the publication was issued is unknown, but several factors point to a late date: (*a*) the publisher of the *Canonic Variations* and other Bach works (Balthasar Schmid of Nuremberg) died in 1749, in which year a further member of the Bach family (J. E. Bach) published through another firm (Haffner); (*b*) Schübler appears to have 'filled a gap' between publishers, working on the engraving of both the *Musical Offering* and the *Art of Fugue* (Wolff 1973 pp17, 20); (*c*) Schübler's 'engraving of the *Six Chorales* is of better quality and certainly originated later' than the *Musical Offering*, which belongs to 1747 (Wolff 1977a p11); (*d*) although the composer paid Schübler promptly for work on the *Musical Offering*, he owed him on his death a further 2 Reichsthaler 26 Groschen (*Dok* II p497), which may have been for (recent?) work on the *Sechs Choräle*, though Kinsky (1937 p59) thinks this unlikely. There are further possible indications of a late publication, though their relevance is even less certain: (*e*) there are sixty-five words on the title-page* (Bach's sixty-fifth birthday was 21 March 1750); and (*f*) the musical style is so strikingly different from the *Canonic Variations* as to suggest complementary publication, i.e. around 1748 or later.

(iii) Order. The published order itself suggests a purpose for the volume, since the texts of the chorales concerned describe a conception of Christian life (Taesler 1969), and the music has been seen to produce symmetries (Currie 1973):

BWV 645 E♭ major, trio, cantus firmus in left hand
BWV 646 E minor, trio, cantus firmus in pedal
BWV 647 C minor, quartet, cantus firmus in pedal
BWV 648 D minor, quartet, cantus firmus in right hand
BWV 649 B♭ major, trio, cantus firmus in right hand
BWV 650 G major, trio, cantus firmus in left hand (?)

While the scoring of the last is problematic (see BWV 650), the framing of the collection by trio settings in major keys with left-hand cantus firmus is probably intentional in view of the similarity of musical style in the first and last chorales of the set (i.e. the quasi-instrumental melodiousness of their obbligato lines). The arrangement of trio–trio–quartet–quartet–trio–trio is then matched by the number of written-out bars in the engraving: the first and last chorales have fifty-four bars each, BWV 645 being laid out on three pages of three systems, each of which has three staves. These and other number-speculations – that there are 14 pages, 14 lines on the title-page, a total of 256 bars (2^7) and a total of 41 lines of musical score ($14 = B+A+C+H$; $41 = J.+S.+B+A+C+H$) – presumably depend on whether it can ever be proved that the composer himself governed the detail of Schübler's engraving work.

The texts can be seen as presenting a theological progression, an order of events for the true believer:

BWV 645 'Wake, o wake' – preparation for Advent

* See p. 180 below for comparative numerologizing.

BWV 646   'Where should I fly, heavy with sin?' The answer is in the alternative text: I will put trust 'In my dear God'

BWV 647   'He...who hopes in God will be sustained'

BWV 648   The soul given grace 'rejoices in God my Saviour'

BWV 649   'Stay with us, Jesu Christ, as the evening draws on'

BWV 650   'Come from Heaven, Jesu...extinguish the flames of Hell'

Though liturgically bound to the end of the church year and the approach of Advent, the texts can also be understood more personally as scanning personal grace and salvation, either in general or in the course of a particular life then in its sixties; 'Advent' and 'Evening' are then symbolic or analogous. Such a cycle of faith explains why the composer changed the title of the final chorale from that of its cantata version (see BWV 650). On the other hand, if the Advent association is taken literally, the work again becomes a complement to the *Canonic Variations* based (as the title-page of that set says) 'on the Christmas hymn *Vom Himmel hoch*' (BWV 769).

That such a plan was not obvious to near-contemporaries is clear from the sources. While some later MS copies such as Danzig 4203/4 (c1754–62?), P 603 (c1755–60) and P 406 keep the printed order, others change it. The order BWV 645, 648, 646, 647, 649, 650 may date only from the early nineteenth century (P 1115, P 424); that of BWV 645, 646, 647, 649, 650, 648 may be older (P 525, P 284). Few of the well-known copyists' names appear in the sources; Oley owned a printed copy, as probably did the others. The composer's own copy of the printed edition, now in private hands in Princeton, N.J., is said to include autograph 'corrections' (*BG* 25.ii) but no changes in the order.*

(iv) Purpose. Like *Clavierübung I*, the *Schübler Chorales* present six varied pieces in different keys, among which relationships may be conjectured (e.g. the three major keys produce the Trinity triad of E♭ major), while the associated texts suggest a clear plan. They are thus unlikely to be 'a merely diverse collection of works in the same genre', as is sometimes suggested (Wolff 1969 p165), even though most buyers might have seen that 'various texts could apply to them' and certainly would not have known the original cantatas (Dürr 1956). No attempt is made to convey on the organ the dynamic variety implicit in the cantata versions; nor do the echo effects and *f/p* changes found in aria scoring appear in the organ versions. Two manuals are avoided for the one chorale (BWV 647) in which the spacing and number of parts make them impracticable.

The result is a collection of pieces mostly very different from the other collections of organ music published by the composer, not easy to play but allowing for more popular tastes in melody than would have been satisfied by *Clavierübung III* or the *Canonic Variations*. Hints about publishing conditions in central Germany can be heard in the

---

* W. Rust, *BG* 25.ii (1878) uses the Peters edition based on the copy 'corrected in the composer's own hand, with addenda concerning the hands, parts and manuals with and on which they were to be played'. These corrections are still considered as autograph (Hans-Joachim Schulze, letter to author 1974); further information in Wolff 1976 p225 and 1977 pp120ff.

remark of G. A. Sorge (preface to *Drittes halbes Dutzend Sonatinen*, *c*1744, dedicated to J. S. Bach) that 'ich habe nur denen Liebhabern meiner. . .Clavier Arbeit etwas zu ihren Vergnügen in die Hände liefern wollen' ('I have only wished to make available to the lovers of my keyboard music something to please them'), although Bach, unlike Sorge, could not have claimed that his collection was 'playable without special trouble' (*Dok* II p413). However, the *Schübler Chorales* were geared to the practitioners of music as much as the *Canonic Variations* were to its philosophers and theorists – a distinction implied by Lorenz Mizler in his final paragraph to the 1754 Obituary (see BWV 769, p. 315 below).

That the *Schübler Chorales* were intended for wide sale is suggested by the 'registration' of BWV 646 and 647; that of BWV 645 is given in 'Bach's corrected copy' and certain later copies. They are not full registrations like those of Kauffmann's published *Harmonische See-lenlust* (1733) but suggest at what basic pitch to play the lines: i.e., they are aids to interpreting the score notation, not directions for specific stops. (The indications for distributing hands in BWV 648 and 650 are comparable, as are the 'registrations' in BWV 600 and the octave displacement in BWV 608.) Forkel (1802 ch.IX) seems to have understood the indications literally, describing those for BWV 646: 'Bey einigen derselben kann man sehen wie Bach im Registriren von der gewöhnlichen Art abging' ('in some of them one can see how Bach in his registration departed from customary practice'). But Forkel may have said this simply because pedal 4' cantus-firmus lines had become rare by 1802, as indeed they had by 1750; it is even possible that he uses the term 'Registriren' to apply to the total interpretation of the three-stave score, since he would hardly have been familiar with pedal lines on inner staves (see BWV 645, 650, 769.iv).

(v) **Musical style.** By 1776, the *Schübler Chorales* were picked out by one writer as 'so schön, so neu, erfindungsreich. . .dass sie nie veralten sondern alle Moderevolutionen in der Musik überleben werden' ('so beautiful, so new, rich in invention, that they will never become out of date but live through all changes of fashion in music'), and his words were repeated by others (*Dok* III pp313, 441). In particular BWV 645, 649 and 650 have a newness of idiom that, though familiar in the Leipzig cantatas, was unique in organ music until direct and indirect pupils of Bach developed it further in organ chorales (J. L. Krebs, J. F. Doles, C. G. Tag). Along with certain distinctive turns of phrase, the chief element of the idiom is its melodious counterpoint, not imitative, devoid of Italian formulae; a counterpoint which combines two themes rather than pretending to do so. Counterpoint upon a cantus firmus, as old as the organ chorale itself, has now achieved independence; the full organization of the obbligato melody into periods gives it the character of a new, independent theme with a logic of its own. The 'new theme' returns ritornello-like between lines of the chorale and ends with ritornello codas (*da capo* in BWV 649, 650) even when the material itself is less melodious (BWV 646, 647) or is so developed as to become a quasi-ostinato (BWV 648). The ritornello coda is an important feature which is occasionally found elsewhere (e.g. BWV 660) but which contrasts with the many codas of ritornello movements that close with a pedal point on the last note of the chorale melody (e.g. BWV 684).

It is still unclear to what extent the composer introduced a new idiom into German organ music with the *Schübler Chorales* or was merely indicating a trend, but the idiom was certainly adaptable to the long-winded *galant* language of such later composers as C. G. Tag (Dietrich 1929 pp87–8). An occasional attempt towards the characteristic form and melody had already been made in Kauffmann's *Harmonische Seelenlust* (e.g. ' Man lobt dich in der Stille '), which Bach must have known and which itself was probably a pale reflection of an ideal type of cantata cantus-firmus movement.

Origins of the style can be found not only in cantata movements but in organ music. The melodic style and form of the *bicinium* ' Allein Gott' BWV 711 are not far removed from (e.g.) BWV 649, though in the latter they are more richly worked; on the other hand, it is to be expected that more fully scored chorales, such as those of Kauffmann and J. L. Krebs for organ and a wind instrument, develop the species at greater length and (with Krebs) in a yet more modern idiom. Other examples of the counter-theme given its own logical organization into periods will be found in (e.g.) BWV 678 or 684. Earlier composers had written organ versions of those obbligato arias in which an instrumental counter-theme (possibly derived from the chorale melody) accompanies the cantus firmus in an inner part. Many parallels can be drawn, as in Ex. 114 (pp. 108–9). The busy lines of the obbligato or counter-melody may have been changed in style by 1731 (BWV 140/645) but not in formal conception; yet it is the very change towards a calmer, self-contained melody that produces the melodic entity of ' Wachet auf '. In this respect, BWV 645 is clearly maturer than BWV 650 or 649, where the ritornello counter-themes begin as paraphrases.

The ' Schübler style ' as seen at its clearest in BWV 645, 649, and 650 thus comprises a texture, a melodic–contrapuntal idiom, and an aria form. (A further example is BWV Anh.55.) The period form is also to be found in BWV 646, 647 and 648, but not the texture (BWV 647 and 648 are in four parts) or the melodic idiom (BWV 646 has more conventional organ figuration). The form itself is important for several reasons. The aria-like pattern of instrumental prelude–interludes–postlude is very unusual in earlier organ music: by nature it evolved in the context of the cantatas, where the distinction between voice and instruments is so strong as to make a quasi-independent form for the instrumental ' accompaniment ' desirable – more so, it seems, than when both cantus firmus and ' accompaniment ' are played on the same instrument. A result is to make the cantus firmus in organ chorales yet clearer: the crucial postlude, though only four bars long in BWV 645, 646, 647 and 648, rounds off a movement in which the unadorned cantus firmus is emphasized by its own tone-colour. The clarity thus given to the cantus firmus by the form and registration, and by the

Schübler Chorales

Ex. 114

(i) Böhm, 'Freu dich sehr o meine Seele', Partita 12 (Kö 15839)

[G   A   B   A   G   F#   E   D]

Ped.

Chorale (man. II)

(ii) BWV 4, *Versus* III (before 1714)

Violin I, II

Continuo

(iii) J. G. Walther, 'Schmücke dich' (P 802)

simplicity and line-by-line regularity of the melody, can no doubt be matched in other chorale types but belongs essentially to the cantata. Bach's other late publication for organ, the *Canonic Variations*, also uses only plain cantus-firmus techniques; but there each movement closes with a pedal point based on the final of the cantus firmus, and despite the canonic techniques the close of the cantus firmus indicates the close of the movement. In this respect alone, therefore, the six *Schübler Chorales* form a contrast to the five *Canonic Variations*, and the two publications are complementary.

Other characteristics of the *Schübler* styles can be seen as resulting from the nature of transcription itself. Although such details as the pedal line of BWV 645, the left hand of BWV 649, or the distribution of hands in BWV 647 may be uncharacteristic of the various genuine Bach organ styles, it could be that other suitable arias in the cantatas would have given the transcriber severer problems. Even the choice of which movements to transcribe was not a wide one, irrespective of the relevance of their text. In addition to the three trio movements arranged in the *Schübler* set (from BWV 6, 137 and 140) only seven* other surviving cantatas have movements in a suitable form, i.e. solo cantus firmus sung and obbligato melody played by instrument(s), above a basso continuo – in BWV 4, 95, 113, 143, 166, 180 and 199. There are other disqualifications in these movements, however: BWV 4 is a pre-Leipzig cantata, as is BWV 199; the arias in BWV 95 and 180 are each part of a longer movement; that in BWV 143 has a compass beyond c''' in the manuals, while in that in BWV 166 neither the cantus firmus (to g'') nor the basso continuo line (moving quavers) is suitable for giving to the pedal; the aria in BWV 113 would be formally suitable but is not melodious in the same way. (The last is the least objective argument.)

The four-part kind of *Schübler* prelude (BWV 647 and 648) is transcribed from a duet with basso continuo, two vocal parts and instrumental cantus firmus; only three further cantata movements of this kind are known – in BWV 163, 172, 185. All three are pre-Leipzig cantatas and were presumably thought unsuitable in idiom as in instrumental figuration. Such arguments do not claim that the composer had no choice as to what he transcribed, or even that he resorted to including one original composition in the *Schübler* set (BWV 646) because he lacked a suitable cantata movement. No doubt the composer could have adapted or transcribed other aria–chorales of the *Schübler* type had he wished. But those that he did transcribe suggest that the qualifications required – a mature Leipzig aria with cantus firmus, of suitable (untransposed) compass, figuration and spacing – limited the choice of both the trio and the quartet movements.

645

Wachet auf, ruft uns die Stimme (*Schübler*)

Published 1748/9? No Autograph MS. For the cantata movement, see below.

Headed 'Wachet auf rufft uns die Stimme p. [= etc] a 2 Clav. et Pedal, Canto Fermo in Tenore'; 'Dextra 8 Fuss', 'Sinistra 8 Fuss', 'Pedal 16 Fuss' in *BG* 25.ii (from the 'composer's corrected copy'); three staves.

The TEXT of P. Nicolai's hymn was published in 1599. It was later often associated with the 27th Sunday after Trinity (Gojowy 1972) and

---

* According to the list of chorale movements in Neumann 1967 p262. Those in which the cantus firmus is instrumental and the obbligato melody sung (e.g. BWV 12, no. 6) often give the chorale too little emphasis.

more generally with the close of the church year; still later associations were with the 'Advent of Jesus as judge' rather than 'as Saviour' (e.g. Freylinghausen 1741 etc).

Wachet auf! ruft uns die Stimme
der Wächter sehr hoch auf der Zinne,

Wach auf, du Stadt Jerusalem!
Mitternacht heisst diese Stunde;
sie rufen uns mit hellem Munde:
Wo seid ihr klugen Jungfrauen?
Wohlauf, der Bräutigam kömmt,
steht auf, die Lampen nehmt!
Halleluja!
Macht euch bereit zu der Hochzeit,
ihr müsset ihm entgegengehn!

'Wake up', there calls to us the voice
of the watchmen high on the battlements,
'Wake up, O city of Jerusalem!
It is midnight';
they call to us in a clear voice,
'Where are you, Wise Virgins?
Arise, the bridegroom comes,
get up, take your lamps!
Hallelujah!
Get ready for the wedding,
you must go out to meet him!'

v2

Zion hört die Wächter singen,
das Herz tut ihr vor Freude springen,
sie wachet und steht eilend auf.
Ihr Freund kommt vom Himmel
*   prächtig,*
von Gnaden stark, von Wahrheit
*   mächtig,*
ihr Licht wird hell, ihr Stern geht auf.
Nun komm, du werte Kron,
Herr Jesu, Gottes Sohn!
Hosianna!
Wir folgen all zum Freudensaal
und halten mit das Abendmahl.

Zion hears the watchmen singing,
her heart leaps for joy,
she wakes and rises hurriedly.
Her friend comes in glory from
    Heaven,
[made] strong by grace and mighty
    by truth,
her light is bright, her star is risen.
Now come, you worthy crown,
Lord Jesu, Son of God!
Hosanna!
We all follow to the hall of joy
and celebrate the Supper.

Verse 3 is a hymn of praise.

Ex. 115
BWV 140, final chorale (simplified)

The MELODY was published with the text but appears to be some years older, not least since its first line is the same as that of *O Lamm Gottes* (Terry 1921 p315): Ex. 115. Bach uses it only in Cantata 140, from which BWV 645 is transcribed:

> Cantata 140 'Wachet auf, ruft uns die Stimme'
> 27th Sunday after Trinity 1731
> Fourth (middle) of seven movements, 'Zion hört die Wächter singen';
>   called 'Chorale' in J. L. Krebs's performing parts (*NBA* I/27 *KB* p152)
> Trio: obbligato melody (violin I, violin II, viola)
>   cantus firmus (tenor)
>   basso continuo, figured

In the absence of authenticated autograph directions, the distribution of manuals and pedal for BWV 645 (as for BWV 650) cannot be regarded as certain. In both, the left hand could take either the bass (16′) or the cantus firmus (8′); that such pedal lines could be written on an inner stave is clear from BWV 769.iv, and the bass line of BWV 645 is unlike those of original organ pieces. The registration hints in the 'composer's corrected copy' make sense, but some organists may have welcomed the choice – given them by the bare score – of where to place the cantus firmus. Further characteristics of the transcription are that (*a*) ornaments in the obbligato line are different (more generous, but inconsistent); (*b*) the cantus firmus is more decorated;* (*c*) the original figures of the bass part (J. L. Krebs's hand) are unrealized; and (*d*) the 'forte'/'piano' signs are ignored or omitted – both those for echo phrases (bb3/24, 15/36) and those indicating the tenor entries. Either (*b*) or (*c*) could have suggested the extra grace-note in b20/41 which disguises the otherwise exposed parallel unisons.

   The achieving of a melody independent of the cantus firmus, though in principle it is familiar in obbligato arias, is here unusually complete. The right hand is developed to a half-close (b12) before the cantus firmus begins to combine with it, and its opening echo is even re-introduced across the cantus firmus in bb15–16: Ex. 116. (As the example shows, the harmony here unrealized is by no means complete.) Such is the strength of the melodic entity that it suffers no sense of hiatus when it has to come to a halt in the interests of the cantus firmus

Ex. 116

b12/33

* Are the ornaments in BWV 645 implicit in BWV 140?

(bb54, 66). That strength is confirmed by the number of tonic entries of either the first main phrase of melody (bb1/22, 3/24, 15/36, 64) or the second (bb5/26, 19/40, 43, 52, 66); the cantus firmus requires that the obbligato melody be modified, and this process leads to a series of phrases which the ear accepts as logical in their own terms (bb47–58). With the first section repeated, the overall key-plan is tonic–tonic–relative/mediant–tonic, and the counter-melody has marshalled the short cantus-firmus lines into a reasoned ritornello form.

The charm of the melody itself has led many performers to hear in it the call of the watchmen, both near and echo-like (Keller 1948 p194); and its springy dance-like character, often syncopated, can be thought to convey the first two lines of v2, thus giving the overall mood or *Topik* (Schmitz 1970 p65) of an aria concerned with Zion's reaction to the watchmen's call. On the other hand, Schweitzer heard the theme as the arrival of the bridegroom: 'le cortege du fiancé – il arrive, il passe' (Schweitzer 1905 p306); and others have seen it as an allemande with characteristically strong up- and down-beats, as in the bass line of Ex. 116 (Steglich 1962 p28).

Several times in the course of the movement, the harmony is in theory sacrificed to the melodies (thirdless chords and leaping passing-notes in bb15 and 16, the unisons of b20, etc) – an effect which itself results in a texture unusual for the organ, and a peculiarly discordant harmonic character. This combined with other details such as the repeated pedal notes of bb1 and 3, the literal 'echo' in bb3–4, and the crotchet bass lines throughout, produces organ effects uncharacteristic of music originally written for the instrument – except perhaps the sort which exploits intricate counterpoint (e.g. the unusual texture at the beginning of BWV 769.v).

---

646 Wo soll ich fliehen hin (*Schübler*)

Published 1748/9? No Autograph MS.

Headed 'Wo soll ich fliehen hin p. od. Auf meinen lieben Gott p. a 2 Clav. et Pedal', '1 Clav. 8 Fuss, 2 Clav. 16 Fuss, Ped. 4 Fuss'; three staves.

The TEXT of J. Heermann's *Busslied* or penitential hymn *Wo soll ich fliehen hin* was published in 1630; it was associated with the 11th, 19th, 22nd and 23rd Sundays after Trinity in Leipzig, Weimar etc (Stiller 1970 p231; Gojowy 1972).

Wo soll ich fliehen hin,	Whither should I flee,
weil ich beschweret bin	since I am weighed down
mit viel und grossen Sünden?	with sins that are many and great?
Wo soll ich Rettung finden?	Where should I find salvation?
Wenn alle Welt herkäme	If [success in] all the world resulted,
mein Angst sie nicht wegnähme.	it could not take away my misery.

v7

Mir mangelt zwar sehr viel:	I am much in need:
doch was ich haben will,	but what I want
ist alles mir zu gute	is all purchased for me
erlangt mit deinem Blute;	with your blood;
damit ich überwinde	with it I overcome
Tod, Teufel, Höll' und Sünde.	death, the Devil, Hell and sin.

VII

Führ' auch mein Herz und Sinn	Lead my heart and mind
durch deinen Geist dahin,	through your Spirit,
dass ich mög alles meiden,	so that I may avoid everything which
was mich und dich kan scheiden,	can separate me from you,
und ich an deinem Leibe	and so that I may ever remain
ein Gliedmass ewig bleibe.	a limb of your body.

The intervening verses develop the theme of salvation for the sinner.

The MELODY, of secular origin, was associated with the text *Auf meinen lieben Gott* from 1609 (Terry 1921 p344) and attached to the present text from 1630. (Both texts are listed but not set in the *Orgelbüchlein.*) The melodic form is shown in Ex. 229 below (see BWV 694). The melody is used for various verses of the text *Wo soll ich fliehen hin* in Cantatas 5, 89, 136, 163 and 199; all the cantatas are for various Sundays after Trinity, the text being a penitential hymn for the 19th, 22nd and 23rd Sundays (Stiller 1970 p231).

The TEXT of *Auf meinen lieben Gott* was published before 1603 in a Lübeck hymnbook, becoming associated with the 17th and 21st Sundays after Trinity (Gojowy 1972).

Auf meinen lieben Gott	In my dear God
trau ich in Angst und Not;	I trust when in fear and misery;
der kann mich allzeit retten	he can always save me
aus Trübsal, Angst und Nöten,	from affliction, fear and miseries,
mein Unglück kann er wenden,	he can turn away my misfortune,
steht alls in seinen Händen.	all is in his hands.

The following five verses express faith, trust and praise.

For a note on the motifs used in BWV 646, see 'Wo soll ich fliehen hin' BWV 694; the resemblances in figure and treatment may support the conjecture that BWV 646 is an original organ movement, not a transcription. However, an instrumental scoring of basso continuo for the left hand, viola or violin(s) for the right, and cantus firmus for voice would not be out of the question, though the right-hand part does not develop in the *cantabile* or expansive manner of many string obbligatos. While the motivic interest of the left hand is no doubt greater than is often the case with a basso-continuo part, BWV 647 shows that such interest is not exclusive to organ music; moreover, the 16' registration strengthens the continuo effect and conforms to the advice of theorists from Mattheson to Adlung:

Das Pedal . . . thut seine guten Dienste, wenn die Noten in der Grundstimme nicht zu geschwinde sind, und der Bass durch ein sechzehnfüssiges Register durchdringender gemacht werden kann . . . [Wenn] die Noten nicht alle mit den Füssen heraus gebracht werden können: so thut man besser, wenn man das Pedal weglässet, und die Grundnoten blos mit der linken Hand spielet (C. P. E. Bach, *Versuch* 1753 p245).

The pedal can be very useful if the bass line is not too lively and the bass itself can be made more penetrating with a 16′ stop. When the notes cannot all be played with the feet, one will do better to ignore the pedal and play the bass solely with the left hand.

C. P. E. Bach was referring to basso-continuo playing, not solo organ music; but the *Schübler* transcriptions act as a link between the two, and such pairs as BWV 649/650 or BWV 645/646 amply illustrate his points.

Either way – whether or not BWV 646 is an original organ piece, and whatever the relationship between it and the earlier BWV 694 – it is something of an exaggeration to see it as simply 'a much-altered new version' of BWV 694 ('eine stark veränderte Neufassung', Dürr 1956 p101). Moreover, if it is an original organ piece it is the only one by Bach that is actually registered for 4′ pedal. Similarly, it is unclear why Luedtke (1918 p68) thought that BWV 646 (or 694?) may have been intended as an insertion or *Einlage* before the final chorale of Cantata 188. Wolff (1977) thinks it perhaps from a lost cantata.

Like BWV 694, BWV 646 is a trio-like movement in which the left hand serves both as bass line and as imitative second voice, the two hands do not cross parts, and the pedal has the separated cantus-firmus phrases. The main semiquaver motif may be derived from the first line of the chorale melody; it is used *inversus*, and its segments create sequences (Ex. 117). Often the *inversus* follows immediately on

Ex. 117

b1   b2   b3

the *rectus* in one or other hand. The characteristic counter-rhythm ♪♩♪ is useful against the cantus-firmus crotchets, and at times the left hand becomes frankly bass-like. Except at the three cadences (bb6, 14, 24), the motif *a* is present in every half-bar of the movement; the effect is not as fluid or 'fleeing' as in (e.g.) 'Nun freut euch' BWV 734, and the composer appears to have been more concerned with inverted and sequential development of the motif found in BWV 694 than with mere graphic illustration. The cadences referred to above occur at comparable points in BWV 694; but in length, metre ($^4/_4$) and contrapuntal use of the motif, BWV 646 is clearly tighter, more concentrated, less 'fleeing'.

647 Wer nur den lieben Gott lässt walten (*Schübler*)

Published 1748/9? No Autograph MS.

Headed 'Pedal 4 Fuss'; three staves.

For TEXT and MELODY see BWV 642.

BWV 647 is transcribed from:

> Cantata 93 'Wer nur den lieben Gott lässt walten'
> 5th Sunday after Trinity 1724, and later performance(s)
> Fourth (middle) of seven movements, 'Er kennt die rechten Freuden-
> stunden'
> Quartet: cantus firmus (violin I, violin II, viola)
> vocal duet (soprano, alto)
> basso continuo, figured

v4

Er kennt die rechten Freudenstunden,	He knows the right time for joy,
er weiss wohl, wann es nützlich sei;	he knows when it is useful;
wenn er uns nur hat treu erfunden	when he has found us to be true
und merket keine Heuchelei,	and sees no hypocrisy,
so kommt Gott, eh wirs uns versehn,	then God comes, before we are aware of it,
und lässet uns viel Guts geschehn.	and lets great good befall us.

The scoring of the cantata movement itself suggests two manuals; but the spacing requires performance on one. At two points (bb39, 46) the alto is slightly altered from its form in BWV 93 (parts copied *c*1732) for convenience in keyboard performance; a comparable alteration in b35 was made in the 'composer's corrected copy'. Probably because the bass figures are not realized in the transcription – which would make the harmonic implication explicit – the inner pedal point of bb39–40 is avoided in BWV 647 and the note shortened.

The two fugally treated obbligato subjects are both derived from lines of the chorale – the first from line 1 but continuing to accompany line 2, the second from line 3 but continuing to accompany line 4. The paraphrase technique is reminiscent of that frequently met with in the organ chorales: Ex. 118. The first was already noted by Marpurg

Ex. 118

b1   b33

(*Abhandlung von der Fuge* (1753), Fig. XLVIII). The relationship of subjects to chorale lines suggests that by 1724 the composer's paraphrase technique had already reached a maturity comparable to that of such late organ chorales as BWV 680. The bass line accompanies the two subjects with very similar material, and also incorporates thematic entries (bb8, 14, 45). Thus, although the first subject re-appears in the final bars (cf. BWV 695), motivic unity is also given to the movement by the bass line itself. Considered as a ritornello section, the opening bars pervade the chorale, moving continuously and not always with closing cadences separating the sections (e.g. no cadence before the first cantus-firmus entry). The rhythmic unit is one of the *motifs de la joie* described by Schweitzer (1905 p352) and could be seen as justified by the first line of the verse of text concerned; but the *joie* is restrained.

---

648   Meine Seele erhebt den Herren (*Schübler*)

Published 1748/9? No Autograph MS.

Headed 'Meine Seele erhebt den Herren p. a 2 Clav. et Pedal'; 'sinistra', 'dextra forte' in *BG* 25.ii (from the 'composer's corrected copy'); three staves.

The TEXT is biblical, the German *Magnificat* (St Luke i, 46–55) used as the chief hymn for Mariae Heimsuchung (the Visitation) (Stiller 1970 p232) and sung after the sermon in the regular Vespers after a 'praeambulo auf der Orgel' (*ibid* p81).

Meine Seele erhebt den Herren	My soul magnifies the Lord
und mein Geist freuet sich Gottes,	and my spirit rejoices in God,
meines Heilandes...	my Saviour...
Er denket der Barmherzigkeit und	He remembers his mercy and
hilft seinem Diener Israel auf.	helps his servant Israel.

The *Magnificat* is the only canticle or psalm to keep intact its original Gregorian MELODY. Its *tonus peregrinus* was simplified in the harmonization BWV 324 as in Ex. 119. Association with Vespers and

Ex. 119

BWV 324

organ-playing gave rise to a major tradition of organ settings of the *Magnificat*, both short settings of the cantus firmus as versets for *alternatim* performance, and longer interludes of a fugal nature. The text was listed in the *Orgelbüchlein*, the melody harmonized in BWV 323 and 324 and used in BWV 733 and the Magnificat BWV 243/243a; the melody is that called *Magnificat noni toni* (9th mode) in such collections as Scheidt's *Tabulatura nova* (1624).

BWV 648 is transcribed from (the score of?):

> Cantata 10 'Meine Seele erhebt den Herren'
> Mariae Heimsuchung (the Visitation) 1724, and later performance(s)
> Fifth of seven movements, Duetto 'Er denket der Barmherzigkeit'
> Quartet: cantus firmus (oboe I, oboe II, trumpet)
>   vocal duet (alto, tenor)
>   basso continuo, figured

The scoring of the cantata movement itself suggests two manuals, as do the extra headings in the 'composer's corrected copy' (see Headings above); but the right hand then has to play on two manuals at once in b13 and also perhaps in b24. Also, to avoid exaggerated or awkward phrasing, it has to change to the left-hand manual in b6 and elsewhere.

Though short, BWV 648 has an intricate and unusual form:

A	bb1–5	outer framework of a solo pedal theme, from which is derived:
B	bb5–9	inner framework of fugal imitation between inner parts
C	bb9–13	three parts in derived (non-fugal) imitation accompany the two phrases of the melody
D	bb14–21	sequential section derived from pedal theme, modulating from F minor to A minor; alto and tenor inverting counterpoint
C	bb22–8	
B	bb27–31	
A	bb31–5	

Thus, although the pedal theme bears the character of a clear-cut ostinato (even *bicinium*-like), it is not so used in the bass, nor is it treated fugally at length or heard intact during the cantus-firmus phrases. The form is unusually symmetrical and much of the detail is uncharacteristic of organ chorales (e.g. the silence in the inner parts bb9–10); nor can the bass line be regarded as idiomatic for pedals.

The chromatic language can lead to many conjectures about its significance, not least since such appoggiaturas as Ex. 120(i) can often

Ex. 120

(i)   **(ii)** BWV 243, 'Suscepit Israel'

be associated with the idea of, or with texts concerning, supplication or mercy (e.g. the aria 'Ächzen und erbärmlich Weinen' in Cantata 13, 1726). Other appoggiaturas (though not chromatic) are used against the same melody for the same verse of the canticle in the Magnificat BWV 243 – Ex. 120(ii). Other details such as the unexpected change to F minor in b13 are not uncommon (cf. B flat Prelude, *Das Wohltemperirte Clavier*, II, last four bars) and need not be directly related to such older composers as Böhm. It is also possible that B–A–C–H is to be heard in the course of the movement, e.g. in the tenor line across the central bars 17–20. The degree to which the counter-melody (bass) is constantly modified yet still preserves its melodic character is typical of the *Schübler* counterpoint.

---

649   Ach bleib bei uns, Herr Jesu Christ (*Schübler*)

Published 1748/9? No Autograph MS.

Headed 'Ach bleib bey uns Herr Jesu Christ p.'; 'a 2 Clav. e Pedale' (*BG* 25.ii, from the 'composer's corrected copy'); three staves. Original parts of the movement in Cantata 6 headed 'Allegro' (Autograph MS) and 'Allegro assai' (late Autograph? – Dürr *NBA* I/10 *KB* pp39–40).

The first verse of the TEXT is a German version (published 1575) of Melanchthon's *Vespera iam venit* (1551), concerned with the evening scene on the road to Emmaus (St Luke xxiv, 29): 'Bleibe bei uns, denn es will Abend werden'. Verse 2 is found in 1602; vv3–9, a prayer for Jesus's help against all dangers, was added by N. Selnecker and was published in 1611. It became often associated with the 1st and (more often) 2nd Days of Easter (Gojowy 1972) and was used during the Reformation Jubilee in 1730 (Stiller 1970 pp226, 232).

Ach bleib bei uns, Herr Jesu Christ,   Ah, stay with us, Lord Jesu Christ,
weil es nun Abend worden ist;   because it is now become evening;
dein göttlich Wort, das helle Licht,   your divine word – the bright light –
lass ja bei uns auslöschen nicht.   may it not be extinguished in us.

v2

In dieser schwern betrübten Zeit   At this sorely troubled time
verleih uns, Herr, Beständigkeit,   grant us, Lord, steadfastness,
dass wir dein Wort und Sakrament   that we keep your word and sacrament
behalten rein bis an das End.   pure to the end.

The MELODY dates from 1589 or earlier, becoming known in several versions, including one used as an alto line to Calvisius's melody *Danket den Herrn*, 1594 (Terry 1921 p85). Its form in the harmonization BWV 253 is as in Ex. 121. Apart from the 1730 Reformation cantata (xvib), the melody appears only in Cantata 6 and BWV 649.

Ex. 121
BWV 253

Cantata 6 'Bleib bei uns, denn es will Abend werden'
2nd Day of Easter 1725
Third of six movements, 'Ach bleib bei uns, Herr Jesu Christ', vv1 and
    2, called 'Choral' in continuo parts (Autograph?)
Trio: obbligato melody (violoncello piccolo)
        cantus firmus (soprano)
        basso continuo, figured

The transcription is changed in form: two verses of text in the BWV
6 setting gave an overall shape of

A (ritornello or introduction)
chorale (v1)
A (repeated)
chorale (v2)
A2 (ritornello, the first five bars replaced by one new linking bar)

which is simplified in BWV 649 to A–chorale–A. As in BWV 648, the
bass and obbligato lines would be suitable for manuals and the cantus
firmus for pedal; but the rarity of 2' pedal stops in c1750 led to a rarity
of pedal soprano melodies (or vice versa), so the cantus firmus is given
to the right hand. As the movement stands – i.e. untransposed – the
obbligato melody is low for right hand and suits the left better; at the
same time the bass is sufficiently continuo-like to suit pedal reasonably
well, so no violence is done to conventional organ scoring.

The obbligato melody is at first derived from the chorale: Ex. 122.
However, the length of the melody leads to a full ritornello-like line,

Ex. 122

somewhat similar in form to BWV 645, 646 and 650. Each of the four
Schübler trios has an obbligato line or lines which combine with the
chorale either intact or (when necessary) modified in some way
(changed intervals, drawn-out phrases); in each of the four, the melody
also reaches clear cadences before two or more chorale entries. But
the details of treatment vary from movement to movement, and BWV
649 is unusually continuous – the cantata version even more so in view
of its greater overall length. The length of the melody itself – which
begins by paraphrasing the cantus firmus – is sufficient to distinguish
such movements from usual paraphrase organ chorales, although in
this respect BWV 660, one of the 'Eighteen Chorales', is comparable.
Between the cantus-firmus phrases the obbligato melody is clearly
recognizable, and the conspicuously different motifs (*a b c d*) together
with the semiquaver patterns ensure apparent unity and thematic
combination even when the melody is in fact much modified (e.g.
bb15–25).

650   Kommst du nun, Jesu, vom Himmel herunter (*Schübler*)

Published 1748/9? No Autograph MS.

Headed 'Kommst du nun Jesu vom Himmel herunter p.'; three staves, cantus firmus on middle stave (beginning at g′); lowest stave headed 'sinistra' in the 'composer's corrected copy' (*BG* 25.ii) and in P 406 and P 284; middle stave headed 'Pedal 4 Fuss und ein 8va tiefer' in P 406 (second half of eighteenth century).

The TEXT of C. F. Nachtenhöfer's hymn was published in 1667; Pietist hymnbooks associated it with the Nativity and the Incarnation (Freylinghausen 1741 etc).

Kommst du nun, Jesu, vom Himmel herunter auf Erden?	Are you coming now, Jesu, from Heaven down to earth?
Soll nun der Himmel und Erde vereiniget werden?	Will now Heaven and earth be united?
Ewiger Gott,	Eternal God,
kann dich mein Jammer und Not	can my misery and need
bringen zu Menschen Geberden?	bring you to take human form?

The following four verses describe the need for the Incarnation.

The TEXT of J. Neander's hymn *Lobe den Herren, den mächtigen König der Ehren* (see below) was published in 1680; each of the five verses begins 'Lobe den Herren'.

v2

Lobe den Herren, der alles so herrlich regieret,	Praise to the Lord, who so gloriously reigns over all,
der dich auf Adelers Fittichen sicher geführet,	who bears you safely on eagle's wings,
der dich erhält	who preserves you
wie es dir selber gefällt;	as you yourself desire;
Hast du nicht dieses verspüret?	have you not become aware of this?

The MELODY appeared in 1665 (to the text *Hast du denn, Liebster*). In the first movement of the chorale-cantata BWV 137 it takes the form in Ex. 123; the melody of BWV 650 follows the form of the second

Ex. 123

BWV 137

movement of BWV 137. With the text *Richte dich, Liebste*, the melody is used in Cantata 57 (2nd Day of Christmas 1725) and was listed (but not set) in the *Orgelbüchlein*; with the text *Lobe den Herren*, it appears in Cantata 120a (wedding cantata, 1729?) and Cantata 137.

The title of BWV 650 – which does not appear in BWV 137, from which the piece is transcribed (from the score?) – may have been chosen because the composer associated the melody with this text and because it conformed to the *Schübler* plan (see p. 105 above).

> Cantata 137 'Lobe den Herren, den Mächtigen König der Ehren'
> 12th Sunday after Trinity 1725, and later performance(s)
> Second of five movements, 'Lobe den Herren, der alles so herrlich regieret'
> Trio: obbligato melody (violin)
>   cantus firmus (alto)
>   basso continuo, figured

The 'composer's corrected copy' of BWV 650 and the original 1725 parts of Cantata 137 show variant readings in the obbligato melody (bb2 is the same as bb15, 25 in BWV 137 and in the original print of BWV 650) and in the ornaments (cantus-firmus trills according to the 'corrected copy'). The print has no trills in the cantus firmus, and its rhythms are notated more simply: ♪♪ not ♪·♪ (b16), ♫♪ not ♪·♫ (b13) or ♫♪ (b52). But the cantus firmus is still sufficiently decorated to qualify as 'the composer's only decorated pedal cantus firmus', if that is what it is. However, the print notates the movement in a kind of open score, with the cantus firmus in the middle – that is, it follows the order of staves in the original cantata.* On the analogy of BWV 646, perhaps, it was early assumed that the cantus firmus was the pedal line; but BWV 646 did not have its chorale on an inner stave, nor is its bass line a simple continuo, despite its 16′ registration. Thus the closest analogy both musically and notationally is with BWV 645, and symmetry is best served if the parts are distributed by the organist in the same way – whichever way that is – in both pieces.

For characteristics of the transcription–ritornello form, see also BWV 645 and 649. The obbligato melody of BWV 650 may be derived at first from the chorale melody in two ways (Ex. 124). As in BWV 645, though

Ex. 124

perhaps less so, the different phrases of the complete obbligato melody occur in various orders and could in theory occur in others. As a whole, the movement combines vocal aria, chorale melody, and obbligato ritornello sections. The figuration itself is clearly violinistic, but it is

* As do the other three-part *Schübler* chorales transcribed from cantata movements.

probably a mistake to imitate violin articulation (clearly marked in the solo part for BWV 137) on the organ. The wider-ranging broken-chord figure which takes over the second half of the introductory melody (bb9–11) was characteristic of obbligato arias – particularly for violin – and brought a new principle as well as a new kind of figure into organ music. Such an opening introduction as that of the long 'Jesus Christus, unser Heiland' BWV 688 is different in its fugal character and contrapuntal intensity and should not be confused with the new contribution to organ music made by such aria transcriptions as BWV 650. The dancing figure of BWV 650, however, presents a problem of textual interpretation, since for the organ transcription the composer changed the original title, a hymn of praise, to a hymn of Advent, of pre-Advent or even of a personal, 'symbolic' Advent (see the plan outlined on pp. 104–5 above). Connections between the two texts can only be conjectured, and it is difficult to see how the obbligato melody could be solemn or subdued.

It is usually assumed that the composer intended the cantus firmus to be read as $^9/_8$ not $^3/_4$ (Klotz 1969a); but unlike the contrapuntal lines in movements elsewhere with similar rhythmic ambiguities,* a cantus firmus is a distinct solo melody, part of whose distinctiveness may have been its rhythm. The manner of pitting a (gentle?) $^3/_4$ aria melody against jig-like violin obbligato lines in $^9/_8$ can also be heard in Cantata 7, no. 4 (1724).

* E.g. Prelude of C minor Prelude and Fugue BWV 546; last movement of E minor Organ Sonata; Gavotte of E minor Partita.

651–668 Organ Chorales formerly called 'The Eighteen'

The primary source of these chorales (P 271) gives no original title for the collection; its 'title-page' is left blank (*NBA* IV/2 *KB* p59) and the group of pieces comprises either fewer or more than eighteen, depending on how or whether it is subdivided:

pp58–99   17 chorales BWV 651–667
                BWV 651–665 copied by the composer
                BWV 666–667 copied by J. C. Altnikol (pupil from
                  1744 to beginning of 1748)*
pp100–6   *Canonic Variations* BWV 769a
                copied by the composer
p106   chorale BWV 668 (MS now breaks off at middle of b26)
                copied by unknown scribe (Anon II)

The present old title-page to P 271 begins 'Achtzehn...' but once began 'Siebzehn' and was subsequently altered. All eighteen chorales have earlier known versions from the Weimar period, and the whole group serves as an example of the composer's methods of re-working – arranging, revising and collecting older material.

Some of the questions concerning the origin and purpose of the chorales BWV 651–668 may be summarized as follows:

(i) Date. Whatever the reasons for Altnikol's copying of BWV 666 and 667 – with or without the composer's foreknowledge – it can be assumed that the nineteen pieces were copied in order, since BWV 664 and 665 show a later stage in the composer's handwriting than the previous pieces (Dadelsen 1958 p109). But while BWV 769a appears to be a later version of BWV 769 published in 1747, a still later stage in Bach's style of handwriting is known from elsewhere (*ibid*). The group contained in P 271 can be dated over the period 1744–8, the last chorale perhaps slightly later.

    The date of the seventeen chorales as originally composed (BWV 651a etc) is still less certain. Their sources, particularly the copies by J. G. Walther (organist in Weimar) and J. T. Krebs (Bach's pupil in Weimar), suggest the period 1710–14 (Zietz 1969 p137), and a somewhat later date for BWV 664a; recent work suggests that while the Walther copies in P 801 and P 802 may be pre-1717, those by Krebs can be dated to c1720–30 (Daw 1975). The absence both of consistent part-writing in certain chorales and of canonic treatment throughout may suggest that they were composed no later than the *Orgelbüchlein*.

* BWV 666–667 added on blank paper left in the same gathering; BWV 769a follows on verso side of BWV 667.

However, although there is no evidence that the chorales were conceived as a group during the Weimar period, their very difference from the *Orgelbüchlein* in length, form, technique and immediacy of expression provides a unifying factor and makes comparative dating uncertain. Certainly they acknowledge more clearly than the *Orgelbüchlein* the heritage of Buxtehude, Böhm and Pachelbel and may thus be earlier; in individual cases the detail suggests a musical idiom much less mature than many *Orgelbüchlein* chorales. The type of figuration and the contrapuntal technique of 'O Lamm Gottes unschuldig' BWV 656 suggest at first an earlier stage in the composer's development than 'O Lamm Gottes unschuldig' BWV 618. Similarly, the length and architecture of BWV 656 result in a simpler texture and idiom than the three-verse 'Christ ist erstanden' BWV 627; however, since BWV 656 may be intended as an 'improved' version of Pachelbel's models and thus essentially less original than BWV 627, direct comparison between the two may well not be justified. Such comparison can therefore imply either that BWV 651a etc pre-date much of the *Orgelbüchlein* or that they were written as a stylistic complement to it.

(ii) **Sources.** For each of the chorales in P 271, at least two versions exist in one or more copies, and some have as many as four versions. Secondary sources suggest that the composer's fair copy contains some errors, a few details unintentionally carried over from earlier versions, and readings improved by the composer himself after the fair copy was prepared. The group of seventeen was not copied as such (in any of the versions) before Kittel and Kirnberger continued the tradition of P 271; however, the Walther–Krebs manuscripts P 801–3 between them contain all seventeen (some more than once), whilst they also contain Weimar works that would have been open to revision at Leipzig had the composer required. The Mempell–Preller manuscript Lpz MB MS 7 contains more than half the group, including two versions of BWV 653.

(iii) **Nature of 'revision'.** Some of the 'Leipzig versions' are longer by whole sections (BWV 651) or by several bars (BWV 652, 653, 656); others were improved in individual motifs, ornaments, rhythm and part-writing. Two had their written note-values doubled (BWV 656 v3, BWV 661), and it is possible that other apparent alterations too are merely notational: the sharper rhythms and specific ornaments of BWV 653, for instance, may reflect the composer's wish to clarify the intended style of playing BWV 653a. But none of these differences necessarily suggest a later, conscious revision; even the relationship between BWV 651 and 651a is not certain or conclusive but is merely based on assumptions drawn from the sources as they stand. The most prevalent of these assumptions – that the collection presents a set of Weimar chorales 'which Bach arranged anew in Leipzig and put together as a collection of seventeen' (Zietz 1969 p10) – cannot be regarded as proved.

(iv) Order and shape of the collection. Certain features suggest that the revised collection of 'about twenty preludes and worked-out chorales for organ' (as P 271 was described in 1790: *Dok* III p496) was made to a certain pattern which the composer's worsening health probably prevented from being completed. The arguments for such a pattern are: (*a*) the first and last pieces are addressed to the Holy Ghost; (*b*) the first and last movements and the putative middle movement (BWV 661) are marked 'organo pleno' only in the Leipzig version;* (*c*) the two other major collections (*Orgelbüchlein, Clavierübung III*) have discernible patterns. The fact that 'organo pleno' is in any case the obvious registration for BWV 651, 661 and 667 (full pedal cantus firmus) does not disturb this 'cyclic' thesis. If BWV 661 were the middle piece, four more chorales would be required for symmetry,† but the 'Weimar sources' do not suggest which. The collection is not arranged according to the church year, or the liturgy, or any particular hymnological pattern (such as the Luther texts and Gregorian emphasis in *Clavierübung III*); it is the musical characteristics of length and technique (paraphrase, ornamental melody etc) that formally distinguish the collection from the others. Several candidates amongst the miscellaneous chorales could have served in what is a collection of rather mixed musical quality, such as BWV 694 or BWV 734; other possibilities are BWV 735 and BWV 712, which resemble BWV 665 and 666 in form (Klotz *NBA* IV/3 *KB* p11). But it is not even certain that the composer's copy is indeed incomplete; it may be significant that the last chorale to be fair-copied by the composer (BWV 665) has a particularly conclusive ending.

(v) Purpose. The musical repertory includes at least six major examples of the paraphrase prelude in which the lines are derived from the cantus firmus (BWV 651, 655, 656, 657, 664, 665) and six of the ornamented prelude in which the melody appears in a decorated version (BWV 653, 654, 659, 660, 662, 663). There are trios (BWV 655, 664), pedal-less cantus-firmus settings (BWV 656 vv1, 2) and plain pedal cantus-firmus settings (BWV 661, 665). These are old Weimar techniques, and cantatas of the period were also moving towards sophisticated paraphrase technique, e.g. Ex. 125. The collection could be seen to acknowledge the forms learnt directly or indirectly from Böhm (BWV 659), Buxtehude

Ex. 125

BWV 161, opening (1715)

* In the Weimar movement BWV 665a the original 'organo pleno' heading was changed to 'sub communione' for BWV 665.
† Five perhaps, if Altnikol added the manual chorale BWV 666 without authorization. The reason for Altnikol's two contributions can only be conjectured; it cannot have been that the composer was totally incapacitated by blindness, since in P 271 BWV 769a follows in his hand and was presumably written later.

(BWV 652, 653, 654) and Pachelbel (BWV 655, 657, 658, 666) and 'developed' by Bach during his Weimar years. As such, the movements demonstrate the treatment of the chorale melody according to tradition – with new elements but without the essential originality of the *Orgelbüchlein* or *Clavierübung III*. Whether commentators have been correct to see weaknesses in the collection (e.g. BWV 652 and 657 in Meyer's opinion (1972)), certain other pieces do seem to shine above the traditions that led to them. Thus BWV 655 and 664 may follow Pachelbel in deriving the lines from the cantus firmus, but the bright Italianate figuration is superior in both conception and working-out. There is often a characteristic relevance to the text: the lines suggest a word (e.g. 'Hallelujah' at the close of BWV 652) or musical allegory (e.g. the ornaments of BWV 654, 'Adorn yourself'). The 'weaker' movements may be the most old-fashioned, e.g. the 'objective' cantus-firmus settings of BWV 657 and 666. Either way, variety in techniques seems to have been a guiding principle of the collection: a kind of mid-eighteenth-century salute to late-seventeenth-century forms. With *Clavierübung III*, the *Schübler Chorales*, the *Canonic Variations* and the *Orgelbüchlein* (recopied in the same period), the student organists of Leipzig would have had a full compositional repertory before them.

---

651   Komm, Heiliger Geist (formerly 'The Eighteen')

Autograph MS P 271; copies of Bach's last alterations in P 1109, P 1160; other late copies in Kirnberger and Kittel circles.

Headed in P 271 'Fantasia super...', 'in organo pleno', 'canto fermo in Pedal.' (added later to title?), 'J. J.' ['Jesu juva', 'Jesus, help']; two staves.

The TEXT contains three verses, the first of which is a fifteenth-century German translation of the Whit antiphon *Veni sancte spiritus*; the second and third verses are Luther's additions (Erfurt 1524). In most hymnbooks (including Leipzig) the chorale was the chief hymn of the three days of Whitsuntide (Stiller 1970 p228), given in Latin in some Dresden and Leipzig books (Gojowy 1972).

Komm, heiliger Geist, Herre Gott,	Come Holy Ghost, Lord God,
erfüll mit deiner Gnaden Gut	fill with the goodness of your grace
deiner Gläubgen Herz, Muth und Sinn,	the heart, spirit and mind of your believers,
dein brünstig Lieb entzünd in ihn'.	kindle your ardent love in them.
O Herr, durch deines Lichtes Glast	O Lord, through the brilliance of your light
zu dem Glauben versammelt hast	you have gathered to the faith
das Volk aus aller Welt Zungen.	people of every tongue on earth.
Das sei dir, Herr, zu Lob gesungen.	Let this be sung to your praise, Lord.
Halleluja, Halleluja.	Hallelujah, Hallelujah.

Verse 2 concerns the holy light and protection from false teaching, v3 the ardour that sustains the faithful.

The MELODY was published with the text in 1524; versions published in 1535 and 1560 include different 'Hallelujah' cadences, the last of which was that used in the present organ chorales (Terry 1921 pp244–5) – it is not known from what source. Otherwise, the organ chorales use the melody as it appears in BWV 226 (Ex. 126). The melody is used

Ex. 126
BWV 226

in Cantatas 59 (Whitsunday 1723 or 1724), 172 (Whitsunday 1714 etc, without text, cantus firmus adapted and abridged) and 175 (3rd Day of Whit 1725 etc, different text) and in the organ chorales BWV 651, 651a, 652 and 652a, and is listed in the *Orgelbüchlein*. J. G. Walther's cantus firmus (*DDT* 26/7, no. 58) is a simplified version of the 1524 form.

The huge continuous fantasia is both musically and dogmatically suitable to open the collection, and the exuberance of motifs gives a striking gloss on the hymn text. Meyer (1972) does not seem to go too far in seeing it as a response to the day of Pentecost as described in Acts ii, 2: 'And suddenly there came a sound from heaven, as of a rushing mighty wind, and it filled all the house where they were sitting.' For its relationship to the shorter version, see BWV 651a; with the repetition (bb55–86 = bb12–43) and the 'new' subject (the *finale alleluiaticum* from b89 onwards), the fantasia remains a highly unified piece, its driving lines derived from the cantus firmus, which itself involves inner repetition or resemblances between the many lines (Ex. 127). Its subsidiary motifs are worked as countersubject to the paraphrase (Ex. 128).

Ex. 127

line 1   C D   CB♭ A C   G
line 2   C D   C   G A B♭ A G F

b91 (cf. motif *b* above)

'Halleluja' G A F D E F

Ex. 128

b25

The nature of the theme prevents toccata elements from gaining independence – e.g., the pedal point at b13 does not develop as far as convention might have suggested: it forms the end of line 1 of the cantus firmus, though in a Pachelbel toccata it might rather have been used as a dominant version of the opening tonic pedal point. Modulations are also bound by the tonic and dominant of the cantus firmus, a fact not quite disguised by even the very skilful control of material at bb17ff (bb60ff) and 34ff (77ff). The episodes give variety of key, as might be expected, and the close of line 4 of the cantus firmus on a bass A (new material b44) gives an important opportunity in the middle of the piece. The so-called newly written sections (bb43–54, 89–104) offer insight into what might be thought the mature style of Bach, notably the simple sequence and thinning of parts in bb56–7 (cf. middle passages in BWV 544, 547), the development of appoggiatura figures in bb49–51 (cf. Fugue of the E minor Partita BWV 830), the constant application of motifs (compare the use of motif *b* above the same cantus-firmus phrase in bb87–8 and 102–3 – an unrelentingly ingenious variety of treatment characteristic of *Clavierübung III*), and the build-up from one part to five in the finale (which exploits all three motifs). That the last three bars of BWV 651a seem more in place at the end of the enlarged BWV 651 than in their 'original' context may reflect on the reliability of the sources or on the skill of the composer in gradually working towards their six parts. Either way, the ab″ in b104 becomes more isolated as the top note of the last six bars in BWV 651, which it is not in BWV 651a. Even the no doubt accidental B–A–C–H becomes apt in a late work, if that is what BWV 651 is: Ex. 129.

Ex. 129 b105

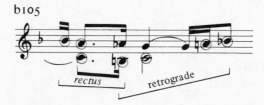

Considered as a whole, however, the piece is particularly admirable for its development of exuberant motifs, logical in their own terms yet conforming to the demands of the cantus firmus. Such a passage as bb82–8 uses its motifs *a* and *b* no doubt less concentratedly than certain *Clavierübung III* movements and with a fitness of harmony and a melodic logic (e.g. the sequence in the soprano bb84–7) that are by no means inferior.

651a Komm, Heiliger Geist

No Autograph MS; copies by J. T. Krebs (P 802) and Walther (Kö 15839), and in a source probably based on Walther (Lpz MB MS 7).

Headed in P 802 'Fantasia super...'; two staves.

The forty-eight bars of BWV 651a amount to less than half of the 'revised' version:

BWV 651:		BWV 651a:
bb1–43 (1st ½)	=	bb1–43 (1st ½)
bb43 (2nd ½)–54 (new)		
bb55–88 (repeat)	=	bb12–45 (repeat)
bb89–103 (new)		
bb104–6	=	bb46–8

Somewhat less than half the cantus firmus, therefore, is given in BWV 651a; but because the melody incorporates several repeated figures its telescoping in BWV 651a is both technically feasible and musically acceptable. Similar repetition within the chorale melody produces shortening of the cantus firmus in two settings of the melody of *Allein Gott* (BWV 664, 715). On the fact that the cantus-firmus finals in the pedal are shorter in BWV 651a than in 651, see also BWV 769.ii (canon at the fifth), where the autograph P 271 has longer notes than the engraved version.

The originality and value of BWV 651a should not be obscured by the majestic length of BWV 651. The pedal point of the opening, rising to the cantus firmus in b8; the convincing and sequential stretto of the two hands; the two pairs of cantus-firmus phrases separated by a modulatory episode; the ease of three- and four-part counterpoint based on the complementary motifs *a* and *b* (see Ex. 127); the overall 'interpretation' of the text – the achievement is unparalleled in the period, though some of these points may be hinted at in the work of Walther or Pachelbel. A further distinction is that the fugal character of the counterpoint is not compromised by the appearance of the cantus firmus in the bass (as it was elsewhere in this period), despite the traditional and ultimately Italianate nature of that counterpoint (e.g. bb28–9).

Since the evidence of the sources cannot be regarded as conclusive, it may be doubted that BWV 651a was later 'enlarged' to BWV 651; the integration achieved in BWV 651 may suggest that the two versions are contemporary. Thus BWV 651a could be a shortened version of BWV 651; this is not suggested by the sources, but nor is it denied by them.

652

Komm, Heiliger Geist (formerly 'The Eighteen')

Autograph MS P 271; also in P 1109, P 1160 and several sources in Kirnberger and Kittel circles.

Headed in P 271 'alio modo à 2 Clav. et Ped.'; three staves.

For TEXT and MELODY see BWV 651. It is possible to see in this second setting of the text a reference to v3:

Du heilige Brunst, süsser Trost,	O holy ardour, sweet comfort,
nun hilf uns, fröhlich und getrost	now help us to remain constantly
in dein Dienst beständig bleiben,	joyful and confident in your service,
die Trübsal uns nicht abtreiben.	[and help us] not to repulse our
	afflictions.

For the relationship of BWV 652 to its earlier version, see BWV 652a. The complete contrast to BWV 651 in the treatment of the chorale is immediately striking: BWV 652 (the longest of Bach's organ chorales) is lyrical in style, sectional–imitative in form, and more supplicatory in mood. Sarabande-like features, such as might be characteristic of a Buxtehude organ chorale, have been heard in it (Dietrich 1929 p63). Each line of the cantus firmus is treated as follows:

> introduction by a derived fugue subject in tenor, answered (against quasi-countersubject) by alto, then pedal (twice in the case of line 1) further tonic 'answer' in soprano, ornamented and like a cantus firmus finally a few cadential bars before next tenor theme

Like BWV 651, the setting aims at musical flow and length despite its sectional nature, but there is less repetition: only line 3 is repeated (as line 7: bb 42–66 = 124–48), not lines 2–4 as in BWV 651. The countersubjects are conceived as an aid to the flow, as shown in (e.g.) the final exposition (b171) where the alto's immediate entry in quavers disguises the true answer, which begins only in b175. The final paragraph, from b171 to the end, contains two sections:

(i) exposition derived from the 'Hallelujah' of the melody (1569 version in Terry 1921 p243): Ex. 130.

Ex. 130
(1569 cadence)

(ii) coda, not obviously derived from any phrase of the cantus firmus. Such sections of various forms and lengths at the ends of chorales were known to north German composers and those influenced by them. Bruhns's 'Nun komm, der Heiden Heiland' (copied in the same source as BWV 652a, Krebs's P 802) has new scale-like patterns in the coda, as has Buxtehude's setting of the same 'Komm, Heiliger Geist' BUXWV 200: Ex. 131. Also in P 802 is Reincken's 'Was kann uns kommen',

Ex. 131
BUXWV 200 (BB 22541/3)
b52

which also shows the tradition of allowing the right hand to wander on its solo manual.

While it may be clear enough that in BWV 652 Bach is attempting to recreate a historic type of organ chorale, the problem for the performer is still to know how sarabande-like the pulse of the piece is and how fast he can convincingly play it. Almost 200 bars incorporate 37 cantus-firmus phrases (9×4 plus an extra pedal phrase in b19 – intended originally as the first of a series?), and the coda seems unsuited to the task of lightening their weight. The chorale is neither a simple Pachelbel 'organ motet' nor a simple Buxtehude ornamental/ paraphrase type, as is often suggested. Its style has elements of the sarabande (e.g. the rhythms ♩ ♩· ♪ and ♩· ♪ ♩); its up-beat version of the cantus firmus results in an implicit lilt (unlike BWV 651); and its ornaments blur the difference between accompaniment and solo lines (unlike BWV 652a). The somewhat doctrinaire nature of the counterpoint should not hide the frequent charm (Ex. 132), which

Ex. 132

b27

depends on a lively tempo. The north German tradition suggests that the coda be marked by greater metric freedom rather than by a change of registration.

652a

Komm, Heiliger Geist

No Autograph MS; copy by J. T. Krebs (P 802) and in a source probably based on Walther (Lps MB MS 7).

Headed in P 802 'a 2 Clav. è Ped.'; three staves.

Because the cadences to lines 2–4 and 6–8 of the cantus firmus are lengthened in BWV 652, BWV 652a is the shorter of the two by six bars:

BWV 652a:		BWV 652:
b39	becomes	bb39–40
b63		bb64–5
b87		bb89–90
b119		bb122–3
b142		bb146–7
b164		bb169–70

This suggests that the composer later lengthened cadences which he felt had been perfunctory. In particular, the first two and the last two of these six cadences underwent considerable alteration.

The more highly ornamented style of the last entry of each 'fugue subject' (i.e. that in the soprano) confirms the traditional aspect of such decorated right-hand solos on a different manual and also helps to lead naturally into the coda. The sources are reliable in respect of this ornamentation (*NBA* IV/2 *KB* p66) and suggest that the different approach to ornaments in BWV 652 is not merely a failing of notation.

653

An Wasserflüssen Babylon (formerly 'The Eighteen')

Autograph MS P 271; also in P 1109 (Penzel), P 1160 and several sources in Kirnberger and Kittel circles.

Headed in P 271 'a 2 Clav. et Pedal'; three staves.

The TEXT is a German translation of Ps. 137 (*Super flumina Babylonis*, Ps. 136 for Vespers), published Strassburg 1525. Not a regular liturgical hymn, the text served analogously as 'the complaint of Zion' (Freylinghausen 1741 etc).

An Wasserflüssen Babylon	By the waters of Babylon
da sassen wir mit Schmerzen;	we sat down in sorrow;
als wir gedachten an Zion,	when we thought of Zion
da weinten wir von Herzen.	we wept from our hearts.
Wir hingen auf mit schwerem Muth	Sorrowfully we hung up
die Orgeln und die Harfen gut	our organs and harps
an ihre Bäum' der Weiden,	on their trees of willow,
die drinnen sind in ihrem Land;	which are in their country;
da mussten wir viel Schmach und	there we had to suffer much shame
* Schand*	and disgrace
täglich von ihnen leiden.	daily at their hands.

The following four verses follow the psalm, ending with curses on Babylon.

The MELODY was published with the text in 1525 (Terry 1921 p101): Ex. 133. The melody is used in BWV 653, 653a and 653b, harmonized

Ex. 133

1525

in BWV 267 and listed in the *Orgelbüchlein*. It was also sung to P. Gerhardt's text *Ein Lämmlein geht und trägt die Schuld* (a Good Friday hymn of the Passion), but its significance for organ music lies more in its use as a hymn at Saturday Vespers in north German *Hauptkirchen*, where organists wove organ pieces from it for concert-like performance. The 1754 Obituary refers to Bach's visit to Hamburg in 1720:

> den Choral: An Wasserflüssen Babylon, welchen unser Bach, auf Verlangen der Anwesenden, aus dem Stegreife, sehr weitläuftig, fast eine halbe Stunde lang, auf verschiedene Art, so wie es ehedem die braven unter den Hamburgischen Organisten in den Sonnabends Vespern gewohnt gewesen waren, ausführte...Reinken...vor langen Jahren diesen Choral selbst, auf die obengemeldete Weise gesetzt hatte. (*Dok* III p84)

> At the request of those present, Bach performed the chorale 'An Wasserflüssen Babylon' extempore, very amply for almost half an hour, in a variety of ways, just as formerly the better amongst the Hamburg organists had been accustomed to play during the Saturday Vespers...

Reincken himself had set the chorale many years previously in the way referred to above.

It is likely that Bach knew the last piece and that this is none other than the extant *Fantasia* preserved in Reincken sources; it is also possible that Bach himself was responsible for the preservation of some of Reincken's music (otherwise rare) in the Möller MS and the *Andreas-Bach-Buch* (Riedel 1960 p191). One or other setting, BWV 653 or 653b, may well be connected with this visit (Schulze *Dok* III p93); however, the report in the Obituary seems rather to refer to a set of variations ('auf verschiedene Art').

BWV 653 is a ritornello chorale conceived as follows:

decorated cantus firmus phrase by phrase *en taille* (in the tenor)
accompanied and introduced by two upper voices, each continuously derived from the first two phrases of the cantus firmus, often in turn; each tenor phrase thus accompanied by one or other theme
pedal continuo bass, often derived from the first line of the cantus firmus (see bb1–2, 4–5, 16–17, 32, 61–2, 77–8), the second (bb27, 50) and possibly others (e.g. line 6 in b39?)

The musical character of the movement is elusive and depends on several elements: (*a*) the sarabande style of the whole; (*b*) the unity of the parts constantly derived from the melody, with very little 'free' writing in any part, but often using strettos (e.g. bb1, 52–3, 65–8) and combinations (b4 pedal = line 1, b5 soprano = line 2); (*c*) the unusual and almost ostinato-like quality of the soprano part, with returning periods at bb1, 12–13 (repeat), 33, 43–4, 58, 66; (*d*) the French character of the pedal, with its striding crotchets and (in bb72–5) its pedal point below a solo *en taille* melody; (*e*) the decided similarity it has with the previous chorale (BWV 652) in melody, use of quaver figures, key and metre, certain rhythmic figures, and the degree to which the upper parts are derived. Of these, (*b*) promises much from close scrutiny.

The deriving of accompanying parts from the cantus firmus was evidently one of the composer's interests in his later years, as in BWV 669, while the constant reworking of the first two lines in the upper voices resembles that of other *Clavierübung III* chorales, e.g. BWV 675 and 682. (There, however, there is no such obvious reference at the end to line 1 as there is at bb77, 80 of BWV 653). The last seven bars present line 1 in the outer parts (imitation at the octave) and contract it in the alto (bb79–80) whilst hinting at line 2 in the upper pedal part (bb81–2), all around a pedal point that closes with a little descending run at the end; though a small detail, this little run may well be a reference to a setting by Reincken or another north German composer. As a whole, however, the movement could scarcely be more different in its continuity from the one Reincken setting that does exist. Whether BWV 653 expresses the text – for example, the languour that commentators have seen as implied in VI of the hymn – can only be conjectured. But its continuity is very striking and is aided by ostinato elements in soprano and bass lines, smoothly moulded accompaniment (e.g., the repeat of bb1–14 overlaps at b12) and similar line-cadences towards G major (cf. bb13, 25, 36).

653a

An Wasserflüssen Babylon

No Autograph MS; copy by J. G. Walther (P 802) and a copy perhaps based on a Walther source (Lpz MB MS 7).

Headed in P 802 'Vers 2 à 4 con 2 Clav. è simp. ped.', 'alio modo à 4', lh 'forte', rh 'piano'; three staves.

The last three bars of BWV 653a become nine bars in BWV 653, adding to the original version two pedal points, several further references to the theme and a richer five-part close. Although BWV 653a did already contain a pedal point, a five-part close and a chromatic penultimate phrase (all as in BWV 653b), evidently they were not thought sufficient, not least because the original b75 is weak. Whether or not the more sharply defined rhythms of BWV 653 reflect a normal style of playing or are there to characterize and make clearer the derived, contrapuntal upper parts, it should be noted that the ingenious and musical use of the cantus firmus was already there in the 'Weimar version', as was the somewhat unusual scoring for manual solo stop *en taille* (*forte*).

Whatever the relationship between BWV 653a and 653b (see below), this four-part setting is more conventionally spaced, with the melody in the tenor and the single pedal a judicious 'reduction' allowing 16′ registration. With one exception, in this version the pedal never goes above d′, which is in keeping with the collection as a whole; the exception is the double pedal eb′ at the close (apparently authentic), which is no longer there in BWV 653, nor in BWV 654/654a (Eb major).

653b

An Wasserflüssen Babylon

No Autograph MS; copy by J. G. Walther (P 802)* and a copy perhaps based on a Walther source (Leipzig MB MS 7).

Headed in P 802 'Vers 1 à 5 con 2 Clav. è doppio pedale'; three staves.

Both sources contain both the five-part and four-part versions, and it can only be conjectured why P 802 calls them *Vers* 1 and *Vers* 2 respectively: perhaps because Walther assumed they were variants or variations, like his own movements but longer. These versions would have served J. T. Krebs as models for his own studies in chorale treatment, as would others in P 802. Spitta's opinion that BWV 653b is an arrangement of 653a (not vice versa) is now discounted, since the single bass line of 653a is thought to be a 'compromise' of the

---

* Zietz 1969 p89: 'later period' of J. G. Walther's handwriting, with many alterations and crossings-out (p141).

two pedal lines of 653b (*NBA* IV/2 *KB* p67), preserving the thematic reference but not the independent figure Ex. 134, already announced

Ex. 134

in b1. Similarly, although the high pedal part does not of itself mean that 653b was not written for the Hamburg organ played in 1720, there is no evidence for Spitta's suggestion (I p606) either that it was sent to Reincken or that it had been adapted from the written-down extemporization in Hamburg, which was later described as lasting 'almost half an hour'.

The double pedal part is different both from Scheidt's suggested scoring of such doubles in *Tabulatura nova* (Hamburg 1624; four parts, cantus firmus in alto) and from Bach's scoring in 'Aus tiefer Noth' BWV 686 (six parts, cantus firmus in pedal); nor does it resemble the distinctive use of double pedal in the concerto transcriptions (e.g. the repercussion effects in BWV 593). Certainly it seems to require 8' stops only (Bruggaier 1959 p148), not least since the spacing is unusual, with the left hand mostly clear of the high upper pedal and constantly crossing the right-hand melody. As it is scored in P 802, there is no particular reason why the cantus firmus is an octave above that of BWV 653a. Comparisons with Buxtehude's double pedal parts are hampered by uncertainty about Buxtehude's intentions; the examples in extant works of Lübeck and Bruhns are clearer, but there double pedals are found rather in preludes and fugues, and the effect is thematic and contrapuntal, not accompanimental.

One can pose two questions about BWV 653b which are to be answered neither by the sources nor by its musical character: was it written before BWV 653a, and was it originally an organ piece? The following points should be remembered.

(i) It is not obvious that the single bass line of the four-part version (BWV 653a) is a 'compromise'. It would not be out of the question to have added a new line to the pedal of BWV 653a, incorporating simple motifs and sustaining the motion. The first two bars of 'Schmücke dich' BWV 654 should warn against regarding a disjunct pedal line as the sign of a compromise. Thus it is still uncertain that BWV 653b is the 'original version' and BWV 653a 'a four-part reduction', as has been said (Emery 1974 p160).

(ii) That the lines of the four-part version are more rhythmically characterized than those of the five-part version may be not because the composer 'revised' the lines of the latter but because he wished to make all the lines of BWV 653b plainer and thus more unified in style. This would be a contrary procedure to that in (e.g.) BWV 608 and 617.

(iii) The spacing alone of the five parts of BWV 653b might suggest that the work is not necessarily or originally an organ piece. As to what it might have been, the character of the pedal lines makes it more possible that it was a composer's exercise than a transcription of some kind, perhaps in the tradition of Buxtehude's 'Mit Fried und Freud' BUXWV 75. There is difficulty too in registering the pedals. However lightly voiced, a 16' stop seems unsuitable; but by c1715 an 8' registration for pedal without cantus firmus was unlikely. Nevertheless, whatever the origins of BWV 653b, it is clear that Walther could plausibly regard it as an organ piece, and that Spitta could also plausibly see it as a reworking of BWV 653a in five parts.

654

Schmücke dich, o liebe Seele (formerly 'The Eighteen')

Autograph MS P 271; also in P 1109, P 1160 and sources in Kirnberger circle.

Headed in P 271 'a 2 Clav. et Pedal'; three staves.

The TEXT is J. Franck's hymn for the Eucharist, published in 1649; it was absent from the usual hymn-plans (Stiller 1970 p233) but was given for the 20th Sunday after Trinity in an Arnstadt book of 1666 (Gojowy 1972).

Schmücke dich, o liebe Seele,	Adorn yourself, dear soul,
lass die dunkle Sündenhöhle,	leave the dark cavern of sin,
komm ins helle Licht gegangen,	come to the bright light,
fange herrlich an zu prangen!	begin to shine in splendour!
Denn der Herr voll Heil und	For the Lord, full of salvation and
Gnaden	grace,
will dich jetzt zu Gaste laden,	wishes to invite you now as guest,
der den Himmel kann verwalten,	he who rules over Heaven
will jetzt Herberg in dir halten.	now wills to make his dwelling in you.

The following six verses speak of the hunger and fear resolved in the Eucharist.

The MELODY by J. Crüger was published with the text and was used in Cantata 180 (20th Sunday after Trinity 1724): Ex. 135. It is listed in the *Orgelbüchlein*, and set in different form in BWV 759.

Ex. 135

BWV 180

Something of a 'Jesus hymn', the organ chorale on 'Schmücke dich' has seemed to commentators 'as priceless, deep and full of soul as any piece of music that ever sprang from a true artist's imagination', in the words of Schumann (David & Mendel 1945 p372); Terry suggested that 'as is invariably the case when the words of the hymn stirred Bach to deep emotion, the *cantus* is treated very freely' (1921 p291). Not as contrapuntally organized as BWV 652, 'Schmücke dich' nevertheless has middle lines of similar lyricism; not as thematically bound as BWV 653, it nevertheless has a rather similar frenchified pedal and overall texture, in addition to sharing the ritornello form. With its homophonic opening and striding continuo-like bass, BWV 654 is even more dance-like than BWV 653; its cantus firmus is simpler, too, though the long notes pass into melismatic figures so as to make the theme virtually unrecognizable. The melody is both ornamented as the cantus firmus and paraphrased in the accompaniment (Ex. 136).

Ex. 136

Intrinsic are the motif derivations from various parts of the cantus firmus, for example Ex. 137. Such a motif as *y* in Ex. 138 below (from the ornamented cantus firmus) also generates development, itself

Ex. 137

originating as an extra melisma when line 5 of the cantus firmus is repeated (see b88 compared with b79). Often the lines seem to be ultimately derived from the cantus firmus as clearly as those of the smaller chorales of *Clavierübung III*, and certainly more directly than those of the *Orgelbüchlein*: line 2, for instance, can be heard in the alto phrase bb5–9.

Quite apart from the length and continuity of the movement, such motivic development produces a work much 'later' in style than that which any Buxtehude-like element in its shape would suggest. Yet the ingenuity gives the impression of being geared towards an expressive end; the cantus firmus is not excessively ornamented, and however ingeniously the closing bars could be shown to be derived from the motifs, their peacefulness seems unquestionable. Few would disagree with Spitta that the piece has a 'strange, puzzling magic' (I p607); yet it should not be assumed that the Eucharist was approached at Weimar in 1715 with the same air of pious solemnity that has been common since the nineteenth century. More objectively, the chorale is remarkable for the reprise-like return of the opening paraphrase theme in bb116ff.

654a

Schmücke dich, o liebe Seele

No Autograph MS; copy by J. T. Krebs (P 802), Leipzig MB MS 7 and several sources in the Kittel circle.

Headed 'Fantasia super...', 'a 2 Clav. è Ped.'; three staves.

The differences between BWV 654 and 654a are slighter than those between BWV 653 and 653a, amounting to variant readings in some rhythms (e.g. b5 more pointed in this 'Leipzig version'), pedal phrases (e.g. soprano pedal point in b105 duplicated in the bass in BWV 654a) and ornamented cantus firmus (fewer ornaments in P 802). The sources doubtless reflect variants in the composer's own manuscripts rather than systematic alterations for the final fair copy.

655

Herr Jesu Christ, dich zu uns wend (formerly 'The Eighteen')

Autograph MS P 271; also in several sources of Kirnberger and Kittel circles.

Headed in P 271 'Trio super...a 2 Clav. et Pedal.'; three staves.

For TEXT and MELODY see BWV 632.

The conception of BWV 655 can be expressed as

> trio for two manuals and pedal, based on material derived from the cantus firmus or chorale melody
> complete cantus firmus in pedal in the last third of the piece
> constant motivic development within a ritornello framework

The melody supplies contrapuntal phrases and is itself quoted complete. The formal difference between such a movement and Pachelbel chorale-fugues is that the counterpoint is trio-stretto, not fugal (Spitta I p604); a detailed difference is that much is derived from the 'subject': Ex. 139. Also derived are the scale-like figures (e.g. descending

Ex. 139

quavers of b40) suggestive of the second and fourth lines of the cantus firmus. Nevertheless, there is not the motivic involvement common in *Clavierübung III*, and the composer has not been at pains to quote the theme overtly until the bass entry in b52.

It is in its episodes that BWV 655 is most like the Trio Sonatas, e.g. bb10ff, 30ff, 45ff. The idea of a trio derived from the chorale melody appears to be highly original; the trio chorales of Buxtehude, Pachelbel, Buttstedt, Kauffmann and others normally give the cantus firmus to the pedal throughout – as here from b52, and as in the similar trios on 'Allein Gott', BWV 664 (at the close) and 676 (periodically). Weimar cantatas show the composer working on paraphrase techniques in upper obbligato instruments (e.g. BWV 161, in five parts) or in the bass line (e.g. BWV 172, no. 5, in four parts) or in a solo instrument (e.g. BWV 199, no. 6, in three parts); a pure trio working seems a logical step for the realm of solo organ music. Various motifs are reminiscent of other Bach organ music of the period, e.g. Ex. 140. The triadic

Ex. 140

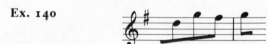

derivatives resemble those of the same chorale in the *Orgelbüchlein*: Ex. 141. Clearly the first is lighter and gayer than the second, owing

Ex. 141

to its simpler texture and harmonic implications, and probably to its tempo (quicker) and key (brighter).

Luedtke (1918 p78) and Terry (1921 p194) see in this 'jubilant' trio a reference to v3 of the text (see under BWV 632); certainly it is not difficult to see the mood as less meditative than BWV 632 and 709 (which have more in common). Keller's view that the movement is 'completely in the style of the Six Sonatas' (1948 p184) needs modification, since the short phrases, the motivic compactness and the use of pedal are more individual; in these respects BWV 664 resembles the Sonatas more closely than does BWV 655. The arranging of invertible trio lines in one-bar phrases also emphasizes the important kinds of repetition in the movement – the immediate inversions of the counterpoint (e.g. bb8–9, 18–19) and the return of material in different keys (e.g. compare bb28, 43). This homogeneity of material is even more pronounced in BWV 664.

655a

Herr Jesu Christ, dich zu uns wend

No Autograph MS; copy by J. T. Krebs (P 802), in a source probably based on Walther (Leipzig MB MS 7) and copies in the Krebs circle (P 1009).

Headed 'Trio super...', 'à 2 Clav. et Ped.'; three staves.

Apart from the occasional minor differences (fewer ornaments in P 802), this 'earlier version' has more angular lines at bb54–5 (left hand) and, most importantly, a different semiquaver countersubject. This not only gives a different aspect to (and sometimes produces parallel fifths in) bb2–3, 8–9, 18–19, 28–9 and 43–4 but also closes the movement in a manner reminiscent of Buxtehude: Ex. 142.

Ex. 142

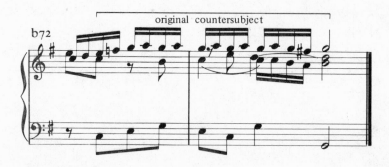

655b

Herr Jesu Christ, dich zu uns wend

Nineteenth-century sources only (Klotz NBA IV/2 KB p70), e.g. Schelble–Gleichauf.

This shortened version is based on the pedal cantus-firmus section of BWV 655. The left hand is an octave lower than in the original. The harmony is often 'banalisiert' (Klotz *ibid*); and the motifs are largely suppressed in the final bars, which are altered to give a perfect cadence in the modern taste.

655c   Herr Jesu Christ, dich zu uns wend

P 285 (*c*1835/40) from a copy of the second half of the eighteenth century.

This shortened version of twenty-nine bars incorporates ornaments characteristic of the 'Berlin School' (Klotz *op cit* p72). Here the motifs are still further removed from the chorale melody (e.g. Ex. 143); and

Ex. 143

the full statement of the cantus firmus in the pedal is omitted altogether. Correspondences are:

BWV 655c:		BWV 655:
bb1–20	=	bb1–20
bb22–5	cf.	bb49–52
bb26–9	cf.	bb70–3

---

656   O Lamm Gottes, unschuldig (formerly 'The Eighteen')

Autograph MS P 271; also in P 1109 and several sources of Kirnberger and Kittel circles.

Headed 'Versus. manualiter', the third verse with 'Pedal' cue; two staves.

For TEXT and MELODY see BWV 618.

The first verse has a somewhat irregular fore-imitation based on a double subject, both parts of which are derived from the cantus firmus (Ex. 144). Although the movement can be seen as subdued, there is no clear evidence that 'a deep Passion atmosphere lies over the

Ex. 144

chorale' (Leutert 1967). The tied quavers of b3 accompany the melody of the soprano, which is unbroken once it has entered. The verse is reminiscent of textures employed by other composers, its idiom found in (e.g.) the opening bars of J. G. Walther's *Harmonische Denck- und Danckmahl* (pub. 1738): Ex. 145.

Ex. 145

J. G. Walther, 'Allein Gott in der Höh' sei Ehr', *Vers* 1

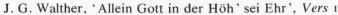

The second verse contains the cantus firmus in the alto; the figuration is livelier but equally conventional, as the sequences of b66 show. Less likely to be found in Walther or conventional composers are the ornamented cantus firmus of b93 (imitated in b97) and the rising line towards the cadence (compare it with that in v3). Nevertheless, the three verses are closer in idiom to chorale variations than to the characteristic courantes of keyboard suites, as has occasionally been thought (Klotz 1962).

In the third verse the cantus firmus is passed down a further step to the pedal, as in other tripartite settings (e.g. the Kyrie–Christe–Kyrie BWV 669–671 of *Clavierübung III*). Its opening three notes may well have influenced the fugal counter-themes: Ex. 146(i). In this melodic

Ex. 146

(i) b104

(ii) b122

shape, with the upward steps and the downward leap, Keller hears a cross motif (Keller 1948 p186 – see BWV 684). Halfway through the verse, the five parts break off for a new theme said to be derived from the cantus firmus – Ex. 146(ii) – and invoking the 'bowed head of the Saviour' (Keller *ibid*), or 'illustrating the act of bearing' sin referred to in the *Agnus Dei* text (Spitta I p602), or suggesting in its repetition 'the multitude of the sins of humanity' (Schweitzer 1905 p357), its ten entries perhaps alluding to the Commandments broken by man then in need of redemption through the Passion of the *Lamm Gottes* (Leutert 1967). Less merely speculative than these interpretations is the graphic reference to the text heard in the penultimate line, 'all Sünd hast du getragen' ('all sin have you borne') – Ex. 147 – which

Ex. 147

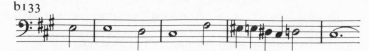

b133

has caught an incipient chromaticism, generating it further almost fugally for four bars (entries on C♯ and F♯). Several examples of such a *passus duriusculus* (see BWV 614) in the cantatas can be found to certain words, e.g. 'quälen' ('torment') in Cantata 63, no. 7. The highly chromatic passage over a pedal C♯, though apparently conventional, is more thematic and rich than (e.g.) that figured as an example by C. P. E. Bach (*Versuch* 1762 ch.24): Ex. 148. The *St Matthew Passion*

Ex. 148

C. P. E. Bach, *Versuch*

setting of the same chorale uses a different form of the melody at this point and does not become strikingly chromatic any more than did the first two verses of BWV 656 at the same word 'verzagen'. But the *Orgelbüchlein* setting (BWV 618) does include an incipient chromatic figure in its bb20–1.

Clearly the last section of BWV 656 is less fraught, corresponding to the last section of the *Agnus Dei* text, which refers to 'peace'. The simple major scales suggest something peaceful, though whether it is a question of angels leading the soul to that peace is doubtful. Nevertheless, the change is dramatic: the sudden return to the tonic, the scale figure (simpler than previous motifs in this movement) and the long pedal point (non-thematic, in that no earlier themes are recalled over it) seem to refer to the last line of the text. No sources suggest a change of organ colour in addition to those of key and figure.

656a

O Lamm Gottes, unschuldig

No Autograph MS; copy by J. T. Krebs (P 802), later arrangement in Leipzig MB MS 7 (from a Walther source?).

Later headed respectively 'Vers 2', 'Vers 3'; two staves.

The differences beween BWV 656 and the 'earlier version' BWV 656a are slighter than those between BWV 653 and 653a, amounting to variant readings (not systematic 'improvements') in the 'later version'. The 'earlier version' has somewhat fewer ornaments, occasionally different readings in detail (b13 inferior in part-distribution; b18 left-hand quavers up an octave), and less 'correct' notation for verse 3 (triplet quavers instead of crotchets). The repeat in verse 2 is shortened by the omission of bb64–70, an omission which may not have been authorized by the composer, and which results in an unusually hasty leap to the next line of the cantus firmus.

It is not certain from P 802 that the three sections are to be understood as one continuous movement, since (*a*) there is a pause on the final beat of VI (b55, third beat – a *signum congruentiae* only, indicating the verse?), and (*b*) the pedal cantus firmus for v3 (= b97 in *NBA* edition) does not begin as the last note of v2 but is taken as a new up-beat to v3 on a new page (Zietz 1969 p145).

---

657   Nun danket alle Gott (formerly 'The Eighteen')

Autograph MS P 271; copies in P 1109 (improved ornaments), P 1160, Walther and Kirnberger sources. 'Weimar version' in P 802 (J. T. Krebs).

Headed in P 271 'à 2 Clav. et Ped. canto fermo in soprano'; two staves (P 271) or three (P 1109, P 1160).

The TEXT of M. Rinkart's hymn was published in 1648 and became associated with weddings, with the Sunday after Christmas or New Year's Day, and in Leipzig with Reformation Day, as the hymn after the sermon (Stiller 1970 pp82, 223, 232).

Nun danket alle Gott	Now let all thank God
mit Herzen, Mund und Händen,	with hearts, mouth and hands,
der grosse Dinge tut	who does great things
an uns und allen Enden,	for us and everyone,
der uns von Mutterleib	who from [the time of] our mother's womb
und Kindesbeinen an	and from our first faltering steps onwards
unzählig viel zugut	has done us immeasurable good
und noch jetzund getan.	and still does today.

Verse 2 refers to the peace and fortitude given by grace, and v3 returns to the praise.

The MELODY is attributed to J. Crüger (1647) and was published with the text. It is harmonized in BWV 386 and the 'wedding chorale' BWV 252, as well as in Cantatas 79 (Reformationsfest 1725 etc) and 192 (Reformationsfest? 1730): Ex. 149.

Ex. 149

BWV 252

Although 'strictly on the Pachelbel model', not graphic/expressive but 'pure to the last note' (Spitta I p602), and despite the opportunities given by the text, BWV 657 is no empty formal copy of the 'chorale-fugue'. While each line of the cantus firmus in the right hand is fugally anticipated in the lower parts in the familiar manner of Pachelbel (cf. BWV 723), the piece has many original elements:

> the imitations are worked out differently each time (stretto in b1, contraction and expansion in bb11–13, dominant quasi-reprise in b39, varied strettos in bb47–8, chromatic alteration in b55, no pedal entry in the final phrase)
> the pedal and inner parts are all more fully developed.

Both pedal and inner parts show a wealth of motifs, somewhat undisciplined. Some develop or suggest further development, others do not. The resulting harmony is usually very expert in a way not far removed from the *Orgelbüchlein* (e.g. bb58–60), but the varied motifs present a patchy appearance. It is easier to believe that 'the piece is probably very old, perhaps already re-worked in Weimar' (Klotz *NBA* IV/2 *KB* p73) than that it 'originated only at Leipzig' (Keller 1948 p186) despite its original, complex treatment of the old Pachelbel technique.

The 'Weimar version' of the work differs only in minor points of detail. It is possible to imagine the composer keeping such a chorale intact in his late collection, as an example of 'modified chorale-fugue'. A penultimate line cannot often have been chromatically altered as in Ex. 150.

Ex. 150

b57   b54

658

Von Gott will ich nicht lassen (formerly 'The Eighteen')

Autograph MS P 271; copies in P 1109, P 1160 and several sources in Kirnberger and Kittel circles.

Lowest of three staves in P 271 marked 'Ped'; in P 1160 (anon, eighteenth century) lowest stave marked 'Pedal 4 Fuss'.

The TEXT of L. Helmbold's hymn was published in 1563; it was sometimes associated later with the 3rd Sunday in Advent (perhaps because of the Christmas associations of the melody) and with the 3rd Sunday after Epiphany – though apparently it had neither link in Leipzig or Weimar (Gojowy 1972).

Von Gott will ich nicht lassen,	I will not abandon God,
denn er lässt nicht von mir,	for he does not abandon me,
führt mich durch alle Strassen,	leading me through all ways,
da ich sonst irrte sehr.	where otherwise I should go astray.
Er reicht mir seine Hand;	He reaches out his hand to me;
den Abend und den Morgen	evening and morning
tut er mich wohl versorgen,	he takes care of me,
wo ich auch sei im Land.	wherever I am.

The following eight verses return to the same ideas of support and faith, praise and trust.

The MELODY was probably adapted from the secular song *Ich ging einmal spazieren* (Terry 1921 p312), though which came first is not established; it resembles other melodies known both in Germany (*Helft mir Gottes Güte preisen*) and elsewhere (*Une vierge pucelle*).* The last two had Christmas associations from at least the early seventeenth century. The melody is harmonized in BWV 417–419, listed in the *Orgelbüchlein* and set in Cantatas 11 (Ascension 1735, different text), 73 (3rd Sunday after Epiphany 1724 etc), 107 and 186a (7th Sunday after Trinity 1724 and 1723): Ex. 151.

Ex. 151

BWV 73 (simplified)

Vigour and continuity are given BWV 658 not only by the figuration and its alternation of scale and broken-chord motifs but by the division

---

* Marpurg also noted the similarity in 1759 and compared Daquin's canonic variations on it with BWV 769, another Christmas chorale (see *Dok* III p127).

of the melody into only three cantus-firmus phrases (four with the repeat). The accompaniment is at times based upon the opening notes of the melody – Ex. 152(i) – but the most prominent feature of the

Ex. 152

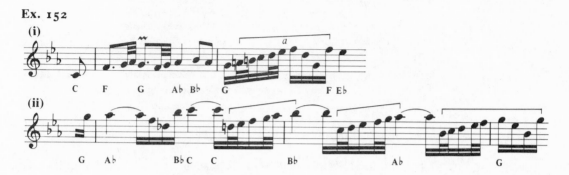

manual parts is the countersubject (motif *a*), which already permeates the texture in bb1–2. While the middle phrase of the cantus firmus may or may not be heard in the soprano in bb23–5, the clearer thematic reference in bb27–9 is coloured by the original countersubject motif *a* (Ex. 152(ii)). Thus the material of b1 is used and rewritten to serve as the 'colouring material' of a different chorale line (cf. BWV 662 and 663) – a paraphrase technique quite distinct from (e.g.) BWV 649, in which the new ritornello melody is much longer than the chorale line which it begins by paraphrasing.

It is noticeable that the bass line of the chorale (left hand) is fairly consistently made up of moving quavers (when it is not coloured by *a*), thus clarifying the crotchets of the cantus firmus (a precaution ignored by J. L. Krebs in his setting of the melody). The pedal line itself is marked '4 Fuss' in the Oley MS, presumably without the composer's authority; however, it is possible, since the scribe was not copying P 271 itself, that he took the direction from another authentic source now unknown. Nevertheless 8' pedal supplies the tenor part otherwise absent, and the other parts seem to make provision for the pedal at written pitch (e.g. bb5–8).

The figure ♪♪♪♪ has inspired much speculation or interpretation: as a 'Seligkeitsrhythmus' or 'beatitude rhythm' reminiscent (or anticipatory) of 'Mit Fried' und Freud'' in the *Orgelbüchlein* (Keller 1948 p187), a 'motif de la joie, un peu plus modéré' than its appearance in such Easter chorales as 'Erschienen ist der herrliche Tag' BWV 629 (Schweitzer 1905 p352), or the *figura corta* of baroque theorists (Schmitz 'Figuren' *MGG*) often used with texts expressing 'Aufwecken', 'wakening'. Similarly, the treatment of the final pedal point is very striking; its harmony is long-spaced, its rhythms new, its motifs more original than that at the end of BWV 656. From the point of view of the phrase structure, the two penultimate bars are not even necessary. The effect – while clearly not as explicitly bell- or clock-like as 'so schlage doch' in Cantata 161 – does accord with others known in Weimar cantatas and could well support Meyer's idea (1972) that the whole chorale is relevant to v6 of the text:

wir werden nach dem Tod　　　　after death we shall be
tief in die Erd begraben:　　　　buried deep in the earth:
wenn wir geschlafen haben,　　　when we have slept
will uns erwecken Gott.　　　　God will wake us.

However, many elements in the chorale take on a different significance if it is seen as an Advent or even a Christmas piece.

658a

Von Gott will ich nicht lassen

No Autograph MS; copy by J. T. Krebs (P 802), J. G. Walther (Kö 15839) and a source probably based on Walther (Lpz MB MS 7).

Headed in P 802 'Fantasia super . . .', 'à 2 Clav. et Ped.'; three staves.

The differences between BWV 658 and 658a are more than notational or simple variants but do not amount to total systematic revision. The opening right-hand paraphrase in BWV 658a is simpler, without ornament; and the bass line is often simpler and higher (no motif *a* in b7, no syncopation in b24; no low Cs in bb4, 7, 8, or low F in b32, etc). The changes of harmony in bb26 and 32 and of alto figuration in b35 suggest that the revisions may have been made at the keyboard. But the opportunity was not taken of amending the repetitive harmony of b8.

659

Nun komm, der Heiden Heiland (formerly 'The Eighteen')

Autograph MS P 271; copies in P 1109, P 1160 and several sources in Kirnberger and Kittel circle.

Headed in P 271 'a 2 Clav. et Ped.'; three staves.

For TEXT and MELODY see BWV 599.

As the cantata movements setting this melody show, the chorale and its associations admit of a very wide variety of treatment, both in technique of composition and in character or mood; BWV 659 is clearly of the meditative kind. The inner parts are derived from the melody,

Ex. 153

both at the beginning (Ex. 153) and throughout the chorale as a whole (Ex. 154). Using such material as accompaniment and introduction to

Ex. 154

b8 (cf. bb16–17)   b9   b24

D   C   F   Eb   D   C [B♮]   Eb   D C D

the ornamented cantus firmus is often described as 'the Buxtehude manner', but in no extant chorale of Buxtehude is the technique developed so fully. Equally original is the pedal, reminiscent more of a string basso continuo than of the moving basses of some *Orgelbüchlein* chorales, despite its quasi-ostinato element (bb1, 8, 9, 16–17, 24). A notable break in the flow of the bass occurs below the ornamented Neapolitan sixth in bb22–3 (cf. the C minor Prelude BWV 546 bb138–9).

The melody spins out of and around the notes of the cantus firmus more in the manner of Böhm (see BWV 682) than of Buxtehude, although the end of BWV 659 must surely refer to Buxtehude's setting of the same melody: Ex. 155. Florid treatments of a cantus firmus often

Ex. 155

Buxtehude, BUXWV 211

Ped.

took the form of a flight to the upper octave, but the expansion of line 1 into the wide, melismatic melody of bb5–8 follows no ready formula. The melismas themselves arise particularly at those points in the chorale melody that correspond to the second- or third-from-last syllables, which is by no means common in such cases. The biggest melismas (bb14ff, 22ff, 32ff) are independent of the cantus firmus and follow on from sequences decorating it, and it is to be expected that such bars as b23 not only resemble free organ pieces of the period (such as the G minor Fantasia BWV 542, bb45–6) but give birth to the most developed of the motifs in the inner parts (motif *a* in Ex. 154 above). That the melismas of BWV 659, despite their occasional similarity to those elsewhere (e.g. Partita BWV 768, Var. 1), require a slower tempo is due in part to the richness of the accompaniment, in part to a quality of beautiful, passionate melody springing from a succession of several conventional and unconventional figures.

While Terry sees the sharpened leading-note in the opening line of the melody as producing the 'diminished fourth...significant of suffering' (1921 pp18–19), it should be noted that the three main extant sources include the ♯ on f' only in b28 and not in b4. If the composer intended it, then the melody here uses the sharpened form of this phrase while the derived figure in the accompaniment uses the unsharpened form (b1); in Cantata 36, nos. 2 and 6, it is the other way round. Also, it is not clear from the notation if a distinction is intended between the ornamentation of b5 and that of b29, though a reason could be conjectured for any such difference.* Less certain still is Spitta's idea that the three settings of 'Nun komm' BWV 659–661 were 'obviously thought of as an interdependent whole' (I p607), since apart from there being no musical reason for this, the Walther sources to which he refers do not include BWV 659 and do include other composers' settings assembled for reasons of convenience not of sequence. The accompaniment itself is so carefully written with such great variety as to encourage notions of imagery. Thus, the 'dragging' motif of bb24–8 could be widely allusive (the 'Saviour bearing the sins of the world'); or the sheer perfection of the three-part writing in bb8–10 could, with more fancy, suggest a reference to the Virgin (Chailley 1974 p198).

659a

Nun komm, der Heiden Heiland

No Autograph MS; copy by J. T. Krebs (P 802) and in a source probably based on Walther (Lpz MB MS 7).

Headed 'Fantasia super...'; three staves.

The difference between BWV 659 and 659a lies chiefly in the ornamented cantus firmus; P 802, for example, gives few ornaments after the first line. The third line has more melismatic decoration in the later version, particularly around the Neapolitan sixth, but the inner parts are left intact. It is possible that when the piece was first written (i.e. as BWV 659a) organists might more readily have noticed how its lines depend on the set *figurae* described by J. G. Walther (*Praecepta* 1708) and others; by the time BWV 659 is supposed to have been composed, it may not have been so obvious that (e.g.) the opening pedal phrase of four bars contains a different four-quaver *figura* in each half-bar, strikingly like those of BWV 680. Such a run as Ex. 156 might also once have been seen as a standard *passaggio* or *tirata*.

Ex. 156

b15

---

* E.g. that b5 represents the composer's later thoughts – BWV 659a has a mordent.

660 Nun komm, der Heiden Heiland (formerly 'The Eighteen')

Autograph MS P 271; copies in P 1109 and sources in Kirnberger and Kittel circles.

Headed in P 271 'a due Bassi è canto fermo'; three staves.

For TEXT and MELODY see BWV 599.

The nature of the two-part 'invention' accompanying the ornamented cantus firmus produces a highly original setting and one open to much speculation. The imitation itself seems to be reminiscent of Pachelbel, the ostinato bass idea of Buxtehude, the coloured melody of Böhm; but the two bass lines and the ritornello plan distinguish the work clearly from any of the possible models. The systematic planning, though on a small scale, is highly unusual:

b1 canonic
b4 sequences
b7 cantus firmus
b11 sequences
b15 canonic
b17 cantus firmus
b20 canonic
b24 cantus firmus
b26 canonic
b30 sequences (to C minor, as in b27 of BWV 659)
b33 cantus firmus and canonic
b39 sequences (inversion of b4)

The canonic imitation contains dispersed within itself the whole first line of the melody (Ex. 157). The ornamented cantus firmus is closer

Ex. 157

to the melody than that of BWV 659; the main melody notes (especially in bb8–9) fall squarely on strong beats, and the basic line is easily picked out as in more naive music. The ritornello sections are also unusual in detail: the sequences are very simple (b4 etc); each section comes to a cadence, having modulated further than the cantus firmus itself demands; sections overlap with the cantus firmus (e.g. bb9ff) and combine.

Questions remain: how did such a movement originate, and what is the stylistic conception behind it? While the idea of a two-part invention accompanying a cantus firmus is found elsewhere (e.g. BWV 675, 688), as are even some of the details of form and figuration (see in particular BWV 646), the use of two bass parts is unique. In principle they suggest the obbligato lines of a cantata aria (voice, cello obbligato, basso continuo) or those of certain trio-sonata textures of the later seventeenth century, with obbligato gamba or cello (Buxtehude, Marais, Legrenzi). In practice, however, the lower bass parts of such works rarely 'compete' with the cello obbligato in the same way. In form, BWV 660 again suggests a cantata aria, particularly in having a closing ritornello – a feature characteristic of the *Schübler Chorales*. But while the concept and form of the piece may be owed to Italian string models, the two basses are certainly conceived in organ terms, suggesting even an ostinato. Their spacing and wide-leaping character may suggest that both be registered 8'; but this is not suggested by any evidence, and the registrations of Kauffmann (1733) make it seem more likely that the manual would have the addition of a 16' stop (Fagott, Quintadena) than that the pedal would be only at 8'. It is equally doubtful that a pictorial expression of v3 is intended (Keller 1948 p188) by the chorale as a whole:

Sein Lauf kam vom Vater her. . .	His course came from the father. . .
fuhr hinunter zu der Höll.	and led down to Hell.

since, as there are no cello arias comparable, it cannot be assumed that in performance the piece has a 'rough' effect as Keller suggests. Also fanciful is the interpretation of the final short chord – curious though that chord is – as 'showing God abandoning his son' (Chailley 1974 p200). In P 271, the last bar is so cramped that both the ♮ sign on B and the arpeggio symbol may have been accidentally omitted; but the fermata is certainly above the final double bar-line, not the final note.

660a

Nun komm, der Heiden Heiland

Autograph MS P 271 (three sides written between 1714 and 1716 and added to P 271 in the nineteenth century: see Dadelsen 1958 p79); copies by J. T. Krebs (P 802) and by Walther (BB 22541/1), and in sources of Walther (Lpz MB MS 7) and Kirnberger circles.

Headed in P 271 'á 2 Clav. & Pedal.'; three staves (as also in P 802).

As is the case with BWV 659 and 659a, BWV 660a has somewhat fewer ornaments (more cursorily written in P 802 than P 271) than BWV 660, and the extra semiquavers and demisemiquavers of the first cantus-firmus line in the 'later version' seem to increase the robustness of the piece. It is not clear either why the composer rewrote the left hand of b33 (did he miscopy the last two beats as if their source had a tenor clef?), or whether the final major chord of BWV 660a was really intended to be minor in BWV 660 (cf. the dominant major in b15 of both versions) and to be played *non arpeggio* (bb15, 42 arpeggiated in earlier version). For a note on the final chord of the 'later version', see BWV 660.

660b   Nun komm, der Heiden Heiland

No Autograph MS; copy by J. T. Krebs (P 802) and probably hence in Walther sources (BB 22541/1–2).

Headed in P 802 'a 2 Clav. e ped.'; three staves, no composer's name.

BWV 660b appears to be an arrangement by J. T. Krebs of BWV 660a already copied into P 802. The two bass parts are in the right hand (up an octave) and left hand respectively, the cantus firmus in long notes (without ornaments) in the pedal. Although this arrangement of the material accords with the style of authentic movements (e.g. BWV 694), the literal transcription, the unconvincing harmony over the new pedal point at the end, and the different form of line 3 of the cantus firmus all suggest that this version is inauthentic, something long agreed upon by the editors (Griepenkerl in Peters VII; Rust in *BG* 25.ii; Klotz in *NBA* IV/2).

---

661   Nun komm, der Heiden Heiland (formerly 'The Eighteen')

Autograph MS P 271; copies in P 1109 and several sources in Kirnberger and Kittel circles.

Headed in P 271 'in organo pleno. Canto fermo in Pedal.'; three staves.

For TEXT and MELODY see BWV 599.

The Full Organ character of the third of the chorales on 'Nun komm' is clear from the registration, the pedal cantus firmus and the nature of the fugal counterpoint. The theme itself is based on the melody (Ex. 158) and passes to sequences (e.g. in the codetta bb7–13) characteristic

Ex. 158

of the big free organ fugues such as the C minor BWV 537. The theme has something of the appearance of the countersubject in a free fugue (see BWV 538), and its motifs (angular four-note groups) are reminiscent of the *messanza*, one of the *musica ornata* figures listed by such theorists as Ahle and Printz (Schmitz 1952 p87): Ex. 159. As in BWV 546, fugal episodes give the movement its breadth; and the inversion

Ex. 159

in b45 is a device similar to one found in such fugues as BWV 547 which lack the second subject (introduced to increase thematic interest) of other long fugues (e.g. BWV 540). In short, several of the details of BWV 661 are those of free fugues – a less common circumstance than might be supposed.

The motifs making up the theme are elastic or variable enough to make it relatively straightforward to combine them with the phrases of the pedal cantus firmus when they enter (e.g. alto in bb24, 26; full soprano entry in b28), including the theme in its inverted form (e.g. tenor in b57; full entry in b60). At b81 is a grand combination: cantus firmus, fugue theme *inversus* (passing to the codetta motif from b8), and adapted fugue theme *rectus*: Ex. 160. Combining a cantus firmus

Ex. 160

with a fugue theme derived directly or indirectly from it occupied the composer in many ways (cf. BWV 670, 686, 695, 733); the intervals of the melody of *Nun komm* made simple combination less straightforward than it was to be in the *Art of Fugue* BWV 1080.ix. More generally, the movement can be seen as a ritornello organ chorale in which the (long) ritornello sections comprise a series of fugal expositions on a theme derived from a cantus firmus (itself used in the place of episodes and coda) and against which the fugue subject is constantly adapted *rectus* and *inversus*.

Naturally it is tempting to see three of the roles of the Saviour evoked in the three Advent chorales BWV 659–661. Quite apart from the chorale text itself, the Catechisms speak in various places of (*a*) 'the only beatifier and Saviour, Jesus' ('der einzige Seligmacher und Heiland Jesus'); (*b*) the Jesus who suffered crucifixion, 'the death on the cross accursed of God' ('der Tod des Kreuzes von Gott verflucht'); and (*c*) the Jesus who 'with his splendour and power' protects us 'against all enemies' ('mit seiner Gewalt wider alle Feinde'). Certainly the cantus firmus passing to the pedal in the last of three chorale settings is often to be found in Bach (BWV 656, 659–661, 662–664, 669–671); and evidence from Kauffmann (*Harmonische Seelenlust* 1733) and Mattheson (appendix to Niedt's *Handleitung* 1721) supports the drawing of reed stops in the pedal *pleno*. On the other hand, the relationship of an organ chorale to the text cannot be regarded as simple, nor the precise shade of eighteenth-century Lutheran interpretation as obvious. But the organist may well keep in mind for BWV 659 the

Saviour as beatifier, for BWV 660 the Saviour as harrower of Hell, and for BWV 661 the Saviour in glory.* Many details of contrapuntal idiom are common to BWV 661 and 733: and as the former is connected with Advent, so is the latter with the Annunciation.

661a   Nun komm der Heiden Heiland

No Autograph MS; copies by J. T. Krebs (P 802, 'improved' in the manner of BWV 661) and by Walther (BB 22541/1–2; Kö 15839) and a source probably based on Walther (Leipzig MB MS 7).

Two staves.

Two major differences between BWV 661 and 661a are (a) that the 'later version' (661) is notated ¢ ♩♩♩♩ instead of C ♩♩♩♩, possibly to confirm the association between *alla breve* signatures and *organo pleno*; (b) that the 'later version' consistently alters the final figure of the original countersubject: Ex. 161. The latter change

Ex. 161

BWV 661a   BWV 661

b3   b6

reduces the number of accented passing-notes, but its purpose is probably to reinforce the angularity of the subject itself or (as in the changes to bb18–19 of BWV 661a) to break the progression of simple spinning motifs. Again, the composer did not take the opportunity to alter what may be regarded as a weakness (soprano bb24–5, or bb48–9 of BWV 661).

---

662   Allein Gott in der Höh' sei Ehr' (formerly 'The Eighteen')

Autograph MS P 271; copies in P 1109 (improved ornaments) and several sources in Kirnberger and Kittel circles.

Headed in P 271 'a 2 Clav. et Ped. canto fermo in Sopr.' (added?); three staves ('adagio' between staves 2 and 3).

The TEXT is an adaptation by N. Decius of the *Gloria in excelsis Deo* (1522), associated in particular with Easter but sung in Leipzig on each Sunday (Stiller 1970 pp77–8, 103) and by tradition associated with the introduction of the Reformation into Leipzig (Leaver 1975). Except on feast-days, when it was replaced by ensemble performance, the

* But see a sceptical comment at the end of BWV 660 above.

hymn was sung in its four verses by choir and congregation after the priest's intonation from the altar (Stiller *op cit*). *Gloria in excelsis Deo* is also associated with Christmas in some Dresden and Leipzig hymnbooks (Gojowy 1972).

Allein Gott in der Höh' sei Ehr'	Alone to God on high be honour
und Dank für seine Gnade,	and thanks for his grace,
darum, dass nun und nimmermehr	since that now and for ever
uns rühren kann kein Schade.	no harm can touch us.
Ein Wohlgefall'n Gott an uns hat,	God is well pleased with us;
nun ist gross Fried ohn Unterlass,	now is great peace without intermission,
all Fehd hat nun ein Ende.	all strife is now at an end.

The following verses address each Person of the Trinity: v2 'Gott Vater, ewiglich', v3 'O Jesu Christ, Sohn eingeborn', and v4 'O Heiliger Geist, du höchstes Gut'.

The MELODY is adapted from the plainsong Gloria of Mass I, beginning after the intonation (*Liber usualis*, Mass I for Easter ('Lux et origo'), in particular the lines 'Et in terra pax hominibus', 'Benedicimus te', 'Adoramus te'). Unlike the plainsong, the chorale melody repeats the opening two lines: Ex. 162. Text and melody appeared

Ex. 162

Vopelius 1682

together in the Leipzig *Gesangbuch* of 1539. The melody is used in more extant Bach organ chorales than any other (BWV 662, 663, 664, 675, 676, 677, 711, 715, 716, 717, the doubtful 771); it is listed in the *Orgelbüchlein*, harmonized as BWV 260 and set to other texts in Cantatas 85, 104, 112, 128 (1725, 1724, 1731?, 1725).

The 'adagio' direction in P 271 already singles out the movement; its treatment of the Gloria or Trinity hymn is thus comparable to BWV

Ex. 163

659's treatment of the Advent hymn. The 'fugue' subject is based on the melody: Ex. 163. Both motifs *a* and *b* have thematic importance – e.g., *a* appears as a pedal motif in b2, and *b* as a tenor motif in b33.

Throughout the chorale, the inner parts show great skill aimed at melodic expression: unlike those in BWV 657, they are highly disciplined, but a listing of their contrapuntal attributes does not of itself suggest their natural beauty, which is curiously enhanced by the many trills.

b1	the overlapping countersubject supplies a motif *a* used elsewhere in the chorale (in the pedal part, or diminished in manual parts), as that of BWV 658 does: the motif itself may spring from the first few notes of the chorale melody
bb6–7	countersubject and subject can appear (alto+tenor) in reversed order
bb8–9	parts 'wait' for the ornamented melody to begin
bb10ff	much motivic imitation between the parts (Pachelbel)
bb33–4	decorative line of alto hides the reference to line 3(5) of the melody (also present, augmented and simplified, in pedal) – i.e., the main theme is altered in outline to serve as a fore-imitation of the third (or fifth) line of the chorale melody (cf. BWV 663, 717)
bb35–7	derived from bb5–7
bb41–2	entries of theme
bb44–5	combination of previous material with a derivation of the last line

The pedal too shows much use of derived material:

bb2ff	throughout the work, much use of motif *a* with its continuation (bb45–6) or without it; motif *a* often inverted
bb6ff	throughout the work, much use of motif *b*, seven times with its continuation*

The melody is decorated to an unusual degree yet remains more recognizable than that of (e.g.) BWV 659. Although its kinds of flourish occasionally look like the obbligato violin or oboe lines of contemporary Weimar cantatas, the resemblance is less than might be expected; essentially the decorative style is a developed form of the coloratura known to other organ composers. Even the unique cadenza (bb51–2) is more an extension of the cantus-firmus coda found in Buxtehude and Böhm (but in BWV 662 on a diminished seventh, not a tonic or dominant pedal point) than a cadenza in any later sense. This is not to deny the aria-like style of the movement, however; as a whole, it can be seen to combine the decorative aria with ritornello form, which is in this case also fugal.

The extent to which motifs are developed in the work may imply a new stage in the composer's development, particularly in incorporating some of the melody's potential motifs into the web of its accompaniment. Such a melody will suggest several very different motifs, and the lines of BWV 663 could hardly be more different from

---

* It could be that the unusual ornament of motif *b* (the *accent*) is given in this form (and not written out) because it is unsuitable for pedal: if it is notated thus, its omission leaves the outline of the theme still visible.

BWV 662. On the other hand, the thematic similarities between BWV 662 and 656 (opening counterpoint) and between BWV 663 and 656 (final cadence) arise from the similar beginnings of the two chorale melodies concerned.

The ornaments of BWV 662, unusual in themselves and in their frequency, seem to suggest a languid mood, particularly in the 'Lombardic rhythm' of motif *b*. Yet whether that same phrase, in its falling shape, expresses either the 'bringing of Heaven down to earth' (Keller 1948 p189) or the 'condescension' of the Trinity (Meyer 1972) is even more conjectural.

662a

Allein Gott in der Höh' sei Ehr'

No Autograph MS; copy by J. T. Krebs (P 802), Walther (Kö 15839), H. N. Gerber (see *NBA* IV/2 *KB* p51) and a source probably based on Walther (Leipzig MB MS 7).

Headed in P 802 'a 2 Clav. e ped.'; three staves; in Gerber MS 'forte' (rh) and 'piano' (lh).

The chief difference between BWV 662 and 662a is that the latter has fewer ornaments. It is not known whether or not the 'later version' (662) clarifies what was earlier taken for granted – that such motifs as the end of b4 would have ornaments, and that the trills would vary with the context. However, the first two of the three characteristic *accents* of motif *b* (see Ex. 163) are already there, sometimes written out in Gerber's copy.

663

Allein Gott in der Höh' sei Ehr' (formerly 'The Eighteen')

Autograph MS P 271; copies in P 1109 and several sources in Kirnberger and Kittel circles.

Headed in P 271 'a 2 Clav. et Ped. canto fermo in Tenore'; three staves ('cantabile' below rh stave).

For TEXT and MELODY see BWV 662.

The fugal theme and pedal part are again both derived from the melody – Ex. 164 – as is the harmony they produce. Again the derived motif *a* is elastic and adaptable (cf. BWV 661); but the conception of the

Ex. 164

movement is original in that the ornamented melody is in the tenor.*
Tenor melodies, whether manual (BWV 653) or pedal (BWV 658), are
not usually ornamented; BWV 663 has further unusual features, prin-
cipally the fluid $^3/_2$ time, the inclusion in the bass part both of derived
motifs (e.g. b1, answered in b4) and of cantus-firmus anticipation (e.g.
bb9, 69), the similar trills at the end of phrase of the cantus firmus,
the sparse accompaniment throughout, the little cadenza before the
'adagio' (cf. BWV 662), and the dividing of the cantus-firmus voice in
b110 (holding up the flow of the melody for this effect). The intention
seems to be to present the much-used theme in a new contrapuntal
setting – cast in ritornello form, but fantasia-like in its constant allusion
to the motifs and even the harmony of the melody. The very rests
in each part are contrapuntal; and the cantus-firmus decorations, built
on scale and *suspirans* figures, are richly melodious and inventive.

While details of the ornamental melody are reminiscent of contemporary or earlier north German chorale fantasias (e.g. in b28/61 the

Böhmian rhythmic phrase ♪ ♫♫♫♫ | 𝅝 | – cf. BWV
662 b9), the whole accords much more closely with the fugal-
paraphrase technique of 'The Eighteen' as a whole. The spacious length
of the treatment is part of this 'technique'. Also, while the canonic
phrase at bb69–79 suggests comparison with J. G. Walther (Var. 5 of
his 'Allein Gott' (1738) contains the same canon, similar to those of
his early Weimar chorales), the pedal motif *b* is used throughout in
a way characteristic of 'The Eighteen' and even of *Clavierübung III*.
Moreover, the final pedal point invites the organist to hear through
it a reference to the last word of stanza 1 ('Ende'), while the 'adagio'
at b97 (approached over the previous two bars?) also draws attention
to the phrase 'ohn Unterlass' ('without intermission').† The part-
writing, with its frequent breaking-off of the tenor on one manual to
take the melody on the other (bb15–16, 77–8, 105–6), may suggest that
the work is earlier in date than (e.g.) BWV 664, as might the divided
tenor line at bb110–13 and the nature of the material itself. But it should
not be missed that some apparently simple material – such as the
detached chords in bb103 and 105 – is derived from motif *b*.

663a   Allein Gott in der Höh' sei Ehr'

No Autograph MS; copy by J. T. Krebs (P 802, P 803).

Headed 'à 2 Clav. è ped.'; three staves.

Apart from a few notational changes (e.g. the filling-out of the
penultimate chord), the 'later version' BWV 663 differs from 663a in

---

* The scribe of BWV 663a in P 802 drew attention to the ornamented melody in the tenor,
  labelling it 'Choral' at b27 and b78.
† 'Adagio' (P 271) can hardly mean more than a temporary slowing – see also BWV 663a.
  On certain similarities between BWV 663 and 656, see BWV 662.

the cadenza and *adagio* passages, regularized in ³/₂. The 'earlier version' treats the passage (bb96–7 of BWV 663) as one loose bar, with the second half marked 'adagio' and the second beat of the next bar marked 'andante'. The last suggests that the overall tempo was understood by Krebs to be not fast, and that the 'adagio' is a temporary effect for three beats or so. 'Cantabile', 'adagio' and 'andante' are directions found in P 802, which appears to be a fairer copy based on that in P 803 (Zietz 1969 p152).

664

Allein Gott in der Höh' sei Ehr' (formerly 'The Eighteen')

Autograph MS P 271; copies in a few sources of Kirnberger and Kittel circles.

Headed in P 271 'Trio sup. . . .', 'a 2 Clav et Ped'; at end 'SDG' ('Soli Deo gloria').

For TEXT and MELODY see BWV 662.

For trio settings of chorales, see under BWV 655. Spitta saw the trio form as an inventive way of using Pachelbel-style fore-imitation in the upper manuals with pedal cantus firmus entering later (Spitta I p604); but apart from the complete shape of BWV 664 as a trio movement, its motifs are both derived and developed in a manner characteristic only of J. S. Bach (Ex. 165). Again a derivative is used as counter-subject

Ex. 165

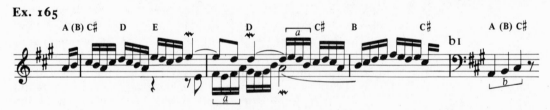

(i.e. delayed double subject – cf. BWV 662), this time with a pedal continuo bass from b1, as in the Sonatas and a later 'Allein Gott' (BWV 676). The paraphrased theme itself is obviously related through its parentage to the chorales BWV 663 and 676, although the different metres (³/₂, ⁴/₄, ⁶/₈) affect the character from the first main beat onwards.

The ritornello demands of a trio-sonata form bring the subject entries at regular moments, but the detail is not conventional:

b1   subject with double subject, over continuo bass; all three derived from cantus firmus. Modified melody for pedal from end of b9 (double subject in right hand at end of b10)

b12 episode, using second half of subject (double subject); pedal motifs as before, including modified theme (end of b16)

b25 entry (including modified pedal answer at end of b28), subdominant b31 episode; motif *a inversus* and *rectus*; b35ff broken-chord play, as in BWV 530.i (said to be 'in the Venetian manner' of violin concertos: Kloppers 1966 p202)

b43 short entry, submediant minor

b46 episode; *a* further expanded, pedal independent of previous motifs

b64 short entry, supertonic minor

b67 episode; *a* further expanded (b68 motif – see C minor Violin Sonata BWV 1017.ii)

b79 tonic entry with answer

b85 first two lines of cantus firmus in pedal; final development of motif above pedal point (cf. BWV 661), including final bar

In the process, an unusual repetition occurs:

bb56–72 = bb35–51 inverted and up a fifth (down a fourth), the two sections ending identically (bb50–2 = bb70–2)

The episodes themselves account for more than half the fugue (over fifty bars); they incorporate sections returning in a different key (cf. BWV 655) and introduce passages with a marked resemblance to the Sonatas (e.g. b35ff).

The shortened cantus firmus in b85 leaves the balance of the movement unimpaired and achieves finality by the fact that the chorale's first and last two lines are similar (cf. BWV 716). It also conforms with other groups of three chorale settings (BWV 669–671, 659–661) in which the pedal takes the final cantus firmus; but this resemblance should not be pressed, since the trio is brighter and gayer than BWV 671 or 661.

664a

Allein Gott in der Höh' sei Ehr'

No Autograph MS; 'second (?) Weimar version' in copy by J. T. Krebs (P 801), other copies in Leipzig MB MS 7 (based on Walther source?) and minor sources (incl. Lpz MB III.8.8, 1740/50).

Headed in P 801 'Trio super . . .', 'à 2 Clav. è Pedale'; three staves (bass and two treble clefs); at end 'SDG'.

While the differences between BWV 664 and 664a do not amount to a systematic revision, the earlier version shows (*a*) fewer ornaments throughout (originally left to the player? – e.g. bb39ff), (*b*) a simpler rhythm in bb1–2 etc (Ex. 166), and (*c*) occasional minor difference in a line (alto continues b79) or motif (b49).

Ex. 166

664b

Allein Gott in der Höh' sei Ehr'

No Autograph MS; 'first (?) Weimar version' in several later copies (Lpz Go.S. 311/1, c1740/50; P 1160; Kirnberger circle and other sources).

This, the 'original version' of BWV 664a (*NBA* IV/2 *KB* p82), differs from it mostly in a few minor details. Two of the more important differences are: (*a*) the pedal is occasionally an octave lower (most of bb40–3) and less smooth (bb31, 41, 42, 60, 61), and (*b*) the theme at first is as Ex. 167. On its subsequent entries, however, the theme

Ex. 167

is as in BWV 664a and 664; it is not known whether the copyists made a mistake or the composer changed it to the other, vastly superior phrase. Together, Exx. 166–7 show a simpler paraphrase of the melody than in BWV 664.

665

Jesus Christus, unser Heiland (formerly 'The Eighteen')

Autograph MS P 271; other copies in Kittel circle.

Headed in P 271 'sub communione. pedaliter' (added?); two staves.

The TEXT is Luther's free translation of the fourteenth-century hymn *Jesus Christus nostra salus*, said to have been written by John Hus; published Erfurt 1524, it served as a doctrinal hymn before the Communion, during which it was sung and played *alternatim* (Luedtke 1918 p87). Schein (1645) and Vopelius (1682) give it as a hymn for Maundy Thursday.

Jesus Christus, unser Heiland,	Jesus Christ, our Saviour,
der von uns den Gottes Zorn wandt,	who turned God's anger away from us,
durch das bitter Leiden sein	through his bitter suffering
half er uns aus der Höllen Pein.	helped us out of the torment of Hell.

Of the following nine verses concerned with the Sacrament and its purpose, v5 concerns resolute faith ('Du sollst glauben und nicht wanken'), v6 grace and mercy ('Solch gross Gnad und Barmherzigkeit'), v9 brotherly love ('deinen Nächsten sollst du lieben').

The MELODY, perhaps of late Gregorian origin, was published with the text in 1524 (Ex. 168); the opening bears a resemblance to the melody *Wir glauben* (see BWV 680, Ex. 198). The melody is used in BWV 665, 666, 688 and 689, is listed in the *Orgelbüchlein*, and is harmonized in BWV 363.

Ex. 168

The form of BWV 665 is regular and in that sense old-fashioned:

> line 1   derived theme in tenor, accompanied by countersubject in manual
>   bass, answered by alto, then pedal (plain notes; manual bass drops
>   out), then soprano (each with countersubject); then freely derived
>   four-part coda
> line 2   as line 1, countersubject begun in upper part
> line 3   as line 2
> line 4   as line 2

Giving each part the melody in the same note-lengths is characteristic
of (e.g.) Böhm, while the bass part moving from manual to pedal (made
clear also in BWV 665a) is known in early Bach (e.g. BWV 549.ii). The
breaks between the lines or sections are clearer than in most sectional
organ chorales; in BWV 666 the breaks between lines are occasioned
by 'interludes' before the following line, rather than by climaxes to
the previous one as in BWV 665. The handling of the harmony is often
masterful (e.g. bb5–6) despite the conventional nature of some of the
figuration. The freely derived coda to each line brings out the allemande-
like character of the texture particularly clearly, e.g. bb11–13.

    The countersubjects have long been seen as giving the chief interest
to the movement, not because they can be traced to the chorale melody
– they cannot – but because they impart different colours to the lines
of the melody. Spitta, who admired the piece greatly (1 pp602–4), saw
it as particularly relevant to the Communion, and Schweitzer found
it easy to see in the countersubjects a representation of key words
from VI of the text:

> God's anger (line 2): Ex. 169(i) (see next page)
> bitter suffering (line 3): Ex. 169(ii)
> resurrection from 'the pain of Hell' (line 4): Ex. 169(iii)

The first line and its countersubject (Ex. 169(iv)) find less agreement
amongst the commentators, and Harvey Grace's idea of it as 'representing the carrying of the Cross' (c1922 p279) is obviously only one
of several possible readings.

    The musical figures which are thought somehow to express these
verbal ideas all gradually work towards the final pedal point – the
biggest close so far in the whole collection. To J. G. Walther, a pedal
point brought 'high pathos' to vocal music (Schmitz 1950 p82). It is

Ex. 169

(i) b14   **(ii) b27**

(iii) b39   **(iv) b1**

possible that the coda is an 'expression' of escape from the 'torment of Hell', though it is in that case rather more rhetorical than the comparable endings of such Weimar cantatas as BWV 161. Similarly, although the chromatic line (b37 etc) is suggestive, it should not be overlooked that the harmony produced is unusually simple, with repeated Gs on the main beats (bb27, 28, 33–7) and repeated Ds in the bars between (bb30–2). There is no good pictorial reason for the line to fall in the particular way it does.

665a   Jesus Christus, unser Heiland

No Autograph MS; copy by J. G. Walther (P 802), also in Lpz MB III.8.11 (1740/50?) and later sources (e.g. J. F. Agricola, Lpz MB MS R 16,4).

Headed in P 802 'in pleno Organo'; two staves.

While the differences between BWV 665 and the 'earlier' 665a do not amount to a radical revision, the sources imply that the composer made two motivic alterations in the 'later version': in bb28, 31, 34 and 36 the demisemiquaver dactyl was added, and in bb49–50 the plain figure became chromatic (Ex. 170). The authority for 'pleno organo' is

Ex. 170   BWV 665a   BWV 665

questionable, since this registration is usually given for continuous, non-sectional movements; perhaps Walther (?) added it in view of the pedal cantus firmus.

666 Jesus Christus, unser Heiland (formerly 'The Eighteen')

No Autograph MS; P 271 (Altnikol); Lpz MB III.8.11 (1740/50?) and later sources including those of Kittel circle and J. F. Agricola (Lpz MB MS R 16,4).

In P 271 cantus firmus labelled 'Choral'; two staves.

For TEXT and MELODY see BWV 665.

The source used by Altnikol seems to have been already revised in Weimar, since some of the later copies also include BWV 665a rather than BWV 665 (*NBA* IV/2 *KB* p84). The chorale melody produces the thematic cell (Ex. 171), but to a lesser extent than usual in 'The

Ex. 171

E B A B

Eighteen'. Also, the technique is motif-imitation rather than fugal. Apart from key, BWV 666 resembles 665 in the manner of the cantus-firmus treatment by anticipation: the tenor entries on lines 2, 3 and 4 anticipate the so-called 'Choral' in the soprano. Altnikol might also have seen resemblances between the semiquaver figurations of BWV 666 and 667, and thus included them.* As in BWV 665, each line has a different countersubject, well developed, and leading to a fuller exposition of the last line followed by a pedal point (cf. BWV 561 Fugue, BWV 718) above which a manual cadenza is built upon the countersubject to the last line. As Spitta pointed out (I p602), the first semiquaver phrase in b10 resembles the organist's interlude-flourish between the lines of congregational hymns, and its development later in the movement is well managed. The impression is of a series of countersubject motifs, quavers and semiquavers in different forms – as if the material that usually emerges over four variations in a chorale partita were now put into one chorale. The second countersubject – Ex. 172 – resembles many by Böhm or Walther and thus suggests a

Ex. 172 b11

more 'objective' treatment of the chorale melody than BWV 665; as in partita movements, it is open to such development as the *inversus* in b12 (bass) but less open to pictorial interpretation than the counter-subjects of BWV 665.

---

* The semiquavers of BWV 666 (e.g. end of b18) also anticipate 'Von Himmel hoch' BWV 769.i, which is in some ways a retrospective movement.

666a   Jesus Christus, unser Heiland

No Autograph MS; copy by J. G. Walther (P 802).

Headed 'alio modo'; two staves.

Walther's version of BWV 666 includes two extra directions to the player: to phrase the opening figure as ⌐ ⌐ ⌐, and to alternate hands in the cadenza figure of b35. It also gives a different form of the motif Ex. 173 in bb26, 28, 31 and 33, suggesting that it may have been altered

Ex. 173   b26

with hindsight after the cadenza was written. These bars were later altered 'according to the newer version' BWV 666 (Zietz 1969 p156).

---

667   Komm, Gott Schöpfer, heiliger Geist (formerly 'The Eighteen')

No Autograph MS; P 271 (Altnikol); copies in sources of Kirnberger circle.

Headed in P 271 'in Organo pleno con Pedale obligato' (added?); two staves.

For TEXT and MELODY see BWV 631.

The two distinct parts of BWV 667 do not amount to independent variations in the sense of Scheidt's and Walther's three-verse partitas; nor do they correspond to the verses of the text, as Spitta already saw (I p601). However, it is not difficult to interpret the second part, at least, as suggesting the same verses in Acts as BWV 651 (Terry 1921 p242). The form is

bb1–8   identical with *Orgelbüchlein* BWV 631: a continuous melody with accompaniment incorporating the *figura corta* and the *syncope consonans desolata* – ¹²/₈ ⌐ ⌐ and ⌐ ⌐ – together symbolizing the *spiritus vivificans* (Meyer 1972)

bb8–12   interlude

bb13–end   cantus firmus in four phrases on the pedal, below loosely imitative accompaniment

The chorale is modal (G-mixolydian) as the term was understood in the eighteenth century by such writers as Kirnberger (*Dok* III pp301–3), but the cadences at the ends of most phrases are diatonic.

Whether or not 'tongues of fire' are painted in the second half (particularly at bb10 and 26), several elements should be noted: (*a*) despite a natural similarity, the second section does not develop the semiquaver figures of the first, but the new figures are associated with compound time as is suggested by the C major Prelude BWV 547; (*b*) the figuration begins at b9 in a quasi-improvised manner not unlike certain simpler (and lower-placed) Pachelbel textures; (*c*) the broken figure in b10 recurs only once (b13) and otherwise gives way to scale-like figures; (*d*) the scale figure when imitated (e.g. bb20–1) resembles in theory that of 'Vater unser' BWV 683, but when placed over a pedal cantus firmus *in organo pleno* it achieves a quite different effect. The pedal itself is specified in Altnikol's copy only when its cantus firmus begins (b13); since the first section also requires it, the intention must have been to put new emphasis on the melody, very likely to be played with added reeds. The theme being in the bass, its harmony naturally differs from BWV 631 and 370, with a characteristic tendency towards diminished sevenths at the cadences (bb18, 21, 26). The cadences themselves are less marked. Whilst the hemiola in the final bar is unexpected (especially at the first tenor f♯'), the overall cadential harmony of the last two bars anticipates a (presumably later) chorale in the same G-mixolydian, BWV 678. However, the close of the G major Fugue BWV 541 suggests that the composer associated such cadences with this key, rather than with any modal or textual quality. Whether the alto in the final bar enunciates a deliberate B–A–C–H line is uncertain, but it does seem that the second half of the movement is a 'response' to the first: the Holy Ghost answers the invitation. Walther's copy of this chorale in P 802 (i.e. BWV 667b) has a clear change of handwriting for the second section (Daw 1975): this may be because Walther wished to reflect the change in musical style and form, because he was aware that the two sections originated at different times, or because he (consciously or not) reflected the style of handwriting in his source, whatever it was.

667a   Komm, Gott Schöpfer, heiliger Geist

No Autograph MS; copy by J. G. Walther (BB 22541/3).

No heading, two staves.

Walther, who included BWV 667a as the first of six settings of the melody by Bach, Pachelbel, Zachow and himself (*NBA* IV/2 *KB* pp34, 85), already incorporated the improvements to BWV 667b made in the 'Leipzig version' BWV 667.

667b Komm, Gott Schöpfer, heiliger Geist

No Autograph MS; copy by J. G. Walther with improvements by J. L. Krebs after 1731 (P 802); fragment in P 801 (probably J. T. Krebs) formerly thought to be autograph (Zeitz 1969 pp103–4).*

No heading, two staves.

P 801, written in haste (Daw 1975), includes bb11–24 only, and its watermark is found in paper of Weimar cantatas of 1714–16 (Dürr 1951 p217), which may or may not suggest a date for it. In its first part BWV 667b differs from both BWV 631 and 667 in having a few evident crudities in the figuration (semitone clashes in bb12, 18), a falling figure at the end of b21, and parallel octaves in b13 (with the tenor in P 802, with the bass in P 801). The parallel octaves are so clear in P 801 (for facsimile, see *NBA* IV/2 p.vi) as almost to suggest that the composer first intended the cantus firmus to be in the alto; at this point in BWV 667, P 271 gives the alto a crotchet rest. See also BWV 667 for a note on Walther's P 802.

---

668 Vor deinen Thron tret' ich (formerly 'The Eighteen')

No Autograph MS; copy by 'Anon II' (Anon 12) in P 271: 25½ bars only, on the lower part of the last page of BWV 769.

Heading 'Vor deinen Thron tret ich pp'; two staves.

The TEXT was published by J. Gesenius and D. Denicke (1646) as a hymn for 'Morning, Midday and Evening'; to Freylinghausen (1741 etc) it was a morning hymn.

Für deinen Thron tret ich hiermit　　Before your throne I now appear,
o Gott, und dich demütig bitt　　O God, and beg you humbly
wend dein genädig Angesicht　　turn not your gracious face
von mir, dem armen Sünder nicht.　　from me, a poor sinner.

v15

Ein selig End mir bescher　　Confer on me a blessed end,
am jüngsten Tag erwecke mich　　on the last day waken me
Herr, dass ich dich schau ewiglich:　　Lord, that I may see you eternally:
Amen, amen, erhöre mich.　　Amen, amen, hear me.

Intervening verses contain prayers suitable for the dying.

* Since this copy is not autograph, it is no longer evidence that the composer ever made a 'Second Weimar Autograph of the Seventeen' in addition to the one which he took to Leipzig and on which he is assumed to have based the revisions found in P 271 (May 1974 p277).

The MELODY is that usually associated with *Wenn wir in höchsten Nöthen sein*: Ex. 174 (cf. Ex. 105, BWV 641). Only BWV 668 gives the

Ex. 174

BWV 431

melody the text *Vor deinen Thron*, which in Freylinghausen's hymn-book is associated with the melodies of *Herr Gott, dich loben alle* and *Herr Jesu Christ, meins Lebens Licht*.

The history of the three-part complex BWV 641/668a/668 has been conjectured to be as follows (*NBA* IV/2 pp102ff and Wolff 1974). 'Wenn wir in höchsten Nöthen sein' BWV 641 was included in the *Orgelbüchlein* and shows characteristic elements: coloratura variation of the chorale melody, three-part accompaniment (developing a motif derived from the melody), but without interludes (the whole only 9 bars long). In *c*1751 the chorale BWV 668a was published at the end of the *Art of Fugue* as a compensation to the buyer for the incomplete fugue closing the collection. This piece, said to have been 'dictated extempore by the deceased man in his blindness to his friend' (*Art of Fugue* preface, *Dok* III p13), contains BWV 641 within itself, enlarging it to 45 bars by means of fore-imitations and interludes, but stripping the melody of its coloratura. In the MS P 271, following the last brace of staves completing BWV 769a and written on the next blank staves (only six of which were drawn by J. S. Bach, presumably for BWV 769a), a somewhat different ('last') version – BWV 668 – was copied by an anonymous scribe;* the manuscript (or the scribe) broke off at the bottom of the page concerned, after only the first 25½ bars of the piece. Since there are in P 271 directs or indications of the next chord, and since the MS has 106 not 108 (27×4) pages, the piece may have been completed on a page now missing.

Between *c*1715 and *c*1750 the steps are conjectural, and questions still unanswered are:

(i) Did the composer work on the piece at all after *c*1715?

(ii) Did he dictate the whole or details of a final chorale? If so, was it BWV 668? or BWV 668a? The copy which was 'dictated a few days before his death to ... Altnikol' (Forkel 1802 ch.IX) has not been identified. But either way, the existence of BWV 641 makes it unlikely that the

---

* Not Altnikol but the copyist of (e.g.) BWV 232, 'Sanctus' continuo part (Dadelsen 1957 p16).

composer did dictate BWV 668 extempore or 'on the spur of the moment' ('aus dem Stegreif') as claimed in the *Art of Fugue* preface.

(^{1} = 1st beat, ^{2} = 2nd beat etc)

BWV 641:		BWV 668/668a:
		bb1–7
bb1–3^1	=	bb8–10^1
		bb10^2–19^1
bb3^2–5^1	=	bb19^2–21^3
		bb21^4–29^1
bb5^2–7^1	=	bb29^2–31^1
		bb31^2–40^1
bb7^2–9	=	bb40^2–42^1
		bb42^2–45

(iii) Why was BWV 668 copied into P 271? When? Why was it given this title?

(iv) Do the differences between BWV 668 and 668a suggest a 'final version' and a 'previous version' respectively, or vice versa, or (since there is no autograph of either) merely variants? Either way, no other copy of BWV 668 is known.

(v) Is BWV 668/668a, like BWV 641, *con pedale*? The layout – especially in view of the de-embellished cantus firmus – allows pedal-less performance with no greater difficulty than (e.g.) BWV 687.

(vi) Who expanded and simplified BWV 641 into BWV 668/668a? When?

The last question is the most difficult and far-reaching, not least because the deathbed associations of the movement have coloured its interpretation ever since it was first offered in the *Art of Fugue*.[*] Already in 1754 the work, as something 'dictated in his blindness', was invoked to do battle with the 'champions of materialism' as an instance of the wonder of human endeavour (*Dok* III p73). Later on Forkel heard it as 'the expression of pious resignation and devotion' (*op cit*), and a more modern mysticism has taken the form of finding in it wonderful numerological reference.[†] However, in relation to the *Orgelbüchlein* chorale, BWV 668/668a shows several curious features.

First, while its form –

> cantus firmus in soprano; fore-imitation and interludes in lower parts based on motifs (*rectus* and *inversus*) derived from each phrase of the melody in turn

[*] The building up of a 'myth' around the chorale has been ably traced by C. Wolff (1974).

[†] For example, line 1 of the melody contains 14 notes (B–A–C–H if A = 1, B = 2, C = 3, H = 8); lines 2–4 contain 27 notes ($3 \times 3 \times 3$ = Trinity); together they make 41 (= J. S. B–A–C–H): see Smend 1969 p173. Or the whole piece can be made to amount to 833 notes (= $7 \times 7 \times (10+7)$), and for the sake of this argument the number 7 can be made to bear several interpretations. See references in *NBA* IV/2 *KB* p105.

– can certainly be seen as a kind of reference to much older organ music, here once and for all immortalized by the master,* the language of the counterpoint itself is much more difficult to ascribe to late Bach. Doubts about its maturity have sometimes been expressed before (Frotscher 1935 p948). Subjectively speaking, it is weaker than that of the smaller 'Aus tiefer Noth' of *Clavierübung III* (BWV 687) in the rhythmic, harmonic and imitative interest of its fore-imitative lines; the resemblance of the cadential bars in BWV 687 to those of BWV 668/668a only underlines this 'inferiority'. Secondly, it is possible to see the harmonic style of the interludes as less original than the 'older' cantus-firmus sections (those already composed by 1715) – for example, compare bb21–7 of BWV 668a with b5 of the *Orgelbüchlein* version. The ends of the cantus-firmus phrases, particularly bb22 and 31–2, do not seem to me worthy of the preceding two or three bars, even when they have been denuded of the *Orgelbüchlein* coloraturas. Thirdly, there appear inconsistencies in the course of the 'new' sections; the suspensions and accented passing-notes of b17, for example, suggest a maturer harmonic style than the following bar, with its simplistic perfect cadence.

That the 'last chorale' is a last salute to an old style is possible, and the final plagal cadence certainly leaves behind a good impression. But its very similarity to BWV 687 – the inverted fugal answers, the plain cantus firmus in the top, the long-held final note, the clearcut openings of sections – leads to doubts as to which was composed first. It is difficult to believe that b14 or b37 of the 'last chorale' was written by Bach nearly half a century after Pachelbel's death, even as a farewell salute.

668a

Wenn wir in höchsten Nöthen (*Die Kunst der Fuge*)

Published *c*1751, no Autograph MS; later copies indirectly as well as directly from printed source.

Headed in the *Art of Fugue* 'canto fermo in canto'; four staves (open score, four different clefs, fifth part at end on lowest stave); described in the preface as 'vierstimmig ausgearbeiteten Kirchenchorals' ('worked-out church chorale in four parts': *Dok* III p13).

For TEXT and MELODY see BWV 641.

BWV 668a differs from 668 in its title, its notation in open score, its complete length of 45 bars (was BWV 668 to have had 45?), and certain details in the musical text. These details are:

---

* It should not be forgotten that BWV 667 is also an enlarged version of an *Orgelbüchlein* chorale, made longer by adding a pedal cantus-firmus verse, i.e. a device as traditional and even old-fashioned as that of adding fugal interludes to BWV 641 to produce BWV 668 (if that is what happened).

b9   tenor a written as two tied quavers in BWV 668a, crotchet in 668; though apparently insignificant, this implies that the original untied quavers of the *Orgelbüchlein* version (BWV 641 b2) were not seen later as being derived from the thematic motif. In b41 the comparable tenor motif has two quavers.*

b26 rh quavers dotted in BWV 668 (like first beat in bass in b9)

b7   imitative semiquavers in tenor added in BWV 668

b10 interrupted cadence in BWV 668

Klotz (*NBA* IV/2 *KB* pp102–3) understands these as the composer's own improvements, from a copy of which the *Art of Fugue* chorale was printed. In view of the questions asked under BWV 668 above, however, other conjectures can be made as to the order and origin of events. Perhaps BWV 668a originated when somebody played BWV 668 over to the composer in his blindness and noted down, from dictation, minor improvements (Wolff 1974 pp293–4).

* Klotz (*NBA* IV/2 *KB* p105) argues that these quavers should be tied since the first note of b42 rises: i.e., bb41–2 (unlike b9) is not a full reference to the original thematic motif of b2 (alto) etc.

669–689   Organ Chorales from *Clavierübung III*

See also BWV 552, 802–805.

Published 1739. Title-page:

Dritter Theil der Clavier Übung bestehend in verschiedenen Vorspielen über die Catechismus- und andere Gesaenge, vor die Orgel: Denen Liebhabern, und besonders denen Kennern von dergleichen Arbeit, zur Gemüths Ergezung verfertiget von Johan Sebastian Bach, Koenigl. Pohlnischen, und Churfürstl. Saechss. Hoff-Compositeur, Capell-meister, und Directore Chori Musici in Leipzig. In Verlegung des Authoris.

Third Part of the Keyboard Practice, consisting of various preludes on the Catechism and other hymns for the organ. Prepared for music-lovers and particularly for connoisseurs of such work, for the recreation of the spirit, by Johann Sebastian Bach, Royal Polish and Electoral Saxon Court Composer, Kapellmeister and Director of the *chorus musicus*, Leipzig. Published by the Author.

Two engravers worked on the volume. The first at times followed closely the style of the composer's handwriting (hence the old claim that the St Anne Prelude etc were engraved by Bach himself); the second was Balthaser Schmid of Nuremberg, publisher of the *Goldberg Variations (Clavierübung IV)* and the *Canonic Variations* BWV 769. The first engraver was responsible for pp1–43 of the 77 pages of music, and the title-page itself, in style of writing, resembles that of *Clavier-übung II* (French Overture and Italian Concerto). The volume appeared towards Michaelmas (29 September) 1739, although in January of that year J. E. Bach had thought that it might be ready for the Easter Fair (*Dok* II p335). The composer's original manuscript, later owned by C. P. E. Bach, is now lost; but his own copy of the published volume has been identified as Lpz BM PM 1403 (Wolff 1977 pp124–5). The volume was published at 3 Reichsthaler, but it is not known if there was a pre-publication price for subscribers, of the kind referred to by J. E. Bach.* The year itself, 1739, was significant to Leipzig in particular, with three Reformation festivals: 25 May (bicentenary of Luther's sermon in St Thomas), 12 August (bicentenary of the Augsburg Confession) and 31 October (the Reformationsfest).

Apart from an older (?) trio on 'Allein Gott in der höh'' BWV 676a, which perhaps shows sufficient resemblance to BWV 676 to be called

* For comparison, a new clavichord in 1745 might have cost as little as 10 Reichsthaler (Dähnert 1962 p231).

an 'earlier version', all the pieces appear to have been specially composed for the published volume. The period of composition – supposing the MS to have been ready by early 1739* – was presumably over the previous year or so; but it may have been earlier (Blume 1973 p248). All the major manuscripts, now widely scattered (e.g. Danzig 4203/4, London B.L. RM 21.a.9, Bologna Cons. G. B. Martini DD.77, the MS bound with part of Oley's copy of *Clavierübung II* and now in Boston Public Library), are direct or indirect copies of the print, complete or incomplete. Hand copies were still being made in the nineteenth century.† Some copies have a different order for the last four chorales (P 216); several include 'corrections' perhaps from a lost autograph MS (Tessmer *NBA* IV/4 *KB*).

Clavierübung III was Bach's first publication for organ. No doubt useful for those who had heard of the composer only by repute were the remarks made in Leipzig a year later by Lorenz Mizler, in his review of the volume in the *Musikalische Bibliothek*:

> Der Herr Verfasser hat hier ein neues Exempel gegeben, dass er in dieser Gattung der Composition vor vielen andern vortrefflich geübt und glücklich sey. Niemand wird es ihm hierin zuvor thun, und gar wenige werden es ihm nachahmen können. Dieses Werk ist ein kräfftige Widerlegung derer, die sich unterstanden des Herrn Hof Compositeurs Composition zu critisiren (*Dok* II p387).

> The author has given here new proof that in this kind of composition he excels many others in experience and skill. No one can surpass him in this sphere, and very few indeed will be able to imitate him. This work is a powerful argument against those who have ventured to criticize the music of the Court Composer.

The last remark is almost certainly a reference to the famous attack made on Bach by J. A. Scheibe in 1737 (see below), although Scheibe had not made any specific reference to organ music. The title *Clavierübung* was still quite common at this period in this part of Germany, and of itself suggests neither that the pieces were suitable for any keyboard instrument nor that the composer was modestly presenting a 'characterless' face on the title-page. The following are some examples of the term used for locally published collections of music:

> J. Kuhnau, *Neuer Clavier Übung* I (Leipzig 1689), II (Leipzig 1692)
> J. Krieger, *Anmuthige Clavier-Übung bestehend in unterschiedlichen Ricercarien...Allen Liebhabern des Claviers wolmeinend mitgetheilt* (Nuremberg 1698)
> V. Lübeck, *Clavier Übung* (Hamburg 1728)
> G. A. Sorge, *Clavierübung...sowohl auf der Orgel, als auf dem Clavicymbel und Clavicordio mit Vergnügen zu hören* (Nuremberg c1739)

---

* I.e. when the composer was still aged 53. There are 53 words on the title-page (cf. the 42 words on that of *Clavierübung IV*, published in 1742).
† How the copying of printed music affected sales of the latter cannot be known with certainty. A few years earlier than this – in 1733 – Vivaldi had told a British visitor that he had decided not to publish more concertos as he was likely to do better by having them distributed in manuscript (*MT* 1973 p893).

*Sperontes singende Muse an der Pleisse in 2 mahl 50 Oden ... zu beliebter
Clavier-Übung und Gemüths-Ergötzung*, I–IV (Leipzig 1736–46)
J. L. Krebs, *Clavierübung, bestehend in verschiedenen Vorspielen und
Veränderungen einiger Kirchengesänge* (Nuremberg n.d.)

In addition, Krebs published in *c*1742 a French Overture and in 1743
an Italian Concerto (cf. *Clavierübung II*); all three works were produced
by Balthasar Schmid.

While *Clavierübung III* is clearly not just a miscellaneous album of
organ chorales, its exact nature as a collection has been in some
dispute, even as to whether it is merely a 'closely knit group of pieces'
or actually in one way or another a 'cycle'. The background to the
questions may be summarized as follows:

(i) Overall plans in which published collections of organ music were
arranged were not uncommon and could take various forms. They might
reflect practical needs in the Mass (e.g. the twenty-one pieces in
Couperin's *Messe pour les paroisses* *c*1690) or the Office (e.g. Kerll's
Magnificat versets in *Modulatio organica* 1686, consisting of seven
versets in each of eight church tones). They might also reflect their
composer's interest in publishing sets of chorales either in various forms
(e.g. J. L. Krebs's *Clavierübung*, containing a free prelude, a chorale
prelude and figured harmonization for each chorale) or in a complex
contrapuntal treatment (e.g. the invertible and mirror harmonizations
of a chorale in Buxtehude's *Fried- und Freudenreiche Hinfarth* 1674).*
Parisian *Messes pour l'orgue* often included Vespers movements
outside the Mass itself (Lebègue, Boyvin, de Grigny etc).

(ii) The common label 'German Organ Mass' is incorrect: (*a*) more
is involved than the Lutheran Missa Brevis of Kyrie and Gloria; (*b*)
it is not an organ mass in the sense of a *Messe pour l'orgue* (nor would
such a collection have been useful); and (*c*) no firm evidence supports
the suggestion that the *Vier Duette* are organ pieces played during
Communion. That there are twenty-one chorales – like the twenty-one
movements of a French Mass – is probably coincidence. While the
Kyrie and Gloria were sung at every main service in Leipzig, it does
not follow that either greater or lesser organ settings were played in
conjunction with choir music or congregational chorale; however, it
is easy to conjecture how they might have been used in this connection.
Hymns sung every Sunday (such as 'Allein Gott in der Höh'' or 'Wir
glauben all'') gave the organist an opportunity to make use of different
keys, as Adlung noted in 1758 (*Anleitung* p726); he reports playing the
Gloria hymn in the keys of E, F, F♯, G, G♯, A and B♭ (three of which
are those used in *Clavierübung III*). The *Missa* or Kyrie pieces in the
collection are to be understood as a reference or dedication to the
Trinity; in the Leipzig hymnbook of G. Vopelius (1682 etc), the *Missa*
is contained in the section of hymns for or 'of the Holy Trinity'.

---

* That Buxtehude's publication was known at least to members of the 'Bach circle' is
clear from J. G. Walther's totally *inversus* pieces likewise called 'Evolutio' amongst
his settings of 'Herr Jesu Christ, wahr Mensch und Gott' (MS Kö 15839).

That the first nine preludes contain three groups of three strengthens this Trinity association, as do the three themes of the E flat Prelude and the three themes/sections of the E flat Fugue.

(iii) The composer's own statement – that the preludes are based 'on Catechism and other hymns' – does not explain why the collection is framed by the E flat Prelude and Fugue or why an organist specifically needed such hymns, since the Leipzig Catechism Examination seems not to have used the organ (Stiller 1970 p242). In 1790, Gerber's *Lexicon* refers to them simply as 'Vorspiele über Kirchengesänge' (*Dok* III p469). Luther's Greater and Lesser Catechisms consisted of a series of questions and answers outlining the principles of faith; from these could be drawn six particular headings, introduced by the German Kyrie and Gloria and set against a background of penitence referred to in (e.g.) the section on baptism:

Luther's reformed liturgy
- Kyrie
- Christe
- Kyrie
- Gloria ('Allein Gott in der Höh')

Luther's reformed doctrine
1. Ten Commandments ('Diess sind')
2. Credo ('Wir glauben')
3. Prayer ('Vater unser')
4. Baptism ('Christ unser Herr')
5. Penitence ('Aus tiefer Noth')
6. Eucharist ('Jesus Christus')

Five of the hymn melodies (1–4, 6) can even be combined in a quodlibet if the notes are juggled somewhat, as a tradition still known in the nineteenth century shows (Hilgenfeldt 1850 p8, table 1). The inclusion of 'Aus tiefer Noth' may or may not be a 'personal catechism' of the composer's: all six hymns are in Luther's hymnbooks and signify the six headings in the Smaller or Lesser Catechism. There is thus little mystery in his inclusion of no. 5 above (Leaver 1975). The six hymns moreover present a front of pure classical Lutheran belief: six pillars of orthodoxy, not only of importance in the Jubilee Year 1739 but a kind of answer to a directive of the Saxon Consistory in 1730 that 'new hymns...shall not be used in public divine services' without permission (David & Mendel 1945 p119). Half the hymn melodies in the *Clavierubüng III* chorales were of Gregorian origin. Leipzig, like Nuremberg, was conservative; the services included major Latin pieces, and liturgical hymns were important in such Leipzig hymnbooks as that of Vopelius.

The term 'Ergötzung', though familiar from title-pages, was more than merely conventional, implying a pious concept of 'recreation' or 'refreshment' of the spirit; music works 'either to the glory of God or of the Devil' (Stiller 1970 pp196, 209), and Bach works *ad majorem gloriam Dei*. The organist, the instrument and his 'refreshed spirit' correspond to the 'knowledge, power and love' that are attributes of the Trinity itself. *Clavier-Übung* thus becomes an organist's corollary to his own *Catechismus-Übung* (Leaver 1975), important in a year celebrating Luther's twin achievement of reformed liturgy and reformed doctrine.

(iv) Despite appearances and despite frequent assumptions, there is nothing to connect the Greater and Lesser Catechisms respectively with the greater and lesser chorale settings. The manual preludes are shorter but not necessarily simpler, unlike the Lesser Catechism; being all fugal in very varied ways, they also present a more unified group than the greater settings. Nor is there any reason to associate the greater settings with the 'connoisseurs' and the lesser with the 'music-lovers' (amateurs) referred to in the title-page; or the first with ecclesiastical, the second with domestic music-making. To some extent the church/home distinction may have been traditional, as suggested in Vetter's collection of 1709/13, *Kirch- und Haus-Ergötzlichkeit* (see note under BWV 770); also, most of the lesser settings do accord with the harpsichord style shown in Book II of *Das Wohltemperirte Clavier*, and in other *Clavierübung* volumes. But more relevant to the volume as *Übung* – 'practice' not 'theory' – is that each of the lesser settings develops a different aspect of fugal form or fugal technique. Only the last (BWV 689) is a fugue fully comparable to those of *Das Wohltemperirte Clavier*, II; the others are shorter or more sectional, offering examples of 'fugal treatment' or 'fugal devices'.

The true relevance of the Catechism aspect lies in the basic claim of the early or orthodox reformers that they were offering congregations three particular gifts: the Bible, the hymnbook and the Catechism. Within the previous decade, Bach had offered major settings of biblical texts (*St Matthew Passion*, *Christmas Oratorio* etc), and collaborated in a hymnbook (Schemelli, 1736); *Clavierübung III* now supplied the Catechism. It would be more than the sources warrant to suggest that the Catechism chorales were an orthodox reaction to the pietist flavour of the Schemelli hymnbook.

(v) While no doubt the musical architecture of *Clavierübung III* was not merely the result of 'esoteric brooding' (Albrecht 1969 p46), any unity that the volume may have is musical rather than strictly liturgical – and theoretical-musical rather than practical-musical. While many of the musical devices, particularly in the treatment of the cantus-firmus melodies, recall those known since at least the time of Scheidt, the whole volume appears as a compendium formally arranged, with cyclic elements more striking to the reader than the player, as has been recently acknowledged (Wolff 1969 p149). The movements suggest various groupings:

552.i	Praeludium	*pro organo pleno*
669	Kyrie, Gott Vater	c.f. in soprano
670	Christe, aller Welt Trost	c.f. in tenor
671	Kyrie, Gott heiliger Geist	c.f. in pedal
		(*con organo pleno*)

672	Kyrie, Gott Vater	$^3/_4$ *manualiter*
673	Christe, aller Welt Trost	$^6/_8$ *manualiter*
674	Kyrie, Gott heiliger Geist	$^9/_8$ *manualiter*
675	Allein Gott in der Höh'	trio in F, *manualiter*
676	Allein Gott in der Höh'	trio in G
677	Allein Gott in der Höh'	trio in A, *manualiter*
678	Diess sind die heil'gen zehn Gebot'	c.f. in canon
679	Diess sind die heil'gen zehn Gebot'	*manualiter*
680	Wir glauben all' an einen Gott	*in organo pleno*
681	Wir glauben all' an einen Gott	*manualiter*
682	Vater unser im Himmelreich	c.f. in canon
683	Vater unser im Himmelreich	*manualiter*
684	Christ, unser Herr, zum Jordan kam	c.f. in pedal
685	Christ, unser Herr, zum Jordan kam	*manualiter*
686	Aus tiefer Noth schrei' ich zu dir	*in organo pleno*
687	Aus tiefer Noth schrei' ich zu dir	*manualiter*
688	Jesus Christus, unser Heiland	c.f. in pedal
689	Jesus Christus, unser Heiland	*manualiter*
802	Duetto I	$^3/_8$ E minor
803	Duetto II	$^2/_4$ F major
804	Duetto III	$^{12}/_8$ G major
805	Duetto IV	$^2/_2$ A minor
552.ii	Fuga	*pro organo pleno*

Note the *organo pleno* framework of the E flat Prelude and Fugue, the three inner groups (Mass, Catechism, Duets), the division of the Mass chorales (three polyphonic, three *manualiter*, three trio), the rising tonality of the trios, the groupings within the twelve Catechism chorales themselves (two canonic c.f., two pedal c.f., two *organo pleno*, the pairings *pedaliter/manualiter*), and the variety within the duets (variety of key, mode and metre).

Several elements in the organization of the volume are thus at work. Some features of the number symbolism can be heard: the three settings of the Trinity hymn (all in three parts, their three keys F–G–A forming a major third); the three themes of the opening Prelude; the three sections of the closing Fugue. Others are graphic: the three flats of the Prelude and Fugue, the 'Third Part' of the title-page. Others can be 'understood' rather than observed: the number of Mass chorales ($3 \times 3 = 9$), the number of pieces as a whole ($3 \times 3 \times 3 = 27$), the progressive triple time of the manual Kyrie preludes ($^3/_4$, $^6/_8$, $^9/_8$). As in other later works of Bach, formal elements of uncertain significance and of uncertain effect will be discovered. Thus the central piece (14th) of the collection is a setting of 'Wir glauben all'' (BWV 681) in the spiky rhythm of a French Overture, at least as it seems to have been understood by J. S. Bach. Does this rhythm express the regal splendour of the God of the Credo? In Cantata 61, the French Overture treatment of a cantus firmus is used for its significance as an overture – a grand opening of the church year on Advent Sunday – not for 'regal splendour' as such. Perhaps the French elements in BWV 681 are there for simple variety? But the central or near-central pieces in all four parts of J. S. Bach's *Clavierübung* have the same French rhythm, three of them in Overtures: the opening of the 4th Partita in D (*Clavierübung I*); first movement of the B minor Suite (*Clavierübung II*); 'Wir glauben all'' BWV 681 in E minor (*Clavierübung III*); *Goldberg Variation* no. 16 in G (*Clavierübung IV*).*

(vi) Despite the symmetries involved both in the work as a whole and in its separate divisions, there is no reason to regard *Clavierübung III* as a cycle. It is possible that the composer intended the chorales as service pieces for Lutheran organists: a repertory to choose from, rather than a single cycle or even two cycles. But as with the *Canonic Variations*, the *Musical Offering* and the *Art of Fugue*, the published order is not obligatory. There was certainly no opportunity in the service at Leipzig or elsewhere for the series of organ chorales to be played as they stand, even omitting the duplications. Nevertheless, the tonalities do suggest groupings: the ear accepts that the larger Kyrie–Christe–Kyrie set follows the E flat Prelude, logic accepts that the smaller Kyrie–Christe–Kyrie set follows the G major chord at the end of BWV 671, and the eye accepts the rising tonalities of the Trinity trios.

The musical style of certain of the pieces has caused some commentators to date them to the Weimar period. But, to take the example of 'Allein Gott in der Höh'' BWV 675 (Keller 1948 p199): its affinity to 'Christ lag in Todesbanden' BWV 695 is purely formal (alto cantus firmus with paraphrase fugal opening). The musical language of the lines themselves is quite different, BWV 675 being much less traditional, nearer to the four Duets BWV 802–805 than to the Two-part Inventions. There is an unconventional, even at times strange, quality about the counterpoint of much of *Clavierübung III*, irrespective of the *stile antico* question (see below) and even perhaps of problems of modality. Already in the 1770s Kirnberger pointed out that only the Trinity trios were firmly put in major keys (*Dok* III p221); and in 1779 A. F. C. Kollmann thought that 'most or all of his Catechism hymns are written in the said modes' (*Dok* III p583). But in practice is BWV 677 (A major) really much more securely diatonic than (e.g.) BWV 674 (E-phrygian)? Both have an ambiguity of 'key' in the first bar. If BWV 674 is in G, why does it begin on the mediant? If in E minor, why is it answered in the supertonic? If modal, how is the diatonic modulation of (e.g.) bb18–22 to be integrated? The so-called modality lies in a kind of diatonic ambiguity exemplified in the cadence, suggested by the key-signature, and borne out in the kinds of lines and imitation. In the A major setting BWV 677, neither cadence nor key-signature is ambiguous in this sense; but despite the anchoring half-cadences (bb7, 16) there is still an uneasy tonality occasioned by the subject itself (cf. the subject of the C major Fugue BWV 547, which contains the same motif in a more clearly diatonic context) and by such details as the mediant harmony of b3, the mediant entries in bb7–8, the slow settling-down of key between b10 and b14. The modality is certainly more pronounced than it is in (e.g.) Telemann's *XX Kleine*

* Note also the pairs of relative keys: D major and B minor, E minor and G major.

Fugen (Hamburg *c*1731), which are supposedly 'nach besondern Modis verfasset' ('composed according to certain modes', i.e. keys). The only 'modal' element in Telemann's fugues is their occasional close on the apparent dominant.

There are other factors contributing to the 'strangeness' of these chorales: the unconventional entries in (e.g.) BWV 673, the lines and spacing of (e.g.) BWV 675, the combination of bold four-part contrapuntal harmony with modal elements in BWV 687, the characteristic lines of BWV 685 that arise from mirror counterpoint. At the same time, several characteristics of motivic development are noticeable: the element of caprice (the flash of semiquavers in b24 of BWV 673), the 'inspired' exploitation of a motif (the tail of the subject of BWV 679, bb18–31), the new treatment of an apparently conventional figure (semiquaver runs in BWV 683, avoiding the common formulae, leaving the opening note isolated, rising more towards the end, etc). Indeed, the motivic development of the shorter preludes is generally much less conventional than that of the greater, despite some obvious parallels. The length and shape of the greater 'Jesus Christus unser Heiland' BWV 688, for example, is such that repetitious extension, rather than capricious *ad hoc* development, is required.

As pairs or, in the case of the Gloria/Trinity hymn, a trio of settings, the organ chorales of the volume offer examples of many very varied techniques: fugue, paraphrase, canon, ritornello, motif development (Williams 1979). The three settings of 'Allein Gott in der Höh'' thus supply a manual trio with inner cantus firmus, a trio-sonata-like movement with partial cantus firmus, and a fughetta based on the first two lines without cantus firmus. They could no doubt have been imitated by pupils but cannot be regarded as blank formal types ready for every composer's individual treatment, as could the so-called 'Pachelbel prelude'. Nor is the volume a compendium of all or even the most up-to-date treatments of chorales. There is no prelude of the decorated-melody type, for example. Whether the *Schübler* preludes were later published to fill such gaps by providing melodious or up-to-date treatments cannot be known, but they certainly go some way in this direction. Yet although by general opinion the obbligato line of (e.g.) BWV 650 is more melodious than the trio line of BWV 676, it could be claimed that the melodic obbligato line is essentially foreign to organ chorales and suggests intrumental music, as here in BWV 650. Those preludes of *Clavierübung III* that approach most closely the obbligato type (BWV 678, 684, 688) use their material imitatively, quasi-canonically or fugally, not 'melodiously'.

The composer's intention of presenting a collection of pieces written in various styles (Williams 1979) is at its clearest in the question of the *stile antico* or 'old style'. No fewer than five of Bach's strictest pieces in the style are contained in *Clavierübung III*: BWV 552.ii (first section, 661–37), 669, 670, 671, 686 (Wolff 1968 p15). It is a style with musical details familiar in the vocal polyphony of Palestrina and in those theorists of the early eighteenth century on whom his influence is most direct, notably J. J. Fux, Caldara and Zelenka – all of whom were admired by J. S. Bach (according to C. P. E. Bach's remarks to

Forkel, *Dok* III p289), and all of whom died between 1730 and 1745. While the clearest signs of the *stile antico* are the larger note-values (⁴/₂ for ⁴/₄),* the style as a whole probably meant, to Bach, a stricter polyphony than usual in keyboard *alla breve* music, a style less dependent on the text and more on the harmonic demands of the counterpoint, and a style for which the tonal ambiguities of so-called modes were particularly suitable. In *Clavierübung III* the *stile antico* pieces resulted in something both old-fashioned and different from the rest: on the one hand they conformed to the composer's well-documented interest in the knowledge of Fuxian styles, then influential at Dresden and elsewhere; on the other they contributed to the array of styles he was setting out to apply in *Clavierübung III*, the B minor Mass and the *Goldberg Variations*.

Bach seems to have acquired his own copy of Fux's *Gradus* soon after it was published in 1725 (Wolff 1968 p28), and others in his circle knew the treatise. His pupil Mizler translated and annotated it in 1742 ('very well' according to Schering 1941 p202) and lectured on it in the University of Leipzig (Wolff 1968 p148). Italian and other *stile antico* Mass movements were performed in Leipzig over the next few decades, and the Dresden court composer Zelenka – in one sense a colleague of Bach's – helped to spread the work of his teacher Fux. But even in *Clavierübung III* it would be a mistake to see J. S. Bach's pieces in *stile antico* as strict textbook demonstrations. While the style of (e.g.) BWV 686 tends towards a more polyphonic texture than the not dissimilar *alla breve* style of the movement based on the same melody in Cantata 38, the rhythms, compass and intervals within a single contrapuntal line in (e.g.) BWV 670 are all outside the Palestrinian mould. Neither in Palestrina nor in Fux is one likely to find a main theme that incorporates two sequences (Ex. 175). Yet although the

Ex. 175
BWV 588

themes of the greater Kyrie–Christe–Kyrie settings are more in the *stile antico*, their working-out may involve passages clearly belonging to the eighteenth century (Ex. 176), and the purity of Bach's *stile antico* ought not to be exaggerated. Conversely, the *alla breve* style in late works such as the six-part Ricercare from the *Musical Offering* is closer to Fuxian counterpoint than earlier examples are, and the opening of the E flat Fugue BWV 552.ii is in a much smoother species counterpoint than previous *alla breve* fugues such as BWV 540 and 538. The E flat

* Fux's *tempo binarium* as distinct from *presto* (2/2) or *allegro* (4/4): *Gradus ad Parnassum* (Vienna 1725) p238.

Ex. 176

BWV 671

b14

Ped.

Fugue is more directly under Fux's influence than the Canzona BWV 588 or the Allabreve BWV 589, which are rather in the common Italianate tradition of Froberger, Kerll, and others (see also Riedel 1968); its second and third sections progressively modify the style until the final pedal entry acknowledges a change of allegiance to newer styles: BWV 552.ii ends with spacious baroque drama.

That the *stile antico* is at least partly a question of notation does not detract from its significance, since much of the pattern-making in Bach's late works is indeed notational – conceptual rather than perceptual. The composer's consciousness of style is beyond question. One of Birnbaum's counter-arguments (1738) to Scheibe's attack on Bach was that the composer understood the 'Italian taste' of Palestrina and others, 'so highly treasured these days' (*Dok* II p305); Mizler pointed out in 1739 that in his cantatas he could both write full inner parts as in the music 'of twenty-five years ago' and compose 'entirely in accordance with the latest taste' (*Dok* II p336); music extemporized or composed for listeners abroad followed various local styles (the old fantasia style for Reincken at Hamburg in 1720, the chromatic 'sighing melody' of the *Musical Offering* for Frederick II at Berlin in 1747). A further key to the concept of *Clavierübung III* is the influence of Frescobaldi's *Fiori musicali* (1635). The direct influence of Frescobaldi on Bach is conjectural in the case of such pieces as the Canzona BWV 588, but the copy of *Fiori musicali* signed 'J. S. Bach 1714' (*Dok* I p269) was evidently acquired at Weimar. Apparent similarities between the two volumes may be misleading – Frescobaldi's use of the term 'alio modo', for example, is not necessarily to be seen as something copied by Bach. Nevertheless, the following characteristics of the *Fiori musicali* suggest a close relationship between the two publications, at least in the mind of the composer – closer than to (e.g.) Scheidt's *Tabulatura nova*.

(i) Purpose. The publication is meant 'mainly to assist organists' ('il mio principal fine è di giovare all organisti') with pieces 'corresponding to Mass and Vespers' ('che potranno rispondere à Messe et à Vespri').

(ii) Shape. *Fiori musicali* consists of three sets of mostly short pieces, the first set of which is as follows:

Toccata before the Mass
Kyrie
Kyrie
Christe
Christe
Christe ($^3/_2$)
Christe
Kyrie
Kyrie
Kyrie
Kyrie
Kyrie
Kyrie ($^3/_2$)
Canzona after the Epistle
Ricercare after the Credo
Toccata Cromatica for the Elevation
Canzona after the Post-communion

The third Mass is followed by a Bergamasca (a *tour de force* of motivic composition, based on a theme resembling one of the Quodlibet melodies of the *Goldberg Variations*) and a Capriccio. But the prelude ('Toccata') before the fugue ('Canzona') after the Mass serve as a framework for the Mass movements, not all of which are required in each service, however liturgical their arrangement may appear.

(iii) *Polyphonic characteristics*. Though short, the Kyries and Christes in particular are written in well-wrought *stile antico* counterpoint of four parts, many with a cantus firmus throughout (and with underived countersubjects), others with held notes that anticipate BWV 669, 687 etc (Ex. 177). Frescobaldi's four-part counterpoint, whether mainly

Ex. 177

Frescobaldi, *Fiori musicali*, first Christe

b9

connoisseur music or not, could have exercised direct influence on (e.g.) BWV 669 without the usual intermediate German traditions of Froberger and others.

(iv) *Some technical details*. While the formal plan of the E flat Fugue BWV 552.ii and the shape of its first theme may well have been influenced by other organ pieces, the principles of mutation and combination of themes were already clear from *Fiori musicali* (e.g. Canzona

of the first Mass, alternative Ricercare of the second) and other works
of that period. Similarly, while the ostinato bass of the Credo fugue
BWV 680 may recall in principle the repetitive bass line of many an
Italian aria (Spitta I p209), *Fiori musicali* already contains a piece with
closer resemblances: a fugue with a simple ostinato bass theme of five
notes ('recercar con obligo del Basso').

Nevertheless, it may well have been only a handful of connoisseurs
who had their spirits refreshed by the greater settings of *Clavierübung
III*. Those who agreed with Scheibe in 1737 that Bach

> seinen Stücken durch ein schwülstiges und verworrenes Wesen das
> Natürliche entzöge, und ihre Schönheit durch allzugrosse Kunst verdun-
> kelte (*Dok* III p280)

> deprived his pieces of all that is natural by giving them a bombastic
> and confused character, and eclipsed their beauty by too much art

may well have been able to point out examples in this volume. It is
an argument sometimes difficult to refute, for the very mastery has
a forbidding air, and the several organ styles were almost unsym-
pathetically old-fashioned – just at the period when Bach himself seems
to have sensed the *galanterie* of the new music, judging by the arias
written for the B minor Mass. Some of the settings seem to have only
a tenuous connection with the text, and it is easier to believe that the
composer was more interested in finding faultless invertible counterpoint or weaving together a theme and its paraphrase. We cannot know
why a certain musical figure sprang to mind, whether there were an
unconscious reference to a particular word or to the general mood of
the text, or how a musical motif is related to anything but itself.
Nevertheless, certain points can be made about many of the pieces
and their relationship to the ideas of the period, particularly their
symbolic or rhetorical reference to the chorale texts and their position
in the musical style and development of their composer. Each movement is an *exemplum* of motivic creation: i.e., it can and no doubt
did serve a composer as a practical demonstration of how to develop
this or that motif (see in particular BWV 678 and 680). If the term
'*Clavierübung*' means not so much 'practical music for performance'
or even 'music for practice'* but *musica pratica* in distinction to *musica
teorica*, the organist–composer of the period could be imagined to have
found here put into written or practical form techniques otherwise
widely scattered, mostly unpublished, inadequately described by the
theorists of the period, and certainly nowhere demonstrated with such
solid skill.

---

* It cannot be assumed that at this period 'üben' was used in the familiar, post-Czerny
sense of 'practising' the piano etc.

669 Kyrie, Gott Vater in Ewigkeit (*Clavierübung III*)

Published 1739, no Autograph MS.

Headed 'Canto fermo in Soprano', 'a 2 Clav. et Ped.'; two staves.

Kyrie, Gott Vater in Ewigkeit is one of three sections of the TEXT first published in the early period of Lutheran hymnbooks (Naumburg 1537) as the German version of the troped *Kyrie summum bonum: Kyrie fons bonitatis* of the Latin Mass II (*Liber usualis*, Mass II for Feasts of the 1st Class, 1). In Leipzig, the German or Latin text was sung after an organ prelude each Sunday (Stiller p103); in pietist hymnbooks, the text was used 'during and after general distress' (Freylinghausen 1741 etc). Strictly, the *Kyrie summum* was sung on Sundays from Trinity to Christmas, the similar *Kyrie paschale* from Easter to Trinity (Luedtke 1918 p82).

Kyrie, Gott Vater in Ewigkeit,	Kyrie – God and Father in eternity,
gross ist dein Barmherzigkeit;	great is your mercy;
aller Ding' ein Schöpfer und Regierer,	sole creator and ruler of all things –
eleison!	eleison!

The text also has specific reference to the Catechisms, e.g. Question 11 from the Heidelberg Catechism:

Ist denn Gott nicht auch barmherzig?	Is then God not also merciful?
Gott ist wohl barmherzig, er ist aber	God is indeed merciful, but he is
auch gerecht...	also just...

The MELODY is adapted from the plainsong, published in 1537 with this text and at Erfurt in 1525 with another (Terry 1921 p250); the three sections of the plainsong share a common second half: Ex. 178. Bach's

Ex. 178

Vopelius 1682

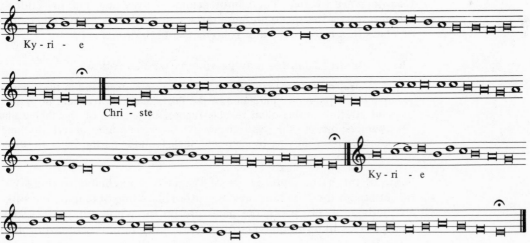

five cantus-firmus paragraphs correspond to the fermata divisions current in hymnbooks (e.g. Dresden 1625 and BWV 371). The melody is not otherwise used by the composer, although BWV 672 is derived from it and BWV 233 carries a theme with a similar beginning. In general, organ settings of any section of the melody are rare; Scheidemann left a four-part 'Kyrie summum' in manuscript, while Scheidt's published Kyrie settings (*Tabulatura nova* III, 1624) use a different melody (so far unidentified).

The three massive $^4/_2$ Kyrie preludes – though they fit into the series of *stile antico* compositions that occupied the composer about 1740, and though in some respects they are related to vocal works (e.g. the tripartite plan, motifs, inversion techniques and cantus-firmus style of the Mass in F BWV 233) – are both unique and intimately keyboard-like in idiom. The form of BWV 669 can be expressed as

> monothematic motet or fugal organ chorale, with theme derived from the first two lines of the cantus firmus, which itself appears augmented, line by line in the top part ('God the Father'); the conception is neither that of the 'organ motet' (one theme is exposed fugally, not a series of lines) nor of the fugue (there are no regular entries fully independent of the cantus firmus)

and its style as

> three-part *alla breve* counterpoint (to which the cantus firmus is a fourth part) incorporating stricter *stile antico* features (see below) in a modal framework (G-phrygian) with frequent diatonic ambiguity (e.g. B♭/E♭ major bb29–35).

In form, the three chorales refer back rather to such works as the little Kyrie–Christe–Kyrie versets of Frescobaldi's *Fiori musicali* and to those which they probably influenced (e.g. *ricercari* of J. K. F. Fischer) than to the usual motet-chorales of Scheidt etc. In style, the chorales relate generally to such works as the Confiteor from the B minor Mass BWV 232, but it is noticeable that the motifs of the Confiteor are livelier. The cantus firmus of BWV 669, moving entirely by step, gives the piece a characteristic smoothness by no means out of place in a movement that follows the Prelude BWV 552.i.

The *stile antico* features may be summarized as follows:

> $^4/_2$ metre, modal character (in the cantus firmus itself and in the opening imitation apparently unrelated to the final cadence), frequent inversions and strettos (rather than regular fugue), the nature of the theme and countersubjects, the high incidence of suspension, dactyl rhythms, crotchet lines moving by step and such features as the inner thirds of the final bars (*canon sine pausa*)

None of the latter features are of themselves exclusive to this style. But although the pedal in particular often has a line of frankly bass-like character (e.g. bb17–18), the parts are on the whole unusually strict: free phrases like the quavers of b36 are more in character with other movements (e.g. E flat Prelude, b70). There are fourteen entries of the theme (with two partial entries) and seven inversions; the seven strettos include a *rectus/inversus* stretto (bb19–20). The subsidiary material is developed very largely from the implied suspensions, the dactyl motif and the rising crotchets of a section of the theme (Ex. 179). Particularly 'effortless' in the working-out are the dactyls and the crotchet lines, which sometimes amount to sub-themes (e.g. b32).

Ex. 179

The whole is developed below a cantus firmus which has the curious feature that the last note of each phrase could be held longer than it is notated. The moulding of the cantus firmus into the movement's theme involves little paraphrase, since such plainchants naturally and traditionally serve as ricercare subjects. While the cantus-firmus lines of BWV 669 and 670 are to be played on a separate manual or set in relief by registration, it is to be noted that the counterpoint is more complete than is often the case with movements of this type; the registration for the accompaniment should be as clear as the solo line (*plein jeu* for the accompaniment, Tierce combination for the solo?). There is a practical utility in reserving the reeds for BWV 671 (cantus firmus in pedal), and this accords with many organs of the period, on which strong manual reeds were unknown.

Fux's own words in *Gradus ad Parnassum* and Mizler's comments in this translation (Wolff 1968 p157) suggest that the intention behind late *stile antico* manifestations was to present music 'grounded on the unchangeable rules of harmony'. The style immediately gave the composer a link with a school of composition then uniquely revered, typical of a high-church music based on plainsong. Whether the style was meant to evoke more – the 'strength of faith' or of orthodox tradition – is uncertain. The desire for a variety of styles as such, however, would not prevent the composer from seeing in the *stile antico* a symbolic or associative reference *ad majorem gloriam Dei*; the *stile antico* even admitted variety within itself:

BWV 669 monothematic, ricercare-like, vocal polyphony
BWV 670 c.f. *en taille*, given freer treatment
BWV 671 several subjects combining in turn with the c.f.

---

670   Christe, aller Welt Trost (*Clavierübung III*)

Published 1739, no Autograph MS.

Headed 'Canto fermo in Tenore', 'a 2 Clav. et Pedal'; two staves.

The TEXT is the second section of the *Kyrie, Gott Vater in Ewigkeit*; see also under BWV 669.

Christe, aller Welt Trost,	Christe – consolation of all the world,
uns Sünder allein du hast erlöst;	you alone have redeemed us sinners;
Jesu, Gottes Sohn,	Jesu, Son of God
unser Mittler bist in dem höchsten	you are our mediator at the highest
Thron;	throne;
zu dir schreien wir in Herzens Begier,	to you we cry in our heart's desire –
eleison!	eleison!

The MELODY is adapted from the plainsong: see under BWV 669. The eight cantus-firmus paragraphs of BWV 670 correspond to the fermata divisions current in hymnbooks, except that the second phrase is divided into two (bb14–16 and 20–2), perhaps on the analogy of bb33–5 and 39–42 (a traditional division of the melody). From b39 to the end, the cantus firmus is virtually the same as that of BWV 669, including the ornaments.

The form, style and features of the *stile antico* of the movement resemble those of BWV 669; the cantus firmus is now in the tenor ('God the Son', the second or 'middle' Person of the Trinity). Twenty-two entries of the theme (similarly derived from the first two lines of the cantus firmus) are countered by only one inversion (b43), perhaps because the angularity of the theme is more obtrusive *inversus* than *rectus*. There is the same ease of counterpoint based on smooth transition, suspensions and counter-rhythms, while the phrygian features again result in some ambiguity of key. The 'B♭ major' of the opening makes it appear that the subject enters on the submediant, and only when the music moves elsewhere (G minor/C minor bb19–22) is there an unambiguous perfect cadence; even the diatonic versions of the theme in soprano and bass bb52–4* do not yield a firmer sense of key or prepare the final cadence. The entries themselves are variously disguised (e.g. alto bb6–7, soprano b28, soprano b52 with alto stretto), and again much is made of the dactyl motif taken from the theme, some passages serving almost as a model of Italianate counterpoint (e.g. bb17–18) and being, in terms of spacing and tessitura, far removed from pure *stile antico* (e.g. bb23–4). The double entry in sixths (b32) is a classic *canon sine pausa* – seen by some as concords symbolizing the term 'mediator' (Chailley 1974 p178). The motifs countering the theme and its cantus firmus in such bars as 46–51 follow the specific *stile antico* types – Ex. 180 – *figura corta* (i), *tirata mezza*

Ex. 180

(i)   (ii)   (iii)   (iv) b50

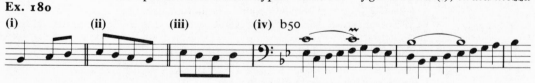

(ii), and *circolo mezzo* (iii), as well as Third Species crotchets (iv), while in general the development of the crotchets produces a pedal line of wider *ambitus* than the other voices. The spacing of this Christe is noticeably different from that of the preceding Kyrie because the

* Compare the versions of bb14–16 (soprano), 20–2, (alto) etc.

soprano is now independent of the cantus firmus, which here appears *en taille*; thus the wide spacing of bb31–2 has no parallel in BWV 669. Quite apart from the general style, however, the similarity of detail in BWV 669, 670 and 671 is bound to result in some similarity of thematic material (e.g. the crotchet motif explored in various ways in BWV 669 (b32, tenor and also *inversus*), BWV 670 (b43, alto and bass *rectus*) and BWV 671 (bb32–3, alto sequence)).

671

Kyrie, Gott heiliger Geist (*Clavierübung III*)

Published 1739, no Autograph MS.

Headed 'à 5 Canto fermo in Basso', 'Cum Organo pleno'; two staves.

The TEXT is the third section of *Kyrie, Gott Vater in Ewigkeit*; see also under BWV 669.

Kyrie, Gott heiliger Geist,	Kyrie – God, Holy Ghost,
tröst', stärk' uns im Glauben	comfort and strengthen us in faith
allermeist	most of all
dass wir am letzten End'	that at the final end
fröhlich abscheiden aus diesem	joyfully we may depart out of this
Elend,	misery –
eleison!	eleison!

The *Kyrie paschale* version of the third section (see BWV 669) bears a reference to the attributes of the third Person of the Trinity:

O Gott, heiliger Geist,	O God, Holy Ghost,
teil' uns mit	impart in us
Weisheit, Glauben und Lieb'	wisdom, faith and love most
allermeist,	of all;
gib göttliche Gerechtigkeit.	give divine justice.

The MELODY is adapted from the plainsong: see under BWV 669. The six paragraphs of BWV 671 correspond to the fermata divisions current in hymnbooks. From b34 to the end, the cantus firmus is virtually the same as that of BWV 669 (but without ornaments).

The form, style and features of the *stile antico* of the movement resemble those of BWV 669; but the five-part fabric, woven (unusually) with two sopranos, and the placing of the cantus firmus in the bass ('God the Holy Spirit') result in a new kind of texture. The ritornello fugal theme (now in four parts) is again derived from the opening two lines of the cantus firmus; it is answered in stretto at the octave by its own *inversus* (a *stile antico* idea) which continues to accompany it (preceding or following) on its eight entries. This pairing of *rectus* and *inversus* may be responsible for the fact that neither theme alone accompanies the cantus firmus, although at certain moments it would have been possible to introduce it (e.g. b24); it is as if the cantus firmus serves as the episodes in a double fugue. (For the registration of this cantus firmus, see p. 189.)

The figures developed in the episodes follow Fuxian types less closely than those in BWV 670, and the composer seems more concerned with sequences of a kind he was using at about that time in Book II of *Das Wohltemperirte Clavier* (compare Ex. 176 with Ex. 181). As

Ex. 181

BWV 892
b88

in BWV 669, however, the simple stepwise nature of the theme pervades the whole texture and its lines, as do the syncopated figures ♩ ♩ ♩ and ♩♩ ♩ ♩ derived from the opening theme and its answer. The continuous quaver motion from b37 to b54 is achieved with several kinds of contrapuntal ideas incorporating both the syncopated rhythm and its stepwise motion: each quaver idea seems to lead to the others, with a fresh beginning at b50 and an abrupt end at b54.

Although this Kyrie is again in G-phrygian, the general character of the movement gives a more firmly diatonic impression because of the sequences, the four- and five-part harmonies, and the cantus firmus being in the bass. The opening of the penultimate cantus-firmus line (bb43–5) is thus clearer diatonically than the same moment in BWV 670 (bb46–8). The last line begins on B♭, but the anchoring effect that this might have (cf. the first pedal entry in the E flat Fugue b14) is immediately countered by the chromatic coda of the last six and a half bars.

This coda is very striking and unexpected. Since the combination of *rectus* and *inversus* themes is reminiscent of Frescobaldi (Kyrie 3 from 'Messa della Madonna' in *Fiori musicali*) it is possible too that the Italian chromatic toccata suggested the final bars of BWV 671, with its *durezza* suspensions and rising/falling semitones. The chromatic semitones themselves are known in other *stile antico* movements (e.g. B minor Mass, 2nd Kyrie b28 and Confiteor b17, etc.), and in the case of BWV 671 they seem curiously apt for the final phrygian cadence A♭/G in the bass. Either way, more is involved than Italian toccata chromatics (see also Wolff 1968 p91–3). The strict five parts develop semitone falls (with or without a falling bass) and lines incorporating diminished thirds, the whole beginning in double stretto (alto/tenor, soprano I/II). The effect is clearly a lament above the final cantus-firmus phrase 'eleison' ('have mercy'), the twelve chromatic steps expressing the *Affekt* of the 'eleison'. The contrapuntal texturing of such chromatics distinguishes the coda from the equally unexpected harmonies at the end of the Confiteor of the B minor Mass, and even more so from the textless chromatic Fantasias BWV 542 and 903. The effect remains more 'vocal' than the falling chromatics above the final pedal point of the Fantasia BWV 903 which, as diminished sevenths, are essentially simpler. In BWV 671 such a progression as that over the bar-line at bb59–60 is unique and has changed the Neapolitan sixth beyond recognition.

672

Kyrie, Gott Vater in Ewigkeit (*Clavierübung III*)

Published 1739, no Autograph MS.

Headed 'alio modo', 'manualiter'; two staves.

For TEXT and MELODY see BWV 669.

The three lesser Kyrie–Christe–Kyrie preludes are usually described merely as fughettas; but their form, style and conception are far less conventional than this term usually suggests. The cantus firmus, in addition to prescribing the E-phrygian tonality, supplies the cadences in bb6–7 and 28–9 and much of the material – Ex. 182 – including the

Ex. 182

falling motif in b8 (top part, an *inversus?*), which can be seen to resemble falling phrases of the cantus firmus (see *a* in Ex. 182). From these motifs are woven four smooth contrapuntal parts in which the three opening notes frequently suggest the cantus firmus (e.g. in b22–3, top part). The four parts create both firm tonalities (G – A minor – D minor – A minor – E-phrygian) and a curious sense of remote sweetness owing largely to the constant series of parallel thirds arising between duplication of theme and countersubject that lead to the doubled F♯ at the beginning of b5, noted by Kirnberger in 1771 (*Dok* III p217) as an example of how 'this great man departs from the rule in order to sustain good part-writing' ('dieser grosse Mann gieng hier von der Regel ab, um einen schönen Gesang in allen Stimmen zu erhalten'). Such passages, slight in themselves, certainly contribute to the character of the movement (cf. similar progressions in the B flat Fugue in *Das Wohltemperirte Clavier*, II, bb64–6 etc) as does the liquefying effect of the triple time itself. The result is that the chromatic semitones of bb8, 9, 25 and 31 extend or express the smoothness of the texture – without the shock effect of the chromatic lines (also often in parallel thirds) at the end of the previous chorale.

673　　Christe, aller Welt Trost (*Clavierübung III*)

Published 1739, no Autograph MS.

Two staves.

For TEXT and MELODY see BWV 669.

That the lesser Kyrie–Christe–Kyrie preludes are to be considered as a group is suggested by the 'progressive' time-signatures, the common cadences on E, and the unconventional fugal form; and it should be noted that BWV 673 and 674 lack separate headings. In addition to its E-phrygian tonality, the cantus firmus supplies much of the material: Ex. 183. Section *a* serves also as first countersubject (cf. that of BWV

Ex. 183

626); and the subject and countersubject create other motifs that are of importance in the texture – *b*, *c* and *d*. The motif *e*, from which so much is developed, may be regarded as deriving from (or at least resembling the shape of) passages in the cantus firmus – Ex. 184(i).

Ex. 184

But the composer does not make many obvious references to the cantus firmus. For example, the final 'eleison' phrase – Ex. 184(ii) – could without trouble have served as a more direct inspiration for the closing bars. Nor does the composer allow motivic development to govern the movement, as in BWV 672: these thirty bars have an original, almost capricious shape quite different from the previous prelude, despite their similar repertory of keys.

Nevertheless, there are many thematic allusions. The irregular bass entry in bb2–3 is related to one motif – Ex. 185 – and most of the other

Ex. 185

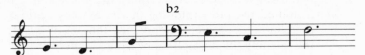

bass phrases have motivic links (e.g. the rising fourths in b23 reflect those in the subject and countersubject). While the spacing of the hands in BWV 673 results in a less consistent texture than in BWV 672, much is again dependent on parallel thirds and sixths. The entries are highly original, on all degrees of the scale but G, in stretto, *canon cum pausa* (bb11–13)* and *canon sine pausa* (bb20–1, 24–5). The lilt given the piece in particular by motif *d* is matched by the semiquaver figure; both the lilt and the semiquaver figure are second nature in $^6/_8$ time, and they justify a tempo at which the quaver in BWV 672 will equal the quaver in BWV 673. As with the two Kyrie fughettas, close inspection will often reveal thematic allusion, or rather will show that the theme has moulded the lines perhaps coloured by motif *e* (e.g. Ex. 186).

Ex. 186

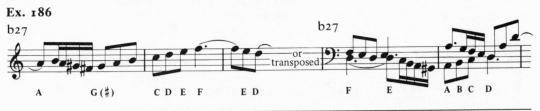

674   Kyrie, Gott heiliger Geist (*Clavierübung III*)

Published 1739, no Autograph MS.

Two staves.

For TEXT and MELODY, see BWV 669; for a note on the grouping of BWV 672–674, see under BWV 673.

In addition to its E-phrygian tonality, the cantus firmus supplies material: Ex. 187. The composer's intention seems again to have been

Ex. 187

---

* The f′/b′ stretto in alto/soprano bb18–19 is disguised in both *BG* and *NBA* editions by the direction of the quaver-tails.

to develop his own themes and motifs from the cantus firmus, working not towards mere intricacy (though most of the phrases of the plainsong melodies can be traced in BWV 672, 673 and 674) but towards a unified texture exploiting motifs as they naturally develop. It is in the character of such composition that motif *a* is developed more than the opening theme itself, appearing as it does in almost every bar, often in thirds and sixths, and once in combination with the opening (b17) – though never *inversus*.

A complement to the other lesser Kyrie preludes, BWV 674 has a comparable smoothness and originality of detail, compact and un-stereotyped. Three details show possible intentions of the composer: (*a*) the turning quaver lines may suggest the final 'eleison' phrase of the plainsong (though there is no clear quotation); (*b*) the quaver motion is constant, perhaps suggesting that BWV 672 ♪ = BWV 674 ♪· and thus that the fughettas are grouped *in proportione* ($^3/_4$ ♪· = $^6/_8$ ♪· = $^9/_8$ ♪· ♪·); and (*c*) the final cadence A/E resembles that of BWV 669 C/G. The last is probable, since the following pattern then emerges:

BWV 669 C/G – BWV 674 A/E
BWV 670 F/G* – BWV 673 D/E
BWV 671 A♭/G – BWV 672 F/E

675

Allein Gott in der Höh' sey Ehr' (*Clavierübung III*)

Published 1739, no Autograph MS.

Headed 'à 3', 'Canto fermo in alto'; two staves.

For TEXT and MELODY see BWV 662.

The three-part BWV 675 is a two-part invention between whose lines – lines characterized by many mobile figures of wide compass and spacing – is introduced the cantus firmus, which is by contrast rhythmically plain and melodically smooth with almost entirely stepwise motion. The 'invention' subject not only contains several important motifs of its own but refers to both the first and fifth lines of the cantus firmus (bb5–9, 26–30): † Ex. 188. The composer makes more of the cantus-firmus upbeat than was customary, and it could be that the prominent opening three notes (FGA) are a reference to the major third formed by the keys of the Trinity trios of *Clavierübung III*. It is unusual too that the paraphrase theme incorporates exactly the same notes and the same length of phrase as the following cantus-firmus line (compare soprano bb1–5 with alto bb5–9). Although sometimes

---

* I.e. as in bb59–60. The cadence of the final bar not only seems out of line with BWV 669 and 671 but unlike them disagrees with the harmonization BWV 371.

† The bar-numbering here (as in *NBA*) excludes the repeat: the first-time bars 19^1–20^1 lead back to b3, and on the repeat b18 leads on to 19^2–20^2–21^2 etc; the movement ends on b48.

Ex. 188

criticized unfavourably as 'not quite worthy' of its surroundings (Keller 1948 p202), the piece clearly conforms to some of the more obvious aims of *Clavierübung III*, particularly its notational references (here to the Trinity) and its ingenious composition of motifs. Thus the motifs are constantly adapted to different harmonic and melodic contexts: e.g., the accent in motif *d* is shifted in bb23–4 (bass), b37 (soprano) and perhaps elsewhere; *d* can be combined with *b* (b18); and the counter-subject motifs *e* and *f* – Ex. 189 – prove particularly versatile, com-

Ex. 189

bining with others (*f* against *d* in b14), perhaps inverted (*f* in b36) or extended (*e* in b15), and running into another motif (*e* runs into a version of *d* in the bass of bb15–16). With three motifs around a cantus-firmus alto, b14 is typical of *Clavierübung III* technique: Ex. 190. Though at times fugal and imitative, the piece is conceived more

Ex. 190

as a play of adaptable motifs, running at times into apparently simple phrases (particularly at the end of each section – a further characteristic of such late works), and throughout highly contrasted with the previous chorale BWV 674, which is based on a single motif.

676

Allein Gott in der Höh' sey Ehr' (*Clavierübung III*)

Published 1739, no Autograph MS; copy by J. N. Mempell (Lpz MB MS 7).

Headed 'a 2 Clav. et Pedal'; three staves.

For TEXT and MELODY see BWV 662.

The movement is a strict trio with dominant answers (as in the Sonatas), incorporating the chorale melody as cantus firmus and paraphrases derived from it: Ex. 191. As the smaller notes in the

Ex. 191

example show, the paraphrase form can also combine canonically with the cantus-firmus form (cf. bb12ff). Integration of the chorale melody is achieved in BWV 676 not only in form (more completely than in other trio settings of the chorale, e.g. BWV 664) but also in the harmony. The melody thus pervades the texture: Ex. 192. Possible references

Ex. 192

to the melody within the trio lines can also be found from time to time, e.g. Ex. 193 (next page).

Despite its difficulty, BWV 676 is one of the more approachable of the *Clavierübung III* movements. Style and texture are reminiscent of the Sonatas; and such features as the figures and rhythms of bb7off

Ex. 193

or the cello-like pedal of bb18ff help towards producing a charm of the kind implied by the writer of the 1788 'Comparison between Handel and Bach' when he thought the Sonatas 'so galant gesetzt... dass sie jetzt noch sehr gut klingen' ('set in such *galant* style that they still sound very well today', *Dok* III p441). Nevertheless, such details as the logical but unconventional cadence in b99 are unknown in the Sonatas, as too is the cantus-firmus species of ritornello form:

bb1–33 trio exposition, lh answering rh; cantus firmus b12 lh
bb33–66 trio exposition repeated but inverted; cantus firmus b45 rh
bb66–78 trio episode modulating but returning to G major for –
bb78–92 next two lines of cantus firmus in canon between pedal and each hand in turn, the other hand in each case being derived from the trio theme (concerning the canon at this point, see BWV 663)
bb92–9 trio episode
bb100– final line of cantus firmus lh (avoiding emphatic tonic) answered
end by rh, followed by short episode, pedal cantus firmus (b114) and rh cantus firmus (b118); then final tonic pedal point

The last section raises most acutely the problem of composing a trio with cantus firmus, since Bach seems to have found it difficult to give the close the sense of finality produced by the ritornello or round shape characteristic of trios in general. This finality eludes BWV 676, despite (*a*) the repeat of the final line of the cantus firmus (heard four times between b99 and the end), (*b*) the return of bb30ff at 119ff, and (*c*) the return of the trio theme, like a coda, in bb123ff. On the other hand, it is to the movement's advantage that the paraphrase theme itself is open to trio-like treatment in such continuous lines – so fluid as to contain a rarely noticed *inversus* of itself (bb30–3 soprano, 63–6 and 119–22 alto).

676a   Allein Gott in der Höh' sey Ehr'

No Autograph MS; not in *NBA*. *BG* 40 uses two sources only: Schelble–Gleichauf (late source, containing many spurious and doubtful works) and Peters VI p2 (*BG* 40 p.lvi; *NBA* IV/2 *KB* pp55–6; *NBA* IV/4 *KB* pp33–4).

Though still often regarded as 'an early Weimar work' serving as the kernel from which BWV 676 was developed, BWV 676a is unlikely to be authentic. The ornaments in bb10, 33 and 40 are not those used elsewhere by J. S. Bach (*NBA* IV/4 *KB* p34), and certain features suggest an ungifted composer's work (reiterated G in the pedal in bb1, 3, 4, 6, 7, 9, 13 etc). The relationship to BWV 676 is as follows:

BWV 676a:	BWV 676:
b1	b1 or 33
bb3–6	bb45–8
bb9–13	bb62–6
bb27–31	bb78–82
bb33–7	bb87–91
bb39–47	bb118–26

The bars between these sections of BWV 676a, and the beginnings and endings of these sections, use material resembling that in BWV 676. Perhaps this piece was extracted from BWV 676 to provide a simpler prelude with right-hand cantus firmus. Although some features show a command of idiom (e.g. the repeat of line 2 in bb39ff), others suggest a patching-up operation (e.g. the recurring d♯' of bb36–9).

---

677   Allein Gott in der Höh' sei Ehr' (*Clavierübung III*)

Published 1739, no Autograph MS.

Headed 'Fughetta super Allein Gott in der Höh' sei Ehr'', 'manualiter'; two staves.

For TEXT and MELODY see BWV 662.

Ex. 194

The work is not a simple fughetta; in the course of twenty bars, it displays several original and complex features:

bb1–7   exposition of subject based (as perhaps is its countersubject) on the first line of the cantus firmus (Ex. 194), which is answered in stretto, and with a second quasi-answer in bb5–6. Countersubject motif *a* developed *rectus* and *inversus* (present in 15 bars of the 20) bb7–16 a second exposition, also beginning and ending in the tonic, based on the first notes of the second line of the cantus firmus (Ex. 195) and developing motif *a* from the first exposition

bb16–20 combination of themes (bb17–18); reference to motif *a*

Ex. 195

Most of the semiquaver phrases (i.e. both countersubjects) can be traced to motif *a*, and again the chorale melody imbues the entire texture. Subject and treatment are surprisingly similar to the opening bars of the C major Fugue BWV 547.

To the player, an important characteristic of the movement is the implied contrast between smooth semiquavers and detached quavers, including those moments when either one is extended (quavers bb6–7, semiquavers bb15–16). The scale figures in bb15–16 and the rising close may, like the runs in BWV 675 and the closing bars of BWV 676, represent the arrival or 'withdrawal of the heavenly host' singing 'Gloria in excelsis Deo' (Terry 1921 p98). On the other hand, touches of chromaticism (b18 – see also bb30–1 of BWV 675) are there to create musical tension before tonics, not for figurative purposes. It is not difficult to see in the several thirds of the theme, as in the emphases on mediant harmonies and entries, a reference to the Trinity hymn. But it should not be missed that the paraphrase theme refers to the melody much less regularly on its main beats than that of BWV 717, based on the same melody; a comparison of the two shows the complexity of *Clavierübung III* paraphrases.

---

678 Diess sind die heil'gen zehn Gebot' (*Clavierübung III*)

Published 1739, no Autograph MS.

Headed 'a 2 Clav. et Ped.', 'Canto fermo in Canone'; three staves.

For TEXT and MELODY (with a note on number symbolism) see BWV 635.

The first of the Ten Commandments settings has received much attention over the last two centuries, reflecting the interests of the commentator concerned. In 1757, Padre Martini quoted the opening as an example of imitation at the octave (*Dok* III p117), although the opening three bars no doubt reminded Italian organists more of organ pastorals. In *c*1776, Kirnberger took the piece to be characteristic of its G-mixolydian mode (*Dok* III p301), in that the dominant is minor (e.g. b40) and the final cadence cannot be perfect. More recent authors have been uncertain of the purpose or character of the movement. Schweitzer saw it as representing order (the canon) and disorder (the upper voices wandering 'without rhythm, without plan'), a representation which he concluded was unsuitable for musical treatment (Schweitzer 1905 p346). Dietrich saw a pre-Fall quietness about the opening, passing through much sinful deviousness before the final salvation at the end; and Schering counted the five phrases of the melody as producing the key number ten when duplicated canonically (Keller 1948 p203). That there are strictly six and not five phrases in the cantus firmus (as in BWV 298 – see Ex. 91 above) endangers Schering's point but allows Dietrich to scan the movement as a whole and to see ten basic sections in it (cantus-firmus phrases plus episodes). One could further claim that number allegory is supported by the 60 bars of the piece (6×10). More objectively, Eickhoff sees the ritornello shape of the movement as highly continuous, with constantly developing material between (or against) lines of the cantus firmus; in this manner, BWV 678 'represents an extreme in the direction of flexible ritornello treatment' (Eickhoff 1967). Naturally, the allegory or pun that Law = Canon has been pointed out; also that canonic imitation of voices implies that the lawgiver of the New Testament (Jesus Christ) imitates the lawgiver of the Old (Moses). This is implied in the text (see also Schmitz 1950 p73) and supports the idea of Christ as the fulfiller of the Law (Leudtke 1918 p83). It is in the nature of *Clavierübung III* in particular to attract such speculation, and much of it accords with other facets of the composer's work. Thus the larger preludes on the Commandments (BWV 678), Lord's Prayer (BWV 682) and Confession (BWV 686) are linked by their canonic devices, as they are by their implications for a Christian.

However, the two incontrovertible elements of the composition are that a canonic cantus firmus is employed, and that the upper voices and bass exploit a long series of musical motifs. The *Orgelbüchlein* setting (BWV 635) already showed that the melody was open to canonic–imitative treatment, while the opening chorus of Cantata 77 gave it in textless quasi-diminished canon between trumpet and continuo, thus underlining the importance of the Commandments proclaimed by the chorus in the Summary of the Law (Terry 1917 p288). The motifs themselves – *a–k* in Ex. 196 below – are very varied, and it is scarcely an exaggeration to see the piece from beginning to end as a kind of fantasia on them, either *rectus* or *inversus*:

motif *a*   see bb1, 15, 21, 22, 23, 37, 38
motif *b*   see bb1, 2, 3, 6, 7, 12, 13, 17, 18, 25, 29, 30, 31, 34, 35, 44, 45, 49, 53, 54, 56, 59
motif *c*   see bb2, 3, 4, 8, 9, 11, 30, 31, 40, 51, 52, 58
motif *d*   see bb5, 6, 7, 9, 11, 12, 14, 16, 17, 18, 21, 22, 26, 34, 35, 43, 44, 48, 49, 50, 53, 55, 59, 60

motif *e* see bb6, 7, 10, 17, 18, 22, 23, 25, 27, 35, 36, 37, 38, 44, 45, 54, 56, 57

motif *f* see bb13, 15, 19, 20, 24, 27, 28, 32, 33, 34?, 37, 38, 39, 46, 47, 48, 51, 52

motif *g* see bb4, 7–11, 18, 35, 36, 40, 41, 42, 51–7, 59

motif *h* see bb5, 10, 16, 25, 36, 43, 55, 56, 57

motif *i* see bb5, 16, 27?, 36, 38, 43, 45, 47, 48, 58, 59

motif *j* see bb6, 7, 11, 12, 17, 20, 21?, 22, 23, 26, 32–4, 44, 49, 50

motif *k* see bb7, 9, 14, 18, 23

Ex. 196

The motifs are naturally not always clearcut; nor does the composer play idly with them – e.g., he could easily have had motif *h* (one or more times) in the last bar, but instead he augments it to two dotted minims.

The two upper voices are like obbligato instruments in a cantata movement; they are not based on the chorale melody and lead to apparently independent music. However, it should be noticed that the opening pedal point is a counterpart of the repeated Gs (and their harmonies) of the following fughetta on 'Diess sind' (BWV 679); and motif *g* also reappears in the fughetta subject. Furthermore, the cantus firmus 'governs' the first four bars of BWV 678 in that it could be played against them – a kind of unspoken allusion. The next two lines of the cantus firmus also could be anticipated in this rather unusual way, though not so convincingly (bb16–19).

The final cantus-firmus phrase of BWV 678 seems to express the 'Kyrie eleison' of the chorale text by the chromatic fall in the upper canonic voice at the end (see a note under BWV 671 concerning 'eleison' codas). The effect is less striking than that in BWV 671 but more so than that at the end of (e.g.) 'Allein Gott' BWV 663, which is simply a harmonic chromaticism. The final phrase of BWV 678, like the chromatic motifs of bb5, 11, 16, 43 and 48, does emphasize the 'purity' of the cantus firmus, particularly when it falls towards the G minor/B flat major of bb51ff. Reaching a relatively remote key at this distance from the end conforms to the plan of other Bach works and is occasioned here by the use of a B♭ in the cantus firmus.* The five-part treatment itself

* The B♭ is rare in the sources of the hymn but is present in BWV 298.

is perhaps 'after the model' of de Grigny (Klotz 1969a), in that the four manual parts are paired off with a distinct colour for each hand (?); see also BWV 682. The conception of *deux dessus* and *deux tailles* (two treble, two alto parts) above a bass is also found in BWV 633/634.

---

679   Diess sind die heil'gen zehn Gebot' (*Clavierübung III*)

Published 1739, no Autograph MS.

Headed 'Fugetta super Diess sind die heil'gen zehn Gebot'', 'manualiter'; two staves.

For TEXT and MELODY (with a note on number symbolism) see BWV 635.

The theme of the fughetta or fugue is derived as shown in Ex. 197. Important motifs follow the part of the subject based on the chorale

Ex. 197

melody, unlike the other *Clavierübung III* fughettas with their stretto' answers; the phrase GABC (= motif *b inversus*) also refers to lines 2 and 4 of the melody (cf. Ex. 91 above).

The movement shows certain resemblances to the previous setting (BWV 678), notably (*a*) the G-mixolydian tonality; (*b*) the pedal point or repeated Gs at the opening; (*c*) the reference to the number ten (ten* entries of the fugue subject, four of them *inversus*); and (*d*) such minor details as the final diminished seventh and plagal cadence. Most striking is a similar sense of motif development: BWV 679 extends and inverts its motifs, particularly the two cells of motif *a* and the countersubject rhythm ♩ ♪. The development of *a* occupies nearly half the composition (bb18–31), obviating the need for more than ten main entries, extending the fughetta to a length that goes beyond chorale-fughetta convention (e.g. BWV 702), mirroring the subject's sequential answers in the previous section, effectively dividing both the movement as a whole and each of its bars into two, and creating a restless three-part invention before the final entries in octave canon. The dissonances arising through the accented passing notes of motif *a* contrast with the triads of the main subject. A very original unity is achieved through the repetitive treatment of the $^{12}/_8$ (cf. the changing figuration and varied texture in BWV 712). The gigue-like liveliness of the movement may well be explained as a reference to Luther's words,

---

* The ten entries draw upon the same kind of 'symbolism' as the eleven vocal entries 'Herr, bin ich's?' ('Lord, is it I?') in the disciples' chorus of the *St Matthew Passion*.

at the close of the Commandments in the Lesser Catechism, that 'we should...cheerfully do what he has commanded' (Leaver 1975) – a more likely explanation, in view of the Lutheran orthodoxy of *Clavier-übung III* as a whole, than that the composer was referring to the pilgrim song *In Gottes Namen fahren wir* (to the same melody: cf. BWV 635), with its text 'in God's name...we go cheerfully' (Steglich 1962 p32). The psalms too speak of 'delight...in thy statutes' (Ps. 119, v. 16) and of rejoicing in the Law (Ps. 19, vv. 7–11; Ps. 119, vv. 14, 54 etc).

---

680 Wir glauben all' an einen Gott (*Clavierübung III*)

Published 1739, no Autograph MS.

Headed 'In Organo pleno con Pedale'; two staves.

The TEXT is Luther's version of the Nicene Creed, published Wittenberg 1524. It is placed in the hymnbooks as if it were a Trinity hymn; as well as being sung after the Gospel on each Sunday by the whole congregation (1526 *Messe*), the chorale was sung after the sermon during the Reformation periods and was later associated in particular with funerals.

Wir glauben all' an einen Gott,	We all believe in one God,
Schöpfer Himmels und der Erden,	maker of Heaven and Earth,
der sich zum Vater geben hat,	who gave himself to be the Father
dass wir seine Kinder werden.	that we might be his children.
Er will uns allzeit ernähren,	He will always feed us,
Leib und Seel auch wohl bewahren,	and will keep us safe in body and soul;
allem Unfall will er wehren,	he will ward off all misfortune;
kein Leid soll uns widerfahren.	no harm shall befall us.
Er sorget für uns, hüt und	He cares for us, guards and watches
wacht,	over us;
es steht alles in seiner Macht.	everything stands in his power.

Verse 2 concerns chiefly 'Jesus Christ, seinen Sohn', v3 'den Heilgen Geist'.

The MELODY, based on the *Credo cardinale* (a free paraphrase of Credo IV in the *Liber usualis*), was popular during the fifteenth century and was published with the text in 1524; Ex. 198. BWV 437 is a

Ex. 198

BWV 437

BWV 680

harmonization of the complete melody, used also in BWV 681 and 765. It is uncertain whether the 'Wir glauben all' an einen Gott' listed in the *Orgelbüchlein* refers to this chorale or to the different text and melody used in BWV 740.

As Ex. 199 shows, the fugue theme is based on the first line of the chorale, its countersubject on the second, its answer perhaps on the

Ex. 199

third. Thus, although BWV 680 is the only one of the larger chorales in *Clavierübung III* that has no through cantus firmus, the chorale melody (which includes repeats of lines 1 and 2) pervades the whole. Also such a fugue has further connotations: it gives an impression of strength and of many voices entering to sing 'Wir glauben...', since the subject uses the opening melisma on 'Wir'. It also includes a strong quasi-ostinato motif in the pedal alluding to 'Firm faith in God' or even to God the creator and giver of life (Leaver 1975). Moreover, the chorale melody would have been impracticably long if set as a cantus firmus – longer than any other melody in *Clavierübung III* – and was rarely set whole in a single movement (there is an example by J. G. Walther). But the chorale in general also seems to pervade the fugue in that the original melody contained both scale-like figures and striding or leaping phrases, the whole against a modified dorian-mode background. Thus although no direct reference is certain, there are decided similarities in outline between the chorale melody and the figuration in the fugue (Ex. 200). These examples – and there are others – are

Ex. 200

not meant to show that the fugue is constrained to use derived motifs foreign to its own melodic idiom but to suggest that, not for the first time in *Clavierübung III*, the organ setting is suffused with its chorale melody.

Quite apart from the paraphrasing technique, the chorale melody itself is difficult to recognize in the fugue subject because the third note is sharpened (as the corresponding note in b1 of BWV 681 is not). The simplest reference to the chorale melody in the whole piece is the second lines heard in the tenor near the end: Ex. 201. The second

Ex. 201

line in the melody is also similar to the last, which has led some commentators to see the tenor phrase in b92 as a reference to the last line.

The general style of the piece seems to show specifically Italian influences. A striding ostinato bass line without pauses (but suggesting more conventional harmonies than BWV 680) accompanies the opening Credo section added by Bach to G. B. Bassani's Mass in F (Wolff 1968 pp202–3) – Ex. 202 – and the possible influence of Frescobaldi has

Ex. 202

Bassani, Mass in F: Credo added by J. S. Bach

already been cited (see p. 186 above). No such examples, however, assimilate the alternate-foot pedal idiom so well as the bass of BWV 680. In general, the idea of a thrusting bass line is common in Bach (Credo and Confiteor from the B minor Mass), although an independent bass line as such below fugal upper parts is more characteristic of Italian vocal and instrumental music (cf. the trio setting BWV 664 b65, etc). The passing of the ostinato phrase into the left hand, for instance, leads to several bars of good but traditional counterpoint (bb76–82), and it is possible that the general suspension style is to be seen as Italianate – highly developed but quite distinct from (e.g.) BWV 679. Moreover, the semiquaver groups throughout BWV 680 show an unusual likeness to those of the *stile antico* repertory of figures (see under BWV 670), almost as if the piece were providing a catalogue of them. Thus all the figures in Ex. 203(i) are used – many of them constantly – in

Ex. 203

(i)

* = retrograde   † = *inversus*

the course of the piece, as a few sample passages show (ii–iii). But most of the semiquaver groups are used imaginatively, with much less repetition than those of (e.g) BWV 684.

Nevertheless, the originality of the whole must not be underestimated. For example, each ostinato passage ends with a two-bar transition in invertible counterpoint (bb8–9, 19–20, 31–2, 44–5, 64–5) moving towards the new key; the structural coherence produced by this device is exceptional. Similarly, thematic reference is pervasive but elusive. Thus, the final tenor reference to the second (or last) line of the melody might be seen as a simplification of the syncopated countersubject to the pedal ostinato as it occurs (e.g.) in b40 (Ex. 204): both have a curiously singing quality that permeates the texture, and the cantus-

Ex. 204

b40

firmus reference in bb91ff (cf. Ex. 201) replaces the countersubject for the final pedal entry. Even the recurring chromatic line *x* (Ex. 204) is allusive, incorporating the falling chromatic fourth of the traditional *passus duriusculus*. Observations on the piece have often led to curious conjectures, such as that the fourteen entries of the subject relate to B+A+C+H (Chailley 1974 p254).

681

Wir glauben all' an einen Gott (*Clavierübung III*)

Published 1739, no Autograph MS

Headed 'Fugetta super Wir gläuben all an einen Gott', 'manualit:'; two staves.

For TEXT and MELODY see BWV 680.

The derivation of the fughetta theme is clearest at the second answer: Ex. 205. Although the key-signature has led Kirnberger and others to

Ex. 205

b3

E B A B   F♯ G   F♯

regard the work (or at least the melody) as being in the E-dorian mode (*Dok* III p302), the key is firmly E minor, complete with sharpened leading-note (and descending D♮C♮) in the tonal answers of bb1 and 5.

The first line of the chorale melody itself is suggested by the recurrent opening motif (e.g. alto b7); moreover, its second line can be heard through the penultimate phrase: Ex. 206.

Ex. 206

b11

A   G   F♯   E   D♯   E

Several misconceptions colour most references to this piece. BWV 681 is not so much a French Overture – such pieces are of quite a different shape – as a kind of fugue using French Overture rhythms for unusual effect. Nor do the left-hand runs or the final appoggiatura imply that it is harpsichord music, for again the composer is working on a pattern-making idea. The organ chorale formed by decorating the opening two lines of the melody with French rhythms serves as a complement to the Italian melodic *figurae* of the previous setting. Like BWV 681, BWV 680 is also a fugue and also uses the first two lines of the chorale melody, but obviously to as different effect as possible – long, fluent, Italianate. Luther's German Creed is thus glossed with French and Italian elements; the E minor setting BWV 681 is no more harpsichord music from this point of view than the D minor (dorian) setting BWV 680 is string music. It is this Italian/French contrast which suggested the French Overture elements, and not a wish to portray majesty, as is often suggested (e.g. Chailley 1974 p255).

---

682   Vater unser in Himmelreich (*Clavierübung III*)

Published 1739, no Autograph MS.

Headed 'à 2 Clav. et Pedal è Canto fermo in Canone'; three staves.

For TEXT and MELODY see BWV 636.

Perhaps the most complex of Bach's organ chorales from both a composer's and a performer's point of view, BWV 682 is a ritornello trio sonata incorporating difficult figures (detached triplets, legato snapped appoggiaturas) above a restless pedal part, through which the cantus firmus appears in slower values in an octave canon between the fourth and fifth voices. The chorale melody itself is paraphrased in the trio theme (Ex. 207). Triple metre is unusual with this cantus firmus; the rhythms are altered here and there, not always for an obvious reason (e.g., the lengthening of the cantus-firmus notes in bb67–8/69–70 is unnecessary harmonically). The canon may allude to the Ten Command-

Ex. 207

cf. Böhm, 'Vater unser'

ments or the Law, the keeping of which Luther (in his commentary on the Lord's Prayer) sees as an aim of constant prayer (Leaver 1975).

The musical language of BWV 682 is as intricate as its form, which Schweitzer curiously described as 'sans architecture aucune' (Schweitzer 1905 p353). Despite Kirnberger (*Dok* III p302) and others, the tonality is E minor rather than the E-dorian implied by the key-signature and the melody itself; its being in the same 'key' as the previous movement suggests a further visual pattern:

BWV 680 (Greater) D-dorian
BWV 681 (Lesser) E-dorian
BWV 682 (Greater) E-dorian
BWV 683 (Lesser) D-dorian

As shown in Ex. 207, the chorale melody is treated in a coloratura style known to other composers connected with Bach (Dietrich 1929 p73). But the technical details of the piece have been insufficiently studied in comparison to its putative symbolisms. On the practical side, few commentators would now argue that the piece requires two players and four manuals, as was once suggested by Keller (1948 p206), who also believed that the snapped appoggiaturas must be played as either ♪♪ or ♪♪ . On the symbolic side, it is still possible to see the first three bars as a picture of 'unsaved man', the appoggiaturas as 'chains of sighs', the bass and its 'uncanny monotony' as the 'foundation of this world', the whole as a state of sin from a catalogue of whose evils the Lord's Prayer is a protection (Weismann 1949–50). It could be that the composer is inviting such interpretations. Certainly the motifs – unlike those of the following chorale – convey a sense of strained effort; and a canonic cantus firmus is associated with the idea of Law or *imitatio*. But more specific questions – such as whether the chromatic lines or the short appoggiaturas are to be seen as rhetorical figures – can be understood only by close attention to the motifs themselves.

A list of motifs on the lines of those indexed for the Ten Commandments prelude (see BWV 678) is also possible for this piece; thus the two settings are closely related in concept and detail. However, the greater length of BWV 682 makes a few pointers perhaps more useful:

(i) The upper parts of the 'trio sonata' are founded on line 1 of the melody (bb 1 and 5, 19 and 23, 56 and 60) and include the motifs shown in Ex. 208 as part of their fugal codetta (motif *a*), countersubject (*b*) and continuation (*c*). All three motifs are curiously characteristic of *galant* flute music. The triplet figure *c* is capable of more variety than *a*. As J. F. Agricola made clear in a review of Löhlein's *Clavier-*

Ex. 208

Schule (1769: *Dok* III p206), J. S. Bach taught players to distinguish between dotted figures and triplets, bringing them together only 'bey der äussersten Geschwindigkeit' ('when the music is extremely fast'). The whole language of the upper parts suggests specific allusion to chamber trios.

(ii) The main 'trio-sonata' ritornello theme preserves the simple repeated note ('Vater') of the cantus firmus, which otherwise contains mostly longer notes than the other parts (in this respect BWV 682 is closer to BWV 684 than to 686). The 'trio-sonata' lines are very homogeneous, constantly developing their few motifs before, during and after the cantus-firmus lines. Although the opening ritornello section is long and rich in thematic detail, it does not recur in a literal repetition; rather, each of the six later ritornello sections introduces motifs from it in order, one at a time. Through the motivic lines specific musical styles are also hinted at, in particular the *Seufzermelodik* or *galant* chromatic sequences at bb33ff and 83ff. A further element is the appoggiatura rhythm itself, recently traced as a device found in the composer's works of the early 1730s – which may or may not be a hint as to when BWV 682 was composed (Herz 1974 p96).

(iii) The continuo-like pedal incorporates important motifs (e.g. the pattern ♪♪♪ | ♪♪) but constantly adapts, taking in other motifs (e.g. inverted motif *b* at b10) and forming passages of invertible counterpoint (e.g. bb6 and 20). Clearer patterns emerge in the pedal during the episodes between cantus-firmus entries, particularly in the sequences following the predominant E minor of the first thirty bars. Only in the section bb30–7 does the left hand resemble the pedal.

(iv) With the syncopated cantus firmus in b54 is introduced a syncopated motif ♪♪♪ . Otherwise little new is introduced, though motif *c* is constantly adapted.

(v) Despite the dominant passage in the middle (line 4 of the chorale melody, from b52), the work repeatedly returns to the tonic, using the motifs with a variety of incomplete cadences to avoid over-strong tonics. The last nine bars are effectively a coda, the texture and chromatic sequence highly reminiscent of the Trio Sonatas, and the final cadence (with the longest notes of the movement) bearing more than a slight resemblance to the close of the E minor Fugue in Book II of *Das Wohltemperirte Clavier*. The coda uses familiar material, but now with a greater sense of finality: compare the bass of bb83–8, for example, with that of bb7–12, based on the same motif but with a less clear series of sequential perfect cadences.

For a note on the distribution of the five parts, see BWV 678.

683   Vater unser im Himmelreich (*Clavierübung III*)

Published 1739, no Autograph MS.

Headed 'alio modo', 'manualiter'; two staves.

For TEXT and MELODY see BWV 636.

As in several *Orgelbüchlein* chorales, the melody is heard as a melodic cantus firmus in the right hand, without interludes between lines, and accompanied by three parts exploiting several motifs. In this case one of the two motifs may be derived from a line of the chorale – Ex. 209.

Ex. 209

willst   das   Be - ten   von   uns   ha'n

The first motif is also inverted, while in its *rectus* form the semiquaver rest (*x*) is often filled by a note immediately above in another part. The second motif appears both with and without its tie. Clearly, the mood is supplicatory, conveyed by the isolated upbeat at the beginning (the similar repeated As that begin (e.g.) BWV 601 and 636 are not left without the accompanying motif); by the thinning of parts at the beginning of each line; by the text of line 4 invoked in the motif itself; and by the low and apparently subdued close. The resemblance that BWV 683 bears to one of the chorale conceptions found in the *Orgelbüchlein* is unmistakable, but the *manualiter* texture seems to give more freedom to the lines. Nevertheless it should not escape attention that the harmonies and general progressions of BWV 636 and BWV 683 are unexpectedly similar – and thus produce in both chorales a sense of lovely, melodious harmony.

683a   Vater unser im Himmelreich

No Autograph MS; later copies only: Schelble–Gleichauf, P 1109 (Hauser; date as P 285), P 285 (*c*1834–40), all containing many spurious and doubtful works (*NBA* IV/2 *KB* pp44, 49; *NBA* IV/4 *KB* pp33–4); Peters V (1846).

BWV 683a is commonly regarded as the 'original' 42-bar version of BWV 683 with extra bars forming prelude, postlude and interludes to the six chorale lines; otherwise the music is the same as BWV 683. Eickhoff

(1967) even sees it, with BWV 691a, as 'Bach's first attempt at using the concertato principle in the organ settings of chorale preludes'. However, the version is unlikely to be authentic. As in BWV 676a, the figuration suggests an ungifted composer's work, in such details as the running bass at the beginning with its prominent Ds, a poor use of semiquaver groups compared with those in BWV 683, etc. Moreover, Bach is not known ever to have shortened an earlier keyboard work when he came to revise it (Tessmer *NBA* IV/4 *KB* p34).

---

684   Christ, unser Herr, zum Jordan kam (*Clavierübung III*)

Published 1739, no Autograph MS.

Headed 'a 2 Clav. è Canto fermo in Pedal'; two staves.

The TEXT is Luther's Baptism hymn published in 1541, often associated in the hymnbooks of Dresden, Leipzig and Weimar with St John Baptist's Day (Stiller 1970 p323; Gojowy 1972).

Christ, unser Herr, zum Jordan kam	Christ, our Lord, came to the Jordan
nach seines Vaters Willen,	according to his father's will,
von Sanct Johann die Taufe nahm,	and was baptized by St John
sein Werk und Amt zu 'rfüllen,	to fulfil his work and office.
Da wollt er stiften uns ein Bad,	There he ordained for us water
zu waschen uns von Sünden,	to wash us of our sins,
ersäufen auch den bittern Tod	and to drown bitter death
durch sein selbst Blut und Wunden;	in his own blood and wounds;
es galt ein neues Leben.	new life was at stake.

The six other verses speak of the gospel narrative ('This is my beloved son, in whom I am well pleased'), of the sending-out of disciples, of damnation for the unbeliever, and of the symbolic nature of water, which

ist vor ihm ein rote Flut,	is for the faithful a red flood
von Christi Blut gefärbet.	coloured with Christ's blood.

The MELODY (by J. Walther?) was published in 1524 and was only later associated with this text (e.g. Wittenberg 1543): Ex. 210. The melody is used in BWV 684 and 685 and Cantatas 7 (Johannistag 1724)

Ex. 210

and 176 (to a different text), and harmonized in BWV 280; the chorale is also listed in the *Orgelbüchlein*.

Though similar in form and technique to other pieces in *Clavierübung III*, BWV 684 has a distinctive conception. The three manual parts together constitute the ritornello, returning between the lines of the chorale melody and constantly combining several motifs, often avoiding firm cadences; from the ritornello, motifs are taken and spun out as accompaniment to the cantus firmus. Below the imitative right-hand parts, the left runs with a semiquaver figure derived from the chorale melody. As in BWV 677 and 681, the melody can be found as if at two different phases lurking behind the semiquaver runs – a kind of double paraphrase (Ex. 211). It is also possible to find references in the other

Ex. 211

parts, e.g. the second line of the melody in the figuration of the right hand in both long and short phrases (Ex. 212). This is not necessarily

Ex. 212

to suggest that the composer was incorporating the cantus firmus as often as and however he could, but that the cantus firmus naturally pervades the idiom. Had the aim been simply to allude or cross-refer, more could have been done with (e.g.) the motif of a rising fourth common to lines 1, 2, 5 and 6 of the melody. Similarly, the top line of bb42ff* could have made a clear reference to the fifth cantus-firmus line, which it accompanies; and the sixth line (cf. pedal bb47ff) could have been made the more obvious source of the right-hand figures at bb50–1 (and the very similar eighth line at bb68–9). Resemblances between BWV 684 and 687 – such as the top part of the former at bb77–9 (with pedal point) and the final bars of the latter – are coincidences suggesting that they may have been composed within a short space of time.

Pace Kirnberger (*Dok* III p302), the tonality is C minor rather than the C-dorian implied by the key-signature; but the cantus firmus itself

---

* Bar-numbering includes repeat. Thus, the second-time bar after the repeated section = b40, the next cantus-firmus entry (minim g) = b47; the piece ends at b81.

is certainly modal. The upper parts are generally diatonic in their treatment of the As of the cantus firmus (bb9, 16), despite moments of insecurity elsewhere (bb15–16, 73–4). On the whole, the purpose of the 'modality' can be seen to be different from BWV 670, where it can result in greater ambiguity of key, and BWV 681, where it is only notational.

The non-stop semiquavers of the setting and the nature of the figures themselves are usually interpreted as representing the flowing Jordan, itself symbolized in the last verse of the text as Christ's blood (Spitta II p695). However, it is not clear how Schweitzer can see 'une eau courante' in the corresponding Cantata 7 (Schweitzer 1905 p345); and the semiquavers of BWV 684 as well suggest the 'sound of a rushing, mighty wind' felt at the presence of the Holy Spirit (Leaver 1975). Others have seen in the lines a connection with the C minor sections of the E flat Prelude BWV 552.i (Trumpff 1963 p470), which again may merely imply closeness in date of composition. Any such suggestions are plausible, since the only two other organ chorales of *Clavierübung III* with (almost) non-stop figures deploy them to very different effect and in a way less open to 'symbolic' interpretation: BWV 676, where the $^6/_8$ trio technique produces many varied figures, and BWV 688, where the three parts use sharply differentiated patterns (minims, quavers, semiquavers). Also open to speculation, however – in this setting of a melody whose text is itself peculiarly symbolic – is the opening motif of quavers: the contours suggest a typical cross figure (Ex. 213)

Ex. 213

signifying the beginning of the movement, as the sign of the cross signifies the beginning of the Order of Baptism itself. Moreover, some significance no doubt attaches to the fact that the cantus firmus of a 'Jesus chorale' appears in the tenor – i.e. a middle voice, for the second Person of the Trinity – as also in BWV 670 and 688.

685

Christ, unser Herr, zum Jordan kam (*Clavierübung III*)

Published 1739, no Autograph MS.

Headed 'alio modo', 'manualiter'; two staves.

For TEXT and MELODY see BWV 684.

The work is not a simple fughetta, and its twenty-seven bars are amongst the most closely reasoned of the collection. Both subject and countersubject are derived from the chorale melody (Ex. 214), and the form is as outlined below:

Ex. 214

A b1   subject and countersubject *rectus*

    b4   subject and countersubject *inversus*, with free middle part

    b8   episode derived from countersubject (which has been answered in bass bb8–9)

B b10   entry of subject (alto) and countersubject (bass, from b12), *rectus*, with episode material continuing against alto entry

   b14   entry of subject (soprano) and countersubject (bass, from b16), *inversus*, with alto derived

   b18   episode derived from countersubject heard intact in soprano

C b20   entry of subject (bass) and countersubject (soprano), *rectus*, with alto derived

   b23   entry of subject (alto) and countersubject (soprano, from b24), *inversus*, with bass derived

The combination of constant inversion, derived motifs and modal progressions (bb1–3, 15–16) results in a highly original composition with unusual harmonic progressions and with a degree of capriciousness about the number of parts, the repetition and the direction it takes that is not suggested by the formal plan above. The antique, Scheidt-like nature of the sequences in b9, however, should not pass unnoticed.

There have been many attempts to find hidden significances in the movement: the turning motif *a* gives the visual appearance of a wave (Schweitzer 1905 p345); the three *rectus/inversus* entries represent the threefold immersion in baptism (Keller 1948 p207); the three *rectus* entries, passing from soprano in turn to bass, suggest a reference to the Trinity (as do the cantus-firmus lines passing from soprano to bass in BWV 669–671), while the three *inversus* entries suggest a play on *inversus/immersus* (Leaver 1975); the two subjects correspond to the Old Adam and the New Man of Lutheran Baptism (Smend 1969 p166). Similar kinds of suggestion could be made for the falling scales of bb4, 5, 13, 18, 20, 21, 24, 25. If the triple-time version of the melody refers to Baptism as 'la manifestation par excellence de la Sainte Trinité' (Chailley 1974 p90), then the triple-time setting of the 'Vater unser' melody in BWV 682 should do so as well; in both cases, direct contrast between the longer and shorter settings is more likely to have been the composer's intention, particularly in view of the four-square *perpetuum mobile* of BWV 684. There is no evidence to support or disqualify these and other speculations about Baptism chorales whose text recounts an act which is itself symbolic.

686   Aus tieffer Noth schrey ich zu dir (*Clavierübung III*)

Published 1739, no autograph MS.

Headed 'a 6', 'in Organo pleno con Pedale doppio'; three staves.

The TEXT is Luther's free and highly personal translation of Ps. 130 (*De profundis clamavi*, used (as Ps. 129) in the Roman Burial Service and Office for the Dead), published Erfurt 1524.

Aus tiefer Noth schrei ich zu dir,	From deep distress have I cried to you,
Herr Gott, erhör mein Rufen.	Lord God, hear my call.
Dein gnädig Ohren kehr zu mir	Turn your gracious ears to me
und meiner Bitt sie öffen;	and open them to my entreaty;
denn so du willst das sehen an,	for if you will take notice of
was Sünd und Untecht ist getan,	what sin and wrong is done,
wer kann, Herr, vor dir bleiben?	who can stand before you, Lord?

v3

Darum auf Gott will hoffen ich,	On God therefore will I place my hope,
auf mein Verdienst nicht bauen;	and not on my deserts;
auf ihn mein Herz soll lassen sich	on him my heart should place its trust,
und seiner Güte trauen,	and on his goodness
die mir zusagt sein wertes Wort;	promised to me by his word;
das ist mein Trost und treuer Hort,	that is my comfort and true stronghold,
des will ich allzeit harren.	for which I will ever wait.

In Dresden, Leipzig and Weissenfels, the hymn was associated in particular with the 21st and 22nd Sundays after Trinity (Gojowy 1972), for which perhaps its striking change of mood in the course of the five verses was apt. By 1525 it was already both a Communion and Burial hymn (Stapel 1950 p176), to which a doxology was added after 1553. In Schein and Vopelius (1645, 1682) it was a Palm Sunday hymn.

The MELODY was published with the text in 1524; the version used in Cantata 38 (21st Sunday after Trinity 1724) preserves the phrygian character – Ex. 215 – and was further used in BWV 687. The chorale was listed in the *Orgelbüchlein*.

Ex. 215
BWV 38

'Aus tiefer Noth' is the grand climax of the so-called organ motet, one of the few six-part pieces in the organ repertory and the only known example by Bach, except for what a writer of 1788 called 'a fugue on the Royal Prussian theme for six voices *manualiter*' (Ricercar *a 6, Musical Offering*; see *Dok* III p439). The authenticity of the double pedal in Bruhns, Buxtehude, Reincken and others is less certain than modern editions suggest, though the older generation of Weckmann and Tunder certainly authorized it (Bruggaier 1959 pp61–2), giving the cantus firmus to the tenor pedal part and the bass to the lower pedal part, as in BWV 686. There are important examples in Scheidt's *Tabulatura nova* (1624), both of them motet movements and both for *organo pleno*.* BWV 686 is the composer's strictest motet piece, a 'model of *contrapunctus floridus*' (Wolff 1968 p69) complete with cantus firmus – as other settings in *Clavierübung III* are models of other techniques. As such, the movement has more parts, its polyphony is more continuous, there are more countersubjects, the expositions are less stereotyped and the final section more keyboard-like than the choral motet movements that the style seems at first to be imitating, such as the opening chorus of Cantata 38 'Aus tiefer Noth'. The cantata movement using the same cantus firmus introduces a chromatic countersubject that, in view of the opening words of the text, is to be understood as expressive – 'penitent chromaticism'. The *stile antico* of BWV 686 is purer, more 'objective'. However, the lively dactyl figures towards the end have been seen as expressing the 'comfort' and 'hope' of the latter part of the hymn – the so-called 'Festigkeits-rhythmus' or *motif de la joie* that might well 'symbolize the fact that after confession of sin comes assurance of forgiveness in absolution' (Leaver 1975), as described in Luther's Lesser Catechism, or 'express the cheerfulness of having survived' the 'standing before the Lord' announced in the last line of VI (Chailley 1974 p76). Whether or not the little rhythms do any such thing, it should not be ignored that – like the other line-by-line countersubjects (in particular that of the second section) – the dactyl figure is a conventional *figura* common enough in *contrapunctus floridus*.

Ex. 216

The form can be expressed as follows:

b1† line 1 (line 3 on repeat), fugally in all voices, including stretto at the octave (b3) and fifth (b9), the latter against augmented cantus firmus in the pedal; countersubjects include syncopated motif *a* (cf. BWV 687) and crotchet motif *b* – Ex. 216 above.

* Which in Germany must always have included at least 16' pedal, normally including reeds.
† The bar-numbering here (as in *NBA*) excludes the repeat; the first-time bar 22¹ leads back to b2, and on the repeat b21 leads on to 22²–23 etc; the movement ends on b54.

b13 line 2/4 (with opening minim or pair of crotchets) in all voices but the top; augmented c.f. in pedal; countersubject as *b* (now *inversus*); most parts moving by step

b22 line 5 in all voices but bottom manual part; augmented c.f. in pedal; countersubject Ex. 217 (i) and *inversus* with further motifs (syncopated and quaver figures)

b31 line 6 in three voices only; augmented c.f. in pedal; countersubject Ex. 217 (ii) (cf. b57ff* of BWV 687) leading to more broken texture

b41 line 7 in all voices, paraphrased (syncopated, partly inverted); augmented c.f. in pedal; countersubject Ex. 217(iii) leading to coda figuration

Ex. 217

(i) b22²   (ii) b32   (iii) b42

But no table shows the idiomatic details – for instance, that the lower pedal part systematically passes on to the countersubject after each subject; that certain rhythmic or melodic shapes suggest that the motifs originated in lines of the melody (see note on BWV 684); that the careful variety in the texture and spacing (increasingly varied in the second section) matches the attention paid to producing good lines (e.g. top parts from b44 to end). The massive opening, though justly admired from at least Marpurg's *Abhandlung von der Fuge* onwards (1753: see *Dok* III pp42–3), presents only one facet of a six-part texture that is constantly varied. That the six parts produce no one unchanging sonority is clear from the fact that the opening single notes gradually widen in texture until the chord of widest extent is reached exactly halfway through (b27 in a work of 54 bars if the repeat is not counted). The lines themselves are constantly allusive; a sample bar (b14) will contain a motet subject derived from a line of cantus firmus, the same in answer, and a countersubject which is like motif *b inversus* but also like the same cantus-firmus line in diminution.

687

Aus tieffer Noth schrey ich zu dir (*Clavierübung III*)

Published 1739, no Autograph MS.

Headed 'a 4 alio modo', 'manualiter'; two staves.

For TEXT and MELODY see BWV 686.

Like BWV 686 a motet organ chorale with augmented cantus firmus and with contrapuntal lines constantly referring to the subjects, BWV 687 has its own characteristic technique:

Line by line, the derived fugue subject is answered in inversion, the expositions of each line closely resembling the others; only in bb11–14

* I.e. the second-time bars after the repeat in BWV 687.

are the lower three parts without a fugue theme, *rectus* or *inversus* or both.

Each exposition begins in close stretto quavers, and each subject is answered at an interval allowing such stretto.

Cantus firmus in top part in notes two beats long (minims), fugue subjects in notes of half a beat (quavers).

Each line or section respectively works towards an increasing motion.

Organ motets with cantus firmus are uncommon for manuals alone; so is the contrapuntal strictness of a movement which, though not in full *stile antico*, is even denser than BWV 686. Melodic cross-references emerge naturally in such textures with such a theme – e.g. the first line *inversus* has much in common with the last line *rectus*. Textures remain sufficiently constant for the semiquaver figures (often beginning with a tied note) to give further continuity. Although the constant inversion may be seen as 'confession...answered by the assurance of forgiveness' (Leaver 1975), nothing in the style or technique suggests a 'mood' for the piece, and any similarity at its close to 'Vor deinen Thron' BWV 668 is of doubtful significance. More important is the comparison in technique with BWV 686: both pieces, similar but different, serve as models of the somewhat misnamed organ motet with cantus firmus. Not the least interesting feature of BWV 687 is its transposition of the phrygian melody to F♯ minor – an uncommon key for organ music, but more feasible than F-phrygian (with G♭ and occasionally C♭).

The modal character of BWV 687 is occasionally conspicuous, as at the two phrygian cadences bb14–15 and 28–9; the same phrygian colour is heard in J. K. F. Fischer's little eight-bar fughetta in *Ariadne musica* (1715), presumably known to Bach – Ex. 218 – which in turn resembles

Ex. 218   J. K. F. Fischer, *Ariadne musica*

certain conventional canzona fugue subjects of the previous century, such as were to be found as late as 1722 in Zipoli's *Collection of Toccates* (Ex. 219). While BWV 687 is founded on a chorale melody,

Ex. 219   Zipoli, *Toccata*

it also shows one of the possible developments of a theme widely known in various forms and contexts, none of which necessarily alludes to any other.

688 Jesus Christus, unser Heiland, der von uns den Zorn Gottes wandt (*Clavierübung III*)

Published 1739, no Autograph MS.

Headed 'a 2 Clav. e Canto fermo in Pedal'; two staves.

For TEXT and MELODY see BWV 665.

By *Clavierübung III* standards, BWV 688 has a straightforward conception:

> fugal through-composed monothematic trio on two manuals, with pedal cantus firmus in long notes (line by line)

But the technique of motif development is particularly mature:

(i) The main trio theme seems to refer to phrases in the melody and is no simple paraphrase – Ex. 220 (cf. Ex. 168). Its thematic reference is thus less clear than most of those in *Clavierübung III*.

Ex. 220

line 1 (end)

line 1 (opening)

(ii) The fugal codetta in the exposition (Ex. 221(i)) supplies much material *rectus* and *inversus* for the rest of the piece, as does the countersubject (bb7–9).

Ex. 221

(i) b6

(ii) b63   b47   b87   cf. b60

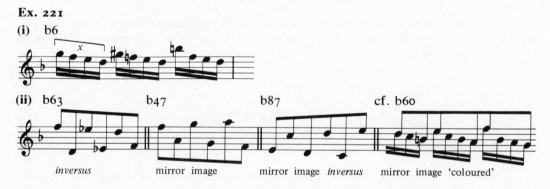

inversus   mirror image   mirror image *inversus*   mirror image 'coloured'

(iii) The main theme (bb1–4, etc) is treated in inversion (bb63ff, 112f lh, etc), mirror image or retrograde (bb47ff, 83ff), mirror-image inversion (bb51ff, 87ff, 104ff, etc), syncopation (bb2of), and syncopated mirror-image inversion (bb112ff rh) – Ex. 221(ii). One form of the theme may alternate with another, e.g. the *inversus* and the mirror *inversus* of bb59–62. Furthermore, motif *x* of Ex. 221(i) can create a 'coloured' version of the main figure, with the leaping intervals filled in (see soprano bb60, 62, 72). In one form or another, the main motif appears some seventy-two or seventy-three times.

(iv) Other, smaller motifs are often inverted (end b27, end b28) or are combined in random ways (e.g. countersubject with the main trio motif in mirror image in b47; codetta motif *x* with the same in b83).

New motifs appear when the main theme is temporarily absent, and the non-stop semiquaver motion is built up from derivatives of both countersubject and codetta, in alternation and in various combinations. On the whole, the movement works gradually towards greater use of scale figures. The coda is unusual for such a ritornello movement, with a pedal point drawn from the last note of the cantus firmus (cf. BWV 684) followed by two ritornello parts to close the piece (cf. BWV 675); ending without pedal is unusual and heightens the dissonant effect of the two upper parts. The final syncopations probably serve as a 'written-out rallentando'. Clearly, motivic inventiveness and combination are the musical aim of the piece, and it could be thought that the composer has deliberately avoided both simple ritornello principles and standard kinds of invertible counterpoint.

How far this treatment can be regarded as relevant to the text or function of the hymn is unknown and has led to much conjecture. Spitta hears in it the 'life-strengthening beliefs' of v5 (Spitta II p694), while others have seen the leaping subject as picturing the separation and coming together of God and Man (Dietrich 1929), or the 'lively exertions' implied in v6 (Steglich 1935 p123), or the 'treading of the winepress' (Isaiah lxiii, 2–3) as a symbol of victory over the cross, whose motif is heard in the first four notes (Leaver 1975) – Ex. 222.

Ex. 222

The brilliant nature of all the motifs has also suggested to some that they picture 'the anger of the Father' which was 'deflected by Jesus' in the institution of Communion (Chailley 1974 p163); but the coda is difficult to interpret in any such way. Despite a certain resemblance of both theme and countersubject to those of the last movement of the E flat Trio BWV 525, no great parallels can be drawn, nor between this organ chorale and those cantata arias in which a cantus firmus is sung between two instrumental lines. Motivic inventiveness may well be not only the nature of the piece but also its purpose, the whole working towards unusual fluid continuity despite the one-bar phrases. Nevertheless, the originality of detail – the one-bar phrases, the inversions, the constant appearance of the subject – has led to fanciful interpretations that at least serve to emphasize that originality (Krause 1965; also H. Reichenbach, *MuK* 1968 pp238ff). Naturally, the number 72 (the number of times the main motif appears) can be found to have Trinity associations ($72 = 1 \times 2^3 \times 3^2$), while the wedge-shaped theme and its inversion (⟩⟨) serve as emblem or monogram for iota–chi, J C, Jesus Christus (Krause 1965): ⟩⟨ . Such interpretation may prevent one hearing in the running semiquavers the running wine-blood of the Eucharist (Kloppers 1966 p41ff), or it may not; such a movement offers to every period, fashion or approach some scope for conjecture.

689

Jesus Christus, unser Heiland (*Clavierübung III*)

Published 1739, no Autograph MS.

Headed 'Fuga super Jesus Christus, unser Heyland', 'a 4 manualiter'; two staves.

For TEXT and MELODY see BWV 665.

The melody supplies the theme for a fugue of greater length and with clearer entries than the previous fughettas of the collection (Ex. 223).

Ex. 223

F   C   C   B♮   C   F   A♭   A♭   A♭   G   F

The sharpened fourth is as found in Vopelius's hymnbook (Leipzig 1682) and helps to transform the modal melody (e.g. as it appears in BWV 688) into a diatonic fugue theme. The countersubject provides much of the quaver material throughout the fugue (Ex. 224), including

Ex. 224

its *inversus* in b19 etc. While a sustained fugue form may well have been suitable for the organ music played before and during Communion, the musical purpose of the piece appears to be to exploit the imitation or stretto of material which in this case (unlike the previous setting) is the chorale melody itself. As in BWV 680 and elsewhere, the first answer is itself a stretto; this sets the pattern for the strettos of the movement, which then occur at varying intervals of time:

bb1–2   middle voices: after six beats (beginning on a down-beat)
b10   upper voices: after one beat
b16   middle voices: after two beats
bb23–4   lower voices: after four beats
bb36–7   upper voices: after five beats
bb37–8   soprano and tenor: after six beats (beginning on an up-beat)
b57   middle voices in a stretto of augmentation: simultaneous

Thus the fugue contains strettos at no fewer than six different distances; the strettos of the (contemporary?) B flat minor Fugue in Book II of *Das Wohltemperirte Clavier* exploit different versions and harmonies in much the same way that BWV 689 exploits different distances. It is particularly convenient for an organ chorale that the augmented stretto in b57 brings in the melody as a kind of rounding-off cantus firmus *en taille*, closing the work except for a deceptively simple coda derived (as in BWV 686) from the counter-motifs. It is notable too that the augmented stretto appears shortly after an imitative episode has used previous material (compare bb30–3 and bb53–4), contracting it and producing a sequence reminiscent of Pachelbel.

Further imitation and strettos concern lesser figures, in particular the dactyl taken from the theme, Ex. 225 – see for example bb41ff –

Ex. 225

and the quaver countersubject *rectus* and *inversus* – e.g. bb35ff (it is possible that the top part of b26 should read as in Ex. 226 and thus

Ex. 226

achieve closer imitation). In the process, the theme is constantly reharmonized – see the bass entries at bb8, 23, 44, 50 – which must be one of the purposes of organ chorales, i.e. to present the chorale melody in varied but always intelligible harmony.

690–713 Organ Chorales formerly called 'Kirnberger Collection'

Accidents of source-material gave this group of chorales its name during the nineteenth century; all are to be found (in a different order) in the MS sources Am.B.72a and Am.B.72, associated with – copied for or at the instigation of – J. P. Kirnberger, a pupil of J. S. Bach in 1748. Am.B. 72a dates from c1760, while Am.B. 72 was made from it for Princess Anna Amalia (May 1974a p99). The group of chorales BWV 690–713 was thus contained in an album of the kind made by several members of the Bach circle. Both the sources and the musical style of many of the chorales themselves suggest that they date from a much earlier period, at least one (BWV 700, like BWV 718 and 741) being perhaps already too old to be included in the well-known albums copied by J. G. Walther and J. T. Krebs (Klotz *NBA* IV/3 *KB* p13). Some pieces in these albums were later known to and copied by Kittel and his circle; some, with others in albums by other copyists, may have been copied from a *Sammelmappe* (collected portfolio) in the composer's possession; and this portfolio may have had the title *Variirte und fugirte Choräle* ('Decorated and fugued chorales'), judging by the collective title in Am.B. 72a and Am.B. 72, P 1160 and P 213 (Klotz *op cit*). Or perhaps the collection of *Variirte und fugirte Choräle* was made only after 1750, at the instigation of J. G. I. Breitkopf (May 1974a p100), and was first advertised in a Breitkopf catalogue of 1764.

Other copies of the 'collection' were made, including the lost MS Danzig 4203/4, probably assembled after the 1764 Breitkopf catalogue was published (May *op cit*), and MSS held by the Breitkopf firm, later owned by Fétis and now represented by Brussels MS II.3919. The copy Am.B. 72a itself may have been based on this 'Breitkopf Collection'. There is, however, no evidence that the twenty-four pieces were themselves defined as a group in any of the sources; at least two can be attributed to another composer and several more are of doubtful authorship. In addition, the extant sources suggest that any *Sammelmappe* would also have included BWV 718, 733, 734 and 741, and even perhaps the 'early versions' of BWV 651–667 and 769 (Klotz *op cit*), which suggests too wide-ranging a survey for any such authentic *Sammelmappe*. From the point of view of musical value, the most promising grouping is that of the seven Advent and Christmas fughettas, a group evidently not completed by the composer (see below, BWV 696). Moreover, Christmas chorales of one kind or another kind make up a group – not homogeneous enough to be called a set – of at least fifteen (BWV *696, 697, 698, 699,* 700, *701,* 703, 704, 710, *713,* 722, 724, 729, 732, 738). Of these, the seven fughettas (italicized numbers) form a distinct set of short, exceptionally skilful pieces, all furthering a contrapuntal style of mature beauty in which a much-used counter-subject provides both motion and ever-new harmonies for chorale melodies also set in the *Orgelbüchlein*. The 'ever-new harmonies' alone show the composer to have stepped beyond the limits of (e.g.) Böhm idioms. While Buxtehude, Bruhns and others presented fugal chorale lines with distinctive countersubjects, the seven fughettas in question develop the technique beyond this, rather in the manner of fully fledged fugues of the type in *Das Wohltemperirte Clavier*, I. While the fughetta as such is clearly part of a common tradition (cf. J. K. F. Fischer's *Blumen-Strauss*, 1732(?); Muffat's seventy-two *Versetl*, 1726) – i.e. short three- or four-part fugues with exposition, episode, one or two final entries, short pedal point etc – the thematic complexity of (e.g.) BWV 698 is unknown elsewhere. It is certainly removed beyond recognition from the Pachelbel fughetta that is still often claimed as the forebear of such pieces (Meyer 1974 p83). If the stretto structure of BWV 697 can also be found in Fischer, its pervasive countersubject, its chorale basis and its modal framework can not. This 'modality' is more a question of ambiguity of diatonic key than of modalism in any real sense, as is also the case with some *Clavierübung III* fughettas. Perhaps even more striking in the seven fughettas is the pervasive counterpoint – the unexpectedly intense and exhaustive use of theme and countersubject in the course of each short movement, particularly in BWV 698 and 701.

It is striking that while the Walther–Krebs MS P 802 contains chorales from the *Orgelbüchlein* and 'The Eighteen' as well as partitas and other chorales (twelve with BWV numbers between 714 and 762), it has none of the twenty-four of the so-called 'Kirnberger Collection'. Perhaps the 'Breitkopf Collection' represented or contained a group of chorales intended by the composer for systematic collection or revision. But whether the 'crudities' or 'improvements' in the detail of various chorales should be accredited to the composer or to the copyist of the source concerned is rarely certain enough for one to be sure whether the composer intended or achieved any such revision.

---

690   Wer nur den lieben Gott lässt walten (formerly 'Kirnberger Collection')

No Autograph MS; copies in Brussels II.3919 (second quarter of eighteenth century), Am.B. 72a (Kirnberger), Am.B. 72, P 1117 (J. L. Krebs), P 1109 (Penzel), P 1116 (Kühnel), Danzig 4203/4 (album c1754/62) and late sources.

Two staves.

For TEXT and MELODY see BWV 642.

Like BWV 683, BWV 690 contains the melody as a cantus firmus in the soprano above a running motif in three and four parts below. The

Ex. 227

suspirans figure (Ex. 227), from which the scales are developed, is not only prominent when the final note of each chorale line is lengthened (e.g. bb4–5) but is itself like the motifs from which interludes are made at the ends of lines in such earlier congregational chorales as BWV 722 and 729. The motif gives the movement the character of a partita variation, e.g. Böhm's 'Wer nur den lieben Gott lässt walten' (nos. 2, 4, 6 and 7) and the *double* of 'Auf meinen lieben Gott' attributed to Buxtehude (BUXWV 179).

As in BWV 695, a simple figured chorale follows, which serves as an appropriate harmonization in $^4/_4$ after a $^3/_4$ or $^6/_8$ setting; however, its original purpose can only be guessed at. But if – as the spacing of BWV 690 in comparison with BWV 683 may suggest – the piece was conceived for domestic keyboard instruments other than organ, a hymnbook-like harmonization could have been particularly useful for that purpose. That there was felt to be some need or use for simple harmonizations – 'beym öffentlichen Gottes-Dienst' ('in a public church service' in church) – is clear from Kauffmann's *Harmonische Seelenlust* (1733), where a plain melody with figured bass is provided for each hymn that is set. In the case of BWV 690, the harmony underlying the counterpoint of the prelude is noticeably more sophisticated than that of the simple chorale.

---

691 Wer nur den lieben Gott lässt walten (formerly 'Kirnberger Collection')

Autograph MS *Klavierbüchlein für W. F. Bach* (early 1720); later copies in P 225 (*Klavierbüchlein für Anna Magdalena Bach*, after 1725), Am.B. 72a (Kirnberger), Am.B. 72, Am.B. 478, P 1116 (Kühnel), P 1160 (Oley), Danzig 4203/4, Sp 1438; also Kö 15839 (J. G. Walther, after 1720?).

Headed 'Choral' in P 225; two staves.

For TEXT and MELODY see BWV 642.

Like BWV 753, BWV 691 may have been written for the W. F. Bach *Klavierbüchlein*, where it appears on fo. 5v. The decorated right-hand melody is without interludes between chorale lines; and the two left-hand parts are not derived from the melody, nor do they develop any one motif consistently. It can only be conjectured whether the unusual nature of the piece depends more on the album's being intended for domestic use or for performance on (e.g.) clavichord; of the two, the latter was probably the stronger influence.

The eight bars contain many (but not all) of the ornaments in the *Explication* or Table of Ornaments placed two leaves earlier in the

W. F. Bach *Klavierbüchlein*; the movement also incorporates many *cantabile* or written-out ornamental figures. The copy in the Anna Magdalena Book is less exact in its ornamentation. The order of pieces in the older album (BWV 994, 924, *691*, 926, *753*, 836 . . .) suggests that the chorales are to supply examples of ornamental effects contrasting with the simpler figuration of the surrounding pieces; they show the technique in miniature. Thus, the first note is plain, as in BWV 622, 641 etc; the next figure (Ex. 228 – see also b9) is familiar (e.g. BWV 656

Ex. 228

b2); the short rest in the melody in b3 is a good example of the *tmesis* figure of musical rhetoric ('cutting', i.e. a break). Nevertheless, the decorated line is unusual in its detail, and though it is similar in principle to the melodic sections of (e.g.) BWV 692, the result is less conventional.

691a   Wer nur den lieben Gott lässt walten

No Autograph MS; later copies only (Schelble–Gleichauf, P 285).

Two staves.

Although some authors have seen BWV 691a as an early attempt at ritornello-chorale style (see BWV 683a), in which they were encouraged by the spurious 'a 2 Clav.' in *BG* 40, the movement is unlikely to be authentic. The same objection can be raised against Spitta's conjecture that BWV 691a was written for use in church services in the earlier part of J. S. Bach's work at Arnstadt and that it showed 'traces of Böhm's manner' (Spitta I pp310, 661). Such bars as 12–13 hardly date from the early eighteenth century; and in addition to the change in stylistic idiom between the interludes and the original phrases from BWV 691, each style seems to require its own tempo (the interludes almost twice as fast). For the sources and type of interpolation, see BWV 683a.

---

692   Ach Gott und Herr (formerly 'Kirnberger Collection')

Copies by J. G. Walther (P 802, Kö 15839, the latter headed 'JGW '), Am.B. 72a (Kirnberger), Am.B. 72, P 1160 (Oley), Sp 1438 and other copyists of the *Sammelmappe*.

See BWV 693, below.

693 Ach Gott und Herr (formerly 'Kirnberger Collection')

Copies in Am.B. 72a (Kirnberger), Am.B. 72, P 1160 (Oley), P 1116 (Kühnel), Sp 1438 and other copyists of the *Sammelmappe*.

M. Seiffert (*Johann Gottfried Walther: Gesammelte Werke für Orgel* (*DDT* XXVI, 1906) pp6-7) includes BWV 692 and 693 as *Vers 4* and *Vers 3* respectively of Walther's seven-movement partita 'Ach Gott und Herr'. Walther himself signed one copy of BWV 692 (see above); BWV 693 is included in a source 'from the end of the eighteenth century' which may have been the first to collect the seven movements in one group (*ibid* p.xxxvii). To be sure, both chorales are included in MSS – Am.B. 72/72a – which are attributed as whole albums to J. S. Bach; moreover, the use in BWV 693 of a motif derived from the melody and made to pervade the whole texture is seen by Spitta as a trait of Bach (I p598). But such total, doctrinaire working of a motif is not characteristic even of chorales in the *Orgelbüchlein*; similarly, the decorated melodic sections of BWV 692 resemble those of (e.g.) BWV 691 only in principle, not in effect. Both chorales demonstrate a technique of treatment pursued without variety or development.

---

694 Wo soll ich fliehen hin (formerly 'Kirnberger Collection')

No Autograph MS; copies in Brussels II.3919 (second quarter of eighteenth century), Am.B. 27a (Kirnberger), Am.B. 72, P 1116 (Kühnel), Danzig 4203/4, Sp 1438 and late sources.

Headed 'à 2 claviers et pédale' (*NBA* IV/3), two staves.

For TEXT and MELODY see BWV 646. The melodic form in BWV 694 is as in Cantata 5: Ex. 229.

Ex. 229

BWV 5.i

Like BWV 646, BWV 694 is a trio-like work in which (*a*) the two hands do not cross parts (and so could easily be played on one manual, like BWV 710 and Var. 7 of BWV 768), (*b*) the left hand serves as a bass line imitative of the right hand, and (*c*) the pedal has separated cantus-firmus phrases. Despite their relative lengths, the ritornello shape of BWV 646 is the clearer of the two because it ends the chorale on manuals alone; but its registration could suit BWV 694 equally well. Of the two, BWV 694 is much longer (and has the slower-moving cantus firmus); and – unlike the maturer chorales in this form, BWV 646, 684, 688 – it contains an extra bar before certain pedal phrases enter (bb9, 25, 40). Also, despite the similarity of motif, BWV 694 exploits inversion much less than BWV 646. For the first forty bars the motif appears only in its *rectus* form as in Ex. 230(i), apart from an isolated *inversus* in

Ex. 230

(i)   **(ii) b84**

(iii) b40

b12; from b40, however, there is an alternation of *rectus* and *inversus* passages as in Ex. 230(ii), comparable to the strict and concise development in BWV 646. Nevertheless, the composer may have intended a reference to the chorale melody in the upper parts: the inversion shown in Ex. 230(iii) occurs at the point at which the cantus firmus has reached line 3.

Despite the length and an occasional harmonic infelicity (e.g. the harmonization of bb73–5 as $\begin{smallmatrix}6\\3\end{smallmatrix}\ \begin{smallmatrix}6\\4\end{smallmatrix}\ \begin{smallmatrix}6\\3\end{smallmatrix}$), the movement shows a conscious attempt at well-knit development of motif, relying almost exclusively either on the *rectus* and *inversus* of figure *a* or on the syncopation of the countersubject (Ex. 231). The amount of repetition is itself graphic

Ex. 231   b1

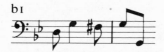

as a description of the text – the 'fleeing' to no avail – more so than is the tightly controlled setting in BWV 646. It suggested similar ideas to such composers as J. L. Krebs when they came to set the same chorale. Some commentators have seen the setting as relating in particular to v7 (Luedtke 1918 p68) – for the text see BWV 646.

695   Christ lag in Todesbanden (formerly 'Kirnberger Collection')

No Autograph MS; copies formerly (?) in Brussels II.3919 (after 1750?), and in Am.B. 72a (Kirnberger), Am.B. 72, P 1109 (Penzel), P 1116 (Kühnel), Danzig 4203/4, Sp 1438 and late sources.

Headed 'Fantasia super...' (*NBA* IV/3), two staves.

For TEXT and MELODY see BWV 625, including a note on the form of the melody.

In shape, the movement is a ritornello chorale in two sections, each a two-part manual fugue or fore-imitation, on line 1 and line 5 of the chorale – Ex. 232 (cf. Ex. 67). The first theme returns in the coda at

Ex. 232

b134 (cf. BWV 647). In motifs, the movement is highly organized, the quaver and semiquaver figures drawn either from the subject (*x* in b62, etc) or developing from other counterpoints (e.g. Ex. 233). The motifs

Ex. 233

themselves are thus only very indirectly derived from the chorale melody, and they go on to produce a coda after the melody is finished – a mature characteristic (cf. BWV 646, 675). The motifs generally produce a texture and line characteristic of the composer's harpsichord music, particularly in the section from b84 on (cf. e.g. the Gigue from the G major Partita BWV 829).

Concerning the plain harmonization of the chorale (found in P 1109, P 1116, Sp 1438) see remarks under BWV 690. Why the melody was not included is unclear; the reason may have to do with the original source (copy of an ensemble *organo* part? insufficient room?) and not with the great familiarity of the melody.

695a   Christ lag in Todesbanden

No Autograph MS; only sources, Schelble–Gleichauf (*NBA* IV/2 *KB* pp55–6) and Peters VI.

Though unknown to have been authorized by the composer, the arrangement with a pedal cantus firmus may well reflect the way in which such manual cantus-firmus chorales were sometimes played by organists, particularly those trained in traditional methods (see also BWV 734). It also shows an unsuspected feature of counterpoint, in that either alto or bass can serve as the bass line; the $^6_4$ chords at the pedal entries, however, are unusual in pieces with a bass cantus firmus (cf. BWV 694). With the chorale melody transposed two octaves lower, it becomes necessary in the interests of good spacing to transpose one or other manual part up or down an octave from time to time. The occasional extra part has been skilfully added. The modifications made to the fugue subject in BWV 695a (bb69, 72, 85, 115) suggests that it is an arrangement of BWV 695, not vice versa.

696

Christum wir sollen loben schon (formerly 'Kirnberger Collection')

No Autograph MS; copies in Brussels II.3919 (after 1750?), Am.B. 72a Kirnberger), Am.B. 72, Lpz Poel 39 (Kittel), P 1108 (Dröbs), Danzig 4203/4, P 1119, Sp 1438 and late sources.

Headed 'Christum wir sollen loben schon oder Was fürchtst du, Feind Herodes, sehr', 'Fughetta'; two staves.

For TEXTS and MELODY see BWV 611.

The first line of the chorale melody supplies the theme – Ex. 234 (cf. Ex. 32) – including both the important motif *a* and the tied/dotted

Ex. 234

(as in P 1119)

fifth note that gives the movement its flow and anticipates that of the D major fugue of *Das Wohltemperirte Clavier*, II. From *a* the countersubject is also derived. Though only twenty bars long, BWV 696 shows a subtle use of motif (particularly *a* – compare the sequence in bb9–10 with bb2–3 of 'Da Jesus an dem Kreuze stund' BWV 621), thematic reference (the final long e' and its cadence refer to the long E-phrygian close of the chorale melody), harmony and counterpoint (strict countersubject accompanying each subject entry). The form is: single exposition, episode and final entry (the last answered at the octave). The use to which motif *a* is put makes it unnecessary to accompany the opening subject with counter-material (as in BWV 698 etc). Compared with most fughettas, these seven for Advent and Christmas have unusually long subjects; that of BWV 696 is arrayed with ornaments (particularly in P 1119) suggestive of some late-seventeenth-century fugue subjects. Despite the final cadence, the 'modality' of such idiom is more a question of ambiguity of key. Thus the answer (bb2–3) implies no clear move to the dominant like that in the harmonization in BWV 121. Moreover, motif *a* introduces unexpected chromaticisms or modulations (e.g. bb6, 7, 15) and at other times moves in thirds and sixths to create mellifluous false relations (e.g. bb4, 10, 11, 15, 18). The harmony and texture in the movement have a richness and originality of style too easily underestimated.

---

697 Gelobet seist du, Jesu Christ (formerly 'Kirnberger Collection')

No Autograph MS; copies in Brussels II.3919 (after 1750?), Am.B. 72a (Kirnberger), Am.B. 72, P 1119, Danzig 4203/4, Sp 1438 and late sources.

Headed 'Fughetta'; two staves.

For TEXT and MELODY see BWV 604.

The fughetta subject is the first line of the chorale melody set as eight quavers, i.e. less metrical than the slower, more canzona-like counterpoint in settings of the melody by Buxtehude, Böhm and others (cf. the same canzona rhythm in the subject of the setting BWV 723). The fourth entry in the exposition is at the fifteenth to the previous entry – an unusual feature. The countersubject supplies the running semiquavers once seen as a 'symbol of the Son of God descending to earth' (Keller 1948 p146) and in any case associated with the 'Engel Schaar' of other Christmas chorales (especially BWV 607, 701). These runs persist until the final chord, combining with the many entries of the theme (twelve times in fourteen bars) to convey the repeated 'Gelobet' given out by the angels.

As in BWV 696, there are characteristic subtleties in the three- and four-part counterpoint: the one-bar subject tends to modulate to the supertonic or relative of the entry; the countersubject can develop *inversus* (bb10, 14); a counter-rhythm of $^7 \, \flat \, \Gamma$ or $^7 \, \flat \, \Box\!\Gamma$ increases both flow and cohesion; the final modal cadence of the chorale melody is retained in the fughetta though the last line of the melody does not appear in the organ setting. A clear tonic is generally avoided, and the sequences (though audible as such: cf. bb8–9 with bb6–7) are somewhat disguised. The form and texture of the resulting movement are too different from those of the *Orgelbüchlein* setting (BWV 604) for easy comparison; but in idiom and motivic complexity BWV 697 is clearly far more developed.

---

698 Herr Christ, der ein'ge Gottes Sohn (formerly 'Kirnberger Collection')

No Autograph MS; copies in Brussels II.3919 (after 1750?), Am.B. 72a (Kirnberger), Am.B. 72, P 1160 (Oley), Danzig 4203/4, Sp 1438 and late sources.

Headed 'Fughetta'; two staves.

For TEXT and MELODY see BWV 601.

The fughetta subject is the first line of the chorale melody (cf. Ex. 10); but as in BWV 696 etc, the term 'fughetta' indicates an intricate miniature developing several motifs with recurrent tonic entries (bb1, 7, 11, 17). The resulting three-part figuration and sequences are more conventional than those of the smaller chorales of *Clavierübung III* but work to similar ends. The countersubject, though not derived from the melody, contains three motifs used throughout: Ex. 235. The

Ex. 235

working-out of the countersubject is particularly inventive. In bb1–2 it is heard in sequence (as a phrase three minims long); in bb3–4 it appears both in the bass (still in the tonic) and in the soprano (motifs *b* and *c* only), and enriched by a subject answer in the dominant (alto). In bb11–12, line 2 of the melody (= the last line) appears in the bass in partial combination with the subject and countersubject above; the bass quavers of bb13–14 are themselves a diminution of the preceding derived crotchet phrase; in bb15–16 the top part has a decorated or paraphrase version of the cantus firmus (Ex. 236); within this para-

Ex. 236

phrase, line 1 of the melody in diminution (semiquavers) is combined with line 2 in diminution (quavers, in the bass) against motif *c* from the countersubject entry begun in b15 (tenor): Ex. 237. Finally, in b18 the second (= last) line of the melody can be heard paraphrased in

Ex. 237

b16

the top part against line 1 in the tenor: cf. Ex. 236. Other thematic diminutions or decorations can probably be found. The figuration against the pedal point of the penultimate bar is also derived, just as every *figura corta* of the piece ( or) can be seen to be derived from motif *a* above. Such complexity is not immediately obvious in a movement whose tessitura and spacing, runs, cadences and thirds all suggest some affinity with the Lesser Catechism chorales in *Clavierübung III* (BWV 669–689). The paraphrase, combination and motif techniques found in this twenty-bar miniature produce a counterpoint of special, unusual flavour.

699

Nun komm', der Heiden Heiland (formerly 'Kirnberger Collection')

No Autograph MS; copies in Brussels II.3919 (after 1750?), Am.B. 72a (Kirnberger), Am.B. 72, Danzig 4203/4, Sp 1438 and late copies.

Headed 'Fughetta'; two staves.

For TEXT and MELODY see BWV 599.

The fughetta subject is the first line of the chorale melody (cf. Ex. 3); on paper the form is little more than exposition, further tonic entry and coda (cf. BWV 696). But the counterpoint has several important features: comparison with lines in BWV 659 suggests that the counter-subject is derived from the subject (particularly the rising fourth); the opening motif of the countersubject produces a figure – Ex. 238(i) –

Ex. 238

(i) b5   (ii) b4

(D   D   C♯   F)

which is developed later; and its second half produces a further figure that achieves independent development in the course of the sixteen bars – Ex. 238(ii). Such independent countersubjects resemble those of the fugal sections in the large chorale fantasias of northern composers (e.g. Buxtehude's 'Nun freut euch' BUXWV 210). A further sign of possible indebtedness to older models is the conventional broken figuration of bb10–11; but the subject itself and its countersubject are strikingly like the double theme of the C sharp minor Fugue of *Das Wohltemperirte Clavier*, I. Certainly, however, the countersubject of BWV 699 looks progressively more like a paraphrase of the chorale subject itself, and its five entries in bb12–15 serve as reminders of that chorale melody.

---

700   Vom Himmel hoch da komm' ich her (formerly 'Kirnberger Collection')

No Autograph MS; copies in Am.B. 72a (Kirnberger), Am.B. 72, Leipzig Bach-Archiv Mus. MS 3 (fair copy, a remnant of Breitkopf MS holdings and formerly thought to be Autograph MS), P 1109 (Penzel), P 1116 (Kühnel), Danzig 4203/4, Sp 1438 and late sources.

Headed 'Fuga sopra...' (P 1109); two staves.

For TEXT and MELODY see BWV 606.

Not least because of the doubling of the left hand in the pedal, BWV 700 is usually described as 'very early' though improved in slight detail during the composer's last decade (Klotz *NBA* IV/3 *KB* p11). The pedal was also doubled in this way in a setting by Pachelbel of the same chorale (*DTB* 58); moreover, the narrow pedal compass in BWV 700 (C–c) may also reflect a 'southern' influence. The form of the movement is unusual and may suggest the composer's youthfulness quite as much as do the square $^4/_4$ rhythms of the whole or the detail of such bars as 31–2 (Pachelbel–Corelli). Bars 1–23 of BWV 700 are a conventional monothematic chorale fughetta; as in the other fughettas, the subject is line 1 of the chorale melody. But in b23 the subject is diminished and is answered by a new subject, itself the diminished line 2 of the melody; the latter in turn has two dominant answers before the clearly marked cantus firmus appears in the pedal/left hand (b34) against its diminished form in the tenor. In b37 a theme derived from line 3 becomes the stretto fugal subject of the next section; other motifs follow which look like derivations of other lines (e.g. the little dactyl figure , perhaps derived from the first four notes of the melody); line 3 then enters in the pedal. In b47, line 4 of the chorale supplies another subject partly in diminution and a last pedal cantus firmus drawing out the end of the line (as in four of the variations in BWV 769). Above the final pedal point is a stretto reference to line 1, now diminished and chromatically coloured. Thus the composer seems already on the path of ingenuity, despite the background of ordinary rhythms (cf. Walther), phased fore-imitations (cf. Pachelbel) and pedal cantus firmus mainly in crotchets (cf. Böhm). Yet the final pedal entry is a feature striking enough to be re-introduced at the end of the mature *Canonic Variations* BWV 769.

---

701 Vom Himmel hoch da komm' ich her (formerly 'Kirnberger Collection')

No Autograph MS; copies in Brussels II.3919 (after 1750?), Am.B. 72a (Kirnberger), Am.B. 72, Danzig 4203/4, Sp 1438 and late sources.

Headed 'Fughetta'; two staves.

For TEXT and MELODY see BWV 606.

Whether or not the scale-like countersubject can be seen as a reference to the angels of vv1–2 and/or the bells of v15 (see also BWV 697), the fughetta is a particularly fluent and musical exercise in the fugal techniques of tonal answers (bb3, 12, 20), in developed countersubject motifs (ascending and descending scales and scale segments), in diminutions of the subject (Ex. 239(i)) and of other chorale-melody

Ex. 239

lines (Ex. 239(ii)), and in thematic combinations. The last is shown in several ways: motif *b* in stretto (bb10–11), *c* in stretto (bb16–18, 21), *b* and *a* (bb12, 14, 20), *c* and *a* (bb15, 24). The countersubject scales run through much of the movement, changing to other motifs only when themes are combined (e.g. b15); and there are often significances in the subsidiary material (e.g., the syncopated alto of b9 appears again later; the alto of b10 is derived from the theme; etc). Thus, although the Christmas scales may seem to the ear to dominate the movement, it does anticipate the intricate motivic and contrapuntal techniques of the *Canonic Variations* BWV 769, and there remains a difference in style or 'tone' between the simple sequential episodes (bb6f, 22ff – both similar to passages in *Das Wohltemperirte Clavier*) and the harmonic turns occasioned by the nature of thematic combination (bb15–16, 19–20). Like BWV 698, BWV 701 is a web of thematic allusion difficult to unravel – see, for instance, Ex. 240 – and this itself becomes a species of musical language, like the canonic techniques on the same chorale in BWV 769. The key to Ex. 240 is as follows:

a chorale line 1 (here functions in turn as fugue answer, subject and entry)
b chorale line 2, in diminution
c chorale line 3, in diminution (subject and answer in succession)
x countersubject, now inverted
y chorale line 4, in double diminution

Ex. 240

But such a passage as Ex. 239(ii) will work only if the tonality is at times ambiguous (b16); or, conversely, a free diatonicism will widen contrapuntal potential.

702

Das Jesulein soll doch mein Trost (formerly 'Kirnberger Collection')

No Autograph MS; copies in Brussels II.3919 (after 1750?), Am.B. 72a (Kirnberger), Am.B. 72, P 406 (based on Kirnberger), Danzig 4203/4, Sp 1438 and late sources.

Headed 'Fughetta'; two staves.

The TEXT of B. Helder's New Year Hymn was published in 1636; Freylinghausen (1741 etc) lists it amongst hymns 'von der Freudigkeit des Glaubens' ('concerning the joyfulness of belief').

Das Jesulein soll doch mein Trost,	The infant Jesus shall be and remain
mein Heiland sein und bleiben,	my consolation, my Saviour,
der mich geliebet und erlost;	who loves and redeems me;
kein G'walt sol mich abtreiben.	no power shall drive me from him.
Ihm tu' ich mich ganz williglich	To him I shall devote myself willingly,
von Hertzengrund ergeben,	from the bottom of my heart,
es mag mir sein weh oder fein,	whether it goes well or ill for me,
mag sterben oder leben.	whether I die or live.

Two more verses follow.

The MELODY was published with the text: Ex. 241. It is used only in BWV 702, whose unusually high final cadence may express the last verse (Terry 1921 p142), particularly the line

Zum Leben fein zu gehen ein.   To enter upon a purer life.

Ex. 241

Freylinghausen

Though excluded from *NBA* IV/3, BWV 702 deserves attention not least since bad opinions of its part-writing and of the pedal line in bb16–18 (Keller 1937) are based on the *BG* edition, which is unlikely to reflect the wishes of the copyist or the composer, whoever they may be. The combination of two fugue subjects derived from the first two lines of the chorale melody is not untypical of J. S. Bach, especially as the resulting counterpoint is Italianate – Ex. 242. Concerning the conven-

Ex. 242

tional nature of the episode material (bb11, 17f) see a note on BWV 701; the upper parts in bb17–18 are derived from the main subject, which enters at the very end of b18. It should also not be missed that both subject and countersubject end with the same motif on a half-close. The well-regulated and varied strettos (bb3–4, 7ff, 12ff, 19ff) are more in line with Bach's development of fugue themes than (e.g.) J. G. Walther's, as are the handling of keys and cadences, the harmony, the development of semiquaver lines, and the rhythmic variety (cf. BWV 693 on all five counts). The very 'irregularity' of the fugue may be considered characteristic of J. S. Bach:

    b1 subject (tenor), countersubject (alto) in dominant
    b3 subject (soprano), countersubject (bass) in tonic
    b4 countersubject (soprano) in octave stretto
    b5 subject (tenor)

b6 countersubject (alto) in tonic to subject in tonic (cf. b1)
b7 subject (bass), answered in following bar by double stretto etc

Strettos remain inventive to the end (bb19–23), as is often the case where a subject begins with repeated notes or rises by step, while the parts 'completing the harmony' (e.g. tenor in last three bars) do so with a fluency typical of the *Orgelbüchlein*.

---

703   Gottes Sohn ist kommen (formerly 'Kirnberger Collection')

No Autograph MS; copies in Brussels II.3919 (after 1750?), Am.B. 72a (Kirnberger), Am.B. 72, Danzig 4203/4 and late sources.

Headed 'Fughetta'; two staves.

For TEXT and MELODY see BWV 600.

Like others of the Advent and Christmas fughettas, BWV 703 is little more than the exposition of a subject derived from line 1 of the chorale melody, followed by an episode developing countersubject material, and closing with a tonic entry – the whole within twenty-two bars. The tonal answer is irregular (as in BWV 701), and the codetta in bb7–9 (like some in fugues of *Das Wohltemperirte Clavier*) develops material used later in the movement – in this case, a semiquaver line derived from the semiquavers of b4 (countersubject) and from then on introduced into every bar of the movement – Ex. 243. Thus the semiquaver motion

Ex. 243   b5

which the chorale subject lacks is supplied by the countersubject, which itself may be derived from the original melody (cf. Ex. 6). Although the semiquaver phrase appears on various degrees of the scale and is of a type with other Advent/Christmas countersubjects (e.g. BWV 701), it makes a distinctive contribution to the harmonic character of this movement in its fluctuation between E♮ and E♭ – the only accidental of the piece, constantly returning and colouring the counterpoint throughout.

---

704   Lob sei dem allmächt'gen Gott (formerly 'Kirnberger Collection')

No Autograph MS; copies in Brussels II.3919 (after 1750?), Am.B. 72a (Kirnberger), Am.B. 72, P 406 (based on Kirnberger), Danzig 4203/4, Sp 1438 and late sources.

Headed 'Fughetta'; two staves.

For TEXT and MELODY see BWV 602. The opening of the melody departs from the traditional form (Ex. 12) in both BWV 602 and 704, the latter perhaps in the interests of forming a fugue subject.

The subject, derived from line 1 of the chorale melody, leads to a fughetta which is comparable in form to the other Advent and Christmas fughettas: exposition (bb1–10), episode (bb10–11), tonic entry (b12), quasi-supertonic entry (b15), quasi-submediant entry (b19) leading to half-close on A. The countersubject (bb4–6) provides material for development in most of the remaining bars, many of which combine its various motifs (e.g. $a+b+$subject in b16, $a+c+$subject in b17): Ex. 244(i). The subsidiary motif in Ex. 244(ii) is also of

Ex. 244

(i) b4   **(ii)** b10

importance, as it is in other fughettas of this group (e.g. BWV 703), especially where it is extended to a longer scale segment – cf. bb20–1 with BWV 697.

The 'modal' close, however, is the most unusual feature of the movement. This final cadence reflects the end of the original plainsong (cf. BWV 696, 602); but that the movement has modal tendencies is also clear from the nature of the theme (beginning on the mediant?), its answer in C and its later entries (b15: G minor, beginning on the tonic). Not only is the subject, with its apparent opening on the mediant, a somewhat remote version of the chorale melody itself, but its final entry is at first harmonized as tonic (not relative minor), and the cadence on A is unconventional. However, the conception may be not so much an 'adaptation of fugal plan to the anti-tonal modality of certain chorales' (Chailley 1974 p187) as a carefully detailed fugue brought to a close on its first middle entry.

---

705   Durch Adams Fall ist ganz verderbt (formerly 'Kirnberger Collection')

No Autograph MS; copies in Am.B. 72a (Kirnberger), Am.B. 72, P 1160, Danzig 4203/4, Sp 1438 and late sources.

Headed in P 1160 'Fuga', 'manualiter'; two staves.

For TEXT and MELODY see BWV 637.

Though excluded from *NBA* IV/3, BWV 705 deserves attention as an example of a traditional type of chorale known from at least the period of Scheidt: an 'organ motet' so similar in style and form to choral movements (e.g. Cantata 2) as to suggest that it may be a transcription (B. F. Richter in *NBG* 26, where it is published as a motet). Whether or not pedal is required, the spacing suggests a less keyboard-like style than that familiar in the traditional German organ motet – a resemblance furthered by the plain figuration, a pure Scheidt form in minims. Each line of the chorale is the subject of fore-imitation, so that the last answer in each case is the soprano statement of the line. The form of the movement thus follows the musical form of the hymn (*ababcade*), just as the final close follows its cadence. Occasional dorian-mode turns of phrase (e.g. bb20 or 42) are more evident than in the cantata settings of the melody; there is less development of motif than in the comparable organ chorale BWV 737. As is often the case in both the ricercare and the capriccio of classical tradition, a repeated-note subject leads to strettos.

---

706   Liebster Jesu, wir sind hier (formerly 'Kirnberger Collection')

No Autograph MS; copies in P 801 (J. T. Krebs), Am.B. 72a (Kirnberger), Am.B. 72, P 1160, Danzig 4203/4, Sp 1438 and late sources.

BWV 706.ii headed 'alio modo' in P 801 (see also BWV 634); two staves.

For TEXT and MELODY see BWV 633.

The usefulness of the text and melody in connection with the sermon (as in the similar case of *Herr Jesu Christ, dich zu uns wend'* – cf. BWV 632) may explain the array of settings which, though varied in technique, leave the melody immediately recognizable. On grounds of key alone, BWV 633, 634, 706.i and 706.ii may appear to belong together; the sources P 801, Am.B. 72a, Am.B. 72a and BB 40037 (Sasse) also group them together, the order in P 801 (pp24–6) being BWV 706.i, 706.ii, 634, 633. As Seiffert pointed out in connection with the Sasse source (*Peters Jahrbuch* 1904), the group is 'very striking'. But there is no question of an organized partita, since the movements are not linked by any clearly marked variation technique. It is more likely that BWV 706 originated as a didactic exercise – perhaps during Bach's teaching of J. T. Krebs after c1710 – and it has been argued that in some way BWV 634 was developed from BWV 706 to become a harmonized chorale with a stylistic character familiar from the *Orgelbüchlein* (Zietz 1969 p130, and see below).

Whilst BWV 706.ii looks like a simple vocal chorale ('un-Bachisch' in Spitta's view, I p588), BWV 706.i harmonizes the melody in a more idiomatic keyboard-like manner. The motifs of BWV 706.i are elementary but give the impression of being liable to develop more independently (e.g. the scale in the final two bars). Although the movement may have originated as a teaching model, it is not easy to see BWV 633/634 as directly developed from it (despite Klotz *NBA* IV/3 *KB* p11) since the *Orgelbüchlein* settings are much less conventional in harmony and are further distinguished by their use of canon.

---

707 Ich hab' mein' Sach' Gott heimgestellt (formerly 'Kirnberger Collection')

No Autograph MS; copies in Am.B. 72a (Kirnberger), Am.B. 72, P 1160, P 1116 (Kühnel), Danzig 4203/4, Sp 1438 and late sources.

Headed 'a 4 manualiter' in P 1160; two staves.

The TEXT of J. Leon's hymn was published in 1589 and became one of the texts concerned with 'death and resurrection' (Freylinghausen 1741 etc).

Ich hab mein Sach Gott heimgestellt,	I have placed my cause in God,
er machs mit mir, wie's ihm gefällt.	he does with me what he pleases.
Soll ich allhier noch länger lebn,	Should I live on earth longer,
ohn Widerstrebn	without resistance
seim Willen tu ich mich ergebn.	I will give myself to his will.

v3

Es ist allhier ein Jammertal,	Everywhere here is a vale of tears,
Angst, Not und Trübsal überall;	all anxiety, distress and trouble;
des Bleibens ist ein kleine Zeit	to dwell here means a little time
voll Müh und Leid,	full of trouble and suffering,
und wers bedenkt, ist stets im Streit.	he who considers it is always uneasy.

VII

Und ob mich schon mein Sünd anficht,	And although my sin troubles me so,
dennoch will ich verzagen nicht;	yet I will not despair;
ich weiss, dass mein getreuer Gott	I know that my true God –
für mich in' Tod	for me – into death
sein liebsten Sohn gegeben hat.	delivered his dearest son.

The remaining fifteen verses trace the conversion of the soul from misery to hope and praise.

The MELODY exists in two versions: that of Cantata 106 is the tenor of a song published in 1589, *Ich weiss mir ein Röslein hübsch und fein*

Ex. 245

BWV 351

(perhaps a variant text of an earlier song); that of BWV 707 and 708
– Ex. 245 – is the soprano, associated with the text from 1598 (Terry
1921 p207). The leap down to the dominant for the fourth note is
already found in seventeenth-century hymnbooks, though BWV 351
preserves an older form.

Excluded from *NBA* IV/3, and – because of its canonic technique in
bb15–16, 72, 97–9 – thought by Spitta to be the work of J. G. Walther
(Spitta I p820), BWV 707 yet bears some resemblance to BWV 705 and
737, not least in the problem of the pedal. The direction 'manualiter'
in P 1160 may reflect the copyist's uncertainty as to any alternative:
the pedal plays the lowest voice all through, or it does not play at all.
However, some of the bass lines are not characteristic of the pedal
(bb13ff, 19, 52 etc), and an organist of 1700 or earlier may well have
played the bass lines of such pieces on either pedal or manual as
convenient. Keller (1937) sees as more Bach-like the chromaticism of
bb52ff and the simple harmonization appended to this piece.
   Although the line-by-line fore-imitation is diffuse, and the infelicities
obtrusive (alto b8, bass b56–8 etc), there is an imaginativeness and
richness of harmony that make the movement difficult to ascribe to
anybody but J. S. Bach. The fore-imitation counterpoint of bb89ff, the
'countersubject' of bb28ff and 108ff, the harmonization of the
unpromising final line (bb128ff) all suggest Bach, though no doubt 'not
from the period of his complete mastery' (*BG* 40 p.xxiii). Although
the countersubjects still remain largely undeveloped, a degree of
cohesion is given throughout the piece by the *figura corta*, ♩ ♫ ,
The countersubjects themselves offer a kind of short repertory:
crotchets or quavers, scale figures or in-turning figures, chromatic,
syncopated, unsyncopated, etc.

---

708   Ich hab' mein' Sach' Gott heimgestellt (formerly 'Kirnberger
Collection')

No Autograph MS; copies in Am.B. 72a (Kirnberger), Am.B. 72,
Danzig 4203/4, P 424, Sp 1438 and late sources.

Two staves.

For TEXT and MELODY see BWV 707.

Despite the high incidence of dominant and diminished sevenths, the
harmonization is scarcely an independent arrangement or 'organ
chorale'. If such harmonizations were useful to organists where the
congregation's hymnbooks gave only the text, more such pieces might
be expected to have survived in similar albums of organists' music;
BWV 708 looks like a vocal arrangement, like countless chorales in
eighteenth-century collections for church congregations.

708a

Ich hab' mein' Sach' Gott heimgestellt

No Autograph MS; copies in Danzig 4203/4, P 424 (nineteenth century?) and late sources.

Two staves.

Though called a 'variant' of BWV 708 in *BG* 40, BWV 708a is a different harmonization in a different metre, found mostly in the same sources that contain not only BWV 708 but also BWV 707, which it follows in the albums. The three harmonizations – BWV 708 and 708a, and the one at the end of BWV 707 – thus present the melody in three different versions in succession.

709

Herr Jesu Christ, dich zu uns wend' (formerly 'Kirnberger Collection')

No Autograph MS; copies formerly (?) in Brussels II.3919, and in Am.B. 72a (Kirnberger), Am.B. 72, Lpz Poel 39 (Kittel), Lpz MB III.8.10 (1740–50?), P 1109 (Penzel), P 1160, P 1108 (Dröbs), Danzig 4203/4, Sp 1438 and late sources.

Headed 'à 2 claviers et pédale'; two staves in the older sources.

For TEXT and MELODY see BWV 632.

Like the *Orgelbüchlein* setting BWV 632, the movement contains a complete statement of the melody in the soprano, but without interludes,* and based on a three-part accompaniment exploiting several motifs in all three parts. In the decorations of its melody (the notes of which can still be heard on the main beats) and in the quality of its accompanying parts, BWV 709 matches several preludes in the *Orgelbüchlein*, although the long notes at the beginning of each melodic line suggest Böhmian origins, as does the final long pedal point. Many of the ornament signs do not appear in the Kirnberger, Kittel, Oley and Penzel sources. The chief contrapuntal idea contains two underived motifs which, as often in the *Orgelbüchlein*, draw attention away from the already disguised melody: Ex. 246(i). Like the further motif *c* (Ex. 246(ii)), motif *b* often affects the melody itself, which also includes

Ex. 246   **(i)**   **(ii)** b3

* From a harmonic point of view, the rests at the ends of the first three lines in BWV 709 could be ignored and the melody note sustained – something not possible at the corresponding points in BWV 632.

several figurations familiar in BWV 622, 641 etc. Such a bar as 18 incorporates *a*, *b* and *c* in one part or another. The degree of imitation between the inner voices is marginally greater than is customary in ornamented chorales while such a bar as 16 (with its thirds, and a counter-motif in the pedal) is close to the conception of texture in certain chorales with undecorated cantus firmus like BWV 602. However, despite the careful texture of (e.g.) b16 (motifs *b* and *c*, the latter in quaver form), its harmony is less advanced than the best of the *Orgelbüchlein*, just as the motifs themselves (e.g. pedal bb17–19) are worked in a more single-minded or doctrinaire manner. The two cadences of bb11–12 and 19–20 are more in the conventional manner of Pachelbel or Walther compared with those of bb4–5 and 14–15, which clearly suggest the composer of 'Nun komm, der Heiden Heiland' BWV 659a.

---

710   Wir Christenleut' (formerly 'Kirnberger Collection')

No Autograph MS; copies in BB 12012/6 (J. L. Krebs), Am.B. 72a (Kirnberger), Am.B. 72, P 1160, P 1116 (Kühnel), Sp 1438 and late sources.

Headed in BB 12012/6 'Vorspiel zum Choral: Wir Christen Leut für 2 Clav. u. Pedal'; two staves.

For TEXT and MELODY see BWV 612. The version of the melody in the Krebs source (B&H edn 6589 p128) includes a repeat of line 1, as do the versions in BWV 40, 110, 142, 248.iii, and 612 (*Orgelbüchlein*). The other sources of BWV 710 omit the five bars concerned (between b4 and b5* of the version in *NBA* IV/3), which led Luedtke to point out that one of the hymnbooks with which the composer seems to have worked (Darmstadt 1699) also omitted the phrase (Luedtke 1918 p48).

A former tradition that J. L. Krebs was the composer – probably arising from BB 12012/6, where Krebs's name appears at the top of the page – is now discounted (Tittel 1966 pp133–4).

As in BWV 694, the technique of two-part invention above pedal cantus firmus gives BWV 710 a unified flow in which the hands do not cross; as in BWV 695, the manual subject is clearly derived from the chorale melody: Ex. 247 (cf. Ex. 35). While the hands themselves tend

Ex. 247

G A Bb A G

* The half-bar at the beginning (semiquavers in rh, rests in lh and pedal) is here counted as 'bar zero' as in *NBA* IV/3.

to follow the contours of the pedal cantus firmus (rising and falling with it), the nature of the theme (along with its motif *a*) appears to develop independently. Neither *b* nor the scale motif of bb3–4 is much developed; what is more striking is the degree of internal 'repetition' – the later appearances of the same motifs or phrases, with different harmonic implications (e.g. bb2f in bb24f, part of an invertible relation between bb23–5 lh and bb0–2 rh), or in inverted counterpoint (b14 partly seen in b42, bb19–20 in bb40–1). The counterpoint of the four bars 28–31 is immediately inverted when the pedal cantus firmus repeats its phrase (bb32–5). Motif *a* is also developed *inversus*, first appearing in that form – Ex. 248 – just before the pedal cantus firmus has the

Ex. 248

same notes – a striking coincidence with the inverted motif of BWV 694. It is obviously motif *a* which dominates the movement, either *rectus* or *inversus*, either in imitation or in thirds, either as a reference to the chorale melody (since it is derived from it) or as a figure varying another (e.g. the alto of b18 contained in the alto of b39).

As often with organ chorales based on melodies moving largely or wholly by step, it is not difficult to find 'thematic references' in the upper parts. The simple descending figure DCBbA can be found in the invertible counterpoint of bb28–35 and elsewhere, as indeed it can in various phrases of the cantus firmus itself (= all of lines 3, 5 and 6, and ends of lines 4 and 7); similar points could be made about the ascending figure GABb or ABbCD.

711

Allein Gott in der Höh' sei Ehr' (formerly 'Kirnberger Collection')

No Autograph MS; copies in Am.B. 72a (Kirnberger), P 1116 (Kühnel), Danzig 4203/4, Sp 1438 and late sources; but not in Am.B. 72.

Headed (*BG* 40) 'Bicinium'; two staves.

For TEXT and MELODY see BWV 662.

While it is true that the figuration of the left hand of BWV 711 is more like that in known *bicinia* of Johann Bernhard Bach (e.g. 'Nun freut euch') than in those of Böhm (e.g. 'Auf meinen lieben Gott'), Walther (e.g. 'Durch Adams Fall') and others, there is no particular reason to ascribe it to J. B. Bach, despite Spitta, Luedtke, Frotscher and Keller (cited by Klotz in *NBA* IV/3 *KB* p41). It is perhaps exaggerating to see the figures of BWV 711 as related to those of BWV 688 (Klotz *op cit*), but the final ritornello does anticipate other chorales (e.g. BWV

646). The piece may have been intended as a partita movement, by itself or with BWV 716 and 717 or other setting(s).

As in J. B. Bach's 'Nun freut euch', the first line of the cantus firmus is paraphrased in the opening (and closing) left-hand theme: Ex. 249

Ex. 249

(cf. Ex. 162). Telemann's *bicinia* (e.g. 'Allein Gott in der Höh'') also involve broken-chord figures; some of them anticipate other lines as well as the first, but others show less derivation. The similarity between the first and penultimate lines of the chorale melody itself aids cohesion in the case of BWV 711; and the left hand is cast in regular ritornello or quasi-ostinato form – i.e., not every chorale line is paraphrased. Though the nature of *bicinia* limits the expressiveness of BWV 711, the composer does try to step outside convention and reach a cello-like style not far removed from obbligato arias (e.g. the transcription BWV 649), though here without a continuo bass. The left-hand line may paraphrase the opening of the chorale melody but soon passes without break or change of direction into its own sequences; thus throughout the piece the thematic allusion is integrated, even hidden.

---

712   In dich hab' ich gehoffet, Herr (formerly 'Kirnberger Collection')

No Autograph MS; copies in Brussels II.3919 (second quarter of eighteenth century), Am.B. 72a (Kirnberger), Am.B. 72, P 1116 (Kühnel), P 1160, Danzig 4203/4, Sp 1438 and late sources.

Two staves

For the TEXT, see BWV 640.

The MELODY is one of two used by J. S. Bach for this text (see also BWV 640), written and published by S. Calvisius in 1581 (Terry 1921 p212): Ex. 250. A simplified version is used in BWV 712 as in Cantatas

Ex. 250

BWV 52

52 (23rd Sunday after Trinity 1726), 106 (funeral, 1707?), the *St Matthew Passion* (BWV 244, no. 38) and the *Christmas Oratorio* (BWV 248, no. 46, Sunday after New Year).

It is possible that BWV 712 belongs with 'The Eighteen' (see p. 126 above): its form resembles that of BWV 665 and 666. From each of

Ex. 251
b2

the six lines of the chorale melody (as it appears in BWV 52 etc) a fugue subject is derived and exposed in four voices:

> A bb1–5: line 1, clearest in soprano and bass (octave canon, b2): Ex. 251
> B bb5–10: line 2, clearest in soprano
> C bb10–15: line 3, clearest in soprano; subject similar to A
> D bb15–19: line 4, clear in all voices
> E bb19–22: line 5, clear in all voices; subject similar to D
> F bb22–end: line 6, clearest in bass (b30)

The increasing tendency towards running figures in the final twelve bars may reflect the melisma at the end of Calvisius' original melody – Ex. 252 – but the chromatic quality is to be found earlier in the

Ex. 252

Calvisius 1581 (transposed from F major)

movement, notably in the countersubject to the last line (b24). Perhaps some reference can be seen here to VI of the text. Since, as in BWV 665 and 666, there is no clearcut cantus-firmus melody as such, whether simple or 'ornamented', the chorale lines that emerge give the appearance of growing out of the fugue subjects, rather than vice versa. The effect is of an organic, very original series of fughettas in which the chorale lines have been made difficult to recognize as melodies outside the fugal context. The fugal character of the sections varies: A and B are regular stretto expositions whose texture becomes smoother when the chorale line emerges; C has a series of answers on three different notes and pursued by further strettos; each of D's answers appears a fifth up; E is similar to D but a step higher; F has an exposition of irregular answers. The lifting of section D up a step three and a half bars later is highly unusual and is only hinted at in the melody itself. The entries or answers or subjects on other than regular tonic–dominant terms (e.g. fifth, octave and seventh over bb10–14) recall middle entries of stretto fugues in *Das Wohltemperirte Clavier* (e.g. C major in Book I, D major in Book II). At least the first of the sections has a fugal theme whose character resembles the C sharp major Fugue of Book II, as does the increase in faster figures towards the end. In diction generally, BWV 712 is close to J. S. Bach's fugal harpsichord music – not only the texture of such passages as bb20–30 but the cell-like motifs themselves, particularly Ex. 253.

Ex. 253

However, such motifs were typical of compound-time chorale fugues (cf. BWV 673, 674) or sections in chorale fantasias (e.g. Buxtehude's 'Wie schön leuchtet' BUXWV 223).

713

Jesu, meine Freude (formerly 'Kirnberger Collection')

No Autograph MS; copies in Brussels II.3919 (second quarter of eighteenth century), Am.B. 72a (Kirnberger), Am.B. 72, P 1109 (Penzel), P 1116 (Kühnel), P 1160, Danzig 4203/4, Sp 1438 and late sources.

Headed 'Fantasia'; two staves.

For TEXT and MELODY see BWV 610.

The form of BWV 713 is unusual:

A   bb1–52, a continuous two- and three-part fugue on a subject which, modified, serves as a countersubject to each of the first six lines of the chorale melody; these six lines appear as cantus-firmus phrases successively in S T B T B S, and are prefaced and interspersed with regular fugal entries

B   *dolce* $^3/_8$, an imitative three- and four-part section paraphrasing (or following the harmonies and outlines of) the final four lines of the chorale melody

Both sections are carefully written to be idiomatic and practicable for the hands alone. The fugal sections themselves are essentially in two voices, the third adding a contrapuntal part between the cantus-firmus phrases; the subject usually appears late and is complete only when there is no cantus firmus. The texture is characterized by intensive use of motifs, particularly the scale-like fragments of semiquavers shown in Ex. 254. The chorale melody appears to restrict fugal development in

Ex. 254

two ways: the key returns constantly to E minor; and, presumably because of the length of the ten-line hymn, there is little interlude development (e.g. no sequential treatment of b46). As in BWV 710, invertible counterpoint forms an important part – for instance, bb26–39 = bb1–14, soprano and tenor inverted (with modifications); but while bb18–19 and 43–4 are closely related, chorale line 6 (b49) is newly harmonized.

The change of metre, style and cantus-firmus treatment at b53 is striking, more so than in the motet BWV 227, no. 5 (verse 3), where at the same point in the stanza the paraphrased chorale melody resembles BWV 713 (Ex. 255). The melody becomes extensile and is

Ex. 255
BWV 227, no. 5
b37

Ex. 256
b53

pulled out over a long phrase (Ex. 256). Spitta described it as 'varied freely in the Böhmian manner' (Spitta I p601), but there are no exact parallels in extant works by Böhm. In the motet,* there is no clean break with the preceding section, nor are the thirds and *empfindsam* motifs so foreign to the work (cf. BWV 227, no. 9 (verse 5)). In the organ chorale, the section becomes a whole movement with its own developed motifs and keyboard cadences (compare the final cadence with that of BWV 695). So subtly do the last three chorale lines pervade the section that several suggestions can be made as to where they fit.

* Since the version of the melody used in BWV 713 is like that of BWV 610 but unlike BWV 227, it is probable that the organ chorale preceded the motet (Meyer 1974 p85). However, the 'Choral' which follows the Fantasia BWV 713 (*NBA* IV/3 p57) has the passing-note of Bach's 'Leipzig arrangements' of the melody – suggesting perhaps that it was added later?

Keller hears the final line in the last ten bars (Keller 1948 p180), but it fits bb77–82 equally well.

In number of bars the two sections are almost the same length; but if – as is possible – a proportional tempo were intended ($^4/_4$ $\wp$ = $^3/_8$ $\wp$ ·), the symmetry would be merely visual, and the playing length would reflect the original structure of the chorale melody, i.e. first section of six lines, second section of three lines. The performer can produce a stylish transition between the sections if the last bar of the $^4/_4$ section incorporates a ritardando so that the last four semiquavers of the $^4/_4$ (left hand) match those in the first bar of the $^3/_8$ section (right hand).

713a   Jesu, meine Freude

No Autograph MS; late copies only, in Schelble–Gleichauf and Peters VI.

BWV 713a differs from 713 chiefly in two respects: the key (D minor), and the fact that the cantus-firmus lines of the first section are all given to pedal in the bass octave, as are cadences and non-thematic phrases in the second section. The resulting trio texture is uncharacteristically spaced, although the key itself is plausible. The source is the same as BWV 691a, 683a etc.

714   Ach Gott und Herr

No Autograph MS; copies in P 802 (J. T. Krebs) and Kö 15839 (J. G. Walther?).

Headed in P 802 'per Canones'; two staves

The TEXT of M. Rutelius's (?) Lenten hymn was published in 1613; the original hymn had six verses, to which J. Gross added four more (Luedtke 1918 pp39, 95), changing the association from Lent to Passion. A few hymnbooks list the text under the 19th Sunday after Trinity (Gojowy 1972).

Ach Gott und Herr,	Ah God and Lord,
wie gross und schwer	how great and heavy
sind mein begangne Sünden!	are the sins I have committed!
Da ist niemand	There is no one to be found
der helfen kann	who can help
in dieser Welt zu finden.	in this world.

v8

Also Herr Christ	So Lord Christ,
mein Zuflucht ist	my refuge is
die Höhle deiner Wunden,	the cave of your wounds,
wenn Sünd und Tod	if sin and death
mich bracht in Not,	have brought me to distress,
hab mich darein gefunden.	I have found myself there.

The MELODY appears in two versions – minor (J. Crüger 1640, BWV 714) and major (Cantata 48, BWV 255, 692, 693): Ex. 257. The chorale is listed in the *Orgelbüchlein*.

Ex. 257

BWV 255

The canon between soprano and tenor is less strict than the ingenuity demonstrated in the *Orgelbüchlein* canons could have made it (e.g. b17); nor is the melody which emerges in bb12–17 quite the same as in any other version. Perhaps the sources are corrupt.* As in BWV 693, the theme and its countersubject incorporate or lead to useful motifs open to development throughout the chorale, *rectus*, *inversus* and diminished. Scale segments suggest that the theme and countersubject are related (Ex. 258). As an unstrict canonic harmonization without

Ex. 258

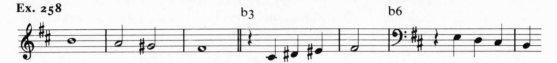

interludes between lines, BWV 714 is similar to such *Orgelbüchlein* chorales as BWV 620 but is less fluent and skilled. The distribution of parts is uncertain and the use of two staves might suggest that the copy is a kind of score which could be played in various ways: the cantus firmus on a separate manual (Klotz *NBA* IV/3 *KB* p39), or the pedal taking bass, tenor or soprano. However, the lowest line (given to pedal in *BG* 40 and later editions) makes an uncharacteristic pedal part, and the four parts can be better played by hands except at bb16–17 – perhaps further evidence of a corrupt text at this point. For a comparison with J. L. Krebs's work, see BWV 744.

---

715   Allein Gott in der Höh' sei Ehr'

No Autograph MS; copy in P 804 (J. P. Kellner).

Two staves.

For TEXT and MELODY see BWV 662.

Like BWV 722 and others, BWV 715 appears to be an accompanimental movement for congregational use, with interludes separating successive lines of the hymn.† However, the chromatic changes in the melody (bb6, 13) and the lengthening of cadence bars (bb4, 9, 16) reduce the convenience of the movement from this point of view, even were a hymnbook to be found which showed clearly that such interludes were desired. Also, not only is the series of chromatic harmonies exceptional, but the inter-line runs do not prepare the following chord (as in BWV 722 etc), and at one point (b2) they agree with neither the preceding nor the following harmony.

---

* E.g., the fifth tenor phrase could have been used in the soprano a bar earlier, with the bass unaltered, if the alto were different.
† Of the kind formerly called *Arnstädter Gemeindechoräle*, but (according to the sources) probably to be dated to the Weimar period (Klotz *NBA* IV/3 *KB* p11); see also a note on J. T. Krebs, BWV 722a.

716   Allein Gott in der Höh' sei Ehr'

No Autograph MS; copies in P 1160 (Oley), P 312.

Headed 'Fuga'; two staves.

For TEXT and MELODY see BWV 662.

The setting BWV 716 (excluded from *NBA* IV/3) appears to be in the tradition of three-part chorale fugues for organ, with sections based on successive subjects:

> b1   exposition of a subject taken from line 1 of the melody, with further bass entry b19
> b29   beginning of second exposition of an unobtrusive subject derived from line 2 (Ex. 259), simplified in bass answer b40
> episode after further soprano entry in b45
> b56   alto re-introduces first subject; countersubject derived from second subject (*a*); bass answer (b70), being a plain cantus firmus (as in BWV 733, 664) on lines 1–2 of the melody, is thus a simplified version of the two subjects in turn
> final treble entry, b82

Ex. 259

b29

Though unambitious in texture, the movement is carefully planned in form, particularly in the pervasive character of the crotchet figures from the entry of the second subject onwards. The use of partial cantus firmus at the close is satisfactory because the chorale melody itself ends as it begins (cf. BWV 664).

---

717   Allein Gott in der Höh' sei Ehr'

No Autograph MS; copies in P 802 (J. T. Krebs), Lpz MB MS 7 (Mempell–Preller).

Two staves.

For TEXT and MELODY see BWV 662.

Like the first part of BWV 713, BWV 717 is a two- and three-part *manualiter* fugue built predominantly on a subject against whose motifs (rather than against the subject itself) all the lines of the chorale appear in plain cantus-firmus form. In contrast to BWV 713, the melody

remains in the soprano, there is no change of direction halfway
through, and the subject is clearly derived from line 1 of the melody
(Ex. 260: cf. Ex. 162). Motifs *a* and *b* remain very important throughout

Ex. 260

the movement in both *rectus* and *inversus* forms, changing the direction
of the second subject which looks at first as if it is to paraphrase line
5 of the melody (Ex. 261). The subject fits both line 6 (b47) and the

Ex. 261

final pedal point, its motifs are open to sequential and imitative
treatment, and the resulting texture is often suggestive of harpsichord
music, particularly the fugal gigues of the English Suites and Partitas
(e.g. bb52–6). A sign of the subtle pervasiveness of the subject, already
admired by Spitta (I pp597–8), is that the motif *b* usually appears on
weak beats, and weak beats are usually characterized by motif *b*. Such
pervasiveness surpasses earlier examples in Scheidt and Pachelbel,
while the simple paraphrase technique (successive notes of the chorale
melody can be heard on each beat of the fugue subject) does not yet
suggest the complex paraphrases to come in (e.g.) BWV 677.

---

718   Christ lag in Todesbanden

No Autograph MS; copies in BB Mus. MS Autogr. Krebs 2 (J. L.
Krebs), sources drawn probably from Kittel MSS (BB 32045; Lpz MB
MS 1), P 281, single sources used in *BG* 40.

Headed by Krebs 'à 2 Claviers et Pédale'; two staves. For manual
registration, see below.

For TEXT and MELODY see BWV 625.

As Klotz shows (*NBA* IV/3 *KB* p42), the sources suggest that the
movement circulated in versions differing in such details as ornaments
in the bass (mordents from b1 onwards in Lpz MB MS 1 etc) and the
melody (appoggiaturas b8 in Krebs's MS), in the passages marked

'forte' (b42 etc in BB 30245, P 281), in the 'Allegro' sign (b24, MB MS 1) and in the marks for the changes of manual:

MB MS 1   *Ob R (Oberwerk, Rückpositiv)*
BB 30245, P 281 *piano forte (piano = Ob; forte = Rp)*
Krebs   *Ow, Uw* or *P (Unterwerk = forte?)*

Variants in notated ornaments and in the named changes of manual probably reflect the copyists' uncertainty as to traditional (and old-fashioned) practices in both respects for the performance of such chorale fantasias. The implications are that lines in a *bicinium* were ornamented, and that two manuals were to be used for such fantasia devices as echo or melody-with-accompaniment.

Since at least the time of Spitta (1 pp210–12), the influence of Böhm has been seen in BWV 718. Spitta himself also heard elements of Pachelbel in the sections which anticipate the following line of the melody (e.g. bb13, 24), and he assumed that the movement was 'conceived for pedal harpsichord', which is doubtful. In form, the movement has been seen to belong to the Buxtehude circle (Keller 1948 p140); but in any case it must be early, perhaps composed too much earlier for J. G. Walther to have known it at Weimar (Klotz *NBA* IV/3 *KB* p13). Other parallels can be drawn between (e.g.) various aspects of the opening bass theme and the continuo arias of earlier cantatas, such as the quasi-ostinato element found also in BWV 4, 71 and 106. As a whole, the movement has been likened to a north German chorale fantasia, in fact the composer's only fantasia (Dietrich 1929 p7). But only the echo passages are truly reminiscent of the north German chorale fantasia; the modest length of the movement and its clearcut sections suggest rather that it is a conscious attempt at surveying some of the repertory of variation techniques known to a fuller extent in the chorale partitas. Thus the short-phrase imitation beginning at bb24ff suggests the traditional simple imitations already found in (e.g.) Scheidt's setting of the same chorale melody.

The form may be expressed as:

A bb1–13   lines 1 and 2, *bicinium* style; for the motifs, ornaments, melodic construction and ostinato–ritornello bass, cf. Böhm's 'Vater unser im Himmelreich'

B bb13–33   lines 3, 4 and 5, two-part accompaniment; not fore-imitation, but melody (still solo rh) anticipated in accompaniment; each line in turn treated at greater length (for the semiquaver figure developed from line 5, see Cantata 4 *Versus* V, bb43–54, also Partita BWV 766 Var. 3)

C bb33–42   line 6, partial paraphrase of melody in triplets, which supply a motif for development; the triplet sequences as in Scheidt, Pachelbel, etc

D bb42–61   line 7, sequential echo development of derived phrase (octave-echo and manual-echo effects), placed beyond the halfway point in the chorale (cf. Buxtehude's 'Gelobet seist du, Jesu Christ' BUXWV 188)

E bb61–73   line 8, three statements in minims (the final on pedal, cf. *Vers* 3 of BWV 656), around which a derived line is developed first in rh, secondly lh, thirdly both; leading to

F bb73–end coda, against the perfect cadence, the rh continues with its figurations, as in fantasias of Reincken, Lübeck, etc (cf. BWV 720).

The sections are articulated by clear tonic or dominant cadences.

The derivation of a conventionally square echo figure from line 7 shows the composer familiar with the principles behind this device (Ex. 262(i)); similarly, the figure in section *E* is moving towards paraphrasing techniques (Ex. 262(ii)). Such figures, turning into a

Ex. 262

(i) b52   **(ii)** b61

countersubject to the minim cantus firmus, are typical of the northern composers. The repetitious echo section is also apt for the text of VI at this point: 'und singen Halleluja' ('and singing Hallelujah'), just as the simple cantus firmus in each voice (bb63, 68, 71) is for the repeat of 'Hallelujah' – the final word of each verse.

Two performance problems arise from the nature of the movement: the tempo, and the distribution of manuals for section *C*. The array of ornaments implies a slower tempo for sections *A* and *B*, hence the 'Allegro' sign (b24) in a source that gives the ornaments (Lpz MB MS I); a later reading may have been to omit ornaments and play at one sustained tempo. However, the sections of longer north German fantasias often seem to require varying tempos, irrespective of ornaments, as too they seem to require varying registration. The choice of manual for section *C* is unclear: both the spacing in b35 and the 'piano' in b41 may suggest that both hands play on the louder manual from at least b35 to the second half of b41 – in which case both hands may also have played on the louder manual from b27 onwards, though this is less likely.

---

719   Der Tag der ist so freudenreich

Only source: MS entitled 'Choraele . . . gesetzet und herausgegeben von Johann Christoph Bachen, Organ: in Eisenach' (*BG* 40 p.xxix).

Spitta, who owned the MS, describes it as written *c*1700 and makes no suggestion that any of its contents is attributed to J. S. Bach (I p99); it is not clear why *BG* 40 included it, why it was arranged on three staves, or what version the melody from b34 was based upon. There are two sections: bb1–24, a fughetta on line 1; bb27–end (after a three-bar flourish), fore-imitation based on line 2 (cantus firmus b34).

---

720   Ein' feste Burg ist unser Gott

No Autograph MS; copies by J. G. Walther (Den Haag 4 G 14 and
Kö 15839) and J. T. Krebs (P 802); earlier (?) copy in *Plauener Orgelbuch* (c1710); later copies in BB 32045 (Dröbs), etc.

Headed in *Plauener Orgelbuch* and Walther MSS 'à 3 claviers et pédale',
by Krebs 'a 2 Clav. e Ped.'; two staves, three for trio sections; for
manual registration as in Kö 15839, see below.

The TEXT of Luther's hymn, a free paraphase of Ps. 46, was written
in 1528, not tied to any particular event (Stapel 1950 pp213ff) but later
becoming associated with Oculi (3rd Sunday in Lent) and also with
Reformation Day (Stiller 1970 p226) – for which, however, few hymnbooks had rubrics (Gojowy 1972).

Ein feste Burg ist unser Gott,	A firm stronghold is our God,
ein gute Wehr und Waffen.	a good bulwark and weapon.
Er hilft uns frei aus aller Not,	He helps us out of all distress
die uns jetzt hat betroffen.	that has come upon us now.
Der alt böse Feind	The old wicked enemy
mit Ernst ers jetzt meint;	means it now in earnest;
gross Macht und viel List	great power and much cunning
sein grausam Rüstung ist,	are his fearful armament,
auf Erd ist nicht seinsgleichen.	he has no equal on earth.

Three further verses combine defiance and faith. Each verse is in two
clear halves (*Stollen/Abgesang*).

The MELODY, said to be adapted by Luther himself from a plainsong,
was published with the text in 1531. Ex. 263 shows that the fantasia

Ex. 263
1535

BWV 720 recalls Klug's version of 1535 (Terry 1921 p153) as closely as
it does the familiar simpler versions. The melody is harmonized in
BWV 302 and 303 and listed in *Orgelbüchlein*; it is used in Cantata
80a (Weimar, cantata for Oculi), and all four verses in Cantata 80
(Reformationsfest 1724 etc?).

Although sometimes likened to the much longer north German chorale fantasia, BWV 720 is, like BWV 718, rather a series of different techniques or methods of developing a cantus firmus:

A bb1–20   lines 1, 2 (3, 4) in dialogue registration (see below), each line one or more times in each hand, decorated or paraphrased
B bb20–4   line 5, paraphrase, two-part imitation above continuo bass
C bb24–33 lines 6, 7 cantus firmus pedal (cf. lines 6, 7 of the text of VI)
D bb35–9   line 8 paraphrase, two-part imitation above pedal
E bb39–end line 9, cantus firmus in *bicinium* texture (cf. BWV 711); then restated in four-part texture (motif as in previous section)

As well as the simple decorations of line 1 in bb1, 4* and 12, and of line 2 in bb8 and 16, there are more paraphrase-like derivations – Ex. 264. As is fitting for the derivative of a line that itself occurs three times

Ex. 264

in the melody (lines 2, 4, 9), the motif *a* can be heard throughout the piece, e.g. in bb4, 6, 15, 27, 28, 33, 34, 52–5, and possibly elsewhere. Line 5 (which can be heard emerging through the complete left-hand phrase bb20–4) and line 8 (ditto, right hand bb35–7) are spun out and disguised, appearing between chorale lines which are treated more simply. The result is that every line of the chorale melody is represented in the movement.

The registration and playing method of BWV 720 and its supposed origin are all interlinked. From Spitta (I pp394–7) onwards, it has often

* The changing of the cadences in bb6 and 9 for the *NBA* edition seems unjustified; *BG* 40 is more correct.

been supposed that the movement was composed for the opening of the rebuilt three-manual organ at the Divi-Blasii-Kirche in Mühlhausen in 1709 and was planned, by the composer/organist who had advised on the instrument, to show its colourful possibilities. Some material facts are:

(i) The musical style of the movement suggests that it was composed earlier than 1709: the squareness of rhythm, texture and parallel motion of such passages as bb50–3 seem even more conclusive evidence than the motifs themselves. However, the conventional *figurae* – though repetitive and partita-like (Frotscher 1935 p934) – are already treated inventively, e.g. two applications of the *suspirans* in bb35 and 51.

(ii) There is no evidence of an opening recital on or dedication of the rebuilt organ.

(iii) The headings and the 'Fagotto' 'Sesquialtera' registration in the Walther and Plauen copies are plausible though (in the nature of sources) not authenticated. Mühlhausen has three manuals and has both the specified stops; but while the compass of the Fagotto is unknown, it may have been only C–c or C–c' (note added by J. L. Albrecht in J. Adlung's *Musica mechanica organoedi* (Berlin 1768) pp92, 260) and thus would be unsuitable for BWV 720. The dialogue Sesquialtera/Fagotto is of a kind known to French composers of the period (viz. Cornet/Cromorne) and was described by later German writers such as Adlung (*Anleitung zur musikalischen Gelahrtheit* (2nd edn, 1783) p588–9), who regarded the Sesquialtera as unsuitable below c' (the lowest note in the relevant section of BWV 720 is c♯', except for the a in b15). The likelihood that a pedal reed is required for the cantus firmus in bb25–32 might reflect the 'gravität' of the new 'Posaunen Bass' as described by the composer himself (*Dok* I pp152–5); but pedal reeds of a suitable kind were more common in the area, both then and later, than the 'Rückpositiv' specified in the sources for the section beginning at b20.

(iv) The movement, with its varying texture and treatment of the chorale melody – cf. 'Ein' feste Burg' by J. N. Hanff (1630–1706) – would certainly give opportunity for important organ effects: dialogue, manual cantus firmus, pedal cantus firmus, and passages in solo, duo, trio and quartet. At the same time, there are traditional central and north German elements, in particular the running right-hand passages leading to the next chorale line (bb33, 48) and the final runs rounding off the pedal point. Such characteristics can be regarded as an argument on either side, as can the fact that in the MS Den Haag 4 G 14 Walther includes BWV 720 with two other settings of the melody (Hanff, Buxtehude).

(v) It is unusual to find both registration and manual indication so explicit in the sources;* but at least one movement by J. G. Walther

* The Plauen and Walther MSS are not necessarily independent evidence on registration, since they are probably related (they contain some of the same works).

('Hilf, Gott, dass mir's gelinge') was registered yet more fully in the *Plauener Orgelbuch* than BWV 720 (catalogue in Seiffert 1920 p373):

Rp (c.f.)	*forte*	Prinzipal 4', Sesquialtera
Ow (accompaniment)	*piano*	Viola da Gamba 8'
Ped (c.f. in canon)		Cornet 2'

All four stops were both at Mühlhausen and in Walther's church at Weimar.

The connection between BWV 720 and the organ at Mühlhausen or elsewhere is not straightforward, though it is still assumed to be so (e.g. Klotz 1975 p386). Even if the (wide-scaled?) Fagotto were of complete compass, it would probably have been at 16';* and it is unclear whether the Sesquialtera had two, three or five ranks – i.e. whether the term were a registration or a stop. In b20, the 'Rückpositiv' seems to apply to both hands (specified for left hand in e.g. P 802), presumably with a *petit plein jeu*; this in turn implies that the Sesquialtera was a *Brustwerk* stop or registration, and the Fagotto on the *Oberwerk*. In b24, the left-hand 'Oberwerk' suggests a chorus of some kind, the right hand still on the *Rückpositiv*. From b25, the two Walther sources have the pedal cantus firmus written on octave lower 'to obtain the effect of the 32' *Untersatz* at Mühlhausen' (Klotz 1975 p386), in which case Walther confused notation with acoustics and produced strange three-part spacing. The free left hand in b34 enables any pedal reed to be taken off. The left-hand sign 'Oberwerk' in b39 suggests that in b35 it plays *Rückpositiv*, which seems desirable from the point of view of texture; whether or not the 'Oberwerk' sign applies also to the right hand of b41 is less certain – from there to the end, the right hand could play either *Rückpositiv* or *Oberwerk* – more likely the former. It could also be that from b50 the left hand also plays on the *Rückpositiv* since that could still be the 'louder' of the two manuals unless an untypical registration change had taken place near b39 or b50. The changing texture of such pieces does allow licence in the use of manuals, as indeed it does in the longer fantasias of Bruhns, Lübeck and others; in BWV 720, rests occur so conveniently in one hand or the other as to make it possible for the Fagotto (or any alternative reed) to belong to any manual. It is not impossible that such adaptability was a purpose of the work and that Walther merely added his own interpretation. That Walther may have meant his registrations merely to 'demonstrate by example how a certain type of composition is to be realised' (Daw 1976 p34) is suggested by the facts that his manual and/or registration signs are uniform (standardized?) in P 801 and P 802, and that he seems to have added them to works copied by others, e.g. J. T. Krebs.

---

* Not that this would make it unreasonable to use it for the opening phrase: the downward run across two octaves (bb2–3) would demonstrate the tone of any reed, and no organist in 1710 was so dominated by the 8' norm as his descendants.

721   Erbarm' dich mein, o Herre Gott

No Autograph MS; only copy, P 802 (J. G. Walther).

Two staves.

The TEXT of J. Hegenwalt's hymn was published in 1524; a translation of Ps. 51, the five verses were generally associated with 'penitence and conversion' (Freylinghausen 1741 etc), and particularly with the 3rd, 11th, 14th and 22nd Sundays after Trinity (Vopelius 1682).

Erbarm dich mein, o Herre Gott,	Be merciful to me, O Lord God;
nach deiner gross' Barmherzigkeit	according to your great mercy
wasch ab mach rein mein Missethat,	wash me cleanly of my misdoing;
ich kenn mein Sünd und ist mir leid.	I know my sin and it grieves me.
Allein ich dir gesündigt hab	Only against you have I sinned,
das ist wider mich stetiglich;	and it is constantly before me;
das Bös vor dir nicht mag bestahn,	evil cannot stand before you,
du bleibst gerecht, ob man urtheile	you are just, however you are
dich.	judged.

The MELODY was published with the text and, like most hymns in Johann Walther's books, was later simplified: Ex. 265. The chorale

Ex. 265

BWV 305

is listed in the *Orgelbüchlein* and harmonized in BWV 305. The sharpened third note (as in BWV 721) occurs also in the work by Busbetzky referred to below.

Though included in *NBA* IV/3, BWV 721 has often been found difficult to accept as authentic on grounds of texture:

> repeated three- and four-part chords, without break from first bar to last, below the cantus firmus (line by line) in long notes in the soprano

No other example in such style is known to have been composed by J. S. Bach – nor any, in quite such simplicity, by his contemporaries. In P 802, Walther specifies neither the pedal nor the two manuals given in *BG* 40, and the movement is playable by two hands on one keyboard – hardly an accident in what is at times a five-part piece. This approach to the setting, whose austerity is clearly appropriate for such a text, incorporates no real paraphrase techniques; however, the harmony expresses the modal cadence of the melody, and the bass does seem to anticipate the chorale line at two places (bb1–2 and b34).

Many suggestions have been made as to the origins of the style of BWV 721. Spitta (I p212) suggested one of Böhm's settings, 'Vater unser im Himmelreich', where, however, the chords are less constant and there is a clear pedal line – radical differences. Terry (1921 p158) and Keller (1937) point to the movement 'Il tremore degl'Israeliti' in Kuhnau's Biblical Sonata no. 1 (1700): one passage, headed 'their prayer to God', in which repeated chords accompany the chorale melody *Aus tiefer Noth*, is much closer to BWV 721. Klotz (*NBA* IV/3 *KB* p47) refers to the repeated chords in the preludes BWV 541, 543 and 549, where, however, there is always either a part moving against them or a held note in the pedal. Mahrenholz (quoted by Klotz *ibid*) claims that the composer was 'stylistically dependent' on the cantata setting 'Erbarme dich mein, o Herre Gott' formerly attributed to Buxtehude but now known to be by Buxtehude's pupil Ludwig Busbetzky (M. Geck *Mf* 1973, p175)* – cf. Ex. 266. Beyond this, the

Ex. 266

Busbetzky, 'Erbarme dich mein, o Herre Gott', 2nd movement

doctrinaire simplicity of BWV 721 invalidates comparison both with general keyboard techniques from Scheidt to J. K. F. Fischer and with the string accompaniment to such pieces as the Sonatina from Cantata 106. Scheidt's *imitatio tremula organi* (*Tabulatura nova, DTÖ* I pp62–3) is a lively *bicinium*, and its repeated notes, superficially resembling BWV 721, do not accompany a chorale. But whatever the influences, the wealth of seventh and ninth chords in BWV 721 makes it likely that its composer was familiar with Italian continuo harmonies in trio sonatas c1700.

---

* Bärenreiter edn 1137, ed. B. Grusnick (Kassel, 1937). In bb5ff Busbetzky writes minims with the direction 'Trem', interpreted by Grusnick (in the light of b4) as repeated quavers. The early-seventeenth-century organ-builder E. Compenius noted that a suitable Tremulant rate was eight times per bar (F. Blume, *Michael Praetorius und Esaias Compenius Orgeln Verdingnis*, Wolfenbüttel/Berlin 1936): this rate perhaps implies a lively tempo.

722   Gelobet seist du, Jesu Christ

No Autograph MS; copies in BB 22541/1 (J. G. Walther), Lpz MB MS 7 (J. G. Preller), Lpz Poel 39 (Kittel) and late sources.

Headed in 22541/1 'man' (*manualiter*); two staves

For TEXT and MELODY see BWV 604.

On this type of movement, see BWV 715. In the spacing of the hands, in the ornaments, and in the incipient motif development (bb5, 10), BWV 722 seems apt for keyboard. The last four bars, outwardly a simple setting of the 'Kyrie eleison' part of the text (see also BWV 604 at this point), nevertheless hint at motif and harmony (e.g. minor subdominant) of bigger chorales. The flourish after each line of the chorale sustains in its first half the harmony of the previous chord, and in its second half anticipates the next (Ex. 267). The third such passage keeps the

Ex. 267

same chord.* Although quick modulatory harmonies are found (b2), those of bb8–9 suggest a language approaching that of some *Orgelbüchlein* chorales. The sources are generous with ornaments. Mempell–Preller collects the piece together with BWV 738, 729 and 732 as 'Vier Weynachts Chorale' (in the same order as BWV 722a, 738a, 729a and 732a in Krebs's P 802), and Walther includes BWV 722 within a group of eight settings of the melody.

722a   Gelobet seist du, Jesu Christ

No Autograph MS; only source, P 802 (J. T. Krebs).

No composer's name; two staves.

The harmonies of BWV 722a, as shown in its figured bass, are closely followed in BWV 722; the chief difference is that the unbarred BWV 722a gives no sign of the half-speed of the last four bars (minim Gs). But

---

* In P 802, the sketch version BWV 722a keeps a held bass note through the second and third inter-line flourishes; but it can only be doubted that the notes 'are to be held during the flourishes' (Zietz 1969 p166).

neither can be presumed to be the earlier version, as each could be drawn from the other, despite the worked-out 'Kyrie' pedal point at the end. That is so of all the four Christmas hymns copied on pp241–2 of P 802 (BWV 722a, 738a, 729a, 732a): the unrealized figured 'sketches' may be reductions rather than drafts, despite what is usually claimed. The sources suggest that the unrealized versions may have been written first, though this is perhaps an accident of preservation; but they suggest Weimar as the place of composition (Klotz *NBA* IV/3 *KB* p11). Two further examples of such chorales occur without attribution in P 802; again the chorale in minims is interspersed with four sets of runs (alternating treble and bass). Perhaps all six are the student work of J. T. Krebs and not, as is often thought (Spitta I p586; Meyer 1974 pp80–1), demonstration pieces in which J. S. Bach showed his Weimar pupils how to play congregational hymns.

723

Gelobet seist du, Jesu Christ

No Autograph MS; copies in Lpz Poel 39 (Kittel), P 409 (*c*1800).

Two staves.

For TEXT and MELODY see BWV 604.

Excluded from *NBA* IV/3, BWV 723 shows the chorale form associated with Pachelbel: each line of the cantus firmus in long notes (here in soprano) is preceded by irregular fore-imitations running through the three accompanying parts, on a theme derived from the melody. The result can be compared with (e.g.) Pachelbel's 'Komm, Gott, Schöpfer, heiliger Geist' (BWV 657 is a further example). But it is to be noted that the composer does not maintain the fore-imitation to the end; there is none for the last line, and before the penultimate line the treatment is less strict. The G-mixolydian key gives tonal ambiguity to the opening fugue: the answer appears to be in the subdominant, and the whole movement wavers between C and G (cf. BWV 697).

It is uncertain whether the heading 'a 2 Clav. e Pedale' in *BG* 40 is justified, since (as often in Pachelbel) the four parts can be played by hands on one manual. Both the contents of Lpz Poel 39 and Kittel's probable access to Bach's own copies (*NBA* IV/3 *KB* pp14, 17) suggest that the attribution to Bach is correct. The four parts are managed with more than competence and without relying on conventional formulae for suspensions etc; but the clear perfect cadences at the end of each line evoke no particular composer, nor do they have any clear textual reference despite the claim that they speak the affirmation 'das ist wahr' of v1 (Chailley 1974 p123).

---

724   Gott durch deine Güte

No Autograph MS; *Andreas-Bach-Buch* (Lpz MB III.8.4).

In tablature (J. B. Bach?).

For TEXT and MELODY see BWV 600. The title is in the *Andreas-Bach-Buch*, but a later hand has added 'Gottes [Sohn] ist kommen' (as in *BG* 40 and Schmieder *BWV*), matching the double title of BWV 600.

The 'early' character of BWV 724 has often been commented upon (*NBA* IV/3 *KB* p11), not least in that no later copies seem to have been made by Walther or Krebs; the technique of contrapuntal accompaniment 'with neither sustained motif nor thematic interludes' is seen by Spitta as 'the most primitive form of organ chorale', as in BWV 737 (Spitta I p595). Nevertheless, the careful four- and five-part texture has points of interest, notably the tentative canonic effects in bb7 and 8, 12 and 13, 17 and 21, 33 and 34, 38 and 39. All of these are worked more strictly in BWV 600, where the composer's grasp of four-part harmony has dealt more imaginatively with canonic problems. The texture of BWV 724 is also written so that the first half is predominantly crotchets, the second quavers, as shown by the syncopations in bb23, 24 etc and the scale motif of b30. While according to *BG* 40 and *NBA* IV/3 the pedal enters in b9 for the fourth (partly free) part, there is no pedal instruction in the tablature until b34, where it is given for the fifth part. Such a pedal entry as b34 agrees with other chorales in which the pedal is withheld until the final two cantus-firmus phrases, e.g. BWV 716, where there is also, as here, some thematic resemblance between the opening and closing lines of the melody. Despite attempts to show some textual reference behind the use of canonic imitation (e.g. bb33 and 34), the composer seems rather to be experimenting with the device: cf. the canon at the fourth in bb1–10 of BWV 716.

---

725   Herr Gott, dich loben wir

No Autograph MS; only source, Peters VI (copy by Forkel).

Three staves in *BG* 40 (five parts).

The TEXT is Luther's translation into rhyming couplets of the hymn *Te Deum*; it was published in 1529. In some hymnbooks (e.g. Weissenfels) it became a hymn for New Year's Day (Gojowy 1972) and in others a hymn of 'praise and thanksgiving' (Stiller 1970 pp223, 232). Luther perhaps saw it as the authority for a confession of faith. The first four of the fifty-three lines are:

Herr Gott, dich loben wir.	Lord God, we praise you.
Herr Gott, wir danken dir.	Lord God, we thank you.

| *Dich, Vater in Ewigkeit,* | You, Father in eternity, |
| *ehrt die Welt weit und breit.* | The world honours far and wide. |

The MELODY – a simplified form of the plainsong (*Liber usualis*, appendix Hymn for Thanksgiving) – appears intact as the top line throughout BWV 725. It was listed in the *Orgelbüchlein*, and sections were used (with different parts of the text) in Cantatas 16 (New Year 1726 etc?) and 190 (New Year 1724 etc), 119 (Council Election 1723), 120 (wedding, *c*1729), and 190a and 120b (200th anniversary of the Augsburg Confession, 1730). The harmonization of the melody in BWV 328 often agrees with that in BWV 725 when the line concerned is not repeated in the former or re-harmonized to the new verse in the latter (e.g. bb1ff, 174ff, 184ff, 244ff);* at one point, however, the melody is slightly different (bb188–202).

Whatever the relationship between BWV 328 (four parts) and 725 (five), the latter does appear to be a written-out organ accompaniment – very likely to provide varied harmonies for a repetitious chant (Spitta I p588). The following points should be noted:

(i) The phrygian modal framework is preserved, as in BWV 328.

(ii) The accompanying parts gradually admit contrapuntal motifs, particularly where repeated lines are concerned; no distinction is made corresponding to the antiphonal division of verse and response which at that period was still the method of singing the *Te Deum* in such churches as the Nikolaikirche in Leipzig (Spitta II p109), traditionally at Mattins (Stiller 1970 p39), in the manner outlined in the 1533 Wittenberg *Kirchenordnung* (Stapel 1950 pp170ff).

(iii) References to the text are certainly to be heard in the music: perhaps the 'angels' in the scale of b18 (cf. BWV 607), 'the incarnation and its purpose' in bb123ff, 'divine power' in the pedal of bb143ff, 'appeal for help' in the chromatic lines of bb163ff, and 'the vigour of belief and praise' (?) in bb193ff.

(iv) A close relation to the text, however, is not in the style of other treatments of *Te Deum* passages (BWV 119, 120); nor would it agree with the modified repetitions within BWV 725, i.e. passages serving two sets of words:

bb143–52, see bb223–32
bb153–7, see bb213–17
bb163–72, see bb233–42

The passages repeated include some of the less conventional harmonies of the movement.

The modified repeats, particularly bb158–9 as altered in bb218–9, may

---

* Bar numbers include repeats, as in B&H edn 6589: i.e., the piece has 258 bars in all, with bb53–62 repeated five times as bb53–102.

be for continuity rather than word-painting. Similarly, the continuity achieved through occasional ties and moving motifs between various lines of the couplets implies that the movement could not be anti-phonally performed unless the organ accompanied both lines. On the other hand, the profusion of cadences hinders continuity – a major difference between the contrapuntal technique of BWV 725 and that of *Orgelbüchlein* chorales that use imitative motifs similar to that in (e.g.) b188.

---

726   Herr Jesu Christ dich zu uns wend'

No Autograph MS; only source, P 804 (J. P. Kellner).

Two staves.

For TEXT and MELODY see BWV 632.

On this type of movement, see BWV 715, which immediately precedes BWV 726 in P 804. Like other examples of the type, BWV 726 has interludes which grow progressively more *arpeggiato*; unlike others of the type, it remains strictly in four parts, of which only the bass is unvocal.

---

727   Herzlich thut mich verlangen

No Autograph MS; copies by J. G. Walther (Den Haag 4 G 14, Kö 15839) and J. T. Krebs (P 802).

Headed in P802 only, 'à 2 Clav. e ped.' (not in J. T. Krebs's hand; perhaps J. L. Krebs, later); two staves.

The TEXT of C. Knoll's hymn was published in 1605, becoming associated with funerals and the Resurrection (Freylinghausen 1741 etc).

Herzlich thut mich verlangen	From my heart I long
nach einem selgen End,	for a blessed end,
weil ich hie bin umfangen,	for I am here surrounded
mit Trübsal und Elend.	by trouble and misery.
Ich hab Lust abzuscheiden	I have a desire to be separated
von dieser argen Welt,	from this wicked world,
sehn mich nach ewgen Freuden,	and I long for eternal joys,
o Jesu, komm nur bald.	O Jesu, come soon.

The ten verses that follow alternate earthly misery with heavenly joy, as in v4 (used in Cantata 161):

Und leben ohne Noth	Living without distress
In himmlscher Freud und Wonne.	in heavenly joy and bliss.
Was schad't mir dann der Tod?	What harm does Death to me then?

The MELODY is that of Hassler's song *Mein G'müt ist mir verwir-ret/von einer Jungfrau zart* (Terry 1921 p196) and was attached to the text from 1613: Ex. 268. Although there are no other organ settings,

Ex. 268

1601

the melody was associated with an unusually large number of texts: *Ach Herr, mich armen Sünder* (Cantata 135, 3rd Sunday after Trinity 1724), *O Haupt voll Blut und Wunden* (four times in *St Matthew Passion*; Cantata 159, Estomihi (Quinquagesima) 1729?), *Befiehl du deine Wege* (*St Matthew Passion*; Cantata 153, Sunday after New Year 1724), *Wie soll ich dich empfangen* (*Christmas Oratorio*, I), *Ihr Christen auserkoren* (*Christmas Oratorio*, VI), as well as *Herzlich thut mich verlangen* (Cantata 161, 16th Sunday after Trinity 1715 etc; also feast of Mariae Reinigung (Purification of the Virgin)); it is also used without text in Cantatas 25 (14th Sunday after Trinity 1723), 127 (Estomihi 1725) and 161 (first movement). Among the unset *Orgelbüch-lein* chorales it is listed as 'Ach Herr, mich armen Sünder'.

The quality of the music, the *suspirans* figures in the decoration (Ex. 269), the *tmesis* figures or gaps in b3 etc, the relationship felt between

Ex. 269

b3

the mood of the music and the 'verlangen' ('longing') of line 1, and the form – soprano melody with accompaniment, without interludes – have all long suggested to players that BWV 727 is very like an *Orgelbüchlein* prelude. However, in its virtual lack of motivic or imitative development in the accompaniment, BWV 727 could only properly be compared to 'O Mensch, bewein' BWV 622, which 'compensates' with its coloratura melody. While in obvious ways BWV 727 differs from the *Klavierbüchlein* pieces BWV 691 and 728, its *suspirans* is found in the former; while it obviously differs from the Tremulant setting BWV 721 (also in P 802), they are very similar in spacing and final cadence. The movement is a harmonized chorale for organ without 'independent' musical devices, lying somewhere between simple four-part harmonies and *Orgelbüchlein* style, though nearer the latter. As a harmonization, its rapt mood is immediate and unequivocal;

what motifs there are (b5 etc) compel a sensitive performance, and the final cadence demands yet further rallentando. This would be so even were the associations of the melody to be still more ambiguous and various.

---

728   Jesus, meine Zuversicht

Autograph MS in P 224 (*Klavierbüchlein für Anna Magdalena Bach*, 1722); later copies e.g. P 643.

Headed 'Jesu, meine Zuversicht'; two staves.

The TEXT of the Easter hymn was published in 1653, becoming one of the death and resurrection hymns (Freylinghausen 1741 etc).

Jesus, meine Zuversicht	Jesus, my trust
und mein Heiland, ist im Leben.	and my Saviour, is alive.
Dieses weiss ich; soll ich nicht	This I know; should I not therefore
darum mich zufrieden geben,	be content with
was die lange Todesnacht	whatever the long night of death
mir auch für Gedanken macht?	makes me think of?

The nine verses that follow contrast death with the afterlife, e.g.

v6

Was hier kranket, seufzt und fleht,	What here is ailing, groaning and beseeching
wird dort frisch und herrlich gehen.	will there be fresh and glorious.

The MELODY was published with the hymn and later attributed to J. C. Crüger (Terry 1921 p238); its version in the harmonization BWV 365 is as in Ex. 270. A varied form was used in Cantata 145 (1st movement, not certainly by J. S. Bach).

Ex. 270

Although the piece in P 224 has the appearance of being a finished fair copy, it may well be that this was the first written-down form of the piece, written out at the moment of creation in 1722 or 1723 (Dadelsen 1958 pp99, 104; *NBA* v/4 *KB* pp11, 20). In form and type it corresponds to the rest of the keyboard book for Anna Magdalena Bach as BWV 691 does to that for Wilhelm Friedemann; whether the composer intended to convey in the decorated melody a subdued mood of death is less certain than that he was incorporating ornaments and figures already familiar from BWV 691 and from the Table of Ornaments in the album for Wilhelm Friedemann – thus perhaps providing practice in florid melodies (Spitta I p585), even a specific *exemplum* for the Table of Ornaments. The cadences of both chorales are their most conventional moments (e.g. the second half of b5 in BWV 728, similar to cadences in J. G. Walther); spacing and type of accompaniment are similar. On the other hand, the melody of BWV 728 shows a greater tendency to rely on groups of small notes and varied decorations of the figure ♪ ♪ .

729

In dulci jubilo

No Autograph MS; copies in Lpz MB MS 7 (J. G. Preller), Lpz Poel 39 (Kittel) and late sources.

Two staves.

For TEXT and MELODY see BWV 608.

Though grouped in some sources with other Christmas hymns with interludes (P 1108, Mempell–Preller), and though similar in form and type to BWV 715 etc, the movement has long been seen to be more developed, to use its interlude motifs more integrally within the piece, and to refer more explicitly to the overall mood of the text, even perhaps to the last verse (Spitta I p587) with its bells and choir of angels. Quite apart from any accident of sources, it is clear that the flourishes between chorale lines that are characteristic of such harmonizations are particularly suited to Christmas settings, none more so than BWV 729. It is much less certain whether the result is suitable for congregational or even choir accompaniment: the breaking of the melody in bb19–21, the irregularly prolonged cadence at bb22–5, the unequal lengths of the interludes (2, 2, 2, 3, 3, 2 bars), the musical rupture that would occur if the organist had to wait for the congregation to pick up the new line at (e.g.) the end of b32, the length of the coda – these suggest an independent organ work. The pedal, though it is not specified, *seems* to be more necessary than in the other chorales of this type, at least for the first ten bars and the last two; the ambiguity, characteristic of such organ music, may imply that only for the pedal point at the end is pedal required, despite the spacings.

The motifs are distinct: the broken scales of the first three interludes may suggest the angel throng (cf. BWV 607) or may be associated with the purpose of Christmas (cf. BWV 600); the broken chords of the fourth interlude suggest the patterns of *bicinium* basses; the moving crotchet bass lines of the fifth resemble those of BWV 600 and 607; and the high full chords of the close are rare outside doubtful or early works (cf. BWV 702, 716).

729a

In dulci jubilo

No Autograph MS; only source P 802 (J. T. Krebs).

No composer's name; two staves.

The figures (harmonies) of BWV 729a are most closely followed in BWV 729; for a note on the relationship between the two, however, see BWV 722. Three major differences between the two versions are: (*a*) like BWV 722a, BWV 729a is without bar-lines, possibly suggesting a freedom for the interludes that is less clear in BWV 729; (*b*) BWV 729a has no interlude between lines 4 and 5 of the chorale (i.e. bb30ff of BWV 729); (*c*) BWV 729a gives no hint of the last five bars (coda) of BWV 729.

730

Liebster Jesu, wir sind hier

No Autograph MS; copy in Lpz Poel 39 (Kittel) and late sources.

Two staves.

For TEXT and MELODY see BWV 633.

Like other harmonizations, BWV 730 preserves the melody above an accompaniment, in this case without either the interludes of (e.g.) BWV 726 or the solo line of (e.g.) BWV 727, but with four or five parts in the manner of (e.g.) BWV 722. Not only does the harmony at times point to the *Orgelbüchlein* (e.g. the diversionary $\frac{6}{4}_{2}$ of b4), but the third (fifth) line of the chorale is treated in a distinct manner anticipatory of certain *Orgelbüchlein* pieces, e.g. BWV 638 (motif, bass line). On this third line, see also BWV 731. In general, the five-part harmonies are of a higher order than the diminished sevenths of BWV 715; dominant and major sevenths and ninths, including the rich effects of b4 and b13, are now more in style. The rising pedal of b13 has suggested to some the words 'von der Erden Ganz zu dir' of VI (Chailley 1974 p185).

731

Liebster Jesu, wir sind hier

No Autograph MS; sources as BWV 730.

Headed 'à 2 claviers et pédale' (*NBA* IV/3); two staves.

For TEXT and MELODY see BWV 633.

Since both settings are found in the same source and since they differ melodically at the third (fifth) line, BWV 730 and 731 must be regarded as distinct pieces, although b1 of BWV 731 reads like a variation of b1 of BWV 730. The tenor and bass lines of BWV 730 and 731 begin with much the same notes as those comprising the characteristic motifs of BWV 633 and 634. Harmonically and melodically, bb11–12 of BWV 730 could replace the corresponding bars of BWV 731, if an organist were to require an ornamented chorale based on the version of the hymn melody used in BWV 730. The juxtaposition of the two settings in the source would also allow this.

The motifs of the inner parts, the moving bass line and the decorative elements (melismas, figures, ornaments) in the melody of BWV 731 seem to be merely woven – albeit skilfully – around the basic four-part harmony. Only in the obbligato-like phrases of bb13–14 does the setting become 'self-contained' in the *Orgelbüchlein* manner, although the accented passing-notes of b3 aleady suggest inventive harmonic treatment resulting from such motifs.

---

732   Lobt Gott, ihr Christen, allzugleich

No Autograph MS; copies in Lpz MB MS 7 (J. G. Preller), Lpz Poel 39 (Kittel), and late copies.

Two staves.

For TEXT and MELODY see BWV 609.

On this type of movement, see BWV 715. As in the case of BWV 729, the conception of such organ chorales is somewhat modified in BWV 732:

b1   typical interlude figure integrated into the harmonization of the chorale

bb2–3 more in *Orgelbüchlein* or partita style, the end of line 1 harmonized with semiquaver motifs

bb6–8 the chorale melody becomes hidden as an alto below a soaring top line (line 3 'today opens his Heaven', according to Spitta I p586)

It is possible too that the downward-running interlude in b8 is a picture of Jesus's descent to earth ('and gives us his son'); but it is uncertain whether the setting should be seen as 'a significant forward step' in the evolution of chorales (Keller 1948 p142), since there is no evidence that the harmonization with interludes came before other chorale forms. Moreover, it is likely that such full-chord technique was earlier than – and led to – the four-part harmonization known in other movements, e.g. BWV 706. The chorale as a whole looks like an improvisation: the short-lived motif development of b1, the change to quavers in b4, the free runs of the interludes, the drawing-out of cadences.

732a   Lobt Gott, ihr Christen allzugleich

No Autograph MS; only source, P 802 (J. T. Krebs).

No composer's name; two staves.

The figures (harmonies) of BWV 732a are followed in BWV 732; for remarks on the relationship, see BWV 722a. There is in BWV 732a no indication of the long closes to lines 1, 2, 3 and 5 of BWV 732 except the fermatas, but the tie to the first note of the first interlude of BWV 732a may well suggest it was taken from BWV 732; the interludes can then be understood as something written in the manner of a typical improvisation of the period.

---

733   Meine Seele erhebt den Herren (Fuga sopra il Magnificat)

No Autograph MS; copies in BB 12014/3, 12014/7 (J. L. Krebs), Am.B. 606 (Kirnberger circle), Darmstadt Mus. MS 525a (Oley).

Headed in two main sources 'Fuga sopra il Magnificat'; also headed in Oley 'Meine Seele erhebet den Herren – pro organo pleno con pedale'; two staves.

For TEXT and MELODY see BWV 648.

Since Spitta (1 p596), writers have related the form of BWV 733 to that of BWV 716; but the two Krebs sources have sometimes led commentators to attribute the work to J. L. Krebs himself, and, in general, the technique of fore-imitation based on a cantus firmus heard later in the movement is associated with Pachelbel. The idea of a loose fugue through which a chorale melody is heard was known both to older composers (e.g. Scheidt's 'Magnificat noni toni' on the same melody, the *tonus peregrinus*) and to contemporaries (e.g. 'Meine Seele erhebet den Herren' by J. C. Schiefferdecker, 1679–1732). But BWV 733 is a far development from its possible antecedents, and despite its texture and idiom it is to be seen rather as a fugal equivalent to the trio on 'Allein Gott in der Höh' sei Ehr'' BWV 664, i.e. a fully worked-out contrapuntal movement based on a theme (derived from the opening line of the chorale) and its countersubject, and crowned by a two-phrase pedal cantus firmus at the close. A further parallel is BWV 661, also using quaver figures.

It is not obvious in what sense BWV 733 is a fugue, nor how (or even whether) fore-imitation is involved. The cantus firmus appears not as a fugue subject but as a series of intonation-like entries, most of them signalling a new part in the texture:

b1	tonic (two parts)
b10	tonic (three parts)
b30	dominant (four parts including countersubject)

bb55–6   stretto
bb75–6   stretto
b98, b119   augmentation, lines 1 and 2 (five parts)

Though different in form, the effect is not at times unlike (e.g.) Contrapunctus IX from the *Art of Fugue*, in which the 'cantus firmus' sounds through the fugue. The opening of BWV 733 sounds fugal, owing to the conventional nature of the 'countersubject', which incorporates very useful ideas – Ex. 271. But it is the motifs that are picked out

Ex. 271

for development rather than the line itself; it is not answered as a fugue subject, nor does it accompany the chorale subject unaltered. More important to an understanding of the movement is the Italianate nature of the counterpoint produced in the first nine bars (two-part), the following thirteen (three-part), and so on until the five parts of b98. Motifs *x* and *y*, for example, are open to sequential extension, inversion and other 'developments'; moreover, like motifs *b c d e f g* and *h* they are familiar from *alla breve* counterpoint in general. Thus *f* is used against the cantus firmus in one of Buxtehude's settings of the *Magnificat* ('Magnificat noni toni' BUXWV 205), *e* and *d* in another (BUXWV 204), *d* in the opening movement of J. S. Bach's Cantata 10, and so on. But more than any movement in (e.g.) Pachelbel's *Magnificat* cycles, BWV 733 is remarkable for its systematic use of such motifs.

Strictly speaking, motifs *e f g* and *h* are not countersubject motifs, as they are themselves accompanied by a motif familiar from *stile antico* counterpoint (Ex. 272). The profusion of usable motifs seems

Ex. 272

to force the composer to rely chiefly on one (motif *a*), and apart from such moments as the cadences in b43 and b65 the other melodic motifs are not much used; those that are (*c, e*) are not particularly melodic or prominent by nature. While *a* is used more or less continuously throughout the movement, it is noticeable that its inversion can be either complete or partial – Ex. 273 – and clearly its chief contribution is its

Ex. 273

fluency. The same and similar quaver themes are used in such diverse contexts as the C minor Fugues BWV 546 and 537, the finale to the *Italian Concerto* BWV 971 for harpsichord, and the Ricercare *a 6* from the *Musical Offering*. In the *Magnificat* fugue BWV 733, the result is a strong, vivid movement quite different in character from vocal movements incorporating the *tonus peregrinus* above fugal or imitative counterpoint (e.g. the 'Suscepit Israel' sections of both the Magnificat BWV 243 and Cantata 10), where the same theme lends an *affektvoll*, plaintive colour quite alien to the *Magnificat* tradition in organ music. The very closing bars would seem, if taken out of context, typical of the major free organ fugues such as BWV 537, 540 or 545. That previous *Magnificat* fugues often end with a major chord prepared in the penultimate bar (e.g. Pachelbel) seems less important than the manner of developing motifs: thus *a* is used to the last to consolidate the tonality of a piece which fluctuates curiously between a minor key and its relative major.

---

734   Nun freut euch, lieben Christen g'mein / Es ist gewisslich an der Zeit

No Autograph MS; copy in P 1117 (J. L. Krebs), P 1160, Danzig 4203/4 and late sources.

Headed in P 1117 'Choral in Tenore'; two staves.

The TEXT of Luther's Advent hymn was published in 1524. Its ten verses form a 'ballad on Christ's Incarnation' (Stapel 1950 pp203ff) containing the 'essence of Lutheran theology' before and after the Incarnation (described in v6); it was later associated with the 13th, 17th and 27th Sundays after Trinity (Schein, Vopelius).

Nun freut euch, lieben Christen gmein,	Now rejoice, dear Christians all,
und lasst uns fröhlich springen,	and let us leap with joy,
dass wir getrost und all in ein	that we – confident and united –
mit Lust und Liebe singen,	sing with pleasure and love
was Gott an uns gewendet hat	of what God has given for us
und seine süsse Wundertat;	and of his sweet miracle;
gar teur hat ers erworben.	very dearly has he purchased it.

The TEXT of Ringwaldt's Advent hymn was published in 1682:

Es ist gewisslich an der Zeit	The time will certainly come
dass Gottes Sohn wird kommen	when God's Son will come
in seiner grossen Herrlichkeit,	in his awful splendour,
zu richten Bös und Fromme.	to judge the wicked and the righteous.
Da wird das Lachen werden teur,	Then jeering will cost dear
wenn alles wird vergehn im Feuer,	when everything perishes in the fire,
wie Petrus davon schreibet.	as Peter writes of it.

The following six verses, ultimately founded on the *Dies irae*, describe Jesus the intercessor on the Day of Judgment.

The MELODY is said to have been derived by Luther from a song *Wach auf, wach auf du schöne* (Terry 1921 p270); it was associated with each hymn in turn. In the *Christmas Oratorio* (part VI, for Epiphany) it is set to yet another text, *Ich steh' an deiner Krippen hier*: Ex. 274. The chorale is listed in the *Orgelbüchlein*, set in BWV 734, 734a

Ex. 274

Christmas Oratorio, VI

and 755, and used without text in Cantata 70 (Sunday before Advent 1723 etc).

BG 40 and some subsequent editions interpret the three-part work on two staves with pedal cantus firmus, perhaps on the analogy of older organ scores. *NBA* IV/3 restores it to manual only, an interpretation which agrees with the sources (e.g. the final bar) and which suits the part-writing (cf. bb36–8 where the left hand can hold the tenor a for five beats but has to abandon it for the next five when the bass quavers go out of reach).

Both the non-stop semiquavers and the continuo-like bass line are unusual. The right hand – e.g. Ex. 275 – is a paraphrase rather than a

Ex. 275

variation (such as Partita IV of BWV 767) and is built on turning motifs called *imitatio violistica* in Scheidt's variations. The left hand occasionally augments and inverts the same figures – Ex. 276 – and helps

Ex. 276

to establish the strong beat at the beginning. Similar motifs, less shapely or pursued less single-mindedly, can be found above pedal cantus-firmus sections of chorales by Pachelbel (e.g. 'Nun freut euch, lieben Christen g'mein') and by those he influenced. The line as a whole can be seen to gloss or refer to more than one line of the chorale (of which, in any case, lines 2, 4 and 7 are the same); moreover, it incorporates elements of ritornello form in its twelve periods and the references back to the 'subject':

b3 dominant
b9 tonic
b30 relative
b36 dominant
b40 tonic
b45 tonic

The closes of each half are also similar. Still more characteristic of the highly organized cell-construction of the melody is that the whole right-hand line consists chiefly of two motifs: the in-turning semi-quavers (*x* in the example) and the scale segment (*y*). Both are immediately adaptable to context and can be varied, as a comparison of b3 with b35 shows.

That BWV 734 slightly resembles the final chorale setting of Cantata 22 (Estomihi (Quinquagesima Sunday)) is due probably to the similarity of the chorale melodies rather than to any particular connection between Lent and Advent. Nevertheless, it is not difficult to see in the exuberance of BWV 734 an allusion to the second line of the chorale (Dietrich 1929). The figured chorale which follows it differs in harmony from the main movement; for one possible purpose of such harmonizations, see BWV 690. It is not clear from the source whether BWV 734 is a prelude to the ensuing harmonization of the hymn, whether the figured chorale (with its keyboard-like bass line) was intended to serve organists whose hymnbooks had no melodies, or whether it had any other purpose.

734a   Nun freut euch, lieben Christen g'mein / Es ist gewisslich an der Zeit

No Autograph MS; late sources (P 285, Schelble–Gleichauf).

It is where the cantus firmus takes a different form, in bb33–5 and 39, that BWV 734a differs from 734. Although the consequent rewriting of other parts is not unmusical, the lines show occasional infelicities: (*a*) in b33, the left hand is given uncharacteristic tenths to stretch; (*b*) in bb32–5, the right hand loses the shaped rise of BWV 734 (where b34 matches b43); and (*c*) in b39, in addition to a premature d″, the right hand leaps uncharacteristically before a beat and breaks the original sequence. Thus BWV 734a is probably inauthentic.

---

735   Valet will ich dir geben

No Autograph MS; reputed Autograph MS 'from Guhr Collection' used in Peters VII; later copies only (p 285, 312).

Headed (in *BG* 40) 'Fantasia super...'; three staves (nineteenth-century sources).

The TEXT of V. Herberger's hymn was published in 1614.

Valet will ich dir geben,	I shall say farewell to you,
du arge, falsche Welt;	O wicked, false world;
dein sündlich böses Leben	your sinfully evil life
durchaus mir nicht gefällt.	I detest through and through.
Im Himmel ist gut wohnen,	To live in Heaven is good,
hinauf steht mein Begier,	and on this stands my desire;
da wird Gott herrlich lohnen	there will God reward well
dem, der ihm dient allhier.	him who serves him here.

The following four verses look to the saviour of the soul:

v4

rück sie aus allem Schaden	bring it from all harm
zu deiner Herrlichkeit.	to your splendour.

The MELODY by M. Teschner was published with the text – Ex. 277
– and took varying forms over the following century (Terry 1921 p297).

Ex. 277
1614

It is listed in the *Orgelbüchlein*, set in BWV 735, 735a and 736,
harmonized in BWV 415 and used in Cantata 95 (16th Sunday after
Trinity 1723) and the *St John Passion* (BWV 245, no. 52).

For the relationship between the two versions of this chorale, see BWV
735a; the authenticity of BWV 735 is not certain enough to justify the
claim that in the rising cadence at the end it was J. S. Bach who was
picturing 'the soul rising to peace' (Keller 1948 p175) in much the same
way that he appears to do in BWV 656. Terry sees the same cadence
as referring to the second half of VI of the text (Terry 1921 p299).

The form of BWV 735 is similar to 'Jesus Christus, unser Heiland'
BWV 665:

> irregular fugal exposition of chorale lines, each of which finally appears
> (not in longer note-values) in the pedal; clear gaps between the expositions
> of lines except 6–7 (see BWV 735a) and 7–8; each fugue (except line 7,
> bb42ff) includes the whole of the chorale line concerned; the whole
> exploiting a few motifs, most of which are announced in the first bars

Although BWV 735 and 665 also share a cantus-firmus decoration and its countersubject (cf. BWV 735 b29 etc with BWV 665 b1), the former appears to be more 'objective' and lacks the passing reference to text lines in BWV 665. On the contrary, the movement is unified by a pair of motifs marked *a* in Ex. 278. Simple motifs familiar from the partitas

Ex. 278

and the *Orgelbüchlein*, they grow in this instance from a decorated chorale line reminiscent of those of Buxtehude and Böhm (Ex. 279).

Ex. 279

Böhm, 'Gelobet seist du, Jesu Christ'

In BWV 735, motif *a* appears *rectus* or *inversus* in the countersubject to every line of the chorale (bb2, 10, 16, 22, 29, 37, 43, 52) as well as on the pedal point in both BWV 735 and 735a; the motif occurs too in the 'old' texture at bars 43–7 (so called because of the broken-chord figure and the incomplete chorale line). Motif *b* is also used (bb12, 15 etc) and seems to influence the falling line in bb60–1, which is reminiscent of that at the end of BWV 564.

735a   Valet will ich dir geben

No Autograph MS; copies in *Plauener Orgelbuch* (c1710), by J. G. Walther (Den Haag 4 G 14, Kö 15839) and later sources (P 281, BB 40037 etc).

Headed 'con Pedale' in *Plauener Orgelbuch*; two staves.

The main differences between BWV 735 and 735a are: certain details in the imitation (dotted figure of BWV 735a b34 also used at bb29ff in BWV 735) and in the accompanying figures (e.g. the two upper parts transposed up and down an octave respectively in bb39f); the contrast between the simple 'old' figure of bb51ff in BWV 735a and running figures developed from motif *a* in BWV 735; and the use in BWV 735 of a final pedal point which is a bar longer and has the final rise based on motif *a*.

Whether the relationship between BWV 735a and 735 is similar to that suggested for the so-called Weimar and Leipzig versions of BWV 651–667 is possible (*NBA* IV/3 *KB* p11) though questionable; see also a note on BWV 736. The alterations of BWV 735 become more radical as the piece progresses, unlike those of 'The Eighteen' (even BWV 651/651a). Thus the motifs of the final pedal point not only suggest that BWV 735 is the 'later version' but also change the conception of the cadence and hence the interpretation of the movement. The final three bars of BWV 735a are clearly 'older' in figuration.

A recent view that BWV 735 may be merely a nineteenth-century arrangement (Lohmann B&H edn 6589 p.vii) is not easily dismissed, since neither the sources nor the nature of the alterations are conclusively against it. All the differences outlined could have been effected by a competent copyist of the Mendelssohn generation. Moreover, the motif-extension in b42 and b52 of BWV 735 disguises the simple sectional form of BWV 735a, in which each line has a distinct beginning. Nor are the 'improvements' in BWV 735 entirely happy: of the four differences listed above, the first produces sequential repetition (i.e., the sequence at bb29–32 in BWV 735 now anticipates the counterpoint of bb34ff); the second interferes with the scale sequences of BWV 735a (bb39–40 an exact dominant answer or sequence to bb37–8); the third may result in a good bass line (cf. BWV 681 bb7–9) but leads only to an infelicitous b53 (based on a motif not heard before); and the fourth creates a thin texture at the end of the piece, and its major change in conception is uncharacteristic of Bach revisions as now known.

---

736   Valet will ich dir geben

No Autograph MS; copies in Lpz Poel 39 (Kittel), Göttweig MS J. S. Bach Nr 30 (mid eighteenth century), and late sources.

Two staves.

For TEXT and MELODY see BWV 735. For the figured chorale added at the end in the Göttweig source, see BWV 690 and 734. That BWV 736, a very accomplished work, is found in the Kittel source may support the suggestion that it was written in Leipzig for the composer's last collection, after BWV 735a or its putative revision had been rejected.

Highly original in general effect, BWV 736 also combines subtle motif and paraphrase techniques. Its form is:

A	bb1–12 (bb13–24)	fore-imitation based on a paraphrase of lines 1 and 2 (3 and 4) of the chorale melody; accompaniment to pedal cantus firmus based almost entirely on motif *a* (see below)
B	bb24–36	fore-imitation based on a paraphrase of line 5 in terms of motif *a* (modified); accompaniment to pedal cantus firmus based on motif *a* (modified)
C	bb36–43	fore-imitation based on theme from B (*inversus* and *rectus*); accompaniment to pedal cantus firmus based on motif *a*
D	bb43–52	fore-imitation based on a paraphrase of line 7 in terms of a further derivative of motif *a*; accompaniment to pedal cantus firmus based partly on motif *a*

E bb52–9   fore-imitation based probably on a paraphrase of line 8 in
terms of motif *a* (*inversus*)

The idea of quick-moving pairs of triplets above a slow cantus firmus
may ultimately derive from Scheidt–Pachelbel types (Dietrich 1929
p62), but some idea of the motivic subtlety of the movement can be
seen in the final cadence, where – looking only at the inner parts –
the last three bars incorporate *a*, *a* inverted, *a* as modified in section
B, and *a* as modified in section *D*, the whole in a texture designed

Ex. 280

to cross-refer to the previous pedal-point cadences: Ex. 280. If the
cantus-firmus lines in *B* and *D* become progressively less obvious as
paraphrases, that of line 8 in section *E* is even more difficult to hear
as such. Only the structural layout of the movement makes it seem likely
that the composer did in fact have line 8 in mind. If the main notes
of the chorale melody did not appear on the beats, the paraphrased
themes of BWV 736 might not be so readily apparent, because the
motivic language is so well integrated in the three-part manual lines.

A further example of the work's unity within variety can be found
in the pedal points at the ends of lines. The final cadence not only
refers back but is given finality by the characteristic brief diminished
sevenths; the middle dominant cadences (b35, b42) are quite distinct,
despite the similarity of motif; and the chorale melody, being in the
pedal (unlike the figured chorale that follows BWV 736 in one source),
leads to cadences whose definition is particularly convenient for
establishing simple overall form: D, D, A, A, F♯/B, D. The gigue-like
figure itself (motif *a*) supports the view not only that the composer
had in mind the second half of VI rather than the first, but also that
the setting dates from the Leipzig period. Kauffmann uses a similar
pattern in 'Komm, heiliger Geist' from *Harmonische Seelenlust* (1733),
naturally more simply (Ex. 281). Of the conjectures to which this
example leads, it seems likely that the composer of BWV 736 knew it,

Ex. 281
Kauffmann, 'Komm, heiliger Geist'
Vox humana + Salicional 8′ + Spillpfeife 4′ (Pedal 16′ + 8′ + 4′ + 2′)
b4

Ped.

possible that he wished to 'develop' its unifying motif, but highly improbable that he required such a discreet registration as Kauffmann's, since BWV 736 looks like an *organo pleno* piece. Whether or not he knew the Kauffman piece before writing BWV 736, it is clear that the latter includes patterns familiar in other compound-time preludes, such as 'In dich hab' ich gehoffet, Herr' BWV 712.

---

737 Vater unser in Himmelreich

No Autograph MS; copy by J. G. Walther (Den Haag 4 G 14, Kö 15839).

Two staves.

For TEXT and MELODY see BWV 636.

Like the doubtful BWV 705 and 707 (both headed 'manualiter' in P 1160), BWV 737 is probably for manual, since Walther gives no pedal indication (*NBA* IV/3 *KB* p59); the four parts are playable by hands alone, and the bass has no clear pedal character.

It is not certain whether Spitta (I p595) is right to see the movement, like BWV 724, as an example of 'the most primitive form of organ chorale...with neither sustained motif nor thematic interludes'. The three accompanying parts include rhythmic and motivic patterns typical of *alla breve* counterpoint in ⁴/₂, and more than once the soprano cantus firmus is anticipated in *alla breve* terms in an inner part: Ex. 282.

Ex. 282   b19

Nevertheless, the opening fore-imitation of b1 (with bass counter-subject) leads the player to expect a motet chorale of the monothematic Scheidt type, as do the inconclusive cadences (e.g. the $^6_4{}_2$ of b28, typical of Pachelbel) and the lengthening of cantus-firmus notes as the piece proceeds. The last line, for example, is typical of Scheidt. The movement progressively resembles a chorale harmonized with many imitative but undeveloped motifs; and if Walther's attribution is correct, BWV 737 must be an early work. But effective cohesion is given to the movement by the increasing use of the dactyl/anapaest figure, just as interest is sustained by the harmony itself, particularly the tension between the modal moments (b3) and the chromatic/diatonic (b28).

738

Vom Himmel hoch da komm' ich her

No Autograph MS; copies in Lpz MB MS 7 (J. G. Preller), Poel 39 (Kittel) and late sources.

Two staves.

For TEXT and MELODY see BWV 606.

On this type of movement, see BWV 715; on running figures in Christmas chorales, see BWV 607, 697 and 701. While the semiquaver figures resemble those of other $^{12}/_8$ chorales – figures used both for interludes between lines (cf. Partita BWV 766 Vars. 2–7) and for accompaniment to the cantus firmus (cf. BWV 666 and 667) – there is little attempt to give the movement unity by developing the same motif. Without the interludes, the movement would be a useful pointer to the *Orgelbüchlein* conception of organ chorale; at least one of the figures themselves was used in other connections with the same chorale melody (see notes to BWV 769, section iv, p. 319 and Ex. 304 below). Although given in Preller's source as one of four Christmas hymns (with BWV 722, 729 and 732), the movement is clearly developed beyond the simple hymn-with-interludes type, chiefly by means of the non-stop semiquaver patterns.

738a

Vom Himmel hoch da komm' ich her

No Autograph MS; only source, P 802 (J. T. Krebs).

No composer's name; two staves.

The figures (harmonies) of BWV 738a are followed in BWV 738; for remarks on the relationship, see BWV 722a. That BWV 738a could be a reduction from, not a draft for, BWV 738 is suggested by the presence in BWV 738a of motifs unlikely to be readily improvised (b3, b4) but the absence of those that decorate pedal points (b10, b20).

739   Wie schön leuchtet der Morgenstern

Autograph MS? P 488 (c1705 – see also BWV 764); copies in *Plauener Orgelbuch* (c1710) and Möller MS (J. B. Bach, c1715?).

Headed in P 488 'a 2 Clav. Ped.'; two staves.

The TEXT of P. Nikolai's hymn was published in 1599; it later became associated in Leipzig with Advent Sunday, the 20th Sunday after Trinity and the 1st and 2nd Days of Whit, and in Dresden with Mariae Verkündigung (the Annunciation) (Gojowy 1972; Stiller 1970 pp220, 228, 231). In Weimar it was associated with the 20th Sunday after Trinity (Gojowy 1972).

Wie schön leuchtet der Morgenstern	How beautifully shines the morning-star,
voll Gnad und Wahrheit von dem Herrn,	full of grace and truth from the Lord,
die süsse Wurzel Jesse.	sweet root of Jesse.
Du Sohn Davids aus Jakobs Stamm,	O Son of David from the lineage of Jacob,
mein König und mein Bräutigam,	my king and my bridegroom,
hast mir mein Herz besessen;	you have taken possession of my heart;
lieblich, freundlich,	lovely, kind,
schön und herrlich, gross und ehrlich,	fair and splendid, great and faithful,
reich an Gaben,	rich in gifts,
hoch und sehr prächtig erhaben.	exalted to high glory.

The six verses that follow continue the enthusiasm of Advent:

v7

Wie bin ich doch so herzlich froh,	But how heartily glad I am
dass mein Schatz ist das A und O.	that my treasure is the alpha and omega.

The MELODY, in part derived from older material, was published with the text and takes slightly varied forms in J. S. Bach – Ex. 283. It is listed in the *Orgelbüchlein*, set in BWV 739 and 763, harmonized in BWV 436 and used in Cantatas 1 (Mariae Verkündigung 1725), 36 (Advent Sunday 1731), 37 (Ascension 1724 etc), 49 (20th Sunday after Trinity 1726), 61 (Advent Sunday 1714, 1723), and 172 (Whit 1714, 124 etc).

Ex. 283
BWV 172

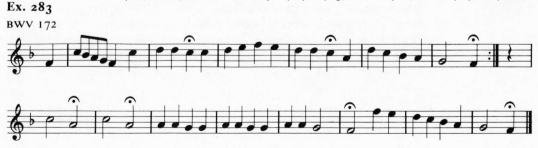

It is not certain that BWV 739 (excluded from *NBA* IV/3) is the work of J. S. Bach, or even that P 488 is in his hand (Dadelsen 1958 p76 – for a note on the watermark see Dürr 1977 p234). The uncertainty is not resolved by considering either that the *Plauener Orgelbuch* also ascribes the piece to J. S. Bach or that he copied out other composers' organ music. Both the secondary sources above contain a large repertory of north German keyboard music.

The form and style of BWV 739 are clearly influenced by the north German chorale fantasia: the kind of figuration, the changing of manuals, and the varied and sectional accompaniment to cantus-firmus lines are reminiscent of Lübeck, Bruhns, Buxtehude, Reincken and others. Like Böhm's 'Christ lag in Todesbanden', however, BWV 739 is shorter than the pure fantasia; like Buxtehude's 'Ich ruf zu dir' BUXWV 196, it maintains continuity while achieving variety not by changes in metre but by a changing texture of two, three or four parts (including a trio of two manuals and pedal). In most respects, the closest parallels to BWV 739 can be found in 'Ein' feste Burg' BWV 720. The form is:

bb1–4	line 1 provides a subject for fore-imitation before it appears as a soprano cantus firmus; line 2 follows after unrelated interlude; much use of motif *a* (Ex. 284 below)
bb14–19	line 3, ditto; similar motif
bb21–35	lines 4–6 in pedal below dialogue parts on two manuals (lh *Rückpositiv*, rh *Oberwerk*); semiquaver figures typical of Pachelbel etc
bb36–40	echo effect on two manuals; harmonies are those of the next chorale line
bb40–54	lines 7–9 in pedal, 8–9 anticipated by their harmony (bb44–5) or melody (bb46–7) on alternating manuals (b43=*Rückpositiv?*); broken chords
bb55–64	line 10 anticipated; scale lines derived from *a*?
bb65–end	line 10 in pedal with free parts above; pedal point ditto

Ex. 284

The last two sections are most characteristic of fantasias, e.g. the linked scales b55, b63. Other figures are more typical of toccatas and preludes than of organ chorales: thus such figures as b42 and b46 can be found in Buxtehude's Toccata in D minor BUXWV 155. Some of the bar-by-bar detail is typical of other schools: thus the counterpoint of b22 and b57 can be found in Pachelbel's setting of 'Wie schön leuchtet der Morgenstern' and is similar to 'Ein' feste Burg' BWV 720 bb29, 35f, 51 etc.

740 Wir glauben all' an einen Gott, Vater

No Autograph MS; copy in Schelble–Gleichauf (*BG* 40).

BG 40 headed 'a 2 Clav. e Pedale doppio'.

The TEXT of T. Clausnitzer's Trinity hymn was published in 1668.

Wir glauben all' an einen Gott,	We all believe in one God,
Vater, Sohn und heilign Geist,	Father, Son and Holy Ghost,
den der Cherubinen Rott	whom the band of Cherubim
und die Schaar der Engel preist,	and host of angels glorify,
den durch seine grosse Krafft,	who through his great power
alles würcket, that und schafft.	accomplishes, does and creates all.

Like Luther's version of the Nicene Creed (see BWV 680), the three verses are expressions of faith addressed to the Persons of the Trinity in turn.

The MELODY was published with the text in 1699 (Terry 1921 p339): Ex. 285. It is set only in BWV 740; the first six words of the title are

Ex. 285
1699

listed in the *Orgelbüchlein* (for this text, or for Luther's version? – see text to BWV 680).

A nineteenth-century edition attributes the four- and five-part versions of the movement to J. L. Krebs, who is often thought to be the composer (Tittel 1966 p133); it is excluded from *NBA* IV/3, though formerly thought (like BWV 710) to be by J. S. Bach (Keller 1937). Naumann (*BG* 40 p. xxxvi) thought that the Krebs version was an arrangement 'for his own purposes' of a 'piece by his great teacher', perhaps for an organ whose pedal went up only to (a much-used) middle c' (Bruggaier 1959 p149). Spitta (I pp598–9) assumed Bach was working to Buxtehude models, particularly the melisma above the closing pedal point.

The melisma, however, does not contain figures typical of either Bach (e.g. BWV 659a) or Buxtehude; even if it did, it would be difficult to ascribe b7 to any composer before J. L. Krebs's generation. While the double-pedal and left-hand parts are not unlike BWV 653b (preserved in a manuscript known to the young Krebs), the general melodic style of the opening, the frequent returns to tonic harmonies, and the occasional change to semiquaver motion are all uncharacteristic of Bach. Nor, apart from the clear thematic references in bb1–3, 11, 13–14, 31–2, 32–4, 38–40, is the cantus firmus incorporated (as in BWV 653b) or the motifs developed. Nevertheless, the composer has attempted some slight element of unity at the close of each half (compare bb9–15 with bb40–3).

---

741   Ach Gott, vom Himmel sieh' darein

No Autograph MS; copies in Brussels II.3919 (second quarter of eighteenth century), Am.B. 72a (Kirnberger), Am.B. 72, P 1116 (Kühnel), Danzig 4203/4, Sp 1438 and late sources.

Headed in Am.B. 72a and P 1160 'in organo pleno'; two staves ('canto fermo in Pedale', P 1160).

The TEXT is Luther's version of Ps. 12, published in 1524; in Leipzig and Weimar it became associated with the 2nd and 8th Sundays after Trinity, in Dresden with the 13th (Stiller 1970 pp228, 230, Gojowy 1972). Like other psalm-versions by Luther, the versification is 'popular', almost folksong-like.

Ach Gott vom Himmel sieh darein	O God look down from Heaven
und lass dich des erbarmen,	and have pity that
wie wenig sind der Heilgen dein,	your saints are so few;
verlassen sind wir Armen.	we wretches are abandoned.
Dein Wort man lässt nicht haben	Your word is not held to be
* wahr,*	true,
der Glaub ist auch verloschen gar	faith is quite extinguished
bei allen Menschenkindern.	among all the sons of men.

The remaining five verses follow the psalm.

The MELODY was published with the text in a second publication of 1524 (Terry 1917 p132): Ex. 286. The chorale is listed in the

Ex. 286

1524

Orgelbüchlein and set in BWV 741, Cantata 2 (2nd Sunday after Trinity 1724) and (to different texts) Cantatas 77 and 153.

The sources are problematic: Danzig 4203/4 attributes the work to J. C. Bach (son of Heinrich Bach), P 1160 has a mutilated copy, and the 'copyists have gradually introduced much that is wrong' although 'we seem to be dealing with a genuine Bach work' (Naumann *BG* 40 p.xlvii), 'obviously one of the rare youthful works of Bach', 'revised between 1739/40 and 1750' (Klotz *NBA* IV/3 *KB* p40). Accepting the authenticity of the movement would have important implications, since it would show the composer achieving individuality; the fantasia-like variety in the number of parts, the character of the themes and the treatment of the chorale are nevertheless combined with a sense of inventive harmony known only to the composer of the *Orgelbüchlein*. However, some of the 'inventive' harmonies are uncertain in the texts as left by the sources.

The form of BWV 741 can be shown as:

> seven cantus-firmus lines in the pedal, each preceded by fore-imitation; the fore-imitation sometimes stretto, with one or two free parts (e.g. b1) sometimes incorporating a cantus-firmus motif (e.g. soprano crotchets b13)

The parts vary from two to five, with the double pedal giving the last two lines in canon – this feature, like the part-writing in general, makes it very unlikely that the pedal should play in the first six bars, despite cues in P 1116 and P 1160. The free chromatic tenor to line 5 of the chorale melody (bb29–36 etc) suggests a reference to the words (line 5 of VI?) as possibly does the harmony of line 6 (bb45–7). That the several incidental harmonic cruxes in the text are unlikely to derive simply from copyists' uncertainties is shown by the last ten bars, where a larger harmonic paragraph is itself unconventional, passing through two dominant steps (C–G minor, G–D minor). Whatever the composer intended in bb45–6, it is clear that a canonic cantus firmus is not yet perfected, and that the harmonies move towards or around diminished sevenths – not surprisingly for the composer of BWV 715. The movement is inconsistent. An original, bare effect is already achieved in b1, and an unconventional progression in b2; but the next four bars are more anonymous in style and even look like a realized figured bass below an absent melody. The harmonic pace is such that triads, sevenths of various kinds and other chords can be found in almost any order, particularly above cantus-firmus sections, while the fugal fore-imitation of bb29–37 suggests a composer able to manipulate harmony more consistently.

---

742   Ach Herr, mich armen Sünder

Copy in BB 40037 (anon).

The source, though related in contents to Dröbs's MSS (*NBA* IV/3 *KB* p35), does not justify the attribution to J. S. Bach any more than it does for BWV 752 and 763, which it also contains. The opening melodic gesture is reminiscent of Böhm (Seiffert 1904) and is uncharacteristic of Bach, as are the repeated semiquavers and the direction 'poco adagio' (Keller 1937).

---

743   Ach, was ist doch unser Leben

No Autograph MS; source in Lpz MB MS 7 (Mempell–Preller) and Lpz MS R 24 (c1800).

Headed in Lpz MB MS 7 'Choral. Pedalio.' in MS R 24 'v. 1. 2 Clav.'

Like BWV 691a, BWV 743 contains a chorale (in this case a harmonization with interludes), prelude and postlude; it is likely to be no more authentic than BWV 691a and 683a, though for different reasons. The figuration is characteristic of such minor central German composers as Armsdorff, Kirchhoff etc and forms a typical partita-like texture. But it is on a scale unusual for such minor composers, and J. S. Bach's influence may well be heard (Keller 1937) not least in the unusual tone-painting of the victorious end (Luedtke 1918 p13).

---

744   Auf meinen lieben Gott

No Autograph MS; copy by J. L. Krebs (P 802) and a late source (P 311).

Headed in P 802 'Chorale Auf meinen lieben Gott per Canonem', followed by a second piece (see below) headed 'alio modo per Canonem'; no composer's name; two staves.

For TEXT and MELODY see BWV 646.

Krebs added BWV 744 to P 802 before 1731 (Zietz 1969, pp93, 160, 170); it includes two short canonic settings, namely BWV 744 and the so-called *Incerta 17* (Kast 1958 p130), both published in B&H edn 6589. The facing pages in P 802 containing the two movements were a replacement made before 1731 (Zietz 1969 pp20, 171), originally entitled only 'Chorale', 'per Canonem'; the title 'Auf meinen lieben Gott' was added later. The authorship is uncertain (Tittel 1966 p135); possibly Krebs was imitating BWV 714 (also in P 802), first in an octave canon, secondly in a canon at the fifth.

In BWV 744, the accompanying motif (treated both in imitation and in parallel sixths, i.e. *canon sine pausa*) resembles that of BWV 714; it is made more use of, though not so rigidly as in Walther's 'Ach Gott und Herr' BWV 693. The strained harmonies resulting from the canon are mostly well managed, except in b12. In the canon *Incerta 17*, the freer accompanying parts lead to more natural harmonies, though they too are not without awkward moments (e.g. b5).

---

745   Aus der Tiefe rufe ich

No Autograph MS; late sources only (P 285, Schelble–Gleichauf).

At b9 headed 'a 2 Clav. e Pedale' (according to *BG* 40); two staves.

At least three texts share this opening line; the one intended is probably G. C. Schwämlein's penitential hymn developed from Ps. 130 and published with the melody below from *c*1676 onwards:

Aus der Tiefe rufe ich   Out of the deep I call
zu dir, Herr, erhöre mich;   to you, Lord, hear me;
deine Ohren gnädig leih,   lend your ears graciously,
werk die flehend Stimm dabei.   may my beseeching voice be effective.

The text glosses the psalm, ending:

v8

Nun mehr hab ich ausgeruft;   Now I have made my appeal:
Jesus kommt und macht mir Luft.   Jesus comes and gives me ease.
Seele, schwing dich in die Höh,   Soul, soar on high,
sage zu der Welt: Ade!   say to the world: Farewell.

The MELODY (Zahn no. 1217) is as in Ex. 287.

Ex. 287
Zahn no. 1217

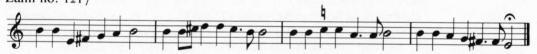

In form, BWV 745 is a unique two-movement partita: a harmonization in full chords (implying pedal), similar to but fuller than BWV 766, followed by a fantasia incorporating separated chorale lines as soprano cantus firmus. While it is just possible that the harmonization is the work of J. C. Bach (1642–1703), to whom the work is sometimes now attributed, the fantasia's harmonies (e.g. augmented sixth in b11), cadences (b12) and melodic detail (bb14–16), and the form and obbligato-like texture of the whole, make it unlikely to be the work of a composer working before 1750–75.

---

746   Christ ist erstanden

Copies in BB 22541/3 (J. G. Walther), P 311 and a lost Penzel source (*BG* 40).

The movement is attributed in Walther's MS to J. K. F. Fischer (*NBA* IV/2 *KB* p34). Published in *c*1715 as a *Ricercar pro festis paschalibus* (Fischer, *Sämtliche Werke für Klavier und Orgel*, ed. E. von Werra

(Berlin, 1901) p97), the movement was one of five such chorale settings, all without pedal cues and all concerned with monothematic fugal treatments of a chorale line (without cantus firmus). As such – and despite similarities in the harmony and part-writing – BWV 746 is unlike chorales which it is often said to resemble (BWV 707, 737 etc).

747

Christus, der uns selig macht

Copy in Lpz MB MS 7 (Mempell–Preller).

The change and even confusion of idiom and form between one part of this chorale and another – modern obbligato melodic opening, antique chorale-fantasia close – makes it most likely to be the work of a young composer c1750. The texture in the middle of the work and the pedal line throughout do not suggest an intimate knowledge of organ idiom.

748

Gott der Vater wohn' uns bei

Copies in Den Haag 4 G 14 (J. G. Walther, headed 'JGW'), Am.B. 72a (Kirnberger), P 1160, P 1116 (Kühnel), Danzig 4203/4 (attrib. to Walther), Sp 1438 and late sources.

Spitta (I p385), who was critical of BWV 748, showed that it was attributed to Walther in his own MS (i.e. 4 G 14). M. Seiffert included it as no. 35 of J. G. Walther, *Gesammelte Werke für Orgel* (DDT 26, 1906). The figuration and its working are similar to Pachelbel's setting of the same chorale.

748a

Gott der Vater wohn' uns bei

Copy in Schelble–Gleichauf and late sources.

Five introductory bars were added to BWV 748 to form BWV 748a (see *BG* 40, p.li).

749

Herr Jesu Christ, dich zu uns wend'

Late source only (P 285) copied from Hauser *Sammelband*? (*NBA* IV/2 *KB* p44).

Anonymous in P 285, the movement is one of three fughettas (the others are BWV 750 and 756) in the manner of J. C. Bach (1642–1703). Keller hears its 'suppleness' as evidence that it may be a youthful work of J. S. Bach (Keller 1948 p144).

---

750 Herr Jesu Christ, mein's Lebens Licht

Late source only (p 285) copied from Hauser *Sammelband*?

See BWV 749.

---

751 In dulci jubilo

Copy in Lpz MB MS 7 (Mempell–Preller).

Two staves.

For TEXT and MELODY see BWV 608.

The unvaried, undeveloped simplicity of the movement makes it unlikely to be the work of J. S. Bach. The pastoral pedal point accompanies two 'verses', tonic and dominant; the last line of the second verse returns abruptly to the tonic for its repeated canonic cantus firmus. The conceit is charming, not least in the association of tonic–dominant musette (a feature of the Italian organ *pastorale*) and the canonic element for the text line 'trahe me post te' ('draw me after you'), for which see BWV 608. Keller suggests a composer under Pachelbel's influence, e.g. Vetter or Zachow (Keller 1937). Frotscher thinks the carillon figure in the third and fourth lines would be helped by a Glockenspiel stop, of the type registered 'with Christmas chorales' (Frotscher 1935 p934).

---

752 Jesu, der du meine Seele

Copy in BB 40037 (anon).

See BWV 742 for a note on the source. Although the attribution of this movement to J. S. Bach is questioned usually on the grounds of the weak canon, its weakest point is the harmony resulting from the canon and its inept keyboard technique.

---

753 Jesu, meine Freude (fragment)

Autograph MS (*Klavierbüchlein für W. F. Bach*; probably early 1720).

Two staves.

For TEXT and MELODY see BWV 610.

The 8¾ bars (14¾ bars including repeat) are not known to have been completed; the fragment appears to be a 'first MS' ('Erstschrift') rather than a fair copy (Plath *NBA* v/5 *KB* p77). For the type and style of such a movement, see BWV 691 and 728. The order of pieces in the W. F. Bach Book is BWV 994, 924, 691, 926, 753, 836: the decorated chorales are thus isolated movements.

It is possible that BWV 691, 728 and 753 were intended to demonstrate variety of detail in such treatments. BWV 753 has long runs of semi-quavers, including the fine example of the *figura messanza* in b13 and

Ex. 288

b14 – Ex. 288. Its inner parts are also well planned, particularly the long rise in the tenor bb2–4 followed by a falling bass.

754

Liebster Jesu, wir sind hier

Copy in Lpz MB MS 7 (Mempell–Preller).

For TEXT and MELODY see BWV 633.

Luedtke (1918 p20) thought that the trio texture and the bass quavers suggested J. G. Walther as composer; but the square phrases, the basso-continuo-like pedal, the melodic detail and the simplistic har-mony suggest rather a less talented composer of a later generation – perhaps the composer of BWV 751.

755

Nun freut euch, lieben Christen

No Autograph MS; late copies only, P 285 (as BWV 734a), P 1119.

Two staves.

For TEXT and MELODY see BWV 734.

The cantus firmus with fore-imitation (but not the fourth in b3) resembles in this instance Pachelbel's treatment of the same melody, and several composers of his 'school' could have composed it. However, Seiffert (1904) thought that it could be a very early work of J. S. Bach, characterized by a 'smoothness in the lower parts and certain turns of harmony' not typical of Pachelbel.

---

756 Nun ruhen alle Wälder

Late source only (P 283) copied from Hauser *Sammelband*?

See BWV 749, 750, 755. Unlike that in BWV 755, the fore-imitation answer (bb2–4) does not contain grammatical errors, but can hardly be credited to J. S. Bach.

---

757 O Herre Gott, dein göttlich's Wort

Copies in P 409, Lpz MB MS 7 (Mempell–Preller; copied end of eighteenth century and grouped with BWV 600, 609).

Although the two sources (from the second half of the eighteenth century) contain genuine Bach works, BWV 757 is unlikely to be one of them. As in BWV 755, the short imitations, bass cantus firmus and semiquaver figures are characteristic of the Pachelbel 'school'; perhaps the piece was a partita movement (Dietrich 1929 p66).

---

758 O Vater, allmächtiger Gott

Only source, P 291 (late eighteenth or early nineteenth century?).

Although the source contains genuine Bach works, BWV 758 is unlikely to be one of them. The techniques applied in each of the four verses can be found in one or more works of J. G. Walther, and while the static quality of the first is uncommon later than 1650, its archaic harmonies are not. The pedal point (bb49–52) must belong to the eighteenth century – hardly a 'very early work of Bach' (*BG* 40 p.lii).

---

759 Schmücke dich, o liebe Seele

Copies in Am.B. 72a (Kirnberger; *NBA* IV/3 *KB* p30), P 1115 (G. A. Homilius), Sp 1438 and several late sources.

The attribution of BWV 759 to G. A. Homilius (1714–85), already noted in *BG* 40, is probably confirmed by the identification of the copyist in P 1115 (Kast 1958 p62). The details of bass line, cadences and decorative figuration, and the level of general competence, suggest a somewhat *galant* composer to whom several of the spurious chorale preludes sometimes attributed to J. S. Bach may actually belong.

---

760 Vater unser im Himmelreich

Copies by J. G. Walther (Den Haag 4 G 14 and P 802, both attributed to Böhm; also Kö 15839); formerly (?) in Brussels II.3919; and in Am.B. 72a (Kirnberger), Am.B. 72, Danzig 4203/4 and late sources.

---

761 Vater unser im Himmelreich

Copies by J. G. Walther (Den Haag 4 G 14 and P 802, both attributed to Böhm); formerly (?) in Brussels II.3919; and in Am.B. 72a (Kirnberger), Am.B. 72 and later sources.

J. Wolgast (*Georg Böhm, Sämtliche Werke* (Leipzig, 1927)) includes BWV 760 and 761 as a two-movement setting by Böhm according to the attribution and arrangement in P 802: 'George Böhme, Vater unser im Himmelreich Versus 1 a 2 Clavier manualiter Versus 2 a 1 Clav. con pedale'. The coupling of a *bicinium* with a fore-imitation setting accords more with Böhm's groups of *versus* chorales than with his chorale partitas. On grounds of style, the pieces could be attributed to J. C. Bach (1642–1703).

---

762 Vater unser im Himmelreich

No Autograph MS; copies in P 802 (J. T. Krebs), Lpz MB MS 7 (Mempell–Preller), BB 30194 (eighteenth century).

Headed in P 802 'à 2 Clav. è ped.'; no composer's name; two staves.

For TEXT and MELODY see BWV 636.

The so-called Buxtehude manner of such a setting (fore-imitation of each line, which is then heard decorated in the top part) has been seen as 'good school-work but no more' (Keller 1937), and criticized as unfree with its literal decoration of a melody whose main notes always fall on the beat, e.g. b16 (Keller 1948 p177). However, the latter is not as conclusive as it seems. Nevertheless, BWV 762 is unlikely to be authentic: the excessive frequency of D minor cadences (or returns to D minor) is difficult to ascribe to J. S. Bach at any age. On the other hand, many of the figures in the accompaniment (b7, b22 etc) suggest that their composer was acquainted with Bach melodies of the Weimar period; and the pedal line suggests an accomplished player. There are fewer ornaments in the oldest source (P 802) than in later copies. Since this part of P 802 is dated 1710–14 by Zietz (1969 pp100, 168) and could be earlier still, the composer may be J. T. Krebs himself; a later date would suggest other pupils.

---

763   Wie schön leuchtet der Morgenstern

Copy in BB 40037 (anon.)

See BWV 742 for a note on the source; see BWV 752 for remarks on the canon technique.

---

764   Wie schön leuchtet der Morgenstern (fragment)

Autograph MS ? P 488 (c1705).

For TEXT and MELODY, see BWV 739.

In the source, BWV 764 follows immediately after BWV 739 (q.v.). No complete copy of BWV 764 is known, but the fantasia-like form of BWV 739 makes it unlikely (though not impossible) that BWV 764 was *versus* 2 in a pair of settings, on the analogy of BWV 760/761. Despite the squareness of its motif (counteracted by the phrase structure but close to the Walther idiom) and the repetition of rhythm, it is not impossible to see BWV 764 as an early work of J. S. Bach. Its harmonic grasp is more competent; there are signs that a new motif is to develop; the main motif accompanying the first three chorale lines is not idly repetitious in either its *rectus* or *inversus* forms, and it seems to be derived from the opening chorale line: Ex. 289.

Ex. 289

---

765   Wir glauben all' an einen Gott, Schöpfer

No Autograph MS; copy in P 801 (J. T. Krebs, four lines of chorale) and Lpz MB MS 7 (Mempell–Preller, two lines of chorale only (i.e. bb1–53)).

Headed in P 801 'à 4 di [—]', in Mempell–Preller 'di J. S. Bach'; two staves.

For TEXT and MELODY see BWV 680.

Like BWV 705, 707, 737 and 746, the movement contains figures characteristic of Scheidt's polyphony and later *alla breve* styles, but develops them much farther. It has been frequently thought to be authentic (*BG* 40 p.liv; Zietz 1969 p136). In P 801 it is anonymous; Krebs gave no composer's name either for BWV 765 or for the

Orgelbüchlein chorales (except BWV 603), and 'di [—]' at least suggests uncertainty.

The form is unusual. From each of the first two cantus-firmus lines, a regular fore-imitation is derived in stretto (cf. BWV 680), and the resulting counterpoint is an accomplished *alla breve* style (e.g. bb8–12). For line 3 of the cantus firmus, a fore-imitation subject in the bass remains only indirectly answered (cf. bb50–2 alto, 48–50 tenor), and the *alla breve* counterpoint continues to give the movement cohesion; line 4 has no subject for fore-imitation. In bb49 and 65, quicker, shorter *alla breve* themes emerge and are answered *rectus*, *inversus* and in stretto; though derived from b4 and referring to the cantus firmus, they become themes in their own right and realize a contrapuntal potential unusual in conventional motet organ chorales. The cohesion is also helped by the cantus firmus presenting only four of the eleven lines of Luther's chorale, an 'abbreviation' made possible by the virtual identity of lines 4 and 11. That the final flourish is more typical of the Buxtehude organ chorale with ornamented soprano than of the plain cantus-firmus type (as here) is not the least original touch of the movement.

766–771 Partitas and Variations

766 Christ, der du bist der helle Tag (*Partita*)

No Autograph MS; reputed Autograph MS once in Guhr Collection and a 'very old copy' in Forkel's (*BG* 40); copies in Darmstadt Mus. MS 73 (first half of eighteenth century), Lpz Scheibner MS 4 (6th movement missing) and late sources.

Headed in Scheibner MS 'Partie diverse sopra il Choral...'; two staves.

The TEXT of E. Alberus's hymn *Christe, du bist der helle Tag* or *Christ, der du bist der helle Tag* is a translation of *Christe, qui lux es et dies* (Lent), later used as an evening hymn (Freylinghausen 1741 etc) and published in 1556.

Christ, der du bist der helle Tag,	Christ, you who are the bright day,
vor dir die Nacht nicht bleiben mag.	before you the night may not endure.
Du leuchtest uns vom Vater her	You illumine us from the Father
und bist des Lichtes Prediger,	and are the preacher of light,
und bist des Lichtes Prediger.	and are the preacher of light.

The six verses that follow are a prayer for safety:

v7

So schlafen wir im Namen dein,	So we sleep in your name,
dieweil die Engel bei uns sein.	while angels are with us.
Du heilige Dreifaltigkeit,	O Holy Trinity,
wir loben dich in Ewigkeit,	we praise you in eternity,
wir loben dich in Ewigkeit.	we praise you in eternity.

The MELODY was published with the text in 1568, differing from version to version: Ex. 290. It is harmonized in BWV 273 and listed in the *Orgelbüchlein*.

Ex. 290

BWV 273

The seven movements (counting the opening chorale)* do not appear to be related to the seven text verses† in any sense of 'picturing' the text; but they could serve as interludes between sung verses. The period of composition is also uncertain; the absence of pedal does not of itself imply that the work originated in an early period, e.g. at Lüneburg (suggested by Spitta I p207). More significant is that some sources omit the variation which is nearest to harpsichord idiom (Var. 5); without the pedal in Var. 6, the partita would match those of a previous period written for domestic music-making. All the movements can be related to variation or *versus* types known to older German organ composers, and the examples referred to below are only chosen as typical of those familiar types. A feature less in the old tradition of chorale partitas is that the variations include interludes between the lines, more integrally incorporated than those in such chorales as BWV 738. Only for the *bicinium* variation in a set (in this case Var. 1) were interludes customary.

Chorale (Partita I)

The harmonies of the chorale, fuller and also more varied than those of the organ partita BWV 768, are less in the tradition of the latter than of Böhm's partitas (e.g. 'Ach wie nichtig', equally or more suitable for harpsichord). The four- to seven-part harmonies seem also to be conceived less distinctively for the organ than those of (e.g.) BWV 715.

Var. 1 (Partita II)

Although there is no preliminary statement in the bass, the conception of the second movement is the traditional *bicinium*, including the anticipatory first phrase before the melody proper of b2 (cf. BWV 768) and the repeated ends of melodic phrases (cf. J. G. Walther's 'Schmücke dich', *Vers* 3) marked 'piano' in the sources (all fairly late). It would be no falsification to introduce the movement by playing over the opening left-hand phrase alone first; the sources may be unreliable on this point. In such ritornello movements the bass line both accompanies and adds its own melody, as in the continuo arias of early cantatas (e.g. BWV 106, 'In deine Hände'). Halfway through the movement (bb15–21), the melody is spun out in sequential imitation, in principle like the corresponding moment in *versus* 3 of Böhm's 'Auf meinen lieben Gott'.

Var. 2 (Partita III)

The chorale lines are here accompanied, occasionally embroidered and all separated by a short motif appearing *rectus* or *inversus* in every

---

* The seven movements of BWV 766 (including the chorale) are numbered 'Partita I' – 'Partita VII' in *BG* 40 and elsewhere. The following discussion refers to 'Chorale' (= Partita I) and 'Var. 1' – 'Var. 6' (= Partitas II–VII respectively), and the Partita numbering is sometimes added in brackets.

† Any more than they do in those partitas of Böhm in which the number of movements is the same as the number of text verses.

bar of the movement. Other motifs give variety to repetition, as does the altered form in the penultimate bar (soprano). A cantus-firmus line incorporating, and disguised by, its own counter-motif – Ex. 291 – is

Ex. 291

common in keyboard partitas, e.g. Böhm's 'Wer nur den lieben Gott lässt walten' Partita 4, and Pachelbel's 'Christus, der ist mein Leben' Partita 1.

Var. 3 (Partita IV)

The right-hand semiquaver variation is a traditional movement (e.g. Böhm's 'Gelobet seist du, Jesu Christ' Var. 2, and Pachelbel's 'Alle Menschen müssen sterben' Partita 2); what is less usual is that the right-hand line within itself develops one or two motifs and incorporates interludes between the lines of the chorale melody. While the manner in which the theme becomes disguised is also characteristic of Böhm, it is striking that the opening right-hand passage is moving towards J. S. Bach's maturer techniques of chorale paraphrase (e.g. BWV 661): Ex. 292.

Ex. 292

Var. 4 (Partita V)

Placing the chorale melody in the middle part (*en taille*), with interludes between its phrases, is familiar from the larger-scaled sets of organ-chorale verses (e.g. Buxtehude's 'Ach Gott und Herr', BUXWV 177); in keyboard partitas, *en taille* variations usually have no interludes (e.g. Pachelbel's 'Herzlich tut mich verlangen' Partita 4). Less usual too is the degree of motivic development in BWV 766. The treatment of the motif announced at first in the right hand is particularly concentrated – several times in each bar, without inversion or replacement. As in Var. 2, the midpoint of the movement sees the fourth line of the melody anticipated and developed before its full entry in b13; it is difficult to see such treatment as justifying Terry's view that 'they are not in the ordinary sense Variations at all, but movements in Fantasia form' (Terry 1921 p112).

Var. 5 (Partita VI)

The influence of such chorale suites as Buxtehude's 'Auf meinen lieben Gott' BUXWV 179 on the gigue movement of BWV 766 is clear, as it is in others using much the same motifs spilling across the cantus-firmus lines (e.g. Partita 9 of Böhm's 'Freu dich sehr, O meine Seele'). While the phrase structure of Var. 5 is curiously *bicinium*-like, the melody itself is completely integrated in a texture even more motif-ridden than Var. 4. The motif (Ex. 293) is fragmentary and versatile, open to

Ex. 293

constant alteration. In the course of the motif's development, the chorale melody changes octave and at one point appears to be interrupted by repetitious tonic–dominant harmonies (between b9 and b12).

Var. 6 (Partita VII)

While the rhythmic shape of the accompanying figure can be found in (e.g.) Böhm's 'Wer nur den lieben Gott lässt walten' Partita 5, the idea of a final bass cantus firmus is familiar in sets of chorale verses by older composers (e.g. Buxtehude's 'Nun lob, mein Seel, den Herren' BUXWV 213) and by Bach himself (BWV 656). Heterophonic doubling of pedal and left-hand bass parts* is not uncommon in Pachelbel chorales; but whether the composer's own manuscript(s) showed that manual–pedal doubling was intended in BWV 766 is not clear from its surviving sources. The highly original treatment of the melody from b10 onwards (the phrases again extended in sequence) gives the movement an effect greater than the sum of its parts and one not difficult to relate to the doxology of the final verse of the text.

---

767   O Gott, du frommer Gott (*Partita*)

No Autograph MS; copy in P 802 (J. T. Krebs) and 'a very old copy' from Forkel's Collection (Peters V).

Called in a catalogue of 1781 'Partite diverse über O Gott du frommer Gott' (*Dok* III p269), movements headed 'Partita' in P 802; two staves throughout.

The TEXT of J. Heermann's hymn was published in 1630; various verses later became severally associated with the 4th, 8th or 9th Sunday after Trinity in hymnbooks of Weimar, Leipzig and elsewhere (Stiller 1970 p229; Gojowy 1972).

* Or are the two basses to be understood as alternatives?

O Gott, du frommer Gott,	O God, merciful God,
du Brunnquell guter Gaben,	fount of good gifts,
ohn den nichts ist, was ist,	without whom nothing is that is,
von dem wir alles haben:	from whom we have everything;
gesunden Leib gib mir	give me a healthy body,
und dass in solchem Leib	and [grant] that in such a body
ein unverletzte Seel	an unviolated soul
und rein Gewissen bleib.	and a pure conscience remain.

The seven verses that follow are a prayer for safety in all dangers, including death:

v7

Lass mich an meinem End	Let me at my end
auf Christi Tod abscheiden...	die in the death of Christ...

v8

lass hören deine Stimm	let your voice be heard
und meinen Leib weck auf,	and waken my body,
und führ ihn schön verklärt	and lead it, beautifully transformed,
zum auserwähltem Hauf.	to the chosen multitude.

A ninth verse or doxology was added by 1659 (Terry 1921 p278).

The MELODY was published with the text in 1646; versions differ, and the form used in BWV 767 (cf. the penultimate phrase) does not appear in Zahn: Ex. 294. The text was listed in *Orgelbüchlein* and is associated

Ex. 294

Freylinghausen 1741

with three melodies used in different Bach works: (i) BWV 767; (ii) Cantatas 24, 71 and 164; (iii) Cantatas 45, 64, 94, 128, 129 and 197a (the last five to different texts).

As with BWV 766, the absence of pedal does not of itself suggest that the partita is as early as 'Bach's years as a schoolboy in Lüneburg' despite the usual view to that effect (Smend 1947 p44; Spitta I p207). Equally conjectural is Schweitzer's interpretation of the last three variations (Schweitzer 1905 pp65–6):*

* As with BWV 766, the movements are cited here as 'Chorale' (= Partita I) and 'Var. 1' – 'Var. 8' (= Partitas II–IX).

Var. 6 falling line 'expressing' the death, burial and rest referred to in v7 of the text

Var. 7 the chromatic motif expressing 'the sad wait for the signal of the resurrection' in v8

Var. 8 the 'imposing animation' of the movement expressing the praises of the Trinity in v9

From such ideas, Smend concluded that the composer kept a special regard throughout his life for settings in which 'he spoke of blessed death' (i.e. the death of one saved). Keller made similar interpretations of the chromatic line and the large-scale finale; unfortunately, his choice of verses to be expressed by these effects (vv7 and 8 respectively) was different from Schweitzer's, and it enabled him to see the unexpected *andante–presto* passages in the last movement as a musical depiction ('Vertonung') of the last two lines of v8, translated above (Keller 1948 p137). More objectively, BWV 767 (like 766) includes many specific figurations and movement types familiar from the chorale variations of Böhm and of such composers in the Bach circle as J. G. Walther; the last movement has been seen as an equivalent to the *dialogues aux grands jeux* of certain French organ Masses (Klotz 1975 p387).*

For further comparisons with the works of Böhm and Buxtehude, see BWV 766.

Chorale (Partita I)

For such harmonies (including strong up-beats), see Var. 1 of BWV 766. The form of the melody as it appears in BWV 767 ($a^1a^1ba^2$) gives a rounded form to each variation.

Var. 1 (Partita II)

Complete with left-hand introduction, an anticipated first phrase in the right hand (bb2–3), repeated phrases in the melody, and a largely continuous ostinato–ritornello theme in the bass, the movement has the hallmarks of the traditional *bicinium*; but here the *bicinium* style shows adaptations which J. S. Bach introduced for partitas – i.e. with the melody rather more cut up than in more conventional examples of the type (BWV 711, 718 first part). Parallels can be made with early continuo arias (see BWV 766 Var. 1); but in BWV 767 Var. 1 a comparison of bb2–7 with 31–42 – i.e. sections based on much the same chorale lines – shows how far developed is the musical device of broken melody in such organ *bicinia*.

Var. 2 (Partita III)

The *suspirans* (Ex. 295) is familiar from several German variation types of the later seventeenth century and can be found in other partita movements (e.g. Var. 5 below), as it can in the *Orgelbüchlein* and in

---

* The parallel cannot be pressed, since French dialogues are not cantus-firmus-based and are simpler in texture; also, dialogues are rarely 'employed for the finales of Mass cycles' (Klotz 1969 p117).

Ex. 295

other organ chorales that through this device take on the appearance of a partita movement (e.g. BWV 690). It sustains motion; it suggests imitations and can be developed *rectus* and *inversus*; and it can be made to imply a thematic reference (e.g. final bar, tenor rising from g to c′).

Var. 3 (Partita IV)

For such movements, see BWV 768 Var. 3 and BWV 766 Var. 3. In the detail – number of parts, continuity of left hand, violinistic character of right hand – the corresponding movements of these three sets present the type in three distinct ways. For the bass motif, cf. BWV 644.

Var. 4 (Partita V)

The *suspirans* is here extended into longer scale sections; this too is known in the partitas of other composers (e.g. Böhm's 'Ach wie nichtig' Partita 4), complete with the broken-chord cadences. Less usual is the resulting octave displacement of the chorale melody, migrating down through two (or even three) octaves in the course of bb9–12.

Var. 5 (Partita VI)

The unusual cello-like bass part may owe its origin to the standard 'left-hand division' (variation with passage-work for the left hand) of the partita tradition, e.g. Böhm's 'Gelobet seist du, Jesu Christ'; but the gestures of the line are more characteristic of aria basses.

Var. 6 (Partita VII)

The triple-time variation may be seen (like Var. 9 of BWV 768) as an equivalent to certain movements in Pachelbel's partitas; but earlier composers such as Froberger had already included ³/₄ dance types in their sets of variations. Although the scale motif of Var. 6 is not always found in such movements, the style of the middle section (beginning with the upbeat to b18, chorale line 5) is not unlike that of the Courante in Buxtehude's 'Auf meinen lieben Gott' BUXWV 179.

Var. 7 (Partita VIII)

Whatever may be conjectured about textual references in this move-ment (see above), chromatic variations near the close of a work were familiar from such sets as Froberger's *Variationen Auf die Mayerin*, which itself merely transmitted an older tradition. The chromatic phrase itself (Ex. 296) was already to be found in the last variation (*choralis*

Ex. 296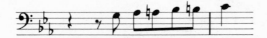

in cantu per semitonia) of Scheidt's 'Da Jesu an dem Kreuze stund' (*Tabulatura nova* 1624); Scheidt also used it in both *rectus* and *inversus* forms, as in BWV 767. The unusual harmonies that such chromaticism may produce (e.g. b19, second beat) were traditionally associated with chromatic countersubjects. The coda, particularly bb17–18, resembles cadences in the instrumental Sonatina from Cantata 106 (1707?).

Var. 8 (Partita IX)

The second manual is used for complete and partial echoes at the same octave, at the octave below, or at the octave above. Its use in bb36–41 is not clear from P 802 (the source for *BG* 40): it seems (*a*) that each hand in turn plays a solo phrase accompanied by the other; but the intention could be (*b*) that a *forte* phrase in one hand is immediately echoed *piano* by the two hands together. Krebs's dynamic markings are too few to show either conclusively; but (*b*) is plausible, since each *forte* statement contains an echo-like repeat and since it seems clear that both hands are *forte* from the middle of b41 and both *piano* from the beginning of b43.

The form of this fantasia-like movement can be expressed:

bb1–3	line 1/3 of the chorale melody; last phrase extended
bb8–9	line 2/4
bb21–4	line 5; echoes within and after phrase
bb29–32	line 6; echoes within and after phrase
bb36–7	line 7 ('Andante' in P 802)
bb45–6	line 8 ('Presto' in P 802)

Like those in French *dialogues*, the short phrases, carefully varied in length, imply that the whole work is nearing its close. As Keller suggests (1948 p137), it is possible that the *andante* section refers to the corresponding line of v8: 'und führ ihn schön verklärt' ('and lead [my body] beautifully transformed'), just as the *adagio* section of Partita 7 of Böhm's 'Wer nur den lieben Gott lässt walten' (Kö 15839) may refer to the penultimate line of v7 of its text: 'Denn welcher seine Zuversicht/auf Gott setzt' ('For who puts his confidence in God'). Such tempo instructions may act as reminders of the text and if so would not imply a change of manual as they do in the French *dialogues*. However, even the changes of manual and/or of stops shown in the MS P 802 may reflect J. G. Walther's convention – as copyist or teacher – rather than the demands of the composer (see notes to BWV 720).

768   Sei gegrüsset, Jesu gütig (*Partita*)

No Autograph MS; copies in P 802 (J. T. Krebs: Vars. 1, 2, 4, 10 only),*
Kö 15839 (J. G. Walther: 11 vars. according to *BG* 40), Lpz MB MS
7 (J. G. Preller: 11 vars. in different order, rich in ornamentation), Lpz
MB III.8.17 (Becker Collection, perhaps from the composer's stock
of MSS 1740–50: 11 vars. in Peters v order), Brussels W.12.102
(Kirnberger: 11 vars. in *BWV/BG* order), Carpentras MS 1086 (for-
merly called Autograph, eighteenth century: 11 vars. in different order),
Am.B. 46 and Am.B. 47 (Kirnberger circle: 11 vars.), and late sources.

Headed in P 802 'Sey gegrüsset Jesu gütig cum 4 Variat.' (two staves
throughout); in Kö 15839 'Choral...O Jesu, du edle Gabe'; Lpz MB
III.8.17 'Sey gegrüsset Jesu gütig p. à diverse Partite per il Organo';
in Brussels W.12.102, 'Sei gegrüsset (Jesu gütig) mit 11 Variationen';
variations labelled 'Partita' in Carpentras MS 1086.

The TEXT of C. Keimann's hymn was published in 1663; several
hymnbooks (e.g. Wagner *Gesangbuch* 1697) relate it to the prayer *Salve*
[or *Ave*] *Jesu, summe bonum*.

Sei gegrüsset, Jesu gütig,	Hail to you, kind Jesus,
über alles Mass sanftmütig,	Beyond all measure gentle,
ach! wie bist du doch zerschmissen,	O, how you are dashed in pieces,
und dein gantzer Leib zerrissen!	your whole body torn to bits!
(R) Lass mich deine Lieb ererben,	(R) Let me inherit your love
und darinnen selig sterben.	and die happy in it.

The hymn exists in versions of five or seven stanzas (Terry 1921
pp292ff), the first five continuous in content and with a common refrain
(*R*); vv6 and 7 have a different refrain:

Singen immer Heilig, heilig:	Sing always Holy, Holy,
alsdann bin ich ewig selig.	then I shall be ever blessed.

J. Böttiger's *O Jesu, du edle Gabe*, a *Jesuslied* for Communion, has a
further refrain:

Dein Blut mich von Sünden wäschet	Your blood washes me from sin
und der Höllen Glut auslöschet.	and extinguishes the fires of Hell.

and is throughout less meditative than *Sei gegrüsset*.

The MELODY appears with Keimann's text in Vopelius's *Gesangbuch*
(Leipzig 1682); that of BWV 410 is very similar: Ex. 297. (The history
of the melody is rather unclear: Grimm 1969 p172.) Both texts are listed
in the *Orgelbüchlein*; the melody is harmonized in BWV 410 and 499;
and it is used as the basis of J. G. Walther's chaconne 'O Jesu, du
edle Gabe' (*DDT* 27 p360).

---

* Movements are cited here as 'Chorale' and 'Var. 1' – 'Var. 11', as in Schmieder *BWV*
and *BG* 40. The order of Vars. 6 and 7 is reversed in Peters v and in some recent
studies on the inner organization of BWV 768 (see below).

Ex. 297

BWV 410

Schweitzer himself saw that BWV 768, because the number and order
of variations differ in the sources, would not serve as an example of
the relation between a text and an organ setting (Schweitzer 1905 p66);
but he accepted Spitta's conclusion that the variations 'are, as one can
see immediately, of different periods' in the composer's output (Spitta
I p594). Luedtke (1918 pp47ff) tried to show, by adding on three verses
from *O Jesu, du edle Gabe*, both that Vars. 8, 9 and 10 were related
to a text and that they were 'added' to the 'earlier' variations. More
recently, Ulrich Meyer has argued that of the arrangements in various
sources –

BG 40/*BWV* (= Brussels W.12.102)	1 2 3 4	5 6 7	8	9 10 11
P 802	1 2 4 10
Kö 15839	1 2 4 10 3 5 7	11 9 6	8
Carpentras MS	1 2 3 4 5 7 11 9	6 8	10
Lpz III.8.17 (= Peters v)	1 2 3 4 5 7 6 8 9 10 11

– it is the last that is 'the latest and most convincing' (Meyer 1973
p478). The pattern may then be expressed:

> ┌── Chorale
> ├─ Var. 1   (bicinium)
> │   Var. 2 ⎫
> │   Var. 3 ⎬ semiquavers ($^4/_4$)
> │   Var. 4 ⎭
> │   Var. 5 ⎱ demi-semiquavers ($^4/_4$)
> │   Var. 7 ⎰
> │   Var. 6 ⎱ compound time ($^{12}/_8$, $^{24}/_{16}$)
> │   Var. 8 ⎰
> │   Var. 9 ⎱ triple time ($^3/_4$)
> └─ Var. 10 ⎰
> └── Var. 11   (Chorale)

Thus the pattern is framed by two simpler chorale settings, the first
in four-part quaver motion and the last in five-part semiquaver motion;
within the framework is a series of settings decorating the cantus firmus,
in various metres and rhythms.

While clearly such a pattern conforms to the present-day quest for
structural plans in Bach's various collections of pieces, it can lead to
assumptions drawn from what are in the first place only conjectures.
Thus in practice the pattern implies (*a*) that both the smaller and larger

groupings of pieces either can be dated to the same period or were later assembled with the pattern in mind; (*b*) that the text is irrelevant; (*c*) that BWV 768 is the first fully patterned organ cycle; (*d*) that the musical characteristics of a variation (e.g. its number of parts, the presence of the pedal) are less relevant than incidental features such as its time-signature; (*e*) that some movements (particularly Var. 1) are of greater formal significance than their style at first suggests. Such implications may or may not be justified in the light of further research. A good source (Mempell–Preller) gives a different order still: 1 2 3 4 5 9 6 8 7 11 10.

Chorale

More keyboard-like than the settings in the partitas BWV 766 and 767, the opening chorale of BWV 768 differs also in form from such chorales with interludes as BWV 715.

Var. 1

Unlike BWV 711, the *bicinium* is organized into three paragraphs, each concerned with two lines of the chorale, with a motif found in the fugue subject of BWV 578.

    bb1–12   lines 1 and 2, to relative major
    bb12–22 lines 3 and 4, to subdominant
    bb22–37 lines 5 and 6

The opening of the melody is anticipated in b4, as in (e.g.) Böhm's 'Vater unser im Himmelreich' and certain arias in Weimar cantatas (e.g. BWV 21). In its ornamented style and spinning-out of the chorale lines beyond their two-bar phrasing, the melody is like that of 'Nun komm, der Heiden Heiland' BWV 659, though presumably its tempo is much livelier than that of BWV 659; the melody also matches the ritornello-like bass in the common close to lines 2 and 6.* The bass itself is constructed from a line which contains two important motifs – Ex. 298 – both of which can be found in such basses as that to J. B.

Ex. 298

Bach's 'Jesus, Jesus, nichts als Jesus' (Dietrich 1929 p71). Although such basses are not unreasonably likened to ostinatos, their development of motif and recognizable returns in different keys are merely characteristic of ritornello themes in general.

* Unclear in some sources; see *BG* 40 p.xxxviii.

Var. 2

In a varying three- and four-part texture based on a new harmonization of the chorale, a motif – Ex. 299 – is exploited *rectus* and *inversus* in

Ex. 299

b1

the inner parts; three times it passes into the melody itself (i.e. more often than in e.g. BWV 653 or 644); it is present in every bar, but the beat on which it enters, its direction and its intervals are all carefully varied.

Var. 3

A two-part variation of a kind known to Pachelbel and others (e.g. J. G. Walther's 'Meinen Jesum lass ich nicht' (1713) Var. 4; Pachelbel's 'Herzlich tut mich verlangen' Partita 7): semiquaver paraphrase in the right hand, non-stop quavers in the left. The semiquavers develop in their own way, and become less clearly related to the cantus firmus – particularly after the 'interlude' bar (b5), where a variant of the basic motif arises.

Var. 4

An accompanying texture which otherwise resembles BWV 644 in its G minor scales is varied by a second semiquaver motif – Ex. 300. When

Ex. 300

b2

this second motif appears, the number of parts always increases to four. Although only a three-note figure, it is not used for mere harmonic decoration (cf. Partita 4 of Pachelbel's 'Alle Menschen müssen sterben', also in Kö 15839). Its harmonic function varies from beat to beat – each of the three notes may or may not be part of the chord (cf. the last two variations of the Passacaglia BWV 582).

Var. 5

There are essentially three lines in Var. 5 – cantus firmus, bass 'division' (following much the same bass line as in Var. 4), and smooth inner parts – but the second half of the variation is enriched by fuller chords in the right hand and by a spilling-over of the accompanying motif into the right hand. Some attempt is made to mitigate the squareness of the bass motif, not least by the suggestive rise at the final cadence; such motifs remain undeveloped and repetitious in earlier keyboard partitas (e.g. Partita 5 of Pachelbel's 'Christus der ist mein Leben'), as in some French *basse de trompette* pieces.

Var. 6

The counter-motif of the $^{12}/_8$ variation – Ex. 301 – occurs in various guises and contexts, both in organ music (e.g. J. G. Walther's 'Jesu

Ex. 301

Leiden, Pein und Tod') and elsewhere (e.g. last movements of F minor and G major Violin Sonatas BWV 1018 and 1019). It is perhaps nowhere so fully exploited as here. Unlike the similar motif in BWV 626, it is taken into the melody itself. Variety of treatment is achieved not by replacing the motif but by breaking it up into sub-motifs (e.g. semiquaver figure *x* on every beat from b12 to the end).

Var. 7

Var. 7 is similar to a trio movement in Böhm's 'Christe, der du bist Tag und Licht' (also found in P 802). After several movements (*versus*), Böhm introduces the pedal for the cantus firmus in a trio whose upper parts exploit motifs imitatively and run together in sixths above the final pedal point. Both composers use the figure ; but the present variation is more continuous, avoiding (like BWV 694 and 710) the crossing of hands. The conception is also similar to Pachelbel's partitas, but the dramatic leap of the lines in BWV 768 Var. 7 is unusual.

Var. 8

Once again a motif – here the familiar curling figure (*circulatio*) – is absorbed into the chorale melody itself, originating there as a melodic paraphrase in b1. The motif is presented along with its own inversion, which becomes increasingly prominent, particularly above (or below) the penultimate chorale line (b10) and the final pedal point. The $^{24}/_{16}$ time-signature is presumably intended to convey a different species of *variatio* from the $^{12}/_8$ of Var. 6.

Var. 9

As in several of Pachelbel's partitas, the cantus firmus sings in the tenor between two highly imitative parts; as in (e.g.) BWV 688, the duo-like manual parts above begin to incorporate inversions of both their figures (compare b1 and b15); and as in BWV 661, the final bars include *rectus* and *inversus* together.

Var. 10

Similarities betwen Var. 10 and other organ works are striking. In its sarabande-like air it is clearly comparable to BWV 652, 653 and 654; the figurations in the accompaniment are particularly like those of BWV 654; and in a more general way, the ostinato-like pedal and chaconne-like motion produce a similarity to Walther's chaconne on the same melody. The form is unusual:

> plain cantus firmus, each line appearing in turn after an ornamented version lasting six bars; from the first of these ornamented lines a figure is derived (Ex. 302 below) which becomes a partial ostinato figure both in the pedal and in the ornamented soprano phrases (canonic treatment of a similar figure can be heard in the Sarabande of the B minor Ouverture BWV 1067)

Ex. 302   b1 (simplified)   b2

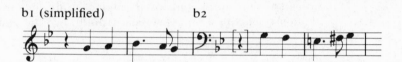

If the right hand is played by a solo manual, so presumably are the last two lines of the melody, when the texture becomes five parts (b75). Alternatively, the plain cantus-firmus phrases could be played on the left-hand manual, the ornamented phrases on a second manual – but the spacing of the hands seems to suggest the exact opposite. In (e.g.) the Brussels source, every chorale line of the cantus firmus is marked 'f' (*forte*), including the 'f. a 2 Voc.' of b75. Apart from bb90ff, the inner parts accompany simply, with surprisingly little overt imitation; and they never make use of the ostinato figure that appears nearly forty times in the pedal (not even in the coda, where the figure does enter in the top part too).

Var. 11

As in J. C. Bach's *Aria Eberliana* of 1690, the last variation is the chorale itself, in which the melody is accompanied with rich harmonies (Meyer 1973 p477). Unlike superficially similar movements in the *Orgelbüchlein* (e.g. 'Jesu, meine Freude' BWV 610), there are five parts without clear development of a motif, either in the pedal or (despite continuous motion supplied by a persistent figure) in the manual parts. The five parts are also more simple and homogenous in Vars. 10 and 11 than the five parts of (e.g.) BWV 633, which imply a distribution in the de Grigny manner (two pairs of manual voices differently registered).

769/769a   *Canonic Variations*, Vom Himmel hoch da komm' ich her

769   *Stichfassung*, engraved version

Published 1747/8. Title-page:

Einige canonische Veraenderungen über das Weynacht-Lied: Vom Himmel hoch da komm ich her. Vor die Orgel mit 2. Clavieren und dem Pedal von Johann Sebastian Bach Königl: Pohl: und Chur Saechss: Hoff Compositeur Capellm. u. Direct. Chor Mus. Lips. Nürnberg in Verlegung Balth: Schmids.

Some Canonic Variations on the Christmas hymn *Vom Himmel hoch da komm ich her*. For organ with two manuals and pedal, by Johann Sebastian Bach, Royal Polish and Electoral Saxon Court Composer, Kapellmeister and Director of the *chorus musicus*, Leipzig. Nuremberg, published by Balthasar Schmid.

769a   Autograph manuscript version

Autograph MS P 271, headed 'Vom Himmel hoch, da komm ich her'; three staves.

For TEXT and MELODY see BWV 606.

The origins, history and order of the pieces in the *Canonic Variations* BWV 769/769a are all difficult questions:

(i) Origins. In the Obituary Notice of J. S. Bach published in 1754, Lorenz Mizler added a note concerning Bach's membership of the Leipzig 'Society for the Musical Sciences' founded by Mizler in 1738:

> In die Societät der musikalischen Wissenschaften ist er im Jahr 1747 Junius...getreten. Unser seel. Bach liess sich zwar nicht in tiefe theoretische Betrachtungen der Musik ein, war aber desto stärcker in der Ausübung. Zur Societät hat er den Choral geliefert: Vom Himmel hoch da komm' ich her, vollständig ausgearbeitet, der hernach in Kupfer gestochen worden. Er hat auch den Tab. IV. f. 16 abgestochenen Canon, solcher gleichfalls vorgeleget...(*Dok* III pp88–9)

> In June 1747 he entered the Society for the Musical Sciences. Certainly our late Bach did not involve himself in deep theoretical speculation but was all the stronger in practical music. He presented to the Society the chorale *Vom Himmel hoch da komm' ich her* completely worked out, and this was afterwards engraved on copper; in much the same way he also presented the canon printed in Plate IV Fig. 16...[= BWV 1076]

The canon BWV 1076, written at least a year earlier (Kinsky 1937 p72), is relevant since it not only shows the interest that Mizler's Society took in such music – in 1747 Mizler had also discussed the Canon BWV 1074 – but actually resembles the melody of *Vom Himmel hoch* in motif and phrase: Ex. 303. The same bass also served as a point of departure

Ex. 303   BWV 1076

for the Canon BWV 1077 (1747), the recently discovered Canons BWV 1081 (Wolff 1976 p240)* and even the first quarter of the *Goldberg Variations* theme. Mizler's Society did not admit 'blosse praktische Musikverständige' ('those expert merely in the practice of music'), but the 'theoretisch Musikgelehrte' ('those learned in the theory of music') could find a place and were doubtless dazzled by BWV 769. Why Bach remained outside the Society for nine years is unknown.† It is also not known whether any or all of the movements of BWV 769 were originally written for Mizler's Society, for private reasons, or for publication, though in the event all three purposes were answered. Smend (1933 p29) is probably right to see the title itself as inauthentic.

(ii) History. According to a recent interpretation (Klotz 1973 pp11ff), the sources suggest the following stages:

A composition of the Canon at the Octave, Canon at the Fifth, Canon at the Seventh, the Augmentation Canon
B composition of the largest Canon with Inversions, perhaps in connection with Mizler's Society
C preparation of the copy for engraving 'in learned showpiece notation' ('in gelehrter Schauwerknotation', Klotz 1966)
D new amended copy of A (known from MSS Sp 1438, Danzig 4203/4 and P 1115)
E final fair copy (P 271) with some C and D readings

Stages C, D and E can be distinguished by differences in the order of movements and discrepancies in the musical text (including ornaments and other details); but each stage also includes both 'early' and 'late' readings.‡ The alto line of the Canon at the Seventh, for example, is more florid in E than in C, involving new motifs generally regarded as characteristic of a revision (i.e. a later stage of composition). However, certain other details suggest that both D and E reflect an earlier reading than C; E also contains errors suggesting it was not

---

* Wolff goes farther and thinks that 'actually, the thematic relationship between the two works [BWV 769 and 1081] suggests that the idea to celebrate the Christmas *cantus firmus* originated as an afterthought in connection with the fourteen canons'. However it should be remembered (*a*) that this chorale melody must have loomed large in the composer's thoughts for over half a century, and (*b*) that he had already attempted several contrapuntal devices with it in BWV 700.

† Details of the Society are given in Schering 1941 pp193ff. It has not escaped numerologists that J. S. Bach was the fourteenth member (B+A+C+H = 14).

‡ The exceptional nature of the sources (primary and secondary MSS on one hand, unusually notated engraving on the other) and the exceptional nature of the music (canons not written out but assumed to be strict, with free parts, the whole open to at least two orders or arrangements) make the customary distinction between 'early', 'late', 'authorized' and 'non-authorized' versions or revisions by no means as certain as is often assumed.

checked. That 1747/8 can be proposed as the date of both E (Dadelsen 1958 p115) and C (Wolff 1973 p20) does not affect the putative sequence, since for C this is the date of publication. Whether or not A and B are demonstrable stages is open to question, but the answer could have a bearing on the order of pieces (see below); so could a yet different interpretation – that D was the last version, with a simpler alto coloratura made for the engraving of the Canon at the Seventh (Emery 1963). Neither speculation nor logical calculation has yet established just how many versions or copies there were.

The two major formal differences between C and E are the order of movements:

C (BWV 769)	I II III IV V
E (BWV 769a)	I II V III IV

and the notation:

C (BWV 769)	I	two staves, lower canonic voices not written in after the first five notes
	II	two staves, ditto after three notes
	III	two staves, ditto after eleven notes
	IV	four staves, open score, four different clefs
	V	three staves
D, E (BWV 769a)		all movements on three staves, all canons written out

Canonic organ chorales in which the canons are not fully written out are difficult to play at sight and demand work 'with the pen at home' (as Marpurg said in 1759, *Dok* III p127); moreover, in the particular case of the engraved version of BWV 769 the music as it stands can scarcely be played, and the publication therefore could not serve as a playing copy. (A similar point could be made about the canons BWV 1074 and 1077.) The opening of movement II shows the problem (see facsimile, next page). Such difficulty further suggests which of Mizler's two categories of musicians the composer had chiefly in mind. The very notation distinguishes the aim of BWV 769 from that of Bach's next publication, the *Schübler Chorales*. Marpurg wrote out the opening of movement II in *Abhandlung von der Fuge* (Berlin 1753), but it is hardly surprising that a year later J. M. Schmidt should think the 'hardest geometrical proof' would not demand deeper meditation than did the *Canonic Variations* (*Dok* III p73).

(iii) **Order.** Although Bach seems himself to have prepared the version for engraving (*NBA* IV/2 *KB* p94), its order of movements is different from the MSS of the D and E versions, including his own. The reason for the discrepancy may be musical: Var. V may have been the last to be written, a crowning imitative piece, incorporating traditional devices of diminution and stretto and ending with pedal point and B–A–C–H reference (*ibid* p91). It also ends with a *forte* registration and a combination of chorale lines comparable to the Quodlibet of the *Goldberg Variations* (Wolff 1969 p156). For publication, Var. V serves as a useful climax – its final ingenuity, alas, clearer to the eye than to the ear, as D. G. Türk pointed out in 1787 (*Dok* III p432). However,

BWV 769 (engraved version), beginning of Var. II (approximately original size) the reason for this order may instead (or also) be notational: the engraving is arranged so that no turn-over is required, and so that each two-page opening admits a different stave system:

p1   title-page
pp2–3   Vars. I, II, III: on two staves
pp4–5   Var. IV: on four staves
pp6–7   Var. V: on three staves
p8   blank

In addition, the central opening (Var. IV), being in open score, becomes a kind of visual climax; that too is a plausible principle of organization for an exceptional work.

The order of movements in the autograph, though independent of layout, is equally logical, in a manner perhaps more to a composer's taste than to a performer's:

I   canon between two upper voices, cantus firmus in pedal
II   canon (derived from melody) between two upper voices, cantus firmus in pedal
V   various inverted canons from the cantus firmus, final strettos and diminution
III canon (derived from melody) + free part, cantus firmus in soprano
IV   canon + free part, cantus firmus in pedal

Canon IV also ends climactically, with two references to B–A–C–H. Thus each order – (*a*) progressive and (*b*) symmetrical – seems authentic and reasoned; and whichever order came first, the composer seems not to have felt bound to it. For quite different reasons, the ordering of movements is also confused in the *Musical Offering* and in the *Art of Fugue* (autograph version) but suggests respectively a progressive and a symmetrical arrangement. The *Goldberg Variations* can be seen to be both, to some extent rising progressively towards Variation 29 and the Quodlibet, to some extent bound symmetrically between the Aria framework (beginning and end) and centring on the French Overture (Variation 16).

(iv) The Music. Previous settings of the melody in BWV 606, 700, 701 and 738 had already brought out motifs open to imitative treatment above or below the cantus firmus. The examples in Ex. 304 are all

Ex. 304

BWV 606 (b3); cf. BWV 769.ii (b19)   BWV 738 (b3): cf. BWV 769.i (b1)

BWV 700 (b37):
cf. BWV 769.iii (b5 etc)   BWV 701 (b1):
cf. BWV 769.v (bb27–8)

in a familiar idiom. Moreover, BWV 700 not only ends with a C major pedal point but, like BWV 701, introduces the combination of lines 1 and 2 of the melody and imitation *per diminutionem* – all features found in BWV 769.

At other moments, BWV 769 resembles the canonic idiom of some of the *Goldberg* movements: compare *Canonic Variation* I with *Goldberg Variation* 3, including the bass line. Melodic lines are occasionally similar (e.g. some phrases of *Canonic Variation* IV / *Goldberg Variation* 13), as are several turns of phrase or actual motifs (e.g. *Canonic Variation* III b13 / *Goldberg Variation* 15 b1). Yet while the resemblance to the *Goldberg Variations* is much subtler than a few shared motifs suggest, the essential technical difference between the two works – one based on a cantus firmus, the other on a series of harmonies – prevents too close an identity. Along with the strict canons of the *Musical Offering* and the two fugal* canons of the *Art of Fugue*, the last half-decade of the composer's life saw the creation of a comprehensive survey of canonic types.

To organists alerted to other significances in Bach, the *Canonic Variations* also offer ground for speculation. Thus Smend observed that throughout the work 49 chorale lines can be heard (7×7) producing altogether 441 notes ($7 \times 3 \times 7 \times 3$) – although it is not clear whether this includes tied notes (Smend 1969 p169). As in BWV 606, 701 and 738, the various scale passages can be seen 'not only [to] represent the ascending and descending angels, but [to] sound joyous peals from many belfries ringing in the Saviour's birth' (Terry 1921 p307). After all, the text of the hymn is sung by an angel who 'sings "the sweet note with heart's pleasure"' (Spitta II p700). The so-called 'dragging' motif in Var. III (see below, Ex. 308, *c*) may be paired with

> dem gleichen bedeutsamen Motiv, das er schon seinem Orgelbüchlein-choral "Christe, du Lamm Gottes" zugrunde gelegt hatte. Weihnachten und Passion sind damit aufeinander bezogen (Klotz 1973 p14).

> the same significant motif already used as the basis for "O Lamm Gottes" [BWV 618 – also canonic]. Christmas and Passion are thus related to each other.

Naturally, the falling lines of Var. I (particularly the beginning and end) could be seen as the descent from heaven to earth, and the rising lines at the end of II and IV as the departing angels or the soul's elevation, etc. Whether or not canons are symbolic in any sense can only be conjectured. Canons were not uncommon for Christmas chorales (e.g. Walther's setting of 'In dulci jubilo' and two settings of 'Puer natus in Bethlehem', as well as BWV 600 and 608); J. H. Schein's *Opella nova* I (Leipzig 1618) had included a setting of 'Vom Himmel hoch' with canonic phrases and intermittent cantus firmus. The superscription to BWV 1077 suggests hidden meanings for at least that particular canon: 'Symbolum. Christus Coronabit Crucigeros'

---

* I.e. canonic theme answered at the fifth (augmented or at the twelfth) in the manner of a fugue subject and answer.

('Symbol: Christ will crown the cross-bearers'),* implying that the musical inversion required symbolizes a Christian tenet – as perhaps also in Var. V of BWV 769.

Neither the 'einige Veraenderungen' of BWV 769 nor the 'verschiedene Veraenderungen' of the *Goldberg Variations* are variations in the familiar sense (the type which Bach elsewhere calls 'double') – despite the addition, in the engraved version, of the label 'variatio' to each movement. Nor is BWV 769 a chorale partita in the sense of BWV 766 or 767. While particularly Var. I, II or IV could serve as *Vorspiel* to the sung hymn, clearly BWV 769 as a whole has more scientific aims; it could be that using the term 'Lied' ('melody') on the title-page, as distinct from the 'Chorale' of the *Schübler* title-page, also expresses the work's non-liturgical purpose. Indeed, in this respect too these last two organ publications of Bach should be seen in apposition to each other. In form, in the nature and ingenuity of their counterpoint, in complexity of notation, in their associations in the church year, and above all in the musical language of the lines and melody (periodic construction, keyboard-like qualities, etc), the *Canonic Variations* must be seen as a contrast to the *Schübler Chorales*. Perhaps the *Schübler* had originally been intended for the same publisher. They require quite as skilful an organist as the *Canonic Variations*, and any player owning both publications could feel that he was being helped to become both 'praktisch Musikverständiger' and 'theoretisch Musikgelehrter'.

(v) The Movements

Var. I: BWV 769 'Variatio 1', 'in Canone all'ottava à 2 clav. et pedal'.
BWV 769a 'Canone all'ottava', 'à 2 Clav: et Pedal.' (added?).

The canon takes the form of a two-part fore-imitation before the pedal cantus firmus, its subject anticipatory of both the first and last lines (cf. BWV 651) and serving to introduce both (bb1, 13): Ex. 305. The

Ex. 305

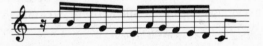

subject and its canonic treatment resemble the opening of 'Christe, du Lamm Gottes' BWV 619. The canon seems particularly successful when the phrases are short or when the cantus firmus is supplying a clear bass line (e.g. bb10–12, 16–18), although compound time enables the composer to deal fluently with the many $^6_4$ chords as they arise (e.g. b3).

* David & Mendel 1966 p36 assume that this refers to the change of mood between the 'sad' chromatic first bar and the 'happy' second bar. However, 'crucigeros' must refer to the cross-bearers themselves (i.e. the notes with sharps before them) not to their 'mood'. The alliteration 'CCC' is reflected in the time-signature C, C, C; the inversion of role from cross-bearer to crown-bearer is implied in the musical inversion. The subject too can be traced to the upper canonic parts.

Pedal 8' is called for, since the style does not demand 16' tone (*pleno*) nor the spacing 4' (solo). Subjectively speaking, BWV 769a supplies the better text across the barline 7–8, neutralizing the chromatic motif of BWV 769.

Var. II: BWV 769 'Variatio 2', 'Alio Modo in Canone alla Quinta à 2 Clav. et Pedal'.
　　　　　BWV 769a 'Canone alla quinta', 'canto fermo in Pedal.'

The canon takes the form of a two-part fore-imitation before the pedal cantus firmus, based on the first line (bb1, 16) and on the second (b10): Ex. 306. As in the Canon at the Second in the *Goldberg Variations*

Ex. 306　　　　　　　　　　　　　　　　　b10

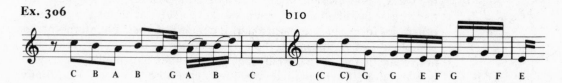

C　B　A　B　G A　B　　C　　(C　C) G　　G　　E F G　　F　E

(no. 6), the canon at the fifth produces a more natural line (with sequences) than a canon at the unison. Bar 12 resembles the sequential figure of BWV 680 (bb72ff), and the imitative use of scales (b5 etc) and leaps (b20 etc) is characteristic of trio sonatas for strings. In b16 the theme returns in the tonic, recapitulation-like (though here syncopated), as in b13 of Var. I.

Pedal registration is as in Var. I; in this movement, the pedal point (which by itself makes both 16' and 4' unlikely) has ascending figuration above in the manual parts, which leave the canon incomplete at the close. The texts do not differ in ways significant to the performer; but the engraved version (because the canons there are not written out) gives no authority for the left-hand sharps in b3 found in other editions.

Var. III: BWV 769 'Variatio 3 Canone alla Settima', 'cantabile'.
　　　　　BWV 769a 'Canone alla settima', 'cantabile'.

On the order, see section iii above.

The canon takes the form of a pair of lower voices running as a kind of ostinato with 'interludes', against a free melodic alto and the cantus firmus in the soprano. The canonic parts begin with the first line of the melody (Ex. 307). The interludes between the appearances

Ex. 307

of the figure in this strict form become themselves somewhat ostinato-like, since they occur approximately when the cantus-firmus lines appear in the top part; the cantus-firmus lines thus appear rather as 'episodes' in a ritornello chorale, as is the case with others in this form (e.g. BWV 662). The alto melody, though not in any formal sense an aria, incorporates motifs familiar in other arias or aria-like contexts – see, for example, several motifs introduced in the first few bars (Ex. 308). Those labelled *a b c d e f* and *g* can all be found in other decorated

Ex. 308

BWV 769

pieces, such as the slow movement of the F minor Harpsichord Concerto BWV 1056, while many cantata and keyboard movements of a *cantabile* character contain the motifs labelled *x y* and *z*. Some, like the dragging motif *c*, may have textual associations (see above, section iv); and the varied appoggiaturas increase the aria-like effect, adding gratuitous clashes (e.g. bb10, 25, 27 in both versions) as if to 'explain' those arising through the canon. At other moments, the free alto line suggests the chorale melody (e.g. b10), as do the inner parts in the final bars. Neither version – nor any reading produced by juggling with accidentals – softens the effect of b19, which is both logical and very striking, the more so as it precedes a simpler passage leading to the lovely *cantabile* close.

The chief difference between BWV 769 and 769a is that the latter has a somewhat more ornate melody, more motifs and motivic allusion as the movement proceeds, and a little more apparent freedom of line (e.g. b6) made easier by being on three staves. While a diatonic interpretation of the unwritten canon* is no doubt correct in the engraved version (quite apart from the evidence of BWV 769a), some notes are more unexpected than others (e.g. f♯′ in b8, c♯′ in b23). The aria-like alto makes a 16′+8′ pedal possible; 'Canon at the Seventh' does not imply that it cannot be a 'Canon at the Fourteenth'.

Var. IV: BWV 769   'Variatio 4 à 2 Clav. et Pedal per augmentation. in Canone all'ottava'.

        BWV 769a 'Canon per augmentationem', 'à 2 Clav: et Pedal.'

On the order, see section iii above; there are no other significant differences between versions.

The canon takes the form of a subject in the soprano followed in

---

* The *f*-like signs in the engraved version above and below the middle of the lower stave of b1 are *signa congruentiae* (cf. Vars. I and II) and do not signify 'forte'.

323

doubled note-values in the manual bass, against a free alto and the cantus firmus in the pedal tenor. The four parts cross more than is usual in BWV 769,* and while the free alto line often imitates one or other of the canonic parts, all three refer to the theme from time to time. Ex. 309 shows a few typical examples; those in the soprano

Ex. 309

are later augmented in the bass. Indeed, the whole variation is a tissue of thematic reference. Those in the meandering soprano part are inconspicuous and mostly *en passant*, becoming clear or striking only when they appear in augmentation in the bass. And the weight of reference is hardly oppressive: the allusions to themes are woven in without seeming repetitive or contrived, so (e.g.) lines 2 and 3 of the melody never appear in undecorated form because their leaps of a fourth could not easily have been integrated.

While in Vars. I, II and III it is the harmonic implications, and in Var. V the canonic potential, of the *Vom Himmel hoch* melody that occupied the composer, in Var. IV it is the melody itself, its simple

---

* It is possible that the composer intended the three manual parts to be barely playable by two hands on three different manuals, particularly on shorter eighteenth-century keys. However, the use of open score cannot be adduced as evidence for this.

melodic cells. Thus it is important that lines 1 and 4 are distinctly similar to each other in their emphasis on scale fragments, while lines 2 and 3 are akin in using fourths and repeated notes. Moreover, if lines 2 and 3 are expressed in a fluid form with passing-notes – Ex. 310 –

Ex. 310   b28 (transposed)

b18 (cf. b22)

they begin to resemble lines 1 and 4. It cannot be known how conscious the composer was of this process; but its results are clear throughout the unusual soprano part of this variation. Every scale passage, every fourth (e.g. b32) invites the hearer to infer an allusion to the chorale melody and hints at the manner in which a subtle composer creates his own melodies from a given theme.

The character of the movement is in some respects more like *Goldberg Variation* 13 than it is like *Canonic Variation* III – the right hand more in the style of Bach's mature harpsichord music than of his organ music. The soprano ranges widely (from c to c‴), and the whole of its second half (from the second half of b21) is free, working towards a particularly good close – rich in harmony and full of thematic allusion. As in Vars. I and II, there is a quasi-ritornello return of the opening melody towards the end (b34, top line, in diminution). The one rather dry moment of the melodic line (b14) produces a very good bass line in bb27–8 and may suggest that the composer's technique in writing canons was to find the bass line first. The final bars, whether or not one sees them as incorporating elements of the theme, are in the organ-coloratura tradition: the last three bars are a developed form of the final pedal point known from (e.g.) Buxtehude's 'Durch Adams Fall ist ganz verderbt' BUXWV 183. On the other hand, the preceding 'dragging' motif in the soprano at bb38f (cf. *c* in Ex. 308) and the fact that the pedal point begins in the 'wrong' key are unlikely outside the works of J. S. Bach.

That the final four bars also refer to B–A–C–H – see Ex. 311(i) – is presumably not an accident, since in the autograph version this is the final piece – in fact, the last bars to be written by Bach himself in P 271. Whether the retrograde in the same part a bar later is a

Ex. 311   (i) b39   (ii) b40

conscious reference is less certain (Ex. 311(ii)). The first in particular shows how the composer prevents the immense motivic ingenuity of the movement from dehydrating the music: b39 combines the 'dragging' motif, two or three motifs *a*, the cantus firmus, the augmented canonic line, and B–A–C–H. Moreover, the melodic line of b20 had to be so managed as to allow the canonic bass part of b39 to combine with B–A–C–H (or vice versa); but the result is one of the best bars in P 271.

Var. V: BWV 769 'Variatio 5', 'L'altra Sorte del' Canone all' rovercio [rovescio], 1) alla Sesta, 2) alla Terza, 3) alla Seconda è 4) alla Nona'.

BWV 769a 'Canto fermo in canone', 'alla Sesta è all' roverscio' [*sic*].

The final movement comprises four complete canonic statements of the chorale in succession, the whole concluding with a coda. The five sections are:

b1 chorale melody in inverted Canon at the Sixth, line by line; pedal continuo bass (probably 16')

b14 chorale melody in inverted Canon at the Third (therefore closely resembling the preceding canon: line 3 similarly drawn out to a four-bar phrase); pedal continuo bass

b27 chorale melody in inverted Canon at the Second between bass and tenor; occasional free part in alto, quasi-imitative; free part in soprano

b40 chorale melody in inverted Canon at the Ninth between outer parts (therefore closely resembling the preceding canon); free part formerly in soprano now in tenor

b52 chorale line 4 in pedal accompanied by *diminutio recta* and *inversa* of line 1; pedal point accompanied by stretto of lines 1, 2, 3 and 4, with *diminutio recta* and *inversa* of line 1

The effect is cumulative, but this description of the coda does not suggest all its musical subtleties: (*a*) the pedal statement of chorale line 4 acts as a confirmation of the previous soprano phrase (cf. BWV 664); (*b*) the pedal point of Var. V produces the lowest note of the five movements (cf. end of BWV 547) and the lowest on the organ itself; (*c*) there are finally six parts, the number having risen from one/two/three (bb1–2) to four (b28) and five (b53); and (*d*) there is at least one B–A–C–H reference (Ex. 312). Moreover, the six parts are all thematic, i.e. including the 2nd soprano running in thirds and the 1st tenor altering line 3 in the final bar and a half. A further detail

Ex. 312   b56   b55

is that the exact form of the chorale melody changes: the cantus firmus is almost the same in the first two canons (especially lines 3–4), and identical in the last two (line 1 is the same in the first canon and the last two). The free parts may ultimately be derived from motifs of the theme (e.g. line 1 in b36, now in A minor), but there is a clear alteration in character from the free semiquavers of b51 to those of the *diminutio* in b52. Very striking is that the two-bar phrase structure of the chorale melody is emphasized throughout by the canonic answer appearing at the same point in each line, i.e. halfway; to counter any unwanted dryness, line 3 is expanded into three bars, and later on non-stop semiquavers and syncopations are introduced. Mizler's phrase 'completely worked out' is thus no empty description of the canonic devices demonstrated in BWV 769.

The versions BWV 769 and 769a do not differ significantly, but the 'forte' signs are problematic. Of versions C, D and E, only E (P 271) has 'forte' at b27; in b39, all versions have 'forte', but the engraving puts it between both staves, and not below the left hand as in *NBA* IV/2. If 'forte' suggests either a louder manual or extra stops, it is difficult to see why it should be in b27, for any or all the parts; at the end of b39, it would apply to both manuals. If, however, it suggests merely a *second* manual, it would be especially relevant to the section bb27–39. It is as if the 'forte' were merely for the two solo-like semiquaver lines accompanied by *piano* canons, 'forte' indicating some solo registration. Either way, the hands must be on the same manual at the beginning of the *diminutio*. The first two canons to some extent resemble the French *dialogues aux grands jeux* (Klotz 1973 pp13–14), so two manuals are obligatory here as throughout BWV 769 (including the other two canons of Var. V). To assume that the 'forte' sign indicates 'loud' is to increase the cumulative effect of the coda in volume as well as in counterpoint – which may well seem to be unlikely.

---

770   Ach, was soll ich Sünder machen (*Partita*)

No Autograph MS; copies in P 802 (J. G. Walther, lacking first two movements), P 489 (first half of eighteenth century).

Headed in P 489 'Partite diverse sopra il Chorale...', two staves; in P 802 'Partita terza' (i.e. first two missing), two staves. Attributed in P 802 'di Giov. Seb. Bach', according to reverse ink impression of (lost) original title-page of the MS (Zietz 1969 p17).

With the possible exception of the last two movements, BWV 770 follows closely the texture and types of figuration characteristic of harpsichord variations c1690 – particularly the chorale partitas of Pachelbel, described by J. G. Walther as having been written 'at a time when there was a raging infection' of such works ('zur Zeit der dazumahl grassierenden Contagion': J. G. Walther *Musicalisches Lexicon* 1732, under 'Pachelbel'). P 489 comprises only BWV 770; P 802 is much more weighted towards organ music than P 801 yet also contains Pachelbel's comparable harpsichord-style chorale partita 'Was Gott thut, das ist wohlgethan'. That the sources themselves do not make the instrumentation more certain is clear from Kö 15839 (J. G. Walther), which contains both BWV 768 and seven of Böhm's and Pachelbel's (harpsichord?) partitas. While it may be true that the older the partita the less exclusively it belongs to either harpsichord or organ, the general idiom of BWV 770 (on a chorale melody not otherwise known to have been used by J. S. Bach) leaves little doubt.* The running bass of Partita V does not appear in Bach's 'organ partitas' though it is common in works of Pachelbel referred to, while the running soprano of Partita VI is outside the idiom of comparable movements in BWV 766, 767, and 768. However, in P 802 Partita X is labelled 'allegro Organ' [sic], a reference to the two (optional?) manuals.

The expanded treatment of the melody in Partita IX includes 'forte'/'piano' directions of doubtful authenticity; apart from echo passages (bb17ff, 25ff), the two manuals are used for a question-and-answer technique known only in later harpsichord music (e.g. B minor Ouverture BWV 831, Echo) and in principle different from that of the last movement of the Partita BWV 767. The technique may be derived from French *dialogues* (e.g. de Grigny, 1699), and such a passage as bb44–9 is particularly characteristic of the French style. Doubt has also been expressed about the manual directions in Partita X, which were probably added later in P 802 (Emery 1970 p168); if so, the intention may have been to make the movement conform to the shorter fantasias that incorporate several organ-chorale techniques (e.g. BWV 718). The fantasy of the movement, however, again seems rather to suggest a harpsichord piece borrowing or adapting treatments from the chorale fantasia for its own idiom. The attribution in P 802 may be the work of J. L. Krebs, who probably copied the first two movements into P 802 – i.e., they were already missing by the time he owned the MS (Zietz 1969 p101).

---

771 Allein Gott in der Höh' sei Ehr' (*Partita*)

Copy in P 1143 (eighteenth century), BB 40035 and late sources.

For TEXT and MELODY see BWV 662.

Though attributed to J. S. Bach in P 1143, the work is unlikely to be authentic; in BB 40035 Vars. 3 and 8 are attributed to N. Vetter (1666–1734), as perhaps the rest of the partita should be (Schmieder

---

* That a distinction was at least sometimes intended between organ and harpsichord chorales is shown on the title-page of Daniel Vetter's *Musicalische Kirch- und Hauss-Ergötzlichkeit...der Choral eines jedweden Liedes auff der Orgel, nachgehends eine gebrochene Variation auff dem Spinett oder Clavicordio* (1709, 1713): 'the chorale of each hymn on the organ, followed by a broken variation on the harpsichord or clavichord'. Vetter was organist of the Nikolaikirche in Leipzig.

BWV). However, these movements show a more primitive use of motif than others, and Spitta accepts BWV 771 as an early Bach work under the influence of Pachelbel, particularly in the number of parts and the treatment of the cantus firmus in Vars. 2 and 11 (Spitta I pp250–1). But weaknesses are evident: Vars. 1, 2, 11 and 13 are less developed than trio or melodic treatments in (e.g.) Böhm's 'Herr Jesu Christ, dich zu uns wend'; there is a reliance on simple, undeveloped motif in Vars. 3, 4 (cf. a figure in the anonymous BWV 743), 5, 6, 7, 9, 13, 14 and 17; the fughetta of Var. 8 has none of the hallmarks of shape, motif and harmony of BWV 716, despite the latter's simpler texture. On the other hand, while the Pachelbel influence on Var. 12 has had little effect (in comparison with BWV 768, Partita III), Var. 10 uses the interesting device of a single accompanimental figure for both the cantus firmus proper and its anticipation.

Additional Organ Chorales

---

n.v.1   O Lamm Gottes, unschuldig

No Autograph MS; copy in P 802 (J. G. Walther), LM 4983.

For headings, see below; two staves.

For TEXT and MELODY see BWV 618.

In P 802 Walther attributes the (first) movement to 'J.S.S.' [*sic*]; in LM 4983 (a MS once in the possession of J. G. Bach) it is attributed to 'Giovan. Sebast. Bach'. P 802 has no second movement ('Choral'), and the first part is followed by empty staves; LM 4983 has the word 'Immanuel' written below b31 of the Chorale;* each source omits ornaments given by the other.

The two pieces treat the chorale melody in distinct ways: cf. BWV 760 and 761, also copied in P 802. The second is no 'Chorale' in the sense of BWV 708, BWV 715 or the figured chorale that follows BWV 695.

> *A* Chorale lines 1–3 are treated in turn as ornamented cantus-firmus answers to fore-imitations; line 4 follows without interlude; line 5 follows without fore-imitation, and it 'dissolves' into motivic paraphrase, bb46–9. Three parts.
>
> *B* The chorale is harmonized, the melody is ornamented, and the final line 'dissolves' across an interlude bb27–31. Basically four parts.

Such 'dissolving' of the final line is not uncommon in fore-imitation chorales of such composers as Böhm (e.g. 'Christ lag in Todesbanden' in Walther's MS BB 22541/3). It is difficult to see in such treatment any intended reference to the final line of the text – 'have mercy on us' or 'give us peace' – although the unusual sequence of bb47–9 of the first movement certainly draws attention to the close of the melody. In both movements, the composer seems more concerned with developing motifs familiar from the *Orgelbüchlein* and elsewhere.

Perhaps the two settings of 'O Lamm Gottes, unschuldig' were part of a set of chorale verses or a partita; the presence of only one movement in P 802 would not argue against this, since that is also the

---

* W. Emery, 'An American Manuscript: Two Unknown Pieces by Bach?' (*MT* 1954 pp428–30) assumes that 'Immanuel' (see facsimile in *NBA* IV/3) applies to the following piece, the first of the Two-part Inventions; but the word also appears on p1 of the MS.

case with several of Walther's own sets represented in this source. The idiom of the first movement to some extent resembles Walther's, though its use of motif is superior. The idiom of the second is more Böhm-like (particularly the coda), although no very similar piece by Böhm is known. Whether the term 'Choral' indicates that it is a hymn accompaniment and whether the 'dissolved' final line looks 'almost inauthentic' are questions that have recently been asked (Meyer 1974 p82), though without much evidence either way.

Anh.55

Herr Christ, der einig Gottes Sohn

Copy in P 801 (J. T. Krebs).

Headed 'a 2 Clav. è ped.'; two staves.

For TEXT and MELODY see BWV 601.

Though anonymous in P 801, where it follows the partita BWV Anh.77, the chorale known as BWV Anh.55 (= *Incerta 23* in Kast 1958 p130) is thought by H. Lohmann (B&H edn 6589 p.viii) to be the work of J. S. Bach on the grounds that the incomplete source Lpz MB MS I was to have included a chorale on this text, ascribed to J. S. Bach and coupled with BWV 765 (which is also included in P 801).
The concept of BWV Anh.55 is unusual:

> chorale in the tenor of a trio texture which includes an obbligato melody (possibly derived from the cantus firmus for the first bar) above a continuo-like bass; the obbligato line used to accommodate the cantus firmus throughout.

Thus, if the movement were composed by J. S. Bach and if it were written out by J. T. Krebs before 1745, it could be regarded as an anticipation on a smaller scale of the *Schübler Chorales* (particularly BWV 645 and 649). Its melodic type and formal concept show closer affinity to the *Schübler* than to the *Orgelbüchlein* preludes (also in P 801) or even to the trio 'Allein Gott in der Höh'' BWV 664a, which it precedes. The bar-by-bar detail is more than competent, not least in the variety-within-unity of the obbligato melody. The angular line may well suggest J. L. Krebs, not least as the musical flow appears to be 'interrupted' for the sake of the repeat in b9, as in Krebs's 'Von Gott will ich nicht lassen'.

Anh.73

Ich ruf' zu dir, Herr Jesu Christ

Copy in P 1149 (c1800) and Lpz MB MS R 25 (second half of eighteenth century – Krause 1964 p53).

Headed in Lpz MS R 25 'Vorspiel auf das Lied Ich ruff zu dir Herr Jesu Christ per il Organo auf 2. Manuale und das Pedal. dell Sig. C. P. E. Bach'.

Like BWV 683a, BWV Anh.73 seems to be the result of a later-eighteenth-century composer adding introductory bars and other material to an organ chorale conceivably regarded as too short for church use at that period – in this case, BWV 639.

Calendar

Phrases in quotation marks are taken from the Obituary or from contemporary documents, all to be found in *Dok* I–III.

1685–1700	(i) Eisenach. Possibly learnt organ from Johann Christoph Bach (1st cousin once removed), organist of the Georgenkirche. (ii) Ohrdruf. Possibly taught by brother Johann Christoph Bach (a pupil of Pachelbel).
Mar. 1700	Lüneburg, chorister of St Michaelskirche; possibly organ lessons there or in the Nikolaikirche or Johanniskirche (where Böhm organist). While there, said to have travelled 'occasionally' to Hamburg and to have heard Reincken there.
c1700	Perhaps learnt 'French taste' at the court of Celle (orchestra of the Duke of Braunschweig–Lüneburg)
1702–3	Applied for post of organist at the Jakobikirche, Sangerhausen.
1703	Few months at Weimar. May have studied Italian string music there. Received commission to test organ in the New Church, Arnstadt (Bonifatiuskirche, organ by F. Wender).
9 Aug. 1703 – 29 June 1707	Organist at Bonifatiuskirche, Arnstadt. Criticized for long interludes in chorales and for too bold and chromatic harmonization. At Arnstadt 'revealed the first fruits of his industriousness in the art of organ-playing and composition'.
1705–6	Winter journey to hear Buxtehude; probably heard special *Abendmusiken* performances (Dec. 1705).
1707 – 25 June 1708	Organist at Divi-Blasii-Kirche, Mühlhausen (organ by Wender, new contract 15 June 1707); possibly tested organ (Reformation Day 1709?).
July 1708 – Dec. 1717	Organist to the court of Weimar, a position enabling Bach to perform 'well-ordered church music'; 'here too he wrote most of his organ works'.
14 Dec. 1713	Invited to post of organist at Liebfrauenkirche, Halle.
2 Mar. 1714	Promoted at Weimar to *Konzertmeister*.
1 May 1716	With Kuhnau and C. F. Rolle, reported on new organ of the Liebfrauenkirche, Halle.
Aug. 1717	On payroll of Prince Leopold of Anhalt–Cöthen as Kapellmeister; allowed to leave Weimar 2 Dec. 1717.
Sept. (?) 1717	Visit to Dresden; extempore competition with Louis Marchand called off.
1717–23	Kapellmeister to the court of Cöthen.
17 Dec. 1717	Reported on the rebuilt organ of the Paulinerkirche, Leipzig.
Oct.–Nov. 1720	Played to Reincken at the Katharinenkirche, Hamburg; 23 Nov. 1720 leaves Hamburg after unsuccessful candidature for post of organist at the Jakobikirche (organ by Arp Schnitger).
1 June 1723	'Entered upon the cantorate' at Thomaskirche, Leipzig.

Calendar

2 Nov. 1723	Inaugurates small new organ at Störmthal (by Z. Hildebrandt, still extant).
25 June 1724	New organ at Johanniskirche, Gera, tested and dedicated by the 'famous Cantor and Kapellmeister Bach' (organ by J. G. Finke).
Sept. 1725	Plays organ of Sophienkirche, Dresden (by G. Silbermann).
14 Sept. 1731	Plays organ of Sophienkirche, Dresden, where eldest son (W. F. Bach) is appointed organist 1733.
Sept. 1732	Examines rebuilt organ of the Martinikirche, Kassel (by H. Scherer, rebuilt by N. Becker).
1 Dec. 1736	Plays large new organ in the Frauenkirche, Dresden (by G. Silbermann), for two hours in the presence of 'many persons of rank'.
Michaelmas 1739	*Clavierübung III* published by the author.
1739	Visits the large new organ of Altenburg Schlosskapelle (by G. H. Trost).
26 Sept. 1746	With G. Silbermann, examines the large new organ of the Wenzelskirche, Naumburg (by Z. Hildebrandt).
1746 or later	*Six Chorales* published by J. G. Schübler (Zella).
c1748	*Canonic Variations on Vom Himmel hoch* published by B. Schmid (Nuremberg).
8 May 1747	Plays organ of the Heiligegeistkirche, Potsdam (by J. J. Wagner).
28 July 1750	Dies in Leipzig, 'mourned by all true connoisseurs of music'.
1751	*Art of Fugue* published.

List of Musical Sources

These notes accompany only the more important MSS referred to in the main text and are designed to give a summary of the origin and contents of those sources. They do not describe every source that is necessary to a complete edition of Bach's organ works, nor do they give details beyond those of a summary. The dispersal of German manuscripts during and after the last war has also meant that some present locations are uncertain or temporary: this summary therefore identifies MSS only by the more familiarly used catalogue numbers. Further information on most of the sources can be found in *NBA* IV/2 *KB*, *NBA* IV/3 *KB*, Kast 1958, Krause 1964, Blechschmidt 1965 and Zietz 1969 (see List of References).

Abbreviations

Am.B   Amalien-Bibliothek (Berlin, Musikbibliothek der Prinzessin Anna Amalia von Preussen)

BB   Berlin, Deutsche Staatsbibliothek, Mus. MSS (previously Preussische Staatsbibliothek (formerly Königliche Bibliothek), Musikabteilung)

LM   New Haven, Connecticut, Yale University Music Library

Lpz MB   Leipzig, Musikbibliothek (including former Musikbibliothek Peters)

P   P-signatures [for 'Partituren' – scores] of BB – dispersed

Am.B. 46: Copy made for Anna Amalia; two vols. (the first with same contents as Am.B. 47); like the other Am.B. MSS, probably copied under the direction of Kirnberger. Includes (1) *Orgelbüchlein, Schübler Chorales* etc and (2) 'The Eighteen' etc with 369 four-part chorales. Like Am.B. 47, probably based at least in part on original copies by J. S. Bach (Klotz *NBA* IV/2 *KB* p50).

Am.B. 47: Copy made by a scribe in the Kirnberger circle (for Kirnberger's use?); contents same as first volume of Am.B. 46, but without *Schübler*.

Am.B. 72: Copy of Am.B. 72a (order and contents slightly changed) made for Princess Anna Amalia before 1788, presumably under the direction of Kirnberger.

Am.B. 72a: MS copied before 1788 and serving as source for Am.B. 72; not in Kirnberger's hand, as is sometimes claimed (Blechschmidt 1965). Entitled *Sammlung von variirten und fugirten Choraelen vor 1. und 2. Claviere und Pedal von J. S. Bach*; the most complete source extant of BWV 690–713. Probably reflects the contents (and order?) of a collection assembled for or by Breitkopf after the composer's death, with a view to publication (May 1974).

Am.B. 478: Copy of *Klavierbüchlein für Wilhelm Friedemann Bach*, made c1760/80.

Am.B. 606: Album of 'Seven Fugues' written by several copyists of the last third of the 18th century; includes BWV 733, 535.ii, 539.ii and 580.

Andreas-Bach-Buch (Lpz MB III.8.4): Important album of over 50 pieces by several composers (including Böhm, Buxtehude, Buttstedt, Kuhnau,

Pachelbel, Reincken), made by unknown copyists around 1710/15 (perhaps mostly J. Bernhard Bach – cf. Möller MS below): provides a unique source for certain pieces. Mostly free keyboard works including several in ostinato form. See also notes to this MS in vol. I.

BB 12012/6, 12014/3, 12014/7: Isolated copies made by J. L. Krebs.

BB 22541/1, 22541/2, 22541/3: Copious albums written by J. G. Walther for his own use, and including organ chorales of more than twenty named central and north German composers; some 17 pieces by J. S. Bach include duplications. Pieces are grouped mostly according to title – the first two albums emphasize Advent/Christmas chorales (e.g. 12 settings, by ten composers, of *Nun komm* in BB 22541/2) including some from *Orgelbüchlein*. See also Kö 15839 and Den Haag 4 G 14. In a letter of 1729 (*Dok* II p193), Walther claimed that J. S. Bach and others (e.g. Buxtehude) had presented him with copies of some 200 of their works.

BB 30194: A few keyboard works of J. S. Bach, copied by an unknown 18th-century hand.

BB 30195: Album of works by various composers, copied by an unknown hand (after *c*1780?).

BB 30245: Album of works by Buxtehude, Vetter etc, once in the possession of Dröbs.

BB 40037 (lost during or after World War II): Album of works by various composers, copied by C. Sasse (begun in 1759 at the earliest), including Kauffmann's *Harmonische Seelenlust*.

BB 40644: see Möller MS.

Brussels II.3919 (Brussels, Bibliothèque Royale de Belgique, MS II.3919): MS W.12.102): Important *Orgelbüchlein* copy by a scribe in the Kirnberger thematic catalogue MS II.3912, and containing two sections: (1) BWV 696–699, 701–704 (second half of 18th century) and (2) BWV 690, 694, 712–713, 741 (second quarter of 18th century) (May 1974a p102).

Brussels W.12.102 (Brussels, Conservatoire Royal de Musique, Bibliothèque, MS W.12.102): Important *Orgelbüchlein* copy by a scribe in the Kirnberger circle (perhaps for use by Kirnberger, whose signature is on the title-page), containing BWV 599–607, 611, 612, 609, 608, 610, 613, 614, 616, 617, 619, 622, 620, 624, 621, 623, 625–627, 629, 628, 630, 633, 632, 635–644 (in that order) as well as the Partita BWV 768. (The order of pieces seems to result from a desire to minimize page-turns, but this is uncertain.) Written mostly on two staves, with the pedal line in red; but three staves for BWV 607, 620, 624, 623 and 633.

Danzig 4203/4 (Danzig (now Gdańsk), former Stadtbibliothek Mus. MS 4203/4, disappeared by or after 1945): Album once thought to have been copied or begun between 1754 and 1762 (Wolffheim *BJ* 1911) 'with the obvious intention of gathering together all the available chorales of Bach' for publication by Breitkopf (Klotz *NBA* IV/2 *KB* p54), but now dated after the Breitkopf catalogue of 1764 (May 1974a).

Den Haag 4 G 14 ('s-Gravenhage, Gemeente Museum MS 4 G 14): A 367-page album of 196 organ chorales by twenty-five named central and northern German organ composers, copied by J. G. Walther as a new enlarged version (?) of the source Kö 15389. Only 5 works are ascribed to J. S. Bach (BWV 737, 601, 727, 720, 735a).

Hauser Sammelband: A lost album, certainly copied by Kittel; sold by auction in 1905, having been part of the collection of F. Hauser, whose several volumes (some now numbered with P-signatures) were much used for the *BG* edition.

Klavierbüchlein für Anna Magdalena Bach (P 224, P 225): Two partly autograph albums of keyboard and vocal music; P 244 probably copied 1722–5, P 225 from 1725 to c1740?

Klavierbüchlein für W. F. Bach (LM): Copied by the composer from 1720, the earliest part including BWV 691 and 753.

Kö 15839 (Königsberg (now Kaliningrad), former Universitätsbibliothek Mus. MS 15839): A 345-page album of organ chorales, copied partly by J. G. Walther; see also Den Haag 4 G 14. Includes a few so-called 'Weimar versions' of 'The Eighteen', miscellaneous chorales and BWV 768. MS not available since 1937.

LM 4719: album devoted chiefly to the *Orgelbüchlein*, copied c1780 and based on Lpz Poel 39 (*NBA* IV/3 *KB* p19).

LM 4840: Album of 34 chorales plus BWV 769a, partly copied by C. H. Rinck (early 19th century) from B&H publication of 1803/6 – see Sp 1438.

LM 4983: Album once owned by Johann Günther Bach, written probably by a single copyist in the mid 18th century; includes music of Buxtehude.

Lpz Go.S. (Leipzig Bach-Archiv, Sammlung Manfred Gorke): Miscellaneous collection of MSS (see Schulze 1977).

Lpz MB MS 1 (Scheibner MS 1): Album of several fascicles, with a few chorales, free organ works (including trios) and keyboard works of J. S. Bach, copied in the Erfurt circle around Kittel, probably by J. A. G. Wechmar. The volume includes works of late composers (e.g. J. L. Krebs, C. P. E. Bach). See also notes to this MS in vol. I.

Lpz MB MS 7 (Mempell–Preller MS x 7): Album of several fascicles, devoted to an important selection of chorales, free organ works and keyboard music of J. S. Bach, copied by J. N. Mempell and J. G. Preller. Dates of 1743 and 1749 appear in the volume; but Mempell's MSS seem to have been written between c1730 and 1740, Preller's c1743–9 or up to 1753 (Schulze 1974). Regarded as a 'Kittel circle' MS, but the sources may derive directly or indirectly from J. G. Walther (Klotz *NBA* IV/2 *KB*) or even, in the case of 'The Eighteen' (copied by J. G. Preller), from the composer's 'Weimar autograph' (May 1974). In general Mempell seems to have been closer to J. P. Kellner's circle, Preller to the Weimar Bach tradition (Schulze 1974).

Lpz MB III.8.4: see *Andreas-Bach-Buch*.

Lpz Poel 39 (Lpz MB Poelchau Mus. MS 39): Album devoted to some 60 organ chorales of J. S. Bach, possibly based on copies by J. C. Kittel; perhaps in the hand of J. N. Gebhardi (from c1803?) or another copyist in the 'Kittel circle' (same hand as BWV 645–650 in Lpz MB Poel. Mus. MS 25).

Möller MS (BB 40644): Album of over 50 pieces (Albinoni, Böhm, Bruhns, Buxtehude, Flor, Lebègue, Reincken etc.), made by several copyists around 1705/10; mostly free keyboard works. Both this and the *Andreas-Bach-Buch* have more pieces by J. S. Bach than by any other composer.

P 224, P 225: see *Klavierbüchlein für Anna Magdalena Bach*.

P 271: Largely autograph album containing groups of works perhaps not originally bound together: the organ sonatas, the first 15 of 'The Eighteen' ('revised' versions), the *Canonic Variations* BWV 769a and (in earlier handwriting, but bound in later) BWV 660a. Two pieces were added by Altnikol (BWV 666, 667), and another by an unknown copyist (BWV 668). The sonata copies are dated c1730 (Dadelsen 1958 p104), the rest variously dated c1744–8 or later. Eventually owned by C. P. E. Bach, though perhaps originally passed to W. F. Bach (Wolff 1974).

P 281: Album of several fascicles written by two copyists, containing two organ chorales, two other keyboard works and the Eight Preludes and Fugues BWV 553–560; third quarter of 18th century?

P 283: Autograph of *Orgelbüchlein*; for dating etc, see introduction to BWV 599–644.

P 284: Album devoted to chorales of J. S. Bach (*Orgelbüchlein*, *Schübler*, some of 'The Eighteen' etc), copied by unknown scribe of the 18th century and based on Kirnberger sources. Most of the *Orgelbüchlein* chorales have pedal part in red ink.

P 285: Album of organ chorales (many as in the Hauser *Sammelband*, q.v.) copied in the 19th century, containing many doubtful and inauthentic works. Works of J. S. Bach are according to versions found in Kittel, Oley and Kirnberger MSS.

P 291: Album of several fascicles of organ music by various composers, copied in the late 18th century; BWV 654a copied by J. C. Kittel.

P 311, P 312: Two albums of organ chorales by J. G. Walther (directly from BB 22541/1?), J. S. Bach and others, written in c1840 by copyists (including J. Fischhof and A. Werner) who assumed that all were authentic works of J. S. Bach. At least some pieces were based on copies of Kittel, Oley etc. 'Probably intended as copy for a publication [filling] the gaps in the B&H print of 1803/6' (Klotz *NBA* IV/2 *KB* p45).

P 406: Album devoted to organ chorales of J. S. Bach ('The Eighteen', *Orgelbüchlein*, *Schübler* and others), written by two copyists of the second half of the 18th century, based on Kirnberger sources. As in P 284, in most of the *Orgelbüchlein* preludes the pedal part is in red ink. Owned by Forkel.

P 409: Small album written by unknown copyists of the second half of the 18th century (c1800?), containing five organ works (BWV 651, 723, 736, 757, 540.ii).

P 424: Album probably copied in the 1830s by one Nitsche and devoted to 30 chorales of J. S. Bach, together with BWV 769a. Copied from B&H publication of 1803/6 (see Sp 1438).

P 488: J. S. Bach's earliest known autograph, containing BWV 739 and 764; c1705.

P 489: A 16-page MS devoted to BWV 770, copied by unknown scribe of the first half of the 18th century.

P 525: Copy of the *Schübler Chorales* only, in an unknown hand of the second half of the 18th century.

P 603: Album of 9 chorales (including *Schübler*) written by an unknown copyist (the 'Anon 300' who was working for C. P. E. Bach c1755–60).

P 643: Copy c1800 of certain movements from P 224 and P 225, made by the copyist of P 1112.

P 801: Important album of several fascicles written chiefly by J. T. Krebs and J. G. Walther, presumably during J. S. Bach's Weimar period; about two-fifths of the contents are works of Bach, the rest by Bustyn, Buxtehude, Kauffmann, J. L. Krebs, Lübeck, Telemann and an important group of French composers (d'Andrieu, d'Anglebert, Clérambault, Dieupart, Lebègue, Laroux, Marchand, Neufville and Nivers), copied mostly by Walther. The *Orgelbüchlein* pieces occupy what are now the first one and a half gatherings, apparently written as a group, followed by BWV 765 and a series of blank pages. The order is BWV 643 (fragment), 640, 616, 617, 637, 638, 601, 642, 606, 609, 706.i–ii, 634, 633, 626, 603, 632, 627, 611, 602, 604, 621, 610, 635, 630, 612, 607, 599, 615, 605, 600; there may once have been others before 643. Perhaps these chorales were copied during their period of composition; at least some were copied from a source other than the surviving autograph P 283 (Daw 1976).

P 802: Important album of several fascicles and possibly several phases, written chiefly by J. T. Krebs (responsible to some extent for copying the music of J. S. Bach?) and J. G. Walther (music of other composers). P 802 seems to be the oldest of the three albums P 801, P 802 and P 803, and about three-fifths of its contents are devoted to J. S. Bach. The rest comprises chorale-based works of Buxtehude, Reincken, J. T. Krebs, Böhm, Walther, Alberti, Leyding, J. and W. H. Pachelbel, Kauffmann, Lübeck, Bruhns, Weckmann, J. B. Bach, J. K. Vogler and anonymous composers. While the dating and chronology are uncertain, it is possible that most of the Bach copies in P 802 belong to the first half of the Weimar period (Zietz 1969); but some, if not all, of the 'Weimar versions' of 'The Eighteen' may well date to later than 1717 (Daw 1976). How P 802 p138 comes to contain a copy of a piece by Kauffmann which was not published until 1733 – the copy is apparently based on the printed version – has not yet been explained; whether or not its copyist was indeed Walther, it does seem to indicate a later date for parts of the MS than that usually suggested (Daw 1976), although Walther's letters show that he was acquainted with Kauffmann.

P 803: Album of several fascicles devoted to free pieces (except for the chorale BWV 663a) which may be for organ or other keyboard instruments; copied mostly by J. T. Krebs, J. G. Walther and J. L. Krebs, but now including some later music. See notes to this MS in vol. I.

P 804: Album written by J. P. Kellner and several other copyists, and containing free organ and keyboard pieces (see vol. I); BWV 715 follows a copy of the Two- and Three-part Inventions, which are signed at the end 'Finis Johann Peter Kellner 1725'.

P 1108: Album written by J. A. Dröbs and devoted to organ chorales of J. S. Bach, including *Orgelbüchlein* (different order) and Advent/Christmas chorales (BWV 722 etc, BWV 769); probably based on Lpz Poel 39 or its source.

P 1109: Album written mostly by C. F. Penzel about 1770 and devoted to organ chorales of J. S. Bach but including some doubtful works added by F. Hauser's copyist after c1830. After a group of *Orgelbüchlein* chorales is written the date '22 Jan 1766'. The copies of 'The Eighteen' are probably based on the 'Leipzig version', i.e. original copies by J. S. Bach.

P 1110: Late copy of 40 *Orgelbüchlein* chorales, approximately (not exactly) in the order of P 283; copied partly by Michel (C. P. E. Bach's copyist), partly by Hauser's copyist (cf. P 1109).

P 1111: Album written by J. A. Dröbs and devoted to 12 organ chorales of J. S. Bach, 5 of which appeared in P 1108; probably based on Lpz Poel 39 or its source.

P 1112: Album of 11 of 'The Eighteen', copied mostly by Michel, with the last page by J. A. Dröbs.

P 1113: Album of 6 *Orgelbüchlein* chorales copied by J. C. Oley.

P 1114: Album of 3 *Orgelbüchlein* chorales copied by J. C. Oley.

P 1115, P 1116: Albums written largely by A. Kühnel (c1800?) and containing (1) 12 authentic Bach chorales (e.g. BWV 664b and 769a – based on drafts by J. S. Bach?), and (2) 14 miscellaneous chorales of J. S. Bach (11 from the 'Kirnberger Collection')

P 1117: Copy by J. L. Krebs of BWV 690 and 734, possibly made between 1727 and 1735.

P 1119: Album of 8 authentic and inauthentic Bach chorales; mostly written by unknown copyists of the late 18th century, but BWV 696 and 697 copied probably before the 1760s.

P 1143: A copy of BWV 771 in an unknown hand of the 18th century.

P 1160: Album written partly by J. C. Oley but mostly by an unknown copyist; devoted to organ chorales of J. S. Bach. Probably based, like Am.B. 47 etc, on original Bach copies and collected while Oley was a pupil (1749–50); 53 pieces, including some *Orgelbüchlein*, 'Eighteen', 'Kirnberger', four-part chorales and doubtful works.

P 1216: Incomplete copy of the *Orgelbüchlein* made by C. G. Meissner before 1730(?); formerly thought to be autograph ('the Mendelssohn autograph copy'). Missing since 1945.

Plauener Orgelbuch (Plauen, Kirchenchorbibliothek III.B.a.No.4): Large album 'written 1708' (according to title-page) by several copyists; includes the work of a large group of composers similar to those in BB 22541, Den Haag 4 G 14 and Kö 15839; originated in Thuringia. The MS contains more works of Buxtehude than J. S. Bach, and in some cases it incorporates careful registrations. Destroyed in 1945; photocopy in BB.

Schelble–Gleichauf (Sammlung Schelble–Gleichauf, formerly in the Mozart-stiftung, Frankfurt am Main): An album (now lost) containing '140 variirte Choräle' of J. S. Bach (title-page) but including many of the doubtful and inauthentic works amongst the chorales listed by Schmieder between BWV 690 and 769.

Sp 1438 (Berlin–Charlottenburg, Hochschule für Musik, Bibliothek Sp 1438): Album from last third of 18th century collected by J. G. Schicht for publication by Breitkopf & Härtel in 1803/6. Based on original Bach copies, at least so far as 'The Eighteen' is concerned. Destroyed in 1945.

List of References

A few sources cited only once or twice in the text (where they are fully identified) are omitted from the following list.

Adlung *Anleitung* | J. Adlung, *Anleitung zur musikalischen Gelahrtheit* (Erfurt, 1758; 2nd edn 1783)

Albrecht 1969 | C. Albrecht, 'J. S. Bachs *Clavierübung Dritter Theil*: Versuch einer Deutung', *BJ* 55 (1969) 46–66

Arfken 1965 | E. Arfken, 'Das Weimarer Orgelbüchlein Johann Sebastian Bachs' (unpublished diss., Göttingen, 1965)

Arfken 1966 | E. Arfken, 'Zur Entstehungsgeschichte des Orgelbüchleins', *BJ* 52 (1966) 41–58

BG | Johann Sebastian Bachs Werke, Bach-Gesellschaft edition (46 vols., Leipzig, 1851–99)

B & H | *Joh. Seb. Bach: Sämtliche Orgelwerke*, Breitkopf & Härtel edition, ed. Heinz Lohmann (Wiesbaden, 1968–, in progress)

BJ | *Bach-Jahrbuch*

C. P. E. Bach *Versuch* | C. P. E. Bach, *Versuch über die wahre Art das Clavier zu spielen*, 2 vols. (Berlin, 1753–62); English trans. W. J. Mitchell, *Essay on the True Art of Playing Keyboard Instruments* (London, 1949)

Bernhard | J. Müller-Blattau, *Die Kompositionslehre Heinrich Schützens in der Fassung seines Schülers Christoph Bernhard* (Kassel, 2nd edn 1963); English trans. W. Hilse, 'The Treatises of Christoph Bernhard', *Music Forum* 3 (1973) 1–196

Besseler 1950 | H. Besseler and G. Kraft, *Johann Sebastian Bach in Thüringen* (Weimar, 1950)

Blechschmidt 1965 | E. R. Blechschmidt, *Die Amalien-Bibliothek: Musikbibliothek der Prinzessin Anna Amalia von Preussen (1723–1787)... (Berlin, 1965)*

Blume 1973 | F. Blume, *Syntagma Musicum* (collected writings; Kassel, 1973)

Bruggaier 1959 | E. Bruggaier, *Studien zur Geschichte des Orgelpedalspiels in Deutschland bis zur Zeit Johann Sebastian Bachs* (Frankfurt, 1959)

Budday 1977 | W. Budday, 'Musikalische Figuren als satztechnische Freiheiten in Bachs Orgelchoral "Durch Adams Fall ist ganz verderbt."', *BJ* 63 (1977) 139–59

BUXWV | G. Karstädt, *Thematisch–Systematisches Verzeichnis der musikalischen Werke von Dietrich Buxtehude* (Wiesbaden, 1974)

Chailley 1974 | J. Chailley, *Les Chorals pour Orgue de J.-S. Bach* (Paris, 1974)

Currie 1973 | R. N. Currie, 'Notizbuch für Studenten – Cyclic Unity in Bach's *Sechs Choräle*: A New Look at the "Schüblers"', *Bach* (Riemenschneider Institute), 4:i (1973) 26–38, 4:ii (1973) 25–39

DDT | *Denkmäler deutscher Tonkunst*

DTÖ | *Denkmäler der Tonkunst in Österreich*

Dadelsen 1957 | G. von Dadelsen, *Bemerkungen zur Handschrift Johann*

Sebastian Bachs, seiner Familie und seines Kreises, Tübinger Bach-Studien 1 (Trossingen, 1957)

Dadelsen 1958 | G. von Dadelsen, *Beiträge zur Chronologie der Werke Johann Sebastian Bachs*, Tübinger Bach-Studien 4/5 (Trossingen, 1958)

Dadelsen 1963 | G. von Dadelsen, 'Zur Entstehung des Bachschen Orgelbüchleins', in *Festschrift Friedrich Blume zum 70. Geburtstag*, ed. A. A. Abert and W. Pfannkuch (Kassel, 1963) 74–9

Dähnert 1962 | U. Dähnert, *Der Orgel- und Instrumentenbauer Zacharias Hildebrandt* (Leipzig, 1962)

David 1951 | W. David, *Die Orgeln Johann Sebastian Bachs* (Berlin, 1951)

David & Mendel 1945 | H. T. David and A. Mendel, *The Bach Reader* (New York, 1945; revised edn with supplement, 1966)

Daw 1975 | S. Daw, private communication.

Daw 1976 | S. Daw, 'Copies of J. S. Bach by Walther and Krebs: P 801, P 802, P 803', *Organ Yearbook* 7 (1976) 31–58

Dietrich 1929 | F. Dietrich, 'J. S. Bachs Orgelchoral und seine geschichtlichen Wurzeln', *BJ* 26 (1929) 1–89

Dok I | *Bach-Dokumente* I, ed. W. Neumann and H.-J. Schulze (Leipzig/Kassel, 1963)

Dok II | *Bach-Dokumente* II, ed. W. Neumann and H.-J. Schulze (Leipzig/Kassel, 1969)

Dok III | *Bach-Dokumente* III, ed. H.-J. Schulze (Leipzig/Kassel, 1972)

Dürr 1951 | A. Dürr, *Studien über die frühen Kantaten J. S. Bachs* (Leipzig, 1951) (cf. Dürr 1977)

Dürr 1954 | A. Dürr, 'Neues über die Möllersche Handschrift', *BJ* 41 (1954) 75–9

Dürr 1956 | A. Dürr, 'Gedanken über J. S. Bachs Umarbeitungen eigener Werke', *BJ* 43 (1956) 93–111

Dürr 1977 | A. Dürr, *Studien über die frühen Kantaten Johann Sebastian Bachs* (2nd, enlarged edn of Dürr 1951, Wiesbaden, 1977.

Ehricht 1949–50 | K. Ehricht, 'Die zyklische Gestalt und die Aufführungsmöglichkeit des III. Teiles der Klavierübung von Joh. Seb. Bach', *BJ* 51 (1949–50) 40–56

Eickhoff 1967 | H. J. Eickhoff, 'Bach's Chorale-Ritornello Forms', *Music Review* 28 (1967) 257–76

Emery 1963 | W. Emery, 'A Note on the History of Bach's Canonic Variations', *MT* 104 (1963) 32–3

Emery 1970 | W. Emery, 'Der Klaviaturumgafang von Bachs Orgeln als Beweismittel für die Datierung seiner Werke', in *Johann Sebastian Bach*, ed. W. Blankenburg (Darmstadt, 1970) 162–77; translation of 'The Compass of Bach's Organs as Evidence of the Date of His Works', *The Organ* 32 (1952) 92–100

Emery 1974 | W. Emery, 'Cadence and Chronology', in *Studies in Renaissance and Baroque Music in Honor of Arthur Mendel* (Kassel, 1974) 156–64

Finke-Hecklinger 1970 | D. Finke-Hecklinger, *Tanzcharaktere in Johann Sebastian Bachs Vokalmusik*, Tübinger Bach-Studien 6 (Trossingen, 1970)

Forkel 1802 | J. N. Forkel, *Ueber Johann Sebastian Bachs Leben, Kunst und Kunstwerke* (Leipzig, 1802)

Freylinghausen 1741 | J. A. Freylinghausen, *Geistreiches Gesangbuch* (Halle, 1741; first publ. Halle, 1706)

Frotscher 1935 | G. Frotscher, *Geschichte des Orgelspiels und der Orgelkomposition*, 2 vols. (Berlin, 1934–5)

Gojowy 1972 | D. Gojowy, 'Lied und Sonntag in Gesangbüchern der

Bach-Zeit: Zur Frage des "Detempore" bei Chorälen in Bachs Kantaten', *BJ* 58 (1972) 24–60

Grace *c*1922 | Harvey Grace, *The Organ Works of Bach* (London, *c*1922)

Grimm 1969 | J. Grimm, *Das Neu Leipziger Gesangbuch des Gottfried Vopelius (Leipzig 1962)* (Berlin, 1969)

Herz 1974 | G. Herz, 'Der lombardische Rhythmus im "Domine Deus" der h-Moll-Messe J. S. Bachs', *BJ* 60 (1974) 90–7

Hilgenfeldt 1850 | C. L. Hilgenfeldt, *Johann Sebastian Bachs Leben, Wirken und Werke* (Leipzig, 1850)

Huggler 1935 | H. E. Huggler, *Johann Sebastian Bachs Orgelbüchlein* (Bern, 1935)

Kast 1958 | P. Kast, *Die Bach-Handschriften der Berliner Staatsbibliothek*, Tübinger Bach-Studien 2/3 (Trossingen, 1958)

Kauffmann | G. F. Kauffmann, *Harmonische Seelenlust . . . Kurtze . . . Praeludia* (Merseburg/Leipzig, 1733–6)

Keller 1937 | H. Keller, 'Unechte Orgelwerke Bachs', *BJ* 34 (1937) 59–82

Keller 1948 | H. Keller, *Die Orgelwerke Bachs* (Leipzig, 1948)

Kinsky 1937 | G. Kinsky, *Die Originalausgaben der Werke Johann Sebastian Bachs* (Vienna, 1937)

Kloppers 1966 | J. Kloppers, *Die Interpretation und Wiedergabe der Orgelwerke Bachs* (Frankfurt, 1965)

Klotz *NBA* IV/2 *KB*, IV/3 *KB*: see *NBA KB*

Klotz 1966 | H. Klotz, 'Über J. S. Bachs Kanonwerk "Vom Himmel hoch, da komm' ich her"', *Mf* 19 (1966) 295–304

Klotz 1969 | H. Klotz, 'Originale Spielanweisungen in Bachs Orgelwerken und ihre Konsequenzen für die Interpretation', in *Bach-Interpretationen*, ed. M. Geck (Göttingen, 1969) 112–18

Klotz 1969a | H. Klotz, 'Les Critères de l'interprétation française sont-ils applicables à la musique d'orgue de J.-S. Bach?' in *L'Interprétation de la musique française aux XVIIe et XVIIIe Siècles*, Colloques Internationaux du CNRS (Paris, 1969) 155–72

Klotz 1973 | Klotz, 'Die "Kanonische Veränderungen" in Entwurf, Reinschrift und Druck', in *Die Nürenberger Musikverleger und die Familie Bach*, ed. W. Wörthmüller (Nuremberg, 1973) 11–14

Klotz 1975 | H. Klotz, *Über die Orgelkunst der Gotik, der Renaissance und des Barock* (Kassel, 2nd edn 1975)

Krause 1964 | P. Krause, *Handschriften der Werke Johann Sebastian Bachs in der Musikbibliothek der Stadt Leipzig* (Leipzig, 1964)

Krause 1965 | J. Krause, 'Die grosse Bearbeitung von Jesus Christus unser Heiland aus Clavierübung III von J. S. Bach', *MuK* 35 (1965) 117–126

Krey 1956 | J. Krey, 'Bachs Orgelmusik in der Weimarer Zeit' (unpublished diss., Jena, 1956)

Leaver 1975 | R. A. Leaver, 'Bach's "Clavierübung III": Some Historical and Theological Considerations', *Organ Yearbook* 6 (1975) 17–32

Leutert 1967 | H. Leutert, 'Betrachtungen über Bachs Choral-triptychon "O Lamm Gottes, unschuldig"', *Musik und Gottesdienst* 21 (1967) 21–5

Luedtke 1918 | H. Luedtke, 'Sebastian Bachs Choralvorspiele', *BJ* 15 (1918) 1–96

Mf | *Die Musikforschung*

MGG | *Die Musik in Geschichte und Gegenwart*, ed. F. Blume, 14 vols. (Kassel, 1949–68) plus Suppl. (Kassel, 1970–)

MT | *Musical Times*

MuK | *Musik und Kirche*

References

Marpurg *Abhandlung* | F. W. Marpurg, *Abhandlung von der Fuge*, 2 vols. (Berlin, 1753–4)

Matteson–Niedt | J. Mattheson, 'Sammlung von Orgeldispositionen', in F. E. Niedt, *Musicalische Handleitung anderer Teil* (Hamburg, 1721)

May 1974 | E. May, 'J. G. Walther and the Lost Weimar Autographs of Bach's Organ Works', in *Studies in Renaissance and Baroque Music in Honor of Arthur Mendel* (Kassel, 1974) 264–82

May 1974a | E. May, 'Eine neue Quelle für J. S. Bachs einzeln überlieferte Orgelchoräle', *BJ* 60 (1974) 98–103

Meyer 1972 | U. Meyer, 'Zur Frage der inneren Einheit von Bachs Siebzehn Chorälen (BWV 651–667)', *BJ* 58 (1972) 61–75

Meyer 1974 | U. Meyer, 'Zur Einordnung von J. S. Bachs einzeln überlieferten Orgelchorälen', *BJ* 60 (1974) 75–89

NBA | [J. S. Bach], *Neue Ausgabe sämtlicher Werke*, Neue Bach-Ausgabe (Leipzig/Kassel, 1954– , in progress)

NBA KB | Neue Bach-Ausgabe, *Kritischer Bericht* (Critical Commentary): IV/2 (H. Klotz, 1957), IV/3 (H. Klotz, 1962), IV/4 (M. Tessmer, 1974)

NBG | *Veröffentlichungen der Neuen Bachgesellschaft* (New Bach-Gesellschaft edition), nos. 22 (1921) and 30.ii (1929), ed. H. Luedtke (Leipzig)

Neumann 1956 | W. Neumann, 'Zur Frage der Gesangbücher J. S. Bachs', *BJ* 43 (1956) 112–23

Neumann 1967 | W. Neumann, *Handbuch der Kantaten Johann Sebastian Bachs* (Leipzig, 3rd edn 1967)

Novello | *The Organ Works of Bach*, Novello edition, ed. W. Emery and others (18 vols., London, v.d., revisions in progress)

Peters | [J. S. Bach], *Compositionen für Orgel, kritisch–korrekte Ausgabe*, Peters edition: vols. 1–7, ed. F. G. Griepenkerl (Leipzig, 1844–7); vol. 8, ed. F. A. Roitzsch (Leipzig, 1852); vol. 9, ed. Roitzsch, rev. M. Seiffert, H. Keller (3rd edn, Leipzig, 1940); further revisions in progress

Paretorius *Musae* | M. Praetorius, *Musae sioniae* IX (Wolfenbüttel, 1610)

Printz 1696 | W. C. Printz, *Phrynidis Mytilenaei oder des satyrischen Componisten anderer Theil* (Leipzig/Dresden, 2nd edn 1696)

Riedel 1960 | F. W. Riedel, *Quellenkundlichen Beiträge zur Geschichte der Musik für Tasteninstrumente in der 2. Hälfte des 17. Jahrhunderts* (Kassel, 1960)

Riedel 1968 | F. W. Riedel, 'Der Einfluss der italienischen Klaviermusik des 17. Jahrhunderts auf die Entwicklung der Musik für Tasteninstrumente in Deutschland während der ersten hälfte des 18. Jahrhunderts', *Analecta Musicologica* 5 (1968) 18–33

Schering 1941 | A. Schering, *J. S. Bach und das Musikleben Leipzigs im 18. Jahrhundert* (Leipzig, 1941)

Schmieder *BWV* | W. Schmieder, *Thematisch–systematisches Verzeichnis der musikalischen Werke von Johann Sebastian Bach* (Leipzig, 1950)

Schmitz 1952 | A. Schmitz, 'Die Figurenlehre in den theoretischen Werken Johann Gottfried Walthers', *Archiv für Musikwissenschaft* 9 (1952) 79–100

Schmitz 1970 | A. Schmitz, 'Die oratorische Kunst J. S. Bachs: Grundfragen und Grundlagen' (1950), in *Johann Sebastian Bach*, ed. W. Blankenburg (Darmstadt, 1970) 61–84

Schrammek 1975 | W. Schrammek, 'Johann Sebastian Bach, Gottfried Silbermann, und die französische Orgelkunst, *Bach-Studien* 5 (Leipzig, 1975) 93–107

Schulze 1968 | H.-J. Schulze, 'Johann Sebastian Bach und Christian Gottlob Meissner', *BJ* 54 (1968) 80–8

Schulze 1972 | H.-J. Schulze, 'J. S. Bach's Concerto-Arrangements for Organ – Studies or Commissioned Works?', *Organ Yearbook* 3 (1972) 4–13

Schulze 1974 | H.-J. Schulze, 'Wie entstand die Bach-Sammlung Mempell–Preller?', *BJ* 60 (1974) 104–22

Schulze 1977 | H.-J. Schulze, *Katalog der Sammlung Manfred Gorke* (Leipzig, 1977)

Schweitzer 1905 | A. Schweitzer, *J. S. Bach le Musicien–Poète* (Leipzig, 1905)

Seiffert 1904 | M. Seiffert, 'Neue Bach-Funde', *Jahrbuch der Musikbibliothek Peters* (1904) 15–25

Seiffert 1920 | M. Seiffert, 'Das Plauener Orgelbuch von 1708', *Archiv für Musikwissenschaft* 2 (1920) 371–93

Sietz 1935 | R. Sietz, 'Die Orgelkompositionen des Schülerkreises um Johann Sebastian Bach', *BJ* 32 (1935) 33–96

Smend 1933, 1969 | F. Smend, *Bach-Studien: Gesammelte Reden und Aufsätze* (collected writings; Kassel, 1969)

Spitta I, II | P. Spitta, *Johann Sebastian Bach*, 2 vols. (Leipzig, 1873–9)

Stapel 1950 | W. Stapel, *Luthers Lieder und Gedichte* (Stuttgart, 1950)

Steglich 1935 | R. Steglich, *Johann Sebastian Bach* (Potsdam, 1935)

Steglich 1962 | R. Steglich, *Tanzrhythmen in der Musik Johann Sebastian Bachs* (Wolfenbüttel/Zürich, 1962)

Stiller 1970 | G. Stiller, *Johann Sebastian Bach und das Leipziger gottesdienstliche Leben seiner Zeit* (Berlin, 1970)

Taesler 1969 | W. M. Taesler, 'Von Zusammenhang in einigen zyklischen Orgelwerken Johann Sebastian Bachs – Beobachtungen eines Orgelspielers', *MuK* 39 (1969) 184–7

Terry 1917 | C. S. Terry, *Bach's Chorals*, II: *The Hymns and Hymn Melodies of the Cantatas and Motets* (Cambridge, 1917)

Terry 1921 | C. S. Terry, *Bach's Chorals*, III: *The Hymns and Hymn Melodies of the Organ Works* (Cambridge, 1921)

Tessmer *NBA* IV/4 *KB*: see *NBA KB*

Tittel 1966 | K. Tittel, 'Welche unter J. S. Bachs Namen geführten Orgelwerke sind Johann Tobias bzw. Johann Ludwig Krebs zuzuschreiben?', *BJ* 52 (1966) 102–37

Trumpff 1963 | G. A. Trumpff, 'Der Rahmen zu Bachs Dritten Teil der Klavierübung', *Neue Zeitschrift für Musik* 124 (1963) 466–70

Vogelsänger 1972 | S. Vogelsänger, 'Zur Herkunft der kontrapunktischen Motive in J. S. Bachs *Orgelbüchlein* (BWV 599–644)', *BJ* 58 (1972) 118–31

Vopelius 1682 | G. Vopelius, *Neu Leipziger Gesangbuch* (Leipzig, 1682)

Walther *Praecepta* | J. G. Walther *Praecepta der musicalischen Composition* [1708], ed. P. Benary (Leipzig, 1955)

Weismann 1949–50 | W. Weismann, 'Das grosse Vater-unser-Vorspiel in Bachs dritten Teil der Kalvierübung', *BJ* 38 (1949–50) 57–64

Williams 1979 | P. Williams, 'The Musical Aims of J. S. Bach's Clavierübung III', forthcoming in memorial volume for Thurston Dart

Witt 1715 | C. F. Witt, *Psalmodia sacra* (Gotha, 1715) = *Neues Cantional* (Leipzig/Gotha, 1715)

Wolff 1963 | C. Wolff, 'Die Rastierungen in den Originalhandschriften Joh. Seb. Bachs und ihre Bedeutung für die diplomatische Quellenkritik', in *Festschrift für Friedrich Smend* (Berlin, 1963) 80–92

Wolff 1968 | C. Wolff, *Der Stile antico in der Musik Johann Sebastian Bachs* (Wiesbaden, 1968)

Wolff 1969 | C. Wolff, 'Ordnungsprinzipien in den Originaldrucken Bachscher Werke', in *Bach-Interpretationen*, ed. M. Geck (Göttingen, 1969) 144–67

References

Wolff 1973 | C. Wolff, 'Die Originaldrucken Johann Sebastian Bachs', in *Die Nürenberger Musikverleger und die Familie Bach*, ed. W. Wörthmüller (Nuremberg, 1973) 15–20

Wolff 1974 | C. Wolff, 'Johann Sebastian Bachs *Sterbechoral*: Kritische Fragen zu einem Mythos', in *Studies in Renaissance and Baroque Music in Honor of Arthur Mendel* (Kassel, 1974) 283–97

Wolff 1976 | C. Wolff, 'Bach's *Handexemplar* of the Goldberg Variations: A New Source', *Journal of the American Musicological Society* 29 (1976) 224–41

Wolff 1977 | C. Wolff, 'Bachs Handexemplar der Schübler-Choräle', *BJ* 63 (1977) 120–9

Wolff 1977a | C. Wolff, Preface to facsimile edn *Johann Sebastian Bach Musicalisches Opfer BWV 1079* (Leipzig, 1977)

Zahn | J. Zahn, *Die Melodien der deutschen evangelischen Kirchenlieder aus den Quellen geschöpft und mitgeteilt*, 6 vols. (Gütersloh, 1889–93)

Zietz 1969 | H. Zietz, *Quellenkritische Untersuchungen an den Bach-Handschriften P 801, P 802 und P 803* (Hamburg, 1969)

Index of Names

Biographical details of composers, organists, copyists, organ-builders, editors and authors before the twentieth century have been collected from *MGG*, *Dok* I–III, Terry, *NBA KB* etc. An organist's appointments ('appts') include his last major post. 'Hymn-writer' includes editors and compilers of hymn-books; normally, no distinction is made between the writer of the text and the composer/arranger of the melody. 'Author' indicates a twentieth-century author. 'Pupil of J. S. Bach', as defined by Hans Löffler (in Besseler 1950), implies those 'owing their musical education wholly or largely' to the composer, those only 'for a short time under his influence', and those 'strongly influenced by though not known to have taken instruction' from him.

Adlung, J., 1699–1762, organist at Erfurt Predigerkirche from 1728, 141, 177, 262

Agricola, J., 1492–1566, hymn-writer, 90

Agricola, J. F., 1720–74, pupil of J. S. Bach, court composer at Berlin from 1751, 11, 33, 166, 211

Ahle, J. G., 1651–1706, predecessor of J. S. Bach at Divi-Blasii-Kirche, Mühlhausen, 155

Alberti, D., c1710–40, Venetian composer, 339

Alberus, E., ?–1553, hymn-writer, 301

Albinoni, T., 1671–1750, Venetian composer, 337

Albinus, J. G., 1624–79, hymn-writer, 98

Albrecht, C., author, 179

Albrecht, J. L., 1732–69?, cantor at Mühlhausen Marienkirche from 1758, 262

Altni(c)kol, J. C., 1719–59, pupil (from 1744) and son-in-law (from 1749) of J. S. Bach, organist at Naumburg from 1748, 124, 126, 167, 169, 171, 337

Ambrose, Bishop of Milan, c340–97, 15

Anna Amalia, Princess of Prussia and sister of Frederick II, 1723–87, 226, 335

d'Anglebert, J. H., 1635?–91, Parisian composer, 338

Arfken, E., author, 8, 11, 14, 16, 17, 28, 44, 71, 75, 77, 88

Armsdorff, A., 1670–99, chorale preludes in P 806 (with Zachow, Pachelbel, Buxtehude etc), organist in Erfurt, 292

Babst, V., hymn-writer (pub. 1553), 20

Bach, Anna Magdalena, 1701–60, second wife of J. S. Bach (1721), 228–9, 272, 336–7

Bach, C. P. E., 1714–88, fifth child of J. S. Bach, by 1740 musician to Frederick II at Potsdam, 1767 succeeded Telemann at the Hamburg Johanneum, 3, 6, 10–11, 70, 103, 115, 145, 182, 314, 337, 338, 339

Bach, J. Andreas, 1713–79, fifth son of J. C. Bach of Ohrdruf and brother of J. B. Bach (below), 135, 268, 335, 337

Bach, J. B., 1700–43, nephew and pupil of J. S. Bach and brother of J. Andreas Bach (above), organist at Ohrdruf Michaeliskirche from 1721, 248–9, 287, 311, 336, 339

Bach, J. C., 1642–1703, cousin of J. S. Bach's father, organist at Eisenach Georgenkirche from 1665, 259, 290, 293, 294, 298, 314, 333

Bach, J. C., 1671–1721, elder brother of J. S. Bach (who lived with him from 1695), pupil of Pachelbel, organist in Ohrdruf from 1690, 333

Bach, J. E., 1705–55, grandson of J. S. Bach's uncle, secretary to J. S. Bach 1737–42, cantor in Schweinfurt from 1743, 104, 175

Bach, Johann Günther, 1703–56, tenor in Erfurt, 337

Bach, W. F., 1710–84, second child of J. S. Bach, organist at Dresden Sophienkirche 1733, Halle Liebfrauenkirche 1746, from 1774 in Berlin, 103–4, 228–9, 272–3, 295–6, 334, 335, 337

Bassani, G. B., c1657–1716, maestro di cappella at Ferrara from 1685, 207

Becker, N., organ-builder in Mühlhausen (first half of 18th century), 334

Bedos de Celles, Dom J. F., 1706–79, French Benedictine organ-builder and theorist, 52

Beethoven, L. van, 1770–1827, 44

Bernhard, C., 1627–92, 'pupil' of Schütz, kapellmeister at Dresden from 1681, 44

Birnbaum, J. A., 1702–48, teacher (*Dozent*) of Rhetoric in Leipzig from 1721, 184

Birnstiel, F. W., Berlin publisher, active c1750–82, 11

Blechschmidt, E. R., author, 335

Index

Index of BWV Works Cited

This index excludes the main reference to each chorale (including the introductory discussion of each collection or group of chorales) and certain simple cross-references (e.g. to the various organ chorales using the same melody); it also excludes the List of Sources (pp. 335–40). Variants (e.g. BWV 651a–667a) are usually subsumed under the main BWV number.